SLAVIC PAGANISM TODAY:
Between Ideas and Practice

Selected Studies by
Dr. Roman Shizhensky

Translated by Jafe Arnold
Edited by John Stachelski

2021

PRAV Publishing
www.pravpublishing.com
pravpublishing@protonmail.com

Translation copyright © 2021 PRAV Publishing

All rights reserved. No part of this book may be reproduced or distributed in any form or by any means, electronic or mechanical, including photocopying, recording, or by any information storage and retrieval, without permission in writing from the publisher.

ISBN 978-1-952671-09-8 (Hardcover)
ISBN 978-1-952671-11-1 (Ebook)

Table of Contents

From the Translator and Publisher   7

Author's Preface   13

I. Conceptualizing Contemporary Slavic Paganism in Russia   19

    Russian Paganism in the Twenty-First Century: Ideologists, Organizations, Trends   21

    Contemporary Russian Paganism as an Example of "Imagined Community"   37

    The Russian Pagan Diaspora: Definitions of Neo-Paganism in Contemporary Russia   51

    On the Question of the Terminology of Slavic Variations of "Indigenous Religions": The Case of the Term "Neo-Paganism"   59

    The Periodization of Modern Slavic Paganism according to the Russian Pagan Diaspora   69

    Aspects of the Codification of Contemporary Slavic Paganism: The Data of Field Studies   83

    Particularities of Studying Contemporary Slavic Paganism: Historiographical Analysis of the Leader of the Koliada of the Vyatichi Community, Nikolai Speransky (Velimir)   99

II. Landmarks of Contemporary Pagan Faith   119

    Yav', Prav', and *Nav'* as Religio-Philosophical Foundations of Slavic Neo-Paganism   121

    The Golden Age in the Works and Preachings of Slavic Neo-Pagans   133

    A Comparative Analysis of the Texts of Alexey Dobrovolsky and Herman Wirth: Toward the Question of the Source Base of Russian Neo-Pagans   143

The Contemporary Russian Priestly-Volkhv "Caste"
seen through the Prism of the Religious Concepts
of Christopher Dawson   151

The Concept of Pagan Re-Mythologization:
The Case of the 'Signs' of the Community
of Nikolai Speransky   175

The Philosophy of Gender in Contemporary
European Paganism   183

III. Symbols and Rituals   197

The Staff of the Volkhv: The Question of the Sacred
Attribute of Twenty-First Century Russian Paganism   199

The Archetypes of Contemporary Slavic Paganism:
The Case of the Fiction Film *Guard Outpost*   209

Christian Mystery and Neo-Pagan Ritual Practice:
The Rites of "De-Baptizing" and "Naming" in
Russian Native Faith Organizations   233

IV. The Pagan Alternative   241

Per Aspera ad Astra: The Beginning of the
International Contacts of Twenty-First
Century Russian Pagans   243

The Slavic Religious Alternative: The Slovenian Variant   257

The Term *Rodina* (Homeland) in the Conceptual
Stock of the Contemporary Pagan Diaspora:
The Data of Field Studies   267

Contemporary Pagan Ratings of Russian Historical
Figures: The Data of Field Studies   277

Pagan Tolerance: The Experience of
Questionnaire Surveying   293

Selected Bibliography   303

FROM THE TRANSLATOR AND PUBLISHER

The present volume, *Slavic Paganism Today: Between Ideas and Practice*, consists of 21 articles by one of the Russian Federation's leading scholars of contemporary Slavic paganism, Dr. Roman Shizhensky. These studies were originally published in Russian in various journals, anthologies, conference proceedings, and online resources between 2008 and 2020. Until now, only one has ever been translated into English.[1]

Introducing such a compilation is conventionally the prerogative of an established academician in the corresponding field(s) who takes upon themself the task of reviewing textual precedents, contextualizing the studies at hand within ongoing scholarly debates and developments, and suggesting ways in which such a publication might contribute to an array of peer-reviewed cumulations. According to custom, such a book can then safely be shelved amongst preceding bibliographies and impending reviews, citations, critiques, and developments. The present book, as a culminating compilation of a reputed scholar's research and contributions within a multidisciplinary field, undoubtedly, by all means deserves such a comprehensive "encircling" by competent scholars. Here, however, I would instead like to, within the purview of PRAV Publishing and as this volume's translator, draw attention to several somewhat broader perspectives concerning this book's publication and relevance.

First and foremost, *Slavic Paganism Today: Between Ideas and Practice* is, above all, a work of translation. On one level, this is a compilation of studies by a Russian scholar translated from the latter's native Russian into English for consultation by Anglophone scholars and readers. Without a doubt, the newfound availability of Dr. Shizhensky's studies in translation will fill an ever-present,

---

[1] An English translation of the article "On the Question of the Terminology of Slavic Variations of 'Indigenous Religions': The Case of the Term 'Neo-Paganism'", featured in this volume in original translation, was previously published as "Paganism and Neo-Paganism of the 20-21st Centuries: On the Terminology of Slavic Variations of 'Indigenous Religions'" in the *Lithuanian Journal of Anthropology 1* (2014).

considerable gap of literature and concepts in translation. This seemingly elementary, self-evident level is in fact of considerable significance: the deeply rooted fact remains that the direction of translations between the Russian and English-language worlds of scholarship and literature remains overwhelmingly in favor of the latter. In the 21st century, any translation in the other direction bears a certain sorely-needed refreshing of perspective and balancing of trajectory, introducing "new" nuances, reflections, and questions. This, moreover, is inextricable from yet another level, namely, the possibility, or rather question, of attempting to translate the terminology, frameworks, styles, discourses, and interests of one world of historico-cultural reflection into another. *Slavic Paganism Today* is fundamentally an attempted work of translating studies of terminologies, ideas, and trends which hail from one cultural, linguistic, religious world into another with its own respective historical baggage of semantics and categorizations, a process which is forever beset by incorrect equivalencies, misperceived analogies, and uniquenesses lacking established standards. It would be misleading, therefore, to preface this collection, like English-language studies of the Slavic world in general, otherwise than as a "work-in-translation", or rather "work-towards-translation." How else, after all, is one to characterize an attempt to translate into English studies on Slavic-Russian religious language, rites, symbols, and concepts which are in their homeland the whole constituent subjects of the relevant fields of scholarship and debates themselves, including down to the very level of etymology and semantics? On the level of translation, therefore, the proposed subtitle of this volume, *Between Ideas and Practice*, is faithful to its context.

Secondly, this volume is in fact many possible books in one. Many of these articles could very well be expanded into monographs on their own. Moreover, the diversity of readers of this book is bound to take it in different forms and directions. Historians of Slavic pre-Christian religion, researchers of "neo-pagan" currents and their permutations, comparative mythologists, linguists, sociologists, and scholars of 20th and 21st-century post-Soviet culture, politics, etc., will necessarily read this book differently from one another, as well as from pagans themselves, curious newcomers to the subject of Slavic religion and culture, and other audiences bound to extract from these pages different threads than those grasped by known and unknown others. This is practically ensured by the very diversity of the present volume: in this collection, Dr. Shizhensky approaches the study of contemporary Slavic paganism from a wide spectrum of theoretical and methodological perspectives and with a no less diverse array of topical subjects, ranging from individual pagan figures to multilevel communities, from cinema, symbols, and rituals to specific creeds and macro- and microcosmic trends. It is this simultaneous plurality of approaches to contemporary Slavic paganism and the diverse outlets of its themes which, in our opinion, make this volume a valuable collection of source material and reflection for all in and between.

The latter two dimensions stand behind the "unorthodox" structure of this volume. The 21 texts presented here, selected for this publication by the author, have been organized not in terms of chronology or methodological contiguity, but rather into four thematic "blocs" under the titles "Conceptualizing Contemporary Slavic Paganism in Russia", "Landmarks of Contemporary Pagan Faith", "Symbols and Rituals", and "The Pagan Alternative." This arrangement has been projected not as a strict "segregation" nor in any form of linear progression, but as a relatively flexible flow between different dimensions of the "contemporary Slavic pagan experience." To maintain both the "polycentricity" and the "unity" of the studies compiled here, footnotes and references have been left with their respective articles, while a selected bibliography encompassing the exemplary source bases of all of the texts has been organized at the end of the volume.

Thirdly, we arrive at the very subject of the book at hand. This volume's publication finds itself amidst a widely-recognized underrepresentation, or rather sheer lack of works in the English language on historical and contemporary Slavic paganism in comparison to many - or, as some might suspect with fair grounds, any - other paganisms and religious studies. Here it is worth recalling that "the first consolidated publication of all the available sources of Slavic paganism"[2] and the first ever such volume in English is only now being released by Brill.[3] This situation led the editor of the (rather tellingly makeshift) volume *New Researches on the Religion and Mythology of the Pagan Slavs* to remark as recently as 2019: "Nothing serious, for decades, has appeared in English concerning the mythology of the pagan Slavs."[4] Meanwhile, the number of English-language scholarly anthologies and fully-fledged monographs dedicated to contemporary Slavic paganism remains countable on one hand.[5] In an equally few number of cases, articles on various cases of contemporary Slavic paganism are "tagged along" in anthologies on other "neo-pagan zones", all the while as, to quote Kaarina Aitamurto's remark in the introduction to her dissertation published as *Paganism, Traditionalism, Nationalism: Narratives of Russian Rodnoverie*, "Despite many similarities, contemporary Paganism in Russia proved to be in several ways quite different from Western Paganism."[6] This comes in addition to the fact noted by the Russian pagan philosopher Askr Svarte (Evgeny Nechkasov) - clearly confirmable by a perusal of any online bookstore - that many Slavic pagan publications which have been "exported" into English, including some of those studied in academic literature, represent "those same pseudo-pagan speculations which adequate and competent representatives of Rodnoverie (Native Faith) here

---

[2] Enrique Santos Marinas, "Reassessment, Unification, and Enlargement of the Sources of Slavic Pre-Christian Religion", *Russian History 40* (2013), p. 40.

[3] Juan Antonio Álvarez-Pedrosa (ed.), *Sources of Slavic Pre-Christian Religion* (Leiden: Brill, 2020-21).

[4] Patrice Lajoye (ed.), *New Researches on the Religion and Mythology of the Pagan Slavs* (Lisieux: Lingva, 2019), p. 5.

[5] For example: Kaarina Aitamurto, *Paganism, Traditionalism, Nationalism: Narratives of Russian Rodnoverie* (London: Routledge, 2016); Kaarina Aitamurto and Scott Simpson (eds.), *Modern Pagan and Native Faith Movements in Central and Eastern Europe* (Durham: Acumen, 2013); Mariya Lesiv, *The Return of Ancestral Gods: Modern Ukrainian Paganism as an Alternative Vision for a Nation* (Montreal & Kingston: McGill-Queen's University Press, 2013); Scott Simpson, *Native Faith: Polish Neo-Paganism at the Brink of the 21st Century* (Kraków: Nomos, 2012). Of course, this recognition of the scarcity of relevant English-language works still says nothing of the hyper-fixations of Western studies (and, as Dr. Shizhensky points out in several of this volume's articles, a definite portion of Russian scholarship as well) on such specific aspects as "nationalism", "constructionism", etc.

[6] Aitamurto, *Paganism, Traditionalism, Nationalism: Narratives of Russian Rodnoverie*, p. 2.

in Russia have been struggling against for many years."⁷ If such pamphlets are easily accessible to English-language readers, then the few scholarly studies available in English on Slavic paganism are confined to the restricted domains of academic publishers, specialist journals, and rare collections which remain generally inaccessible and often unaffordable to the much broader circles of those interested in the religious heritage of one of the world's rich cultural-linguistic families and its contemporary spiritual seekers. In this context, Dr. Shizhensky's *Slavic Paganism Today* is being made available in the spirit of an orientation which in the Slavic-speaking world is known as "scholarly-popular."

These grander contexts and this scholarly-popular orientation shaped the specifics of the procedure adhered to over the course of this volume's translation. Recognizing at once the prevailing lack of rigorous studies on Slavic paganism, the de facto absence of precedents for countless questions of translation, as well as the broad interest in this world of inquiry being made accessible, I have pursued a middle ground between heavy-handed translator's interjections and strict "scientific" transliteration systems on the one hand, and loose, familiar "renderings" on the other. On this note, sincere thanks are due to John Stachelski of Yale University's Department of Slavic Languages and Literature for editing this volume with an eye towards ensuring its "scholarly-popular" balance.

It is in light of and for all of the above-mentioned directions that PRAV Publishing presents Roman Shizhensky's *Slavic Paganism Today: Between Ideas and Practice.*

- Jafe Arnold,
PRAV Publishing
9 January 2021

---

7   Askr Svarte, *Polemos: The Dawn of Pagan Traditionalism* (trans. by Jafe Arnold; PRAV Publishing, 2020), p. 20. It is to Mr. Nechkasov that I owe my first acquaintance with Dr. Shizhensky's scholarship.

AUTHOR'S PREFACE

Slavic paganism is one of the most interesting worldview phenomena of our time.[8] Yet, problems with studying this phenomenon had already begun, so to speak, "as soon as the hero entered Baba Yaga's hut." Since the late 1970s, scholars have not been able to arrive at a unified opinion not only on classifying pagan groups and their orientations, but also the terminology of this movement and its chronology of emergence. Considering the reasons why an individual joins the pagan social world and examining the particularities of their creed, ritual practices, and attributes is left in second place. As follows, the appearance of researchers at holiday festivals and attempts at reaching new associations and individual pagans are often met with hostility. People wait for the "catch" and expect uncomfortable questions from scholars. I have probably been lucky in this regard, and I was pleasantly surprised when the majority of young-pagan (*mladoiazychniki*) groups not only responded to the survey questionnaires of our research laboratory[9], which were short-term, one-time actions, but also agreed to longer-term cooperation and, what's more, even granted us full access to their archives!

Note should be made of the fact that in the new pagans' mythology and holiday-ritual complexes, there is much more than pure constructing emerging as a result of the loss of first-hand sources; there are also attempts at reconstructing "the original ancestral paganism." For the sake of realizing this utopian project, even ethnic belonging, which has long been an axiomatic postulate, recedes into the background. The young pagans mix different traditions without issue, by virtue of which archaism emerges as

---

[8] The author expresses his sincere gratitude to the Russian Academic Excellence Project at Immanuel Kant Baltic Federal University for supporting his research during the creation of this book.

[9] The "New Religious Movements in Contemporary Russia and Europe" scientific-research laboratory, founded by myself, operated out of Kozma Minin Nizhny Novgorod State Pedagogical University from 2013 to 2020. As part of the laboratory's work, expeditions were organized among the most famous pagan associations in Russia, Ukraine, Belarus, and the Baltic countries.

equal to truth. Accordingly, the so-called *Rodnover* can easily wear Thor's hammer while covering his body with Permian animal style tattoos, playing the jaw harp, etc. In addition to this worldview and "practical" syncretism, yet another particularity which has drawn scholars' attention to paganism can be highlighted, namely, the development of this phenomenon precisely amidst urban culture. What compels a metropolitan resident in the 21st century to bang on a tambourine and jump over a bonfire? Scholars should be able to answer this question.

The development of paganism today is, no matter how strange such may sound, directly dependent upon its fragmentation. The vast majority of Native Faith community leaders have spoken in favor of the movement's decentralization and the impermissibility of the emergence of dogma and the creation of one "pagan church." This chosen "course" has allowed for partial rebranding and the shifting of a series of emphases in both the worldview and practice of the new pagans. For instance, the ideological project of the "*Shuynyi put'*" ("Left-Hand Path") launched in 2010, which I have evaluated as a pagan reform (a modern, exaggerated analogue of the reform of 980), has allowed for the movement to not only draw in youth from the quasi-pagan milieu - the potential "flock" of adjacent new religious movements - but also significantly expand the geographical distribution of followers (into Siberia and the Volga region) as well as launch new readings of "tradition" (such as "magical cosmopolitanism" and "primitive paganism"). Finally, the "*Shuynyi put'*" has partially contributed to the individualization of religious practices and, as a consequence, the mass discovery of definite sacred space (temple complexes).

In characterizing Russian paganism at the present stage of its development, attention should also be paid to its structural changes. "New school" formations have been added to the "standard" strata of communities, unions of communities, confederations, settlements, pagan families, conferences, and lone ideologues. Some of the ideologists who previously figured among respondents have moved into the status of being interviewers and engaged in their own studies.

Internet resources headed by pagan bloggers are also actively developing, bringing together relevant global information about the worldview under consideration. A specialized school is also in operation, the graduates of which have founded around 30 new communities. Pagans have since made it onto the "big screen", participating in polemics with representatives of the world confessions. Syncretic Veche fellowships are also taking shape, uniting representatives of different orientations. All of the above testifies to the absence of a process of stagnation in today's variation of Slavic paganism.

In my opinion, over the course of its development in the near future, contemporary Slavic paganism will not move beyond the scope of its diasporic functioning and existence - it will remain a "worldview for its own." However, large holiday festival events (such as the summer solstice) with definitive scenarios and ethnic coloring continue to draw dozens and hundreds of ordinary people, which, without a doubt, will contribute to paganism's broadening "way to the people." Due to the number of those who "vacation" at such "ethno-grill-outs", we cannot judge the actual number of "Native Faith" adherents. The festival ends, and then what?

Contemporary Slavic paganism's lack of mainstream traits at the present stage is at once a problem and a way out of this problem. Slavic *ethnica* is still too young. If we were to attempt to describe this phenomenon's level of development with one term, then the most fitting of all would be a definition borrowed from one of the "natural sciences", botany: "prolification", or the sprouting of a flower out of another that has finished its development. It is altogether difficult to determine how and where 21st-century Slavic nativism will "sprout" further. A number of communities, unions, and circles are now in a stage of developing their worldview bases, amidst which some have already decided on a range of tasks and a program for life in Russian reality while others are undergoing a stage of division. In other words, paganism is now more "interim" than invariant, which is to say that it finds itself in a formative process - but this does not mean that such will always be the case.

I hope that the present publication will allow readers to immerse themselves into the world of contemporary Slavic paganism and familiarize themselves with the peculiarities of this worldview, its holiday-ritual practices, the structure and attributes of young-pagan associations, and the philosophy of the ideologists of this movement.

- Dr. Roman Shizhensky
Immanuel Kant Baltic Federal University
Kaliningrad
12 December 2020

I. CONCEPTUALIZING CONTEMPORARY SLAVIC PAGANISM IN RUSSIA

RUSSIAN PAGANISM IN THE TWENTY-FIRST CENTURY: IDEOLOGISTS, ORGANIZATIONS, TRENDS[10]

Besides the traditional presence of the world religions, the religious space of the Russian Federation in the second decade of the 21st century is characterized by an "inflorescence" of new religious movements. One of the most vivid manifestations of this new religiosity is contemporary Russian paganism. Let us note that from a chronological standpoint this phenomenon is nothing new, either for Soviet or post-Soviet Russia, and in fact, is presently passing its 40th anniversary.[11] Yet, the peculiarity of the Russian variant of this movement, previously noted by the author in 2011 as characterized by "worldview-prolification" (akin to the growth of one plant out of another which has completed its growth), is hyper-relevant in the present time.[12] Twenty-first century Russian polytheism (pantheism, supremotheism, etc.) represents a kaleidoscope of personalities, trends, and ideologies which have generated en masse the sporadic phenomenon of constructed "young paganism" (*mladoiazychestvo*).

Despite this movement's propensity for endless transformations, the statistically average Russian pagan retains a "constant portrait." As a result of the comparative analysis of questionnaire surveys conducted in 2014 and 2015 - a study facilitated by the research team of the "New Religious Movements in Contemporary Russia and Europe" laboratory of Kozma Minin Nizhny Novgorod State Pedagogical University, which aimed to

---

10   Article first published in *Vestnik slavianskikh kul'tur [Bulletin of Slavic Cultures]* 50 (2018).
11   R.V. Shizhensky, *Filosofiia dobroi sily: zhizn' i tvorchestvo Dobroslava (A.A. Dobrovol'skogo)* (Moscow: Orbita-m, 2013), p. 30. A different point of view is maintained by the scholar of religion A. Gaidukov, who dates the emergence of the first groups of followers of contemporary Russian polytheism only to the late 1980s: A.V. Gaidukov, *"Slavianskoe novoe iazychestvo v Rossii: opyt religiovedcheskogo issledovaniia"* in E.S. Elbakian, S.I. Ivanenko, I.Ia. Kantherov, and M.N. Sitnikov (eds.), *Novye religii v Rossii: dvatsat' let spustia. Materialy Mezhdunarodnoi nauchno-prakticheskoi konferentsii* [Moscow: Dom Zhurnalista, 14 December 2012] (Moscow: Drevo zhizni, 2013).
12   A Belov, *"Uzok ikh Krug"*, *Nezavisimaia gazeta* (21/12/2011) [http://www.ng.ru/problems/2011-12-21/5_krug.html].

determine the social portrait of members of the contemporary pagan movement - the following conclusions can be drawn: first of all, the question of gender affiliation showed that the male component is predominant at Kupala festivals: 138 (59%) of the total number of respondents in 2014 and 257 (60%) in 2015 were male. Secondly, the most prevalent age among adepts of the pagan worldview was 31. Thirdly, the question of education level revealed that the overwhelming majority of respondents had higher education. Fourthly, in the sphere of professional employment, the most widespread occupation was a middle-management position. Fifthly and finally, the most common answer to the question of the contemporary pagan's place of residence was "city of federal significance", which confirms the scholarly community's thesis that this movement has emerged out of the urban environment.[13]

The function of the singular regulator shaping the foundation of the worldview of a particular association is, as in most new religious movements, assumed by the leader of the community - the *zhrets* ("priest"), *volkhv*[14], or *verkhovod* ("high-leader").[15] According to the data of questionnaire surveys conducted among participants of the Kupala festival held in the area of Ignatyevskoe village in the Maloyaroslavets district of the Kaluga region in 2015, out of the five answer options of "religious", "administrative", "household-economic" (*khoziastvennaia*), "informational" and "other", the average respondents of pagan communities attached priority to the leadership function in the following way: the largest number of pagans pointed to the religious function as the

---

[13] See Roman Shizhensky, "Contemporary Pagan Ratings of Russian Historical Figures: The Data of Field Studies" in this volume; R.V. Shizhensky M.Y. Shliakhov, "Pis'mennye istochniki sovremennykh rossiiskikh iazychnikov po dannym polevykh issledovanii", *Istoricheskie, filosofskie, politicheskie i iuridicheskie nauki, kul'turologiia i iskustvovedenie. Voprosy teorii i praktiki* 8:3 (58) (2015), pp. 210-214.

[14] The Old Slavic *volkhv'*, related to Russian *volkhvovanie* ("magic", "conjuring", "divining"), *volshebstvo* ("magic") and cognate of the Old Norse *völva* ("seeress"), referred to a priestly figure among the Slavic peoples (e.g. Belarusian *vl'khva*, Ukrainian *volkhv*, Polish *wołchw*, Bulgarian *v'lkhva*, Slovenian *volh/volhva*), whose title might be translated as "magus", "wizard", or "wiseman." - Trans.

[15] R.V. Shizhensky, "Zhrechestvo v sovremennom russkom iazychestve", *Vestnik udmurtskogo universiteta. Seriia istoriia i filologiia* 5:2 (2008), p. 148; See also Roman Shizhensky, "Contemporary Pagan Ratings of Russian Historical Figures: The Data of Field Studies" in this volume.

determining type of activity. This answer was preferred by 179 out of 429 respondents, amounting to 41.7%. In second place, in the opinion of the movement's adepts, is the informational role. This position was voted for by 89 (20.7%) of respondents. Forty-four (10.3%) identified the dominant function of the community leader to be administrative. In last place was the economic role of the pagan "chief." Thirty-nine (9.1%) of respondents present at the festival chose the latter. It is also noteworthy that 69 (16.1%) of respondents proposed their own alternative variants for describing the "leadership function." The most interesting of these responses, in our opinion, included the following: "the community leader is both father, brother, and prince", "sexual education", "religio-social", "peacekeeping", "traditional", "*vedovskaia*"[16], and "ethico-moral."[17]

As such universal and "indispensable" figures reflecting the movement as a whole, determining association leaders' range of reasons for coming to paganism is therefore of extreme importance. An online survey posing the question "Why did I become a pagan?" was conducted among leaders of Slavic communities between 7 May 2015 and 16 April 2016. The survey engaged 25 respondents (21 men and four women) representing the following unions, communities, and associations: the Veles Circle (*Velesov Krug*), the Union of Slavic Communities of Slavic Native Faith (*Soiuz Slavianskikh Obshchin Slavianskoi Rodnoi Very*), Great Fire (*Velikii Ogon'*), the Circle of Pagan Tradition (*Krug Iazycheskoi Traditsii*), the Union of Venedi (*Soiuz Venedov*), *Troesvet, Svetovid,* the Koliada of the Vyatichi, Landmark of Veles (*Velesovo Urochishche*), Land of Dazhdbog (*Zemlia Dazhd'boga*), *Rodunitsa, Khorovod,* the Slavic Circle, the *Svarozhichi, Svarte Aske* ("Black Ash"), and Heritage (*Nasledie*). In addition, this

---

16   *Vedovskaia* is an example of the multifaceted saturation of contemporary Russian pagan language, or the "newspeak" discussed by the author below, as this term can connote: (1) pertaining to "magic", "sorcery" or "witchcraft", i.e. *vedovstvo*, (2) "knowing", "conscious", or "governing" from the Russian *vedat'/vedanie*, or (3) in the spirit of so-called "Slavic-Aryan" and "Hindophile" trends among neo-pagan circles can be interpreted as a loose allusion to "Vedic" - Trans.

17   R.V. Shizhensky and O.S. Tiutina, "*Proektsii institutsional'noi samoidentifikatsii v sovremennom slavianskom iazychestve po dannym polevykh issledovanii*", *Mezhdunarodnyi zhurnal prikladnykh i fundamental'nykh issledovanii* 1-2 (2016), pp. 278-282.

open question was answered by representatives of the pagan or sympathetic press, such as the publishing house *Russkaia Pravda* ("Russian Truth"), the newspaper *Rodnye prostory* ("Native Expanses"), and *Za Russkoe delo* ("For the Russian Cause"). In geographical terms, the survey was participated in by citizens of the Russian Federation (from Moscow, Saint Petersburg, Novosibirsk, Krasnoyarsk, Ryazan, Kaluga, Rybinsk, and Perm), Slovenia (Ljubljana), Czechia (Prague), Ukraine (Zhitomir), and the Republic of Belarus (Minsk). The responses received over the course of the interviews were categorized into the following blocs: (1) "It is fate or destiny to be born a pagan (e.g. a *rodnover*)"[18], (2) national self-consciousness, (3) spiritual seeking, (4) the adoption of faith thanks to a friend or outside person, and (5) family influence.[19]

According to this survey, the foremost reasons influencing respondents' choice of worldview were fate/destiny and national self-consciousness. It should be noted that this choice by the religious group in question is in line with the established pattern. The "passionarity" and "excessivity" (notions presently being operationalized and developed by the scholar of religion L.I. Grigoryeva) of group leaders is manifest in the constitution of their own re-mythologized worldview, their consciousness of their pagan "I." The latter, without a doubt, includes elements of escapism, if not rooted in such altogether. Accordingly, the discernment of fate or destiny as the first-rank factor that awakened these future movement leaders to turn to paganism should be considered in a holistic context alongside their own theses on the continuity of tradition and a "Golden Age." In believing himself to be a "traditional" pagan following established rules, the proselyte axiomatically believes that these rules were primordial. The national aspect being seen as the primary reason for "entering" the pagan worldview is a trend that has been established in the

---

18 *Rodnover* - "Native Believer", from the self-designation of Russian Slavic paganism *Rodnaia Vera* or *Rodnoverie*, "Native Faith" (the history and semantics of this term are discussed throughout the author's studies in this volume). - Trans.

19 R.V. Shizhensky, R.V. and E.S. Surovegina, "'*Pochemu ia stal iazychnikom*': opyt oprosa liderov diaspory", *Istoricheskie, filosofskie, politicheskie i iuridiceheskie nauki, kul'turologiia i iskustvovedenie. Voprosy teorii i praktiki 6:68* (2016), pp. 214-215.

movement since its very emergence in the late 1970s. Here we might refer to the ideas of the "pagan of politics", V.N. Emelyanov, and the "politics of paganism" of Alexey Dobrovolsky (Dobroslav). The historicity of this component (i.e. contemporary neophytes' acquaintance with the pagan national world first and foremost through the print products of the "*didaskalia*") is intensified by the quest for the "Golden Age" and logically conditioned experiences associated with the Russian's (or Slav's) sense of loss of a dignified place in socio-political realities. Determining the degree of the radicalization of pagan nationalism remains a paramount aim of a number of Russian scholars today.[20]

In examining the role of leaders in 21st-century Russian paganism, we cannot lose sight of the most important "weapon" allowing leaders to both retain adepts and attract neophytes. The role of this "ideological magnet" has recently been successfully fulfilled by "newspeak." The language of contemporary pagans represents a complex, multifaceted phenomenon formed at the intersection of philology, ethnography, and history. The new language of the new pagans should be understood first and foremost as the sacred language used by contemporary volkhvs in religious practice[21], which constitutes an eclectic ensemble of elements derived from preserved ethnographic, folkloric, and mythological sources alongside the *zagovory* ("ritual discourses" and texts[22]) of the movement's ideologues. Secondly, this "newspeak" is an ethnic identifier whose terminology defines the identity-construction of a given community.[23] Thirdly, this new

---

20 V.A. Schnirelmann, *Ariiskii mif v sovremennom mire - tom I* (Moscow: Novoe literaturnoe obozrenie, 2015): pp. 272-469.
21 V.S. Kazakov, *Imenoslov* (Moscow: Russkaia Pravda, 2011); Veleslav. *Veshchii Slovnik: Slavleniia Rodnykh Bogov* (Moscow: Institut Obshchegumanitarnykh issledovanii), 2007. At the present time, the scholarly community has not endeavored to analyze pagan "newspeak", although an exception to this is G.S. Samoilova's article which examines pagan names: G.S. Samoilova, "*Antroponimy kak sposob samovyrazheniia v novykh iazycheskikh techeniiakh*" in *Iazychestvo v sovremmennoi Rossii: opyt mezhdistsiplinarnogo issledovaniia* (Nizhny Novgorod: Kozma Minin Nizhny Novgorod State Pedagogical University, 2016): pp. 190-200.
22 *Zagovory* refer to magical, ritual, and folk-medicinal speech, such as incantations or prayers. - Trans.
23 D.A. Gavrilov, N.P. Brutal'sky, D.D. Avdonina, and N.N. Speransky, *Manifest iazycheskoi Traditsii* (Moscow: Ladoga-100, 2007), pp. 14-19; D.A. Gavrilov and S.E. Ermakov (eds.), *Russkoe iazycheskoe mirovozzrenie: prostranstvo smyslov. Opyt slovariia s poiasneniiami* (Moscow: Ladoga-100, 2008), p. 18.

language is a kind of "driving force" of the new pagan history, forming a "correct" past out of a "blend" of academic data and the personal histories of Native Faith leaders.[24]

The structure of contemporary Russian paganism deserves particular scrutiny. Over the whole history of this type of Russian new religious movement, the following types of "pagan functioning" can be distinguished: the pagan individual, the lone ideologue, the pagan family, the *veche* ("assembly") or *sovet* ("council"), the union of communities, the pagan confederation, and the pagan settlement. To dwell on the first type, that of the "pagan individual", we can cite the general trend in modern religious consciousness toward the individualization of religion, which has been discerned by scholars (such as Thomas Luckmann and Robert Bellah) to be characterized by the individual's aspiration for faith without organization, the emergence of "patchwork beliefs" (*à la* Danièle Hervieu-Léger) based on books, Internet sites, and lectures[25], and Jasper's "blind faith", or faith without content. Moreover, the predominance of the individual in Russian paganism is confirmed by the materials of surveys.[26]

---

24 Veleslav, *Radeniia v Khrame Moreny* (Moscow: Amrita, 2014); Ibidem, *Rodnye Bogi Rusi* (Moscow: Rodoliubie, 2009); Ibidem, *Slavianskaia Kniga Mertvykh* (Moscow: Svet, 2015); M.S. Vasil'ev, D.Zh. Georgis, N.N. Speransky, and I.G. Toporkov, *Russkii iazycheskii manifest* (Moscow: Vyatichi, 1997).

25 K.A. Kolkunova, "Novye religii v postsovetskom sotsiume" in E.S. Elbakian, S.I. Ivanenko, I.Ia. Kanterov, and M.N. Sitnikov (eds.), *Novye religii v Rossii: dvatsat' let spustia. Materialy Mezhdunarodnoi nauchno-prakticheskoi konferentsii* [Moscow: Dom Zhurnalista, 14 December 2012] (Moscow: Drevo zhizni, 2013), pp. 103-112.

26 "One of the blocs of surveys conducted in 2015 set as its goal determining the community status of those present at the Kupala festival. The question caused difficulty for 47 respondents (11% of the total). The predominant number of pagans, 321 (74.5%) were not members of a community structure. Accordingly, only 61 respondents (14.2%) were members of a pagan organization. Fifty-two respondences indicated the name of their community structure, while nine preferred not to disclose this information. Without a doubt, one peculiarity of the composition of participants from the community-union milieu was their altogether modest share of the total number of those present at Kupala. Both researchers and followers of 20th-21st century paganism have yet to understand the reasons for this observed individualization. However, based on the above, one can speak of a certain blurring of religion-worldview orientations among representatives of contemporary pagan religiosity. The observed terminological bricolage that characterizes the religious views of respondents is, in our opinion, directly related to the weak institutionalization of Slavic paganism, which once again testifies to the motley structure and heterogeneity of this phenomenon both in form (the absence of developed community structure) and content (the majority of adepts lack both a dogmatic and ritual creed)." - Shizhensky, *Filosofiia dobroi sily: zhizn' i tvorchestvo Dobroslava (A.A. Dobrovol'skogo)*, pp. 279-280.

The "lone ideologue" is an original, indispensable type peculiar to this worldview phenomenon. The current Russian trend of pagan seeking was established by the efforts of one individual, Dobroslav (Dobrovolsky), who came to "his paganism" over a series of events which included: working for a year and a half as a salesman in the natural sciences department of Moscow's largest second-hand bookstore; his purchase of a library in 1969 and fascination with esoterica, parapsychology, and history; his study of the pre-Christian worldview of the Slavs starting in the late 1970s; his move from Moscow to Pushchino in 1986 and the development of his own systematic practice of healing; his establishment of the Moscow Pagan Community in 1989, followed by the beginning of his "enlightening-educational" outreach activities; and his period of reclusion from 1990-2013. The case of Dobrovolsky's paganism is unique. Choosing the path of "enlightening" and "educating", Dobrovolsky remained outside of structured pagan organizations (including the spontaneous-amorphous "Russian Liberation Movement" of which he was appointed head) and ultimately implemented the "pagan family" type, beginning and ending his voluntary reclusion surrounded by children sharing his worldview. Moreover, in direct relation to Dobroslav the Yarilo's Arrows (*Strely Yarila*) society emerged as an association of Dobrovolsky's readers, and a first attempt was made at establishing a permanent pagan settlement. Also of great interest are the pagan paths of the ideologues Velimir (Nikolai Speransky) and Veleslav (Ilya Cherkasov). An "individual pagan", carver, artist, and writer, Velimir became the leader of Koliada of the Vyatichi, a member of the council of the Circle of Pagan Tradition, and the *de facto* founder of the cultural center Zhivitsa, after which he departed from all of these associations, continuing to publish works dedicated to his own paganism and from time to time holding rituals for both non-community groups and former associates. Aside from his co-leadership of the Veles Circle, Veleslav has led the de facto "one-man community" Rodoliubie and has published doctrinal literature en masse under his own "ideological brand" of the "Left-Hand Path" (*Shuynyi Put'*). Thus, lone ideologues are a constant type that can be traced across all stages of the phenomenon of the modern pagan movement. At the same time, they also represent an extremely variable type contingent upon and adjusting to specific external and inner factors, capable of manifesting in different chronological segments of the life and creative works of a given pagan ideologue. The "fixed impermanence" of this type of Russian nativism under consideration confirms the thesis of the universal role of the ideologue-leader in this movement as the one who "leaps" from type to type and is capable of assuming a new capacity for a significant amount of time.

The experience of "Native Faith families" has been implemented in the Ryazan community Troesvet, the backbone of which was composed of seven families (currently four).[27] In total, the community counts 25 adults, the majority of whom are around 30 years of age. Let us note that the children of this community, i.e. the second generation, participate in the association's festival and ritual cycle, and many of them bear pagan names (e.g. Miroslav, Yarosvet), wear reconstructed attire, etc.

Yet another example of the "pagan family" type is the community settlement PravoVedi. This "*rod* village"[28] is located near Kolomna and numbers approximately 50 people, the core of the community being constituted by the relatives of the leader, Ma-Lena (Elena Martynova). The community's members have developed their own calendars and basic mythology, and Ma-Lena has authored ritual texts, festival scripts, etc. As noted by one scholar of this association, A.A. Ozhiganova, PravoVedi is distinct from other Russian pagan associations by virtue of a number of peculiarities:

> Firstly, Russian nationalist ideology is totally foreign to Ma-Lena and her followers and, moreover, they deny the existence of nations in principle. Secondly, having only secondary professional education, Ma-Lena is in no way relatable to the circle of intellectuals and connoisseurs of old Russian culture and history, and she relies not so much on books as on her instinct or 'gift.' Finally, many scholars have

---

27 R.V. Shizhensky, "*Interv'iu s Bogumilom (B.A. Gasanovym)*", *Colloquium Heptaplomeres 2* (2015), pp. 102-116.
28 *Rod* - "kin", "clan", "tribe", "folk", "ancestral line", "*genus*" - Trans.

noted that Russian neo-pagan groups are exclusively male societies... the matriarchal structure of PravoVedi and Ma-Lena's assumption of priestly functions run counter to the pronouncedly patriarchal precedents of Russian neo-pagan subculture.[29]

Without a doubt, the percentage of Russian pagan families in the present is extremely insignificant, first and foremost because the movement itself is young and exhibits the instability of worldview peculiar to that "neo-pagan" social sphere which does not aim for transmitting "tradition" to the younger generation and whose adherents "exit the game" before their child is born or comes of age. However, examples do show that pagan orthodoxy spreads into the sphere of family relations as well, and pagan children have been raised under the influence of parents holding a certain rank in an organization, whether priestly or volkhv. Accordingly, in this case as well, the ideologue-leader is the foremost attribute of the pagan microcosm.

The *veche* or *sovet* is a type of structured pagan association which emerges for a short period of time as a deliberative body uniting representatives of independent groups and lone pagans. The reasons for the meetings and resolutions which result from such convocations can be altogether diverse. For instance, the official statement of the Circle of Pagan Tradition and the Union of Slavic Communities of Slavic Native Faith, "On the Substitution of Notions in the Language and History of the Slavs and Pseudo-Paganism" (2009), was aimed at delineating "pseudo-paganism" in the form of a number of contemporary authors from contemporary "real paganism" and its representatives. Also relatable to this structural type are the experiences of the joint statement of the World Congress of Ethnic Religions and the Circle of Pagan Tradition from the summit of their religious leaders, "For Dialogue between the Leaders of Ethno-Natural and World Religions" (2006), and the 2008 Moscow convention which gathered members of the Circle of Pagan Tradition, the Veles Circle, the Union of Slavic

---

29 A.A. Ozhiganova, "*Konstruirovanie traditsii v neoiazycheskoi obshchine 'Pravo-Vedi'*", *Colloquium Heptaplomeres 2* (2015), p. 37; Velimir, "*Poezdka v volshebnuiu derevniu*", *Derevo zhizni: Gazeta etnicheskogo vozrozhdeniia 41* (2009), pp. 1-2.

Communities, Slavia, and *Skhron Ezh Sloven* ("Togetherness of all Slavs"), which was devoted to addressing the desecration of the temple complex in Tsaritsyno Park.[30]

The latter type is altogether close to that of the "pagan confederation", which also entails the joint participation of autonomous associations. Unlike the *veche/sovet* type, however, a confederation is more focused on practical problem-solving and is characterized by a longer "actual lifespan." The three years of cooperation between the Union of Slavic Communities of Slavic Native Faith and the Veles Circle, during which the two groups held joint festivals in 2013-2014, can be considered a unique experience of contemporary pagan confederation. This experience saw consideration paid to "communal-associative specifics", which provided for the holding of joint celebrations of Kupala at the shrine complex of the Veles Circle", i.e. of "Veles' zealots", and "Perun Day" at the shrine of those venerating this deity of the Union of Slavic Communities of Slavic Native Faith. We can also associate with the confederation type the establishment in 2016 of a new pagan fellowship and *veche* center as a result of the convocation of "advocates of Traditional culture - the Slavic, Hellenic, and North-Germanic branches of Tradition - and followers of European Witchcraft"[31], as well as the emergence of the Siberian Veche unifying the *Rodnovery* of Siberia.[32]

The "pagan confederation" type has been spreading since the very emergence of the movement. For instance, Dobrovolsky delivered educational lectures in Kirov, and the Union of Venedi has held conferences in Saint Petersburg. One characteristic trend over the past ten years has been the holding of international conferences for pagans of all possible currents and tendencies of ethnic orientation. For example, the international scientific-practical seminar "Ancestral [*Rodovye*] Foundations of the Russian World" and the international scientific-practical

---

30 Yggeld, "*Soveshchanie na 'baran'em Lbu*'", *Derevo zhizni: Gazeta etnicheskogo vozrozhdeniia 37* (2008), pp. 2-3.
31 Triglav, "*O soveshchanii predstavitelei riada izvestnykh iazycheskikh ob'edinenii 27 Augusta 2016 goda*" [http://triglaw.livejournal.com/138195.html].
32 "Soiuz slaviano-rodnoverov 'Svet Svaroga' - Ustav Sibirskogo veche", Soiuz slaviano-rodnoverov 'Svet Svaroga'. [https://www.serebryanyi-serp.org/index.php/novosti/30-ustav-ssr-svet-svaroga].

conference "Imminent Rus: The Way to World *Lad*"[33] have been regularly organized across the territories of three Slavic peoples. Let us note that the organizational forms of such events copy those of academic conferences (e.g. sending out information letters, programs, sections, summations, the submission of resolutions to authorities, award systems, etc.). Organizers try to invite as participants and members of the organizing committees as many "real" representatives of the scholarly community (independently of specializations) as possible, to acquire administrative buildings for conferences, and to gain coverage of the event in official media (for example, the "Key of Veles" roundtable is regularly covered by the Yoshkar-Ola press).

Despite the diversity of manifestations of Russian pagan structures, the most popular forms of association remain the "traditional" urban communities and unions between them. In order to avoid the unnecessary duplication of the numerous existing studies on specific "neo-pagan" associations, we will present only the most characteristic traits of the contemporary pagan community and communal fellowship. Characteristic of the majority of associations of this type are the presence of an internal structure, sometimes documented in the form of "charters" or "provisions" (concerning the leader, the group, neophytes, and sympathizers), an average group size of 5-15 people, the presence of symbols (in some cases authored by the community[34]), fixed (manmade or natural) places of cult, and the practice of "following the annual cycle (*kolo*)", i.e. regularly holding community holidays, festivals, rituals, gatherings, and lectures. One of the foundational, key arrangements of contemporary Russian paganism which allows adepts to assimilate religious ideas "not in words, but in deeds" ought to be recognized in the festival-

---

33   In Russian Native Faith, *Lad* is one of several terms taken to be the Slavic analogue of the Germanic Wyrd or Hindu Dharma, i.e. cosmic order, fate/destiny, harmony. - Trans.

34   We can cite as examples the symbol of the Ber Circle priestly-volkhv group consisting of bear claws, a "Venedic rune", and the amulet of the council of the Circle of Pagan Tradition in the form of a piece of wood painted in red and depicting *Ognebog* ("Fire-God") in the figure of the winged wolf-snake hybrid, *Semargl*. - R.V. Shizhensky, "*Materialy interv'iu s S.A. Dorofeevym*" in *Indigenous Religions* (Nizhny Novgorod: Kozma Minin Nizhny Novgorod State Pedagogical University, 2010), p. 106.

ritual array. In our opinion, it is precisely holiday and festival activities[35] that unite followers of "traditional" faiths as a kind of generally accepted (or community-accepted) religious core. For the majority of groups residing in megapolises, a holiday festival is often the only opportunity for members to have contact with like-minded people, co-religionists, and to feel themselves to be pagans. In addition, deliberations on the most important veche issues demanding the presence of the majority of a religious fellowship's members, such as matters associated with the inner, everyday life of the community as well as external relations, are generally timed to coincide with a significant holy event. The role of holidays is also undoubtedly important in the, so to speak, chronological dimension. By virtue of the cyclicality and definite systematic scheme of the main holiday dates, a pagan is able to speak of a certain stability inherent not only to their community, but also their doctrine and worldview as a whole. The ritual practices of contemporary nativists are an integral part of festive ceremonies with few exceptions (in some groups, rites of naming, de-baptizing, and others are organized separately to isolate the neophyte to a certain extent from the rest of the community).[36] Rites timed for one or another especially important event bear a fundamentally active and spectacular charge. The latter comprises the so-called "external components" which accompany a rite. In our opinion, these secondary components (e.g. paraphernalia, attire, praises [*slavleniia*], etc.) impart such religious actions

---

35 Representatives of the Circle of Pagan Tradition have offered the following definition of the notion of "holiday" or "festival" (*prazdnik*): "The holy day (*sviato*) is one of the main concepts of the traditional calendar alongside weekdays. It is a day celebrated in honor of an event or a significant point in the annual circle (*kolo*)... The main difference between a holiday and the days of everyday life lies in that worldly, human time is replaced on such days by the 'time of the Gods.'" - Gavrilov and Ermakov, *Russkoe iazycheskoe mirovozzrenie*, p. 132.

36 In the opinion of the authors of the *Russian Pagan Worldview* dictionary, ritual means "special actions established by custom which accompany important moments in the life of a person and society (community). A rite is intended to designate and mark these moments on the one hand, and to, on the other, give the Cosmos a sign that the person or people involved have experienced or passed these moments. The meaning of all rites that have come down from antiquity without exception, as well as all modern reconstructions, is based on the idea that over the course of performing such man reproduces the Divine act - the 'primordial deed', the 'first action'- and thereby becomes like the Divine ancestor" - Gavrilov and Ermakov, *Russkoe iazycheskoe mirovozzrenie*, p. 121.

with a "stage-charge" that allows communities to approach the reconstruction and construction of disappeared traditional Slavic rites as authors. Through rite and its various interpretations, the modern pagan praises a deity, an ancestor, a hero or, moving along the hierarchical ladder, can finally bid farewell to a deceased comrade. The whole series of various initiations (for warriors, volkhvs, etc.) can also be considered among such rites. At the present stage of the Russian variation of paganism's development, the foremost among numerous initiations ought to be recognized as, despite its banality, the rite of joining a community. Unlike other "initiations", this act fulfills the most important practical function of drawing in new adepts, which, without a doubt, has been the fundamental task of paganism from its emergence up to our days.

At the present time, particular interest is also peaked by syncretic pagan associations. For instance, the head of the Rodunitsa community of Rodnovery founded in Krasnoyarsk in 2009, Liutoslav (whose name from his shamanic initiation is Akh Puur Deer Kham), remarked in an interview for the present author on a peculiar religious duality:

> I consider myself to belong to Russian Native Faith, but in my personal views this is combined with Siberian shamanism. This does not give rise to dissonance, since there are many traces of shamanism in our paganism, and it is difficult to overstate the importance of connection with a living ecstatic tradition for understanding one's inner essence and recreating spiritual practices. As a shaman, in my work with people, I directly employ the techniques of Tuvan and Khakas shamanism... In 2013, at the Kurultai in Abakan, I was chosen to be the head of the Wolf Spirit (*Puur Eeren*) Interregional Brotherhood of Shamans.[37]

Two other pagan leaders identify their worldview with a Northern variation of polytheism (e.g. Odinism). D.A. Gavrilov (Volkhv Yggeld) is one of the founders of the Ber Circle (founded in 2000-2001) and the Circle of Pagan Tradition (founded in 2002), and is a member of the Pagan Federation International (founded in

---

37 From an online interview with R.V. Liutoslav, 21 January 2016, author's personal archive.

1971). E.A. Nechkasov (Askr Svarte) heads the Novosibirsk pagan fellowship Svarte Aske (founded in 2011). It bears noting that, as in the previous case, the choice of worldview committed by these leaders in professing Scandinavian-Germanic paganism (Odinism, Asatru) is not necessarily axiomatic for ordinary members of their associations, who are otherwise focused on grasping the Slavic tradition. It is also noteworthy that this syncretism observed among pagan currents bears certain historical parallels with the paradigms of dual-faith (*dvoeverie*). One medieval example of the latter can be cited in the words of one of the heroes of the Icelandic sagas, Thorir the Hound: "If I go into battle [between St. Olaf and recalcitrant locals] I will give my help to the king, for he has most need of help. And if I must believe in a God, why not in the white Christ as well as in any other?"[38] Alternatively, we can refer to field records from across the 19th-21st centuries of ethnographers who recorded the presence of icons in sacred groves and sacrifices in honor of Orthodox saints made by followers of the traditional Mari religion.[39] At the same time, however, in referring to the presence of this claimed parallel, we should not forget that the leaders of these contemporary communities construct their own "Scandinavian-shamanic-oriented" field of mythology, or broader worldview, taking into account modern realities and "one's own 'I' in tradition." This "mix" of historical (from source materials), personal, recommended, and inspired fragments in the case of the head of a community is transmitted to an association's adepts who have arrived in their spiritual seeking at Slavic paganism. The resultant re-mythologized worldview product - including the eclecticism of the ideologue and associated practices - has yet to be the subject of both internal (pagan) and scholarly reflection.

Unions of communities are in turn characterized by the presence of a hierarchy of administration (including a veche, council of elders, council of volkhvs, finance department, etc.) and corresponding organizational documents which prescribe

---

38 Snorri, Sturluson, "Saga of Olaf Haraldson", *Internet Sacred Text Archive*. [https://www.sacred-texts.com/neu/heim/08stolaf.htm].

39 P.V Znamensky, "*Gornye cheremisy Kazanskogo kraia*", *Vestnik Evropy 4* (Saint Petersburg: 1868), p. 34; N.S. Popov and A.I. Tanygin, "*Sovremennye predstavlieniia mariitsev o Boge*" in *Iumyniüla (Osnovy traditsionnoi mariiskoi religii)* (Yoshkar-Ola: GUP Mariiskii poligr.-izdat. komb., 2003), pp. 132-140.

the goals and objectives of the fellowship, the rights and duties of communities, and procedures for adopting new members and sanctioning offenders. A union generally has an Internet resource, a print periodical publication, and a "brand-symbol" marking the narratives of its leaders and presented on the association's advertising products. Unions go through several stages in their "lives": establishment, a period of dynamic development (increasing the mass of believers and expanding geographically, even on an international level), stagnation characterized by stricter rules for admitting new groups, conflict situations within the union's leadership or between a number of communities, and decline. Despite the presence of all of these identified problems, the most successful unions in the present time are the Union of Slavic Communities of Slavic Native Faith and the Veles Circle. Meanwhile, the Circle of Pagan Tradition, which in 2010 counted 19 communities in Russia and Ukraine along with representatives in Germany, Moldova, and the United States, has now virtually exited the "pagan historical scene."[40] The same could be said of the Union of Venedi, which now represents a small "circle of interests" of a matured intelligentsia.

Thus, contemporary Russian paganism as an object of religious studies is characterized by the following particularities:

- Firstly, the statistically average member of a pagan group is a male Rodnover who is around 31 years of age, has higher education, and is an employee, worker, or businessman living in a city of federal significance. This individual does not belong to a structured religious association (a community or union). The main motivations inspiring this Rodnover to attend pagan festivals are recreation, participation in ritual practice, and interacting with like-minded people.

- Secondly, the main factors influencing the choice of worldview of the leaders of existing ethnic-oriented

---

40   Shizhensky, "*Materialy interv'iu s S.A. Dorofeevym*", p. 100; Liubomir, "*Sovmestnoe zaiavlenie WCER i KYT k sammitu religioznykh liderov*", *Valhalla* [http://valhalla.ulver.com/f63/t5731.html].

pagan groups pertain to fate (destiny) and national self-consciousness.

- Thirdly, the Russian pagan worldview in the second decade of the 21st century represents a vivid example of a new religious movement. The new religiosity of this phenomenon is manifest through a set of discourse-codes, among which figure the developed institution of charismatic ideological leaders, a fixed, systematized "pagan thesaurus", and a specific "newspeak."
- Fourthly, on the territory of the Russian Federation the following types of "pagan functioning" are observable at the present time: the individual pagan, the lone ideologue, the pagan family, the *veche/sovet*, the pagan conference, the pagan Internet resource, the community, the union of communities, the pagan confederation, and the pagan settlement.

***

CONTEMPORARY RUSSIAN PAGANISM AS AN EXAMPLE OF "IMAGINED COMMUNITY"[41]

The circle of questions associated with the ideological projects of the pagan "microcosm" is both de jure and de facto fundamental for both the masses of this worldview's representatives and the scholarly community engaged in studying the phenomenon of contemporary Russian polytheism. In turn, the question of whether nationalism is a critically important element of the ideology of young-pagan groups remains open. Defining the "degree" of a "nationalist-izing pagan" should be seen as a key topic of both Russian and foreign scholarly studies devoted to Russian Rodnoverie[42] (the term composed of *rodnaia*, "native", and *vera*, "faith"[43]) in the last third of the 20th century and the early 21st century. In this regard, it is of great interest to examine the main nationalist discourses within contemporary Russian paganism through the hypothesis of the British political scientist, Professor Benedict Anderson, presented in his famous book *Imagined Communities: Reflections on the Origin and Spread of Nationalism*.

Anderson's theoretical theses find confirmation in a particular pagan parallelism to the ideational stock established by this scholar already at the stage of notional arrangement. In the section "Concepts and Definitions", the British scholar examines the nation as the key element of the system of nationalism. A nation, in Anderson's view, is:

> an imagined political community - and imagined as both inherently limited and sovereign. It is imagined because the members of even the

---

41 Article first published in *Vestnik Moskovskogo gosudarstvennogo lingvisticheskogo universiteta* [Bulletin of Moscow State Linguistic University] 1:789 (2018).

42 V. Schnirelmann, *Russkoe rodnoverie: neoiazychestvo i natsionalizm v sovremennoi Rossii* (Moscow: BBI, 2012); Kaarina Aitamurto, *Paganism, Traditionalism, Nationalism: Narratives of Russian Rodnoverie* (London: Routledge, 2016).

43 See Roman Shizhensky, "Particularities of Studying Contemporary Slavic Paganism: Historiographical Analysis of the Leader of the Koliada the Vyatichi Community, N.N. Speransky (Velimir)" in this volume.

smallest nation will never know most of their fellow-members, meet them, or even hear of them, yet in the minds of each lives the image of their communion.[44]

Let us note that the role of Anderson's nation is, when applied to the contemporary Russian pagan community, fulfilled by both the entire movement as a whole as well as individual associations or communities. One of the most vivid universals typical of young-paganism is, without a doubt, self-determination constructed upon a hyperbolized antithesis of "ours" and "foreign." Moreover, in Anderson's opinion a community or nation is imagined as both limited and free. The discourses allowing for the 21st-century pagan to limit their "I" within the community and, at the same time, to consider themselves a member of a free society, the "pagan world", are extremely diverse and belong to a whole line-series of source strata. The latter include external, quickly recognizable elements which we designate as "primary", such as ritual dress, everyday attire "enriched" with pagan attributes (ethnic and pseudo-ethnic embroideries, accessories, slogans, etc.), jewelry depicting pagan symbolism or relics of a "Golden Age", characteristic tattooing, as well as - most revealingly and emphatic of the element of pagan authenticity - the amulet or talisman. Accordingly, the inner or "secondary" signs include the the movement's proselytes use of a particular language and onomasticon[45], direct participation in the ritual cycle, the creation of pagan symbols of faith, and immersion in the specialized ecumene of literature, cinema, music, and Internet networks. Finally, we can highlight a 'tertiary' element that allows for the consolidation of the diverse associations and individual adepts of this phenomenon into a common community of pagans. This element is represented by the ideological figures of contemporary polytheism, their charisma, oratorical and intellectual baggage, and the ideological projects of pagan leaders which remind their flocks of their

---

44 Benedict Anderson, *Imagined Communities: Reflections on the Origin and Spread of Nationalism* [Revised Edition] (London: Verso, 2006), p. 6.
45 See: V.S. Kazakov, *Imenoslov* (Moscow: Russkaia Pravda, 2011).

unity at particular times. In this regard, attention should be paid to the recent creation of particular supra-community advisory bodies, such as the Siberian Veche Association of Pagan Communities of Siberia (established 31/3/2015), the Veche Center of Fellowship of Pagan Associations of Russia (founded 27/6/2016), and others.[46] Moreover, "traditional" unions have also actively developed, such as the Union of Slavic Communities of Slavic Native Faith (founded in 1997) and the Vcles Circle Fellowship of Communities (established in 1999), and pagan authors such as Nikolai Speransky (Velimir), V.S. Kazakov (Vadim), I.G. Cherkasov (Veleslav), B.A. Gasanov (Bogumil), M.I. Ionov (Beloyadr), D.A. Gavrilov (Yggeld), E.A. Nechkasov (Askr Svarte), and others have continued their quest for new worldview forms.[47]

Anderson's definition of the nation comes close to the pagan component of the Russian religious map in the late 20th and early 21st centuries in terms of yet another trait: common to both is the imagination of both the nation and the contemporary Russian pagan diaspora as a community in terms of "deep horizontal comradeship."[48] The majority of Russian polytheistic groups and lone-leaders give preference to Veche forms of administration in their statutory documents.[49] In addition, horizontality is manifest in gender relations: the women of Russian pagan communities share economic responsibilities, form mythologemes on equal terms with males, take an active part in ritual practices, occupy leading

---

46 The Siberian Veche is active on the VKontakte social network [https://vk.com/sibveche], as is the Information Group of the Veche Center [https://vk.com/club133279720].

47 See: R. Shizhensky, "Interv'iu s Velimirom", *Colloquium Heptaplomeres 1* (2014), pp.171-176; "Interv'iu s Bogumilom (B.A. Gasanovym)", *Colloquium Heptaplomeres 2* (2015), pp. 102-116; "Interv'iu s Veleslavom" in ibidem, pp. 177-184; S. Surovegina, "Interv'iu s Beloiarom" in ibid, pp. 117-1120.

48 Anderson, *Imagined Communities*, p. 7.

49 See: Velimir, *Darna - uchenie o zhizni v Prirode i obshchestve* (Troitsk: Trovant, 2009), p. 52; Volkhv Velimir, *Rodnoverie* (Moscow: Samoteka, 2012), p. 50; "*Ustav SSO SRV*", Soiuz Slavianskikh Obshchin Slavianskoi Rodnoi Very [http://www.rodnovery.ru/dokumenty/ustav-sso-srv]; "Tekushchi sostav Piatiglava pereizbran na novy dvukhletnii srok", *Informatsionnyi portal Iazycheskoi Traditsii* [http://www.triglav.ru/news.php?readmore=78, accessed on 10.01.2017].

positions in the priestly "estate" of cult, and realize their "own paganism" through, among other means, narratives.⁵⁰

The parallelism between the nationalism of imagined communities and contemporary Russian paganism is not limited to the existence of common provisions between the nation and community or movement as a whole. In many senses, the cultural roots of these concepts are largely identical. As Anderson notes: "No more arresting emblems of the modern culture of nationalism exist than cenotaphs and tombs of Unknown Soldiers... Yet void as these tombs are of identifiable mortal remains or immortal souls, they are nonetheless saturated with ghostly national meanings."⁵¹ Heroization, both anonymous and personal, is another vivid pattern in contemporary Slavic paganism. We can refer as examples to the narratives of the "first- and "second-wave" nativists, A.A. Dobrovolsky (Dobroslav), V.S. Kazakov, and N.N. Speransky (Velimir). The works of these ideologists glorify the feats of the Baltic (e.g., the Rani/Rujani and Wends) and Eastern (e.g., the Vyatichi) Slavs in their opposition to Christianization and remark on the role of Russian sects and robber-gangs as fighters for the people's freedom.⁵² Nor do these nativist writers pass over the symbolism of the Great Patriotic War, in which they find pagan elements in the Eternal Flame and Motherland monuments, the cult of victory and weaponry, and the symbolism of military posters and the artistic cinema of the era.⁵³ We can place on the top of this ladder the anonymous man of the pagan "Golden Age", those eras chronologically lost

50 See: Vereya (Svetlana Zobnina), *Russkaia vera - Rodoverie* (Moscow: Ladoga-100, 2006); *Arina Vesta: Sviashchennyi smysl iazycheskikh obriadov* (Moscow: Veligor, 2015).
51 Anderson, *Imagined Communities*, p. 9.
52 See: Volkhv Velimir, *Dar shamanizma - dar volkhovaniia* (Moscow: Veligor, 2012), p. 271; Dobroslav, *Iazychestvo: Zakat i Rassvet* (Kirov: Viatka, 2004), p. 67; Dobroslav, *Svetoslavie (ocherki iazycheskogo mirochuvstvovaniia)* (Kirov: Viatka, 2004); V.S. Kazakov, "*Slavianskie obriady i obychai na Kaluzhskoi zemle*", Soiuz Slavianskikh Obshchin Slavianskoi Rodnoi Very (1998) [http://www.rodnovery.ru/stati/91-slavyanskie-obryady-i-obychai-na-kaluzhskoj-zemle].
53 N.N. Speransky (Volkhv Velimir), *Volkhvy protiv globalizma* (Moscow: Samoteka, 2014), p. 210; A.E. Nagovitsyn and D.A. Gavrilov, "*O sovremennykh tendentsiiakh vozrozhdenia traditsionnykh politeisticheskikh verovaniy*" in *Schola-2004, Sbornik nauchnykh statei filosofskogo fakul'teta MGU* (Moscow: 2004).

between the Paleolithic and the establishment of Christianity on the lands of the Slavic tribes. Accordingly, the equivalence between cultural roots and the cult of roots is an inalienable part of both nationalism and paganism in their contemporary manifestations. Moreover, pagan and national "namelessness" is reinforced by the idea of supreme sacrifice, fatality, and dying for the Homeland.[54] This silent history is written in the same way among pagans and nationalists: "from the present to the past." Developing this provision, the British scholar highlights "reversed ventriloquism", or the capacity to speak on behalf of the anonymous deceased, as another constant of nationalism. Contemporary Russian paganism also actively uses this method, especially in its *belles-lettres*. Very suggestive in this regard is the monologue of the Kievan prince Vladimir Svyatoslavich, the historical antihero of Russian polytheists, in the pen of one of the first young-pagan poets, I.I. Kobzev:

> Suddenly, Vladimir hit the table:
> "Did you hear our words, singer?
> Have you decided to go your own way?
> Your Dazhbog is not god. And Perun is not a god.
> The Russian folk invented them like fairy-tales.
> Henceforth neither in word nor in the ringing of strings
> shall we hear of these idols!
> We command to honor another lord.
> Enough praying to the black demon!
> Today we will burn all Peruns in fire
> As damned, impure forces!"[55]

In this context also fits the mass of pagan demotivators with images of nameless Slavic knights, declaring in captions: "I DIED IN BATTLE AND MADE IT TO VALHALLA; and you will pray, fast, and die a slave, a Judeo-Christian."[56]

---

54 Anderson, *Imagined Communities*, p. 144.
55 I.I. Kobzev, *Padenie Perun* [http://www.ikobzev.ru/].
56 R.V. Shizhensky, "*Iazycheskii demotivator - 'mirovozzrencheskaia nagliadnost' sovremennoi Rossii*" in *Istoriia, iazyki i kul'tury slavianskikh narodov: ot istokov k griadushchemu: material mezhdunarodnoi nauchno-prakticheskoi konferentsii 25-26 noiabrya 2012* (Penza/Koling/Belostok: Nauchno-izdatel'skii tsentr "Sotsiosfera", 2012), pp. 77-78.

Further research led Anderson to analyze religious communities. This cultural system (or system of coordinates), in the scholar's opinion, was "in its heyday" a "taken-for-granted frame of reference, very much as nationality is today."[57] It is quite natural that 20th-21st century paganism has to a significant degree been a religious phenomenon, harboring a definite set of characteristics that are intrinsic to religious communities and holding the latter to be, in the spirit of this British scholar's hypothesis, "sacred language and written script", or the "trueness" and "non-randomness" of written signs which, in Anderson's opinion, allowing for social units of the past to speak of "our faith" as the "true faith" and with this connotation to juxtapose "ours" as "true" with "theirs" as "false."[58] As noted above, contemporary Russian pagans also actively modulate their own language and introduce projections of sacred texts into circulation, e.g. ritual books, various "books of foundations", and "books of teachings." The latter contain not only symbols of faith, ritual calendars, pantheons, etc., but also shape the "pagan I" by procedurally forming a "true native believer." As an example we shall cite some of the provisions for characterizing the "pagan self." The ABCs for a Beginning Pagan By Skrytimir Volk (S.S. Lifantyev), who considers himself a representative of the classical current, draws attention to such worldview peculiarities of this group as the following:

> (2) Given the presence of sexual magic, sexual relations outside of marriage are, mildly speaking, not welcomed among us, and severe punishments are envisaged for various perversions, for "opposing Christian hypocrisy" contradicts the pagan essence of sexual intercourse - conception and fertility - as well as the pagan principle of universal and equal responsibility. Therefore, we have much less depravity than modern "civilized people." (3) Nature itself - forest, water, and earth - serves as the altars and images of the gods. For beginners to have a better perception of a god and for the sake of individual psychological moments, we put up idols, but we always

---

57 Anderson, *Imagined Communities*, p. 12.
58 Ibid, pp. 13, 17.

remember that the image is not the god himself...(5) While being tolerant of other faiths since the bloody baptism and priestly disbelief, the majority of us are fighters against Christ. Others do not hold Christ to be guilty, but blame the distortion of his teaching and the ensuing consequences of other Christian ideologies from the ancient apostles to the modern clergy...(7) Most importantly, we venerate Truth, which is the set of laws determining the being and purity of the world - and Truth before which both the gods and people are equally responsible for their actions. We live in harmony with the truth: we do not lie, we do not kill for sport, we do not take away another's property, we do not kick the weak, we do not abandon the sick and lonely; we help friends and strangers in every way we can, and we do not tolerate non-Truth, and if such happens we suppress it and eliminate the consequences of its manifestation...[59]

Or in the words of Ilya Cherkasov (Veleslav):

What does it mean to be a Rodnover? It means living according to Conscience, in harmony with oneself and surrounding Nature...Giving every effort to be Strong, Wise, and Healthy, worthy of the glory of our Ancestors... It means Knowing, directly experiencing reality, and not blindly believing in chimeras. Knowing and remembering that you are a Son of God, a Glorious Kin of the Family of the Gods, and not a humiliated, unworthy "servant of God."[60]

Or in the words of the Union of Slavic Communities of Slavic Native Faith: "The foundations of the worldview of Rodnovery are: the world was created by the Gods; spirit and matter are one and are in ceaseless interaction; the world is simultaneously one and many; nature has a spiritualized element; people are the descendants of the Gods."[61]

One cannot but agree with the professor on the matter that a nation, or in our case a pagan group (or all of Russian paganism today), is only "thinkable" thanks to images: visual and acoustic, and always personal and particular. The choice of one's own god

---

59 S.S. Lifant'ev, *Azbuka nachinaiushchego iazychnika* (2003), pp. 675-676.
60 Volkhv Veleslav, *Osnovy Rodnoveriia. Obriadnik. Kologod* (Saint Petersburg: Vedicheskoe Nasledie, 2010), p. 19.
61 Union of Slavic Communities of Slavic Native Faith, *Slavianskaia Rodnaia Vera* (2014), p. 21.

from among the vast pantheon, the creation of one's own drum, one's custom cut and embroidery of a ceremonial shirt, viewing one's topical demotivators, collective singing at festivals - all of this is rapidly absorbed by the mass of community members and over time shapes the pagan history and turns imagined paganism into something tangible (formulated by Anderson as the "experience of simultaneity"). Anderson pays special attention to linguistic community as the foundation of a nation by which "one could be 'invited into' the imagined community."[62] "Seen as both a historical fatality and as a community imagined through language, the nation presents itself as simultaneously open and closed."[63] This status is held by Russian paganism today: neophytes are invited to festive events under conditions of simultaneous insularity, diasporicity manifest on both the micro-level (e.g., the admission of new members into a community) as well as the macro-level (common nostalgia for the lost homeland of the Golden Age).

The source bases of national consciousness (*à la* Anderson) and contemporary pagan constructs are also identical. The role of the "reactive element" in both cases is perfectly fulfilled by print publications, or rather "prints-as-goods." If for the British scholar the first bestselling author who managed to sell new books by relying on his own name was Luther, then in the Russian pagan field of the late 20th century such a figure was, without a doubt, A.A. Dobrovolsky (Dobroslav), who over the years of his educational activities managed to publish more than 40 works. As in the case of Protestantism, one of the most important factors in the dissemination of ideas through books in the Russian pagan case was the cheap cost of Dobroslav's publications. Over time, the baton of pioneering the pagan printed word would be taken over by V.S. Kazakov, N.N. Speransky, B.A. Gasanov, I.G. Cherkasov, and many others. Specialized publishing houses, such Ladoga-100, Veligor, and others, have emerged and actively work with polytheist writers. As Anderson notes:

> These print-languages laid the bases for national consciousness in three distinct ways. First and foremost, they created unified fields

---

62   Anderson, *Imagined Communities*, p. 145.
63   Ibid, p. 146.

of exchange and communication...[people] became capable of comprehending one another via print and paper. In the process, they gradually became aware of the hundreds of thousands, even millions, of people in their particular language-field, and at the same time that only those hundreds of thousands, or millions, belonged. These fellow-readers, to whom they were connected through print, formed, in their secular, particular, visible invisibility, the embryo of the nationally imagined community.[64]

Two of these ways of aggregating functional characteristics are identical to the process of the emergence of Russian paganism in the 20th century. Let us highlight one way that is characteristic of the influence of the "pagan print language." If at the dawn of this phenomenon the "communication field" connecting individual ideologists consisted of epistolary sources, declarations[65], samizdat leaflets and handwritten and copied *volkhovniki*[66], then subsequently consciousness of the existence of a unique pagan world in Russia, albeit not numbering in the hundreds of thousands, manifested itself, as already noted, through the narratives of leaders, newspaper and journal periodicals[67], and through one of the most important inventions of the late 20th century: the Internet.

---

64   Ibid, p. 44.
65   On this matter we cite a passage from an interview with, V.S. Kazakov, the leader of one of the first pagan groups: "In 1993, when tanks were firing at the White house, I decided that something had to be done, and I wrote to Vyacheslav Palmin that I wanted to joint a Russian-pagan party. We met and talked in September 1993 on Saltykov-Shchedrin Street near Kemz club. I asked him how many people were in the Russian-pagan party in Kaluga, he responded that three were. I said that I also want to join and something needs to be done with this. We didn't need to create a party, because of the tense political situation, but a religious organization. There was relative freedom here then - the White Brotherhood, Jehovah's Witnesses, and many others made their rounds. To attract people, they started writing articles in the newspaper Znamya, the former newspaper of the Communist Party. I sent an article in and signed it 'Vadim Kazakov, Kaluga Slavic community.' Then we printed advertisements calling on all Slavs to join the Kaluga Slavic community...The advertisements were posted on homes, facades, and there is even a photo where we - Palmin, Igor Alekhin, and I - are standing with the advertisements and passing the leaflets out to passer-by." - E.S. Surovegina, "*Interv'iu s volkhvom Vadimom*", *Colloquium Heptaplomeres 3* (Nizhny Novgorod: Minin University, 2015), pp. 93-94.
66   For a recent example, see *Rodoliubie, Koliada Viatichei Volkhovnik 1* (2000).
67   Koliada of the Vyatichi, *Derevo zhizni: Gazeta etnicheskogo vozrozhdeniia* (Troitsk); Union of Venedi, Slava! *Vestnik Rodovogo Slavianskogo Vecha* (Saint Petersburg); *Zhurnal "Rodnoverie"* (Moscow, Kaluga), etc.

Secondly, according to Anderson, "print-capitalism gave a new fixity to language, which in the long run helped to build that image of antiquity so central to the subjective idea of the nation."[68] Taking into account the fact that "antiquity" and "primordiality" are notions that shape contemporary Russian paganism already on the instinctive level, the search for the archaic and accounting for a high percentage of equivalence between "historical" Slavic paganism and today's allow ideologues to construct an image of ancientness. Historicity is attained either through the direct assertion of an absence of discontinuity in pagan tradition, the preservation of pagan views in one or another form over the course of Russian history[69], or through secondary channels of perceiving this postulate, for instance through the publication of historical sources and historiographies dedicated to studying the paganism of the ancient Slavs on the same page as contemporary narratives, as the fruit of the creativity of today's volkhvs. The most successful examples of such eclecticism belong to I.G. Cherkasov (Veleslav), the high-leader of the Rodoliubie Russian-Slavic Native Faith Community. In his monograph, *Praises in the Temple of Morena*, the author's chapters "From the Book of the Great Nav" and "From the Secret Sayings in the Temple of Morena" are followed by the altogether voluminous chapter "The Faces of Mara/Morena in the Works of Russian Historians and Ethnographers in the 18th-20th Centuries."[70] The same principle lies at the core of Veleslav's works *The Slavic Book of the Dead*, *The Native Gods of Rus*, etc.[71]

It bears noting that the uniqueness of the emergence and functioning of Russian pagan groups claiming authenticity of Slavic worldview is not limited to the influence of disseminating print-language. Travel also figures alongside printed language in parallel: according to Anderson, "in a pre-print age, the reality of the

---

68 Anderson, *Imagined Communities*, p. 44.
69 D.A. Gavrilov, N.P. Brutal'skii, D.D. Avdonina, N.N. Speransky, *Manifest Iazycheskoi Traditsii* (Moscow: Ladoga-100, 2007), p. 1; M.S. Vasil'ev, D.Zh. Georgis, N.N. Speransky, and I.G. Toporkov, *Russkii iazycheskii manifest* (Moscow: Vyatichi, 1997).
70 Veleslav, *Radeniia v Khrame Moreny* (Moscow: Amrita, 2014).
71 Volkhv Veleslav, *Slavianskaia Kniga Mertvykh* (Moscow: Svet, 2015); *Rodnye Bogi Rusi* (Moscow: Rodoliubie, 2009).

imagined religious community depended profoundly on countless, ceaseless travels."[72] The "know-how" of young-paganism lies in the absence of chronological continuity, in syncretism, and in the simultaneous coexistence of these two sources in shaping this "imagined community." Analyzing images of traveling in the case of one such model, the pilgrimage, the British scholar identified two system-forming characteristics of such trips: the perception of religiously significant cities (e.g., Rome, Mecca) as centers of sacred geographies, and the experience, the "visual embodiment" of centrality "by the constant flow of pilgrims moving towards them from remote and otherwise unrelated localities."[73]

The establishment of sacred centers is also characteristic of the Russian pagan community, and has been since the very birth of this phenomenon. One of the first experiences of the creation of a "pagan Constantinople" should be recognized in the project of the Dobrovolsky family, who organized a community in the forests of Kirov in the vicinity of Vasenevo in 1990. Over time, Dobrovolsky's (Dobroslav's) home became a seasonal center for festival-ritual practice (such as the Kupala festival and rites of debaptizing and name-giving) and a permanent lecture hall which annually gathered pagans from different regions across the Russian Federation.[74] Presently, one of the most actively developing seasonal centers of Russian nativists is Krasotynka (Kaluga region), the site of a complex of religious objects belonging to one of the oldest Native Faith associations in Russia, the Union of Slavic Communities of Slavic Native Faith. Alongside this, the imagined communities of the eras prior to printing "coincide" with the pagan movement in terms of the "double aspect to the choreography of the great religious pilgrimages": "a vast horde...provided the dense, physical reality of the ceremonial passage; while a small segment of literate bilingual adepts drawn from each vernacular community performed the unifying rites, interpreting to their respective followings

---

72 Anderson, *Imagined Communities*, p. 54.
73 Ibid.
74 R.V. Shizhensky, *Filosofiia dobroi sily: zhizn' i tvorchestvo Dobroslava (A.A. Dobrovol'skogo)* (Moscow: Orbita-m, 2013), pp. 33-35.

the meaning of their collective motion."[75] Accordingly, the difference between the communities under consideration in this case boils down to the connotation of "bilingualism." If for Anderson bilingualism is understood literally as knowing two languages, then in the case of nativism we understand bilingualism to mean the mythologico-ritual "upgrade" of the priestly-volkhv estate which provides for one possessing sacred knowledge and initiating neophytes into it.

Another parallelism between imagined communities and Russian paganism is the topographic anomalousness of sacred space. "It was precisely because temples, mosques, schools, and courts were topographically anomalous," the British scholar says, "that they were understood as zones of freedom and - in time - fortresses from which religious, later nationalist, anticolonials could go forth to battle."[76] The operating shrine complexes and hypothetical pagan schools and monasteries (the most belabored vision of a "Great Shrine" pagan monastery is presented in the works of N.N. Speransky[77]) established in hard-to-reach zones of urban forest parks and on private property (for example, on residential lots) allow for urban nativists to escape for a brief period of time - such as for holiday festivals - to be a part of a kind of pagan union of freemen. Their freedom, religion, and nationalism is the material embodiment of the old, "mocked" gods, the use of officially forbidden symbols, Veche assemblies of equals, and the sacred language of the praises and rites of the new volkhvs.

Professor Anderson counts the lexicons of kinship and home among the idioms of nationalism:

> Both idioms denote something to which one is naturally tied...[I]n everything 'natural' there is always something unchosen. In this way, nation-ness is assimilated to skin-colour, gender, parentage, and birth-

---

75 Ibid.
76 Ibid, p. 170.
77 Velimir, "*Iazycheskii religioznyi tsentr, ego zadachi i problemy sozdaniia*", *Informatsionnyi portal iazycheskoi traditsii* [http://triglav.ru/forum/index.php?showtopic=399]; "*Iazycheskaia tserkov', kto Za i kto Protiv? - vyskazyvaemsia*", *Informatsionnyi portal iazycheskoi traditsii* [http://triglav.ru/forum/index.php?showtopic=428].

era - all those things one can not help. And in these 'natural ties' one senses what one might call 'the beauty of *gemeinschaft*.'[78]

The overwhelming majority of Slavic (or, more broadly, European) pagan associations construct socio-political projections upon these idioms. For example, the cult of the Homeland (*Rodina*), one's native home, and the community compose the foundational discourse of the nativism of Volkhv Velimir (Speransky) and the masses of ordinary adepts. Skin-color and pedigree (racial or national belonging) as "natural ties" are fundamental elements of the Aryanism and eco-anarchism of Dobroslav (Dobrovolsky), Odalism (whose name comes from the Old Norse term for "homeland", "hereditary property", "family nobility"), as well as the works of the radical Norwegian pagan writer Varg Vikernes.[79]

Moving on to conclusions, it should be noted that nationalism is unconditionally present in the ideological constructs of the Russian pagan associations of the last fourth of the 20th century and the first decade of the 21st century. Moreover, when applied to the Russian reality, Benedict Anderson's concept of the origins and spread of imagined communities is distinguished by a significant "nationalistic percentage" covering virtually all of the main loci of the existing political, socio-cultural, and religious phenomenon of Russian paganism. The most striking manifestations of this nationalism include the following:

Firstly, a commitment to establishing a unique microcosm that is partially isolated from Russian society (horizontal comradeship). The very principle of such a community's isolation is based on the idea of defining identity through the hypertrophied

---

78   Ibid, p. 143.
79   "*Patriotizm i lichnostnoe sovershenstvo*", *Derevo Zhizni 34* (Troitsk: 2008); Velimir, "*Smysl i perspektivy iazycheskogo dvizheniia*", *Derevo Zhizni 44* (Troitsk: 2009); R.V. Shizhensky, *Pochvennik ot iazychestva: mirovozzrencheskie diskursy volkhva Velimira (N.N. Speranskogo)* (Nizhny Novgorod: *Tipografiia Povolzh'e*, 2015), pp. 49-731; R.V. Shizhensky, "*Ia iazychnik! - k voprosu o samoopredelenii prozelitov slavianskogo pagan-dvizhenia (na primere iaroslavskoi obshchiny 'Velesovo Urochishche'*" in *Mirovozzrenie naseleniia Iuzhnoi Sibiri i Tsentral'noi Azii v istoricheskoi retrospektive 7* (Barnaul: Altai State University, 2014), p. 197; Dobroslav, *Tsyplenki tozhe khochu zhit'!*, pp. 16-18; Varg Vikernes, *Rechi Varga II* (Tambov, 2011), pp. 15-16, 122, *passim*; Varg Vikernes, *Skandinavskaia mifologiia i mirovozzrenie* (Tambov, 2007), p. 77, 104, *passim*.

notion of "our" and "their" space, and, as follows, the application of this antithesis on all levels of socialization. Accordingly, this horizontality or "equality" is conceived in the ranks of today's pre-Abrahamic worldview adherents as achievable through folk (Veche) law and gender equality that is realized, among other ways, in the segment of cult priests.

Secondly, the creation and axiomatization of distinct pantheons of nameless and historically recorded heroes (whether tribes, members of various religious and political associations, or individual personalities). This constitutes an active search for an historically, chronologically integral (uninterrupted) pagan cult of roots and truth of homeland that has been lost or is other.

Thirdly, proceeding from the previous point, the creation of projections of alternative history, such as those founded on yearning for a Golden Age and the utopias of ideologists aiming to build a new pagan "*Civitas Solis.*" This includes the heroization of "favorable" historical events and the dominance of a subjective inclination in interpretations of "mute" history.

Fourthly, emphasis on "pagan tangibility" and pagan "signification" through the detailed elaboration of ceremonial and ritual components. This includes the active use of print-language (leaders' monographs and lectures, leaflets, calendars, etc.). Finally, this also concerns pilgrimage and the creation of zones of pagan freedom, such as shrines, temples, lecture spaces, and hypothetical pagan monasteries.

***

THE RUSSIAN PAGAN DIASPORA: DEFINITIONS OF NEO-PAGANISM IN CONTEMPORARY RUSSIA[80]

One of the ideological innovations and worldview "breakthroughs" to sweep Russia in the 20th century was the religio-philosophical movement known in the scholarly community as neo-paganism. The etiological key of this term dates back to 1908, when it was coined in Cambridge by the artist Gwen Raverat and the Georgian poet Rupert Brooke[81], who saw in modern paganism only the worship of nature and everyday rural life. In "bestowing" the term "neo-paganism" upon the world at the beginning of the last century, these artists could not have anticipated how the external formulation and semantic meaning of their "brainchild" would change over the course of a few decades. In the 1970s, the process of reanimating native faith came to embrace Russia as well. The increasing activity (especially in the 1980s-'90s) and unexpected longevity of the Russian variant of this movement has drawn public attention to the phenomenon of Slavic neo-paganism.

The scholarly community has grappled with terminological definitions for this religious current. Gradually, a striking peculiarity of the Russian approach to studying Slavic nativism has emerged, namely, the fact that interest is being exhibited in the new pagans not only by professional scholars, such as historians, scholars of religion, political scientists, scholars of culture, etc., but also by representatives of the so-called Abrahamic religions (first and foremost Christianity). Moreover, significant contributions to grasping the semantics of the term have been provided by the

---

80 Article originally published in two parts: (1) in the conference volume *Dialog gosudarstva i religioznykh ob'edinenii v prostranstve sovremennoi kul'tury* [*Dialogue between the State and Religious Associations in the Space of Contemporary Culture*] (Volgograd, 2009), and (2) in R.V. Shizhensky (ed.), *Indigenous Religions. 'Rus' Iazycheskaia': etnicheskaia religioznost' v Rossii i Ukraine XX-XXI vv. [Indigenous Religions. "Pagan Rus'": Ethnic Religiosity in 20th and 21st-century Russia and Ukraine]* (Nizhny Novgorod: Nizhny Novgorod State Pedagogical University, 2010).

81 O.O. Tupik,"*Neoiazichnitstvo na storinkakh presi*", *Visnik Akademii pratsi i solsial'nykh vidnosin Federatsii profsilok Ukraini* 2:15 (2002), p. 259.

leaders of contemporary Slavic paganism themselves. Numerous websites and Internet forums have become a widely accessible and frequently revisited field of discussion. The "worldwide web", as a constantly updated experimental platform, contains the largest number of versions and theories disclosing the essence of the notion of "neo-paganism." In summating the hypothetical material of these three interested research groups - the scholarly community, representatives of the Orthodox Church, and the ideologists of contemporary paganism - we acquire an altogether interesting set of rudiments which are en masse shaping the complex, ambiguous phenomenon in the life of contemporary Russia that is Slavic neo-paganism. According to materials across the Internet, contemporary Slavic paganism encompasses a broad range of associations including:

- "ancient pagan cults
- Eastern philosophy
- esoterica
- Slavic mythology
- Hinduism
- occultism
- Theosophy
- Rosicrucian doctrines
- Zoroastrianism
- Vedantism
- ancient Egyptian magic
- Extrasensory perception
- elements of ancient naturalistic beliefs
- pre-Abrahamic local-ethnic beliefs and cults alongside traditional social institutions
- folklore
- numerous historical tales
- the individual visions of contemporary pagans
- pre-Christian forms of worldview
- Social Darwinist views
- ethnocentric tendencies
- the ancient beliefs and rites of patron gods
- ancient spiritual practices

- Gnosticism
- non-traditional cults
- distorted imitations of elements of rite
- a playful game of religious entourage
- pantheism and polytheism
- pre-civilizational archaisms
- retrotopia
- mystical-racist doctrines"

By deliberately and for greater clarity not combining these definitions into semantic blocs before turning to characterizations of the notion of "neo-paganism", we acquire a significant terminological spread. Particularly noteworthy is the presence of scholarly doubts on identifying the chronological framework of the notion under study. Some authors draw attention to the deep, archaic roots of contemporary paganism, while others look for the soil of this phenomenon in the recent past, and still others claim that neo-paganism is a new religious "remake." Determining the ethnic roots of the rudiments of this movement under study is also a matter of great difficulty, as the range of these roots is colossal. According to scholars, beyond the autochthonous population, any ethnos or any nation of the globe could have influenced the formation of contemporary Slavic paganism. Naturally, the existence of such "neo-pagan eclecticism" is conditioned by the presence of multiple research groups, each of which approaches the study of this phenomenon with its own ideological, religio-spiritual, historical, and other systems. It can be said with confidence that both in the present time and in the near future this variability in identifying and determining the characteristics features of neo-paganism will continue. This is tied not as much to the absence of one line of research as to the "underdevelopment" of the movement itself. Neo-paganism today is still young, it is still undergoing its formative period and developing its main institutions. In the course of this process, Slavic Native Faith will shed its intermittent (temporal), old, and unnecessary shells in the form of various hypotheses, doctrines, and false prophets until its core is exposed. Only then will it be possible for this phenomenon to be adequately characterized. Given contemporary conditions, providing an one hundred-percent accurate definition of the new Slavic paganism is, in our opinion, simply impossible.

The difficulties of unambiguously evaluating the term "neo-paganism", especially given the extensive, diverse "rudimentary baggage" associated with it, allow for this notion to be described in terms of one indisputable peculiarity, namely, this phenomenon's multifaceted nature and versatility. In describing the characteristics of the new paganism, scholars have spoken of it as a synthesis, a spiritual-religious seeking, and as a totality of religious, para-religious, socio-political, and historico-cultural associations and movements. The ambiguity of neo-paganism allows for some specialists to see in it signs of an integral worldview, while others draw attention to the pluralism of contemporary paganism. Others consider neo-paganism to be a syncretic phenomenon, a kind of "entanglement of opposites." Of great interest is yet another point of view, according to which Slavic neo-paganism is related to subculture: "By virtue of its multi-leveled diversity, neo-paganism is not reducible to a religion as such, nor to a social or political movement, and therefore it can be considered a kind of subculture representing an autonomous entity within the dominant culture."[82]

In our opinion, at its present stage of development the new Slavic paganism bears many traits of another phenomenon and term, that of a "diaspora." Definitions of this term are present in the majority of contemporary specialized reference publications, where it is interpreted with minor variations to mean the presence of part of a people (an ethnic community) outside of their country of origin, and refers to their preservation of a sense of identification with their homeland. Despite the apparent popularity and prominence of this term, however,

---

[82] A. Gaidukov, "*Molodezhnaia Subkul'tura slavianskogo neoiazychestva v Peterburge*" in V. Kostiushev (ed.), *Molodezhnye dvizheniia i subkul'tury Sankt-Peterburga: Sotsiologiia i anthropologicheskii analiz* (Saint Petersburg: Institute of Sociology of the Russian Academy of Sciences, Filial, Norma, 1999) [http://subculture.narod.ru/texts/book2/gaidukov.htm].

according to a survey by the Public Opinion Foundation the notion of "diaspora" remains a mystery for half of Russians. The semantic content of this term appears to be altogether abstract and encompasses: people united by national criteria (24%), people united by confession (4%), criminal groups (1%), people united by kinship and family (1%), and people united by social status (1%), etc.[83] Nor is there any unambiguous treatment of "diaspora" in the scholarly world. Currently, professional ethnographers, political scientists, sociologists, historians, geographers, journalists, and others approach this question from multiple positions. While some scholars have tried to develop their own universal definitions of this notion, others have limited their interpretations of this term to the phrase "socio-cultural phenomenon." Some altogether decline to impart "diaspora" with clear terminological content, and still others (the majority) hold that due to the complexity and multifaceted quality of this phenomenon, deducing any comprehensive, universal definition of "diaspora" is simply impossible.

The examination of contemporary paganism as a diaspora therefore cannot be based on a classical, generally accepted schema. This comparison does not fit into the mass of existing definitions due to the fact that contemporary paganism does not possess one of the main criteria of a diaspora, namely, the physical presence of part of a population outside of its country. However, this distance does indeed occur on the ideological front. In this case, under the influence of centrifugal processes, a certain cohort of people who reject the contemporary culture-historical environment crystallizes in the hope of returning to or restoring a former way of life - restoring and, accordingly, returning to, at the very least, a virtualized, presently non-existent homeland. In identifying neo-paganism as a "diaspora", we can cite the definition of this term proposed by V.A. Tishkov:

> A diaspora is a culturally distinct community based on the idea of a common homeland, the collective ties built on this basis, group solidarity, and a demonstrated relation to the homeland. If there are

---

[83] "Poniatie "Diaspora"", Fond "Obeshchetvennoe mnenie" (15/11/2000) [https://bd.fom.ru/report/map/dd003030].

no such characteristics, then there is no diaspora. In other words, a diaspora is a style of life-behavior, not a rigid demographic or ethnic reality, and it is by virtue of this that this phenomenon differs from all other routine migrations.[84]

Without a doubt, contemporary paganism and its Russian variant fully fit into this proposed definition and possess all of the above characteristics. There is no doubt that contemporary pagan associations (communities, movements, etc.) represent a "culturally distinct community" with their own specific sets of formats that are distinct from the rest of the population. To date, the majority of neo-pagan groups have developed not only their own holiday-ritual complexes, but also their own calendars, sacred texts, symbols, clothing, and even language. They have determined and set up their own places of cult, they choose their priests, and, finally, they are forming their own conceptions of behavior for both within the community and in the "outside world." In other words, the leaders of Native Faith have tried to create their own socio-cultural environment. It can be proposed that over time the strengthening "pagan world" will be able to remove its proselytes from constant contact with the dissident environment. Moreover, the "demonstrated relation to the homeland" is manifest in attempts both in words (narratives and electronic communiques) and deeds (personal example, community examples) to restore pre-Christian Rus, the pagan "Golden Age." Their relation to the contemporary Russian state is generally negative. For them, today's homeland is in need of reforms in all spheres and on all levels. Here we can summate neo-paganism under yet another obligatory component of the concept of diaspora proposed by T.V. Poloskova[85], namely, the notion of "state exodus" (in our case pre-Vladimir Rus, the state institutions of the Baltic Slavs, etc.) and the aspiration to preserve a connection with the latter, most often of all not in a physical but a spiritual sense. The following features are common to both of these phenomena: religious community,

---

[84] V.A. Tishkov, "*Fenomen postsovetskikh diaspor v Rossii*", paper presented at the Moscow conference "*Rossiiskaia diaspora v XIX-XX vv.: vyzhivanie ili ischesnovenie?*" (20-21 April 1999).

[85] T.V. Poloskova, "*Diaspory i vneshniaia politika*". *Mezhdunarodnaia zhizn'* 11 (1999).

belonging to a minority of the population, corporatism, infringement upon rights, the presence of a "cementing core" (historical memory or the mythologization of the lost homeland), the preservation of ethno-national culture, the presence of a national ideal, etc. Practically all of these traits are included in the peculiar self-consciousness of the diaspora (in its variations, such as group-based or national) without which, in the opinion of most scholars, the very existence of a diaspora is impossible.

Neo-paganism as a diaspora also fits into the general classification of this phenomenon and can be attributed to the so-called "new diasporas." In his study "Ethno-National Diasporas and Diasporic Entities: Essence and Structure", I.V. Zalitailo determined the time of the emergence of such "new" diasporas to be the late 20th century.[86] Zalitailo distinguishes the main reason for their development to be the collapse of unified polyethnic states and the accompanying deterioration of both the domestic political and socio-economic situation, and the development of "re-assimilation." It is precisely in the late 20th century that neo-paganism in Russia entered a new phase of development. The adepts of traditional faith consolidated and alongside their ideologues took shape organizations in the likes of communities, unions, etc. However, in addition to the collapse of polyethnic states, the reasons for the emergence of diasporas in general and the neo-pagan diaspora in particular should also include the consequences of the process of globalization. "The gradual disappearance of borders and the activation of free flows of goods, people, and ideas" in "a world of crisscrossed economies, intersecting systems of meaning, and fragmented identities"[87] is a consequence of globalization that is unacceptable to the contemporary pagan community.

Having already existed for several decades and developed in a "foreign ethnic environment as well as in the environment of its own ethnos", and, like similar entities, being a universal form, the

---

[86] I.V. Zalitailo, *"Etnonatsional'nye diaspory i diasporal'nye obrazovaniia: sushchnost' i struktura", Analitika Ku'turologii 2* (2005), pp. 59-67.

[87] Roger Rouse, "Mexican Migration and the Social Space of Postmodernism", *Diaspora: A Journal of Transnational Studies 1* (University of Toronto Press, 1991), p.8.

neo-pagan diaspora has skillfully adapted to the changing world. The "vitality" of Russian neo-paganism can be explained in terms of the cohesion of its followers based on the activity of Native Faith organizations, the presence of a "cementing core", the development of the foundations of a creed, and the presence of spiritual and de facto leaders, etc. Moreover, a significant role in not only the preservation of contemporary paganism but also its development in Russia has been played by, according to the classification of I.V. Zalitailo, one of the internal functions of ethnic diasporas: the "preservational function." This function encompasses the following features: (1) the preservation of a people's language and (2) the preservation of ethno-national culture (rites, traditions, lifestyles, domestic arrangements, dances, songs, holidays, national literature, etc.). With regards to Russian neo-paganism, this function can be only partially characteristic, as contemporary Slavic nativism is based not only on reconstruction, but also on the construction of a desired past.

In thinking through the prospects of the neo-pagan movement in Russia, let us take note of the fact that the "wave of re-assimilation" so popular in the post-Soviet space has reached a part of the Russian population as well. In the initial formation of the foundations of its ethnic self-consciousness, contemporary paganism has (with all of its minuses) played a significant role in trying to interest and, as far as such is possible, bring a marginal section of the population (first and foremost various groups of youth) on track toward Russian self-consciousness. Taking into consideration this circumstance, as well as the peculiarities of the emergence and development of the neo-pagan diaspora's "Russian pagan world", there is every reason to presume that this historical phenomenon has long-term prospects in Russia.

***

ON THE QUESTION OF THE TERMINOLOGY OF SLAVIC VARIATIONS OF "INDIGENOUS RELIGIONS": THE CASE OF THE TERM "NEO-PAGANISM"[88]

The "religious salute" that burst the quiet, dormant spiritual space of Russia in the last decades of the 20th century has shone with new force in the new millennium. The kaleidoscope of Russians' spiritual predilections is altogether diverse and, at present, represented by a broad range of currents of both indigenous and foreign origins. One of the hundreds of "religious projects" extant and developing in contemporary Russia is the religious and socio-political phenomenon of Slavic paganism. However, it bears noting that this current, which has taken its place in the hearts and souls of a definite part of Russian society and, as a result, made its way into both scholarly and popular lenses in the past century, does not have a generally accepted terminology to this day. At the core of this problem lies the presence of "competing groups" represented by whole blocs of scholarly associations, representatives of the press, researchers from other confessions, and, finally, the leaders of Slavic paganism themselves. This problem is further complicated by the fact that in describing this phenomenon each of these interested parties tend to initially treat it with certain biases, examining it through the prisms of their respective religious, political, ethnic, and other predilections. As a result of this "terminological splitting" within these groups, new interpretations are appended to the usual (established) definitions. Moreover, a completely new terminological series is being created based both on foreign borrowings as well as the encyclopedic baggage of individual researchers. No less important of a drawback is to be recognized in the kind of "definitional radicalism" of interest groups. In the majority of cases, a researcher either simply ignores parallel

---

88 First published in *Etnichna istoriia narodiv Evropi: Zbirnik naukovikh prats'* [*The Ethnic History of the Peoples of Europe: A Compilation of Scholarly Works*] (Kiev: UNISERV, 2010).

terminological hypotheses or, comparing them to their own, presents the definitions of opponents in an unfavorable light. It also bears adding to the category of shortcomings the degree of ideological influence under which virtually all research groups fall and to which they adhere in their publications on Slavic paganism, such as unambiguous evaluations along the lines of "bad vs. good" and "white vs. black."

For the sake of "insuring" against such one-sided views on the matter, and in order to create (or select from the already created) a more concrete "terminological trunk", it is necessary to abandon as much as possible the frequently historiographically declared issue of dividing the conceptual apparatus in alignment with the professional, political, and, naturally, religious predilections of one or another scholar. By using the "depersonalized" mass of definitions (and not their systems of evidence) we can thus move out from under the therein arising subconscious pressure of judgement. In addition, it is worth immediately emphasizing the ambiguity and versatility of 20th-21st century Slavic paganism. In connection with this condition, which has been noted on more than one occasion by Russian specialists, the set of definitions of this socio-religious phenomenon should, in our opinion, include several rudiments which take into account the opinions of all interested parties. Beyond creating a purely scientific, objective definitional basis, this approach is also substantiated by an elementary sense of tact.

The most widely-used term in the bloc of the Russian Humanities which has to one degree or another touched upon the question of Slavic paganism over the past two centuries is, without a doubt, "neo-paganism." Presently, this notion claims the role of a kind of universalizer that most fully reveals the essence of the phenomenon under study. However, the seeming clarity and specificity of "neo-paganism" harbors several pitfalls which do not allow us to fit this notion into the series of terminological standards for studying contemporary Russian paganism. Examining the history of this term in their monograph, *A History of Pagan Europe*, Nigel Pennick and Prudence Jones draw attention to the following peculiarities: "The term 'neo-

Paganism' is often applied to all contemporary Pagan practices, especially by American commentators. But it was applied first, in a rather pejorative way, to the artists of the Pre-Raphaelite movement. Later, there was actually a group that called itself the Neo-Pagans. Founded in Cambridge in 1908, it included the artist Gwen Raverat and the poet Rupert Brooke."[89] Over time, this English term, initially having a negative semantic significance and narrow artistic specialization, was transformed and packed with its contemporary ring. The *Encyclopedia Britannica* associates "neo-paganism" with "nature religions." Taking "neo-paganism" to mean practically any spiritual current from Europe and the Middle East aiming to restore ancient polytheistic religions, the authors of the *Encyclopedia Britannica* entry see the main difference between "neo-paganism", "ritual magic", and "modern witchcraft" in followers of neo-paganism's aspiration to reconstruct the genuine pantheons and rituals of ancient cultures.[90] The encyclopedia recognizes "Wicca" or "modern witchcraft" to be the closest spiritual current to neo-paganism, although distinct from it. However, in a number of publications by the ideologues of modern witchcraft, particularly in the works of Scott Cunningham, Anodea Judith, and Gus diZerega, there is no border between neo-paganism and Wicca. "Witchcraft" thereby functions as an analogue of neo-paganism, as one of the movement's diverse variations. Moreover, Western adherents of the "nature religions" have imparted the term "neo-paganism" or "new paganism" (*à la* Cunningham[91]) with rudiments which clearly do not fit even into divergent Russian conceptualizations of Slavic paganism. For instance, Judith believes neo-paganism to be a religion, not a worldview[92], while Cunningham speaks of reborn pagan religions in the modern world, and Gus diZerega speaks of an enormous influence on the new pagans by Christian culture

---

89   Nigel Pennick and Prudence Jones, *A History of Pagan Europe* (London: Routledge, 1995), p. 216.
90   "Neo-Paganism" in *Encyclopedia Britannica* [https://www.britannica.com/topic/Neo-Paganism].
91   Scott Cunningham, *Wicca: A Guide for the Solitary Practitioner* (St. Paul: Llewellyn Publications, 2003).
92   Anodea Judith, *The Truth about Neo-Paganism* (St. Paul: Llewellyn Publications, 1994).

and the discontinuity of their tradition.⁹³ Despite its European origins and substantive divergences in semantic context, the term "neo-paganism" has penetrated the environment of Russian followers of nativism as well as circles of Russian researchers of this socio-religious phenomenon. Representatives of 20th-21st century Slavic paganism are divided on the "neo-pagan question" into supporters of using this term, naturally in its "new European variation", and ardent opponents of "new paganism."

One of the first authors to use the term "new pagans" in the 20th century was the literateur Lev Gomolitsky, who dedicated several stories, poems, and essays to Slavic paganism.⁹⁴ However, as was the case with its Western analogue, Gomolitsky's "new paganism" did not go beyond literary fantasy and, in Yuri Miroliubov's opinion, was merely a literary device.⁹⁵ The ideologist of contemporary Russian polytheism, Alexey Dobrovolsky (Dobroslav), refers in his works to "neo-paganism" in its current ring. Dobroslav sees nothing wrong with this term's use by representatives of Slavic paganism. The semantic content of this notion in Dobroslav's works is practically identical to the definitions of Western representatives of "nature religions", who see in "neo-paganism" a traditional worldview adapted to modern conditions.⁹⁶ This point of view was developed by A.M. Shcheglov in his work The Return of the Gods.⁹⁷ Accepting the term "neo-paganism", the author nevertheless believes that in the future this notion will be streamlined, modified, and restored to its original point: "neo-paganism" will become customary for "paganism."⁹⁸ A. Shiropaev has authored an article on this terminological question with regards to the correlation between the notions of "neo-paganism" and "Native Faith." In Shiropaev's opinion, "pagan futurists" are adherents to an integral worldview. Intrinsic to them is a total

---

93 Gus diZerega, *Christians and Pagans: The Personal Spiritual Experience* (St. Paul: Llewellyn Publications, 2001).
94 Lev Gomolitsky (Leon Gomolicki), "*V navi zreti*" (1938).
95 Yuri Miroliubov, *Slaviano-russkii fol'klor* (Munich, 1984), p. 9.
96 Dobroslav, *Prirodoliubivaia religiia budushchego* (Kirov, 2004), p. 15
97 A.M. Shcheglov, *Vozvrashchenie bogov* (Moscow, 1999), p. 3.
98 A.M. Shcheglov, *Iazycheskaia zarya* (Moscow, 2001), p. 20.

rehabilitation of life, a oneness of world-feeling, aesthetics, and a socio-political idea. For this author, "neo-paganism" is the domineering racial and revolutionary vanguard of the rebirth of European paganism.[99] As in his earlier works, Shriopaev holds the main criteria of "neo-" to be the impossibility of reproducing and repeating lost ancient tradition. Overall, the position of supporters of prefixing paganism with "neo-" against the camp of "nature religions" is encapsulated in the capacious phrase of the French philosopher Alain de Benoist: "The new paganism must be truly new."

On 20 February 2005 in Moscow's Tsaritsyno forest park, opponents of the use of the notion "neo-paganism", including the leaders of 12 pagan groups, adopted the public appeal "On 'neo-paganism' and contemporary paganism: Against the clericalization of the humanities." Referring to the opinions of Church leaders, or "clerical-minded authors" claiming that the traditional (pagan) worldview was lost by Russians long ago and, as follows, the term "neo-paganism" is fully "legitimate", the authors of the appeal proclaimed the following as a counter-argument: "We recognize the foundation of our faith to be not a form of ritual (liturgy, initiation, mystery), but kinship with our ancestors and descendants, with our Gods and all of Nature, within and outside of us... We live in Russia and we are upholding the uninterrupted tradition of kinship, language, and shared, deep symbolic meanings from distant ancestors down to our days."[100] In addition, the pagan leaders remarked that the use of the term "neo-paganism" implants into mass consciousness false notions of a link between contemporary Slavic pagans and radical right-wing movements. Devoting separate consideration to the history of the notion of "neo-paganism", the authors hone their attention on the foreign origins of the term "neo-pagan" and justifiably understand such to mean "a social process associated with the preservation and reconstruction of elements of ancient nature beliefs and the

---

99 A. Shiropaev, *"Neoiazychestvo i 'rodnoverie'"*, *LiveJournal* (18/6/2007) [https://shiropaev.livejournal.com/8643.html].
100 *Krug Iazycheskoi Traditsii*, *"Tsaritsynskoe obrashchenie"* [http://slavya.ru/delo/krug/05/neo.htm].

ethnic culture of the peoples of Western Europe and America."[101] The word "pagan", in the opinion of these pagans, comes from the medieval designation of the common folk, and correspondingly the Russian *iazychestvo* from the root *iazyk*, i.e. "people" (*narod*) or "tribe" (*plemia*). Based on the above-cited peculiarities of the emergence of the notion of "neo-paganism" and "paganism", members of the Circle of Pagan Tradition have built their own case of evidence for the unacceptability of using the term "neo-paganism." For the authors of the appeal "On 'neo-paganism' and contemporary paganism", neo-pagans are people who seek new forms for embodying the elements of traditional culture, who uncritically accept the terminology of academic religious studies and try to construct their own new tradition."[102] The opinion that "neo-pagans" are a group interested in tradition but accepting the pagan worldview on a "profane" level is shared by Rodoslav (A.A. Zinchenko), one of the elders of the Russian polytheist movement. In his work *The Winding Paths of Tradition*, Rodoslav deems the main distinctive parameter of "neo-" to be "bookishness", or in other words, unlike true, "natural" pagans, "neo-pagans" comprehend tradition from books and engage in the reconstruction of native faith by the data of various written sources and literature.[103] This point of view is shared by G.N. Botseniuk ("Prince Ogin"), the leader of Slavic pagans abroad represented by the spiritual current of "Great Fire." In Botseniuk's opinion, neo-pagans are reconstructionists or re-enactors whose attempts to revive the Slavic folk faith on the basis of scientific data are doomed to failure. At the core of this problem is the suspicion that the political press to one extent or another affects all scientific research, and therefore the opinions of scholars are turned into dogma while there remains an absence of direct transmission of pagan tradition.[104] Another wholly important addendum to the "neo-pagan affair" is contained in the anonymous article, "The Russian Spirit and How it is being Defamed", which was published

---

101 Ibid.
102 Ibid.
103 Rodoslav, *Izvilistye puti Traditsii* (Moscow, 2006), p. 26.
104 Online interview with G.N. Botseniuk (10/10/2010) from the author's personal archive.

in *Tree of Life: Newspaper of Ethnic Renaissance* in 2007. The anonymous author of the article, sharing the opinion of the Tsaritsyno appeal, firstly deems the precise date of appearance of this unacceptable term to be 1999, and, secondly, draws attention to the scholarly community's lack of informedness on issues within contemporary Russian paganism. For this author, the terminological equation and reduction of all currents of Russian paganism to the unacceptable and offensive term "neo-paganism" is the result of poor immersion.[105] In their collective article "An Analysis of Contemporary Mythmaking in the Newest Studies on Paganism", C.V. Zobnin, D.Zh. Georgis, D.A. Gavrilov, and V.Y. Vinnik relate the substantive shortcomings of this notion, or rather the shortcomings of those scholars who use it (such as V.A. Schnirelmann), to a "terminological monopolization" in scholarship. The world of scholarship is seen as not wanting to use other terms, such as "ethnic faiths", "ancestral faiths", or "Native Faith" to characterize contemporary paganism.[106] Calling "neo-paganism" an "absurd phraseology" and replacing such with the Russian analogue "new paganism", Volkhv Mezgir of the "Rodoliubie of the Koliada of the Vyatichi" Slavic Native Faith community insists on the incorrectness of both notions. In Mezgir's opinion, the prefix "neo-" is rather typical of representatives of the monotheistic religions, as an example of which the volkhv cites an episode from Russian history: the schism in the Russian Orthodox Church which divided Orthodox into the "Old Rite" or "Old Believers" and "New Believers."[107]

Thus, at the present stage, the Russian pagan movement has not developed a single, final point of view on the question of the legitimacy of using the term "neo-paganism" / "new paganism." This problem remains unresolved both in terms of recognizing "neo-paganism" to be a common "self-identifying" definition as

---

105 *"Russkii dukh i kak ego shel'muiut"*, *Drevo Zhizni* 29 (Troitsk, 2007), p. 2.
106 C.V. Zobnin, D.Zh. Georgis, D.A. Gavrilov, and V.Y. Vinnik, *"Analiz sovremennogo mifotvoerchestva v noveishikh issledovaniiakh po iazychestvu (kritika stat'i V.A. Schnirelmanna 'Ot 'Sovetskogo naroda' k 'organicheskoi obshchnosti': obraz mira russkikh i ukrainskich neoiazychnikov'"*, *Analitika kul'turologii* (2015).
107 Mezgir', "Otkrytoe pis'mo. Otvet 'neopravoslavnym'm 'neoiudeiam', a takzhe 'neozhurnalistam' i 'neoistorikam'" in *V zashchitu drevnei Very (Vedy) russko-slavianskoi* (Moscow, 2002), p. 51.

well as in terms of pagan leaders' evaluations of the term's use in scholarly and quasi-scholarly literature.

For their part, the scholarly community, the press, and researchers from other confessions studying the issues of contemporary paganism are overwhelmingly inclined to use the term "neo-paganism." The main argumentation of this term's defenders boils down to the following provisions:

1. Slavic pagan tradition in its authentic form disappeared without a trace and, as follows, the absence of any direct reproductive line allows for the contemporary movement to be seen as a new (neo-)paganism.[108]

2. 20th-21st century Slavic paganism includes diverse religio-philosophical doctrines.[109]

3. The pagan community's propensity towards heterogeneity, constant development, "division", and modernization, the absence of stagnation factors, and its syncretism and eclecticism are characteristic traits of a new Slavic paganism.[110]

4. Attempts by modern adepts of polytheism to reconstruct, rebirth, and construct ancient Slavic rites and rituals are taken by scholars to be a new, artificial paganism.[111]

5. Representatives of this religious "ethnos" have a characteristic approach to the historical process, the ideology and political course of the state, and the Abrahamic traditions, hence the development of "neo-pagan" national patriotism, environmentalism, and anti-globalism.[112]

---

108 V.B. Meranvild, *Slaviano-goritskoe dvizhenia kak Edna iz form proiavleniia russkoi natsional'noi kul'tury*, (dissertation for Candidate of Philosophical Sciences; Yoshkar-Ola, 2002), p. 5.

109 V. Cherva, *"Neoiazychestvo i molodezhnaia kul'tura: v poiskakh novykh religioznykh i kul'turnykh orientirov"* in *Differentsiatsia i integratsiia mirovozzrenii: filosofskii i religioznyi opyt: Mezhdunarodnye chteniia po teorii, istorii i filosofii kul'tury 18* (Saint Petersburg: Eidos, 2004), p. 439.

110 A. Bundina, P. Kozlov, A. Mukhin, *Religioznye organizatsii Rossii* (Moscow, 2001), p. 104.

111 O.I. Kavykin, *'Rodnovery': samoidentifikatsiia neoiazychnikov v sovremennoi Rossii* (Moscow, 2007), pp. 164, 168.

112 *"Stenogramma vystupleniia pravoslavnogo istorika i publitsista V.A. Larionova na vstreche s chitateliami v muze Maiakovskogo, 2/12/2000", Prosvetitel' 1:8* (2002), p. 5.

6. The urban variant of the movement is the most widespread.[113]

It is wholly natural that these declared signs of the new Russian paganism, together with the shortcomings of this term already considered, cannot contribute to any recognition of "neo-paganism" as a leading notion for Slavic "pan-pagan" self-identification. Contemporary pagans have never recognized a temporal rift with tradition, and the vast majority of Russian nativists do not agree that they are immersed in foreign religious doctrines.

One particularity of the notion of "neo-paganism" which confirms the ambiguity and lack of clear criteria of this definition is manifest in the frequent mixing by both researchers and pagans themselves of the terminological base. Most frequently, "neo-paganism" is replaced (substituted) by the phrase "contemporary paganism." Despite the fact that the words "contemporary" and "new" have different meanings in most cases (or coincide only in the sense of related to the present time) and respectively denote "pertaining to one time, one era, to the present time, or to the present era" and "created or made for the first time, recently appeared, rediscovered"[114], many authors use both words to "reveal" the notion in sight. As a result of such "detailing" in literature on revived paganism, one can observe not only the substitution of "neo-paganism" with "contemporary paganism", but also the simultaneous use of the terms "contemporary neo-paganism"[115], "contemporary Russian neo-paganism"[116], "contemporary Slavic neo-paganism"[117], "contemporary neo-pagan parties"[118], etc. Thus, in considering both of these words in the same meaning (pertaining to a given time), we acquire the following phraseology: "new neo-paganism" or "new new

---

113 V.A. Schnirelmann, *"Perun, Svarog i drugie: russkoe neoiazychestvo v poiskakh sebia"* in *Neoiazychestvo na prostorakh Evrazii* (Moscow, 2001), p.13.
114 *Obshchii tolkovyi slovar' russkogo iazyka* [http://tolkslovar.ru/n8895.html].
115 O.V. Aseev, *Iazychestvo v sovremennoi Rossii: sotsial'nyi i etnopoliticheskii aspekty* (dissertation for Candidate of Philosophical Sciences; Moscow, 1999), p. 13.
116 Ieromonakh Vitaliy (Utkin), *Rossiia i novoe iazychestvo* (Moscow, 2001), p. 45.
117 A.V. Prokof'ev, *"Sovremennoe slavianskoe neoiazychestvo (obzor)"* in *Entsiklopediia sovremennoi religioznoi zhizni Rossii*.
118 *"Sovremennye neoiazycheskie partii i organizjatsii v Rossii i messianskaia ideologiia"* in *Slavianskii pravovoi tsentr* [http://www.rlinfo.ru/projects/seminar1200/13.html].

paganism." In the case of recognizing the semantic differences between "contemporary" and "new", we arrive at "present, newly appeared paganism." The first variant is impractical by virtue of both linguistic and semantic pun (new neo-paganism is akin to saying "buttery butter"), while the second treatment, which emphasizes the newness of neo-paganism, its recent origin, once again stresses a lack of continuity between "old" and contemporary paganism. Both phraseological forms, in our opinion, are used by a certain scholarly and quasi-scholarly audience to hyperbolize (exaggerate) a one-sided, deliberately non-objective attitude in society towards 20th-21st century Slavic paganism.

To summarize this examination of the term "neo-paganism", it bears dwelling on those arguments which emphasize the bias of this definition. First of all, "neo-paganism" in the sense of "new paganism" is a notion which arose in European culture and initially designated artists of the pre-Raphaelite movement. Secondly, European neo-paganism, in its contemporary interpretation and in terms of its foundational worldview arrangements, bears a number of serious differences from the contemporary Slavic pagan movement. Thirdly, among the proselytes of Russian paganism as well as in the scholarly world, this notion harbors different, frequently mutually-exclusive semantic charges. Fourthly, since its emergence up to the present time, "neo-paganism" has been a notion with a pronouncedly negative connotation (especially in Russian). All of the above considerations, in our opinion, do not allow us to use this term to characterize the contemporary Slavic pagan movement in the Russian Federation.

***

THE PERIODIZATION OF MODERN SLAVIC PAGANISM ACCORDING TO THE RUSSIAN PAGAN DIASPORA[119]

At the present time, perspectives on the question of the chronology of contemporary paganism are being voiced not only by academic scholars, publicists, and masses of interested people, but have also concerned (and continue to concern) the people leading the Russian Native Faith movement themselves. The latter views of the question differ radically from the majority of scholarly, so to speak, "official" versions. One of the fundamental worldview bases of contemporary Russian paganism is the argument, elevated to the rank of an axiom, that pagan tradition has never been interrupted. This position draws outright skepticism from the scholarly community which holds that, firstly, Slavic paganism was cast into oblivion with the adoption of Christianity (with archaic rudiments at best being preserved in so-called "dual faith"), and, secondly, that contemporary paganism or neo-paganism does not have the right to claim the role of the receiver and successor of the ancient Slavic worldview due to a lack of written primary sources of the "pagan basis." Scholars' hypothetical assertions that the new Russian paganism contains religious and political influences from abroad, such as in the form of "flirtations" with Aryan ideals from the time of Nazi Germany, Eastern mysticism, etc., have also contributed to this "unmasking." Finally, the constructs, "religious fantasies", and seekings of ethnic religiosity's contemporary preachers themselves are not left without attention. Despite the reluctance of the greater part of the scientific community to recognize the pagan history of Rus and Russia and, as follows, pagan chronology, the ideological leaders of the movement have developed their own version of the life of the ancient Slavic tradition and paganism's journey over the centuries.

---

[119] Article first published in R.V. Shizhensky (ed.), *Indigenous Religions. 'Rus' Iazycheskaia': etnicheskaia religioznost' v Rossii i Ukraine XX-XXI vv. [Indigenous Religions. "Pagan Rus'": Ethnic Religiosity in 20th and 21st-century Russia and Ukraine]* (Nizhny Novgorod: Nizhny Novgorod State Pedagogical University, 2010).

For example, in his work *De-Zionization*, Valery Nikolaevich Emelianov, who in the opinion of a number of researchers was one of the founders of Russian political paganism in the 20th century, held the *Tale of Igor's Campaign* and the *Book of Veles* to be the most important sources of pre-Christian literature. This Arabist scholar recognized the physicist V.I. Skurlatov to be the main "reconstructor" of the traditionalist worldview foundation of the triworld of *Yav'*, *Prav'*, and *Nav'*. The date of the "return" of this philosophico-religious model was 1977, when Skurlatov published his notes on the pagan trinity in the eighth issue of the journal Youth Technology.[120] Emelianov cited the poet of "The Fall of Perun", I. Kobzev, and one of the main propagandists of the *Book of Veles*, S. Lesny (Paramanov), as among the leaders of this movement.[121]

One of Emelianov's associates, the "patriarch" of the pagan era and theorist of primordial socialism, Dobroslav (Alexey Dobrovolsky), deemed one of the main sources allowing for the preservation of tradition to be "ancestral" or "genetic memory": "Paganism is perceived by the heart, intuitively, on the level of genetic memory. This memory is inherited, and it manifests itself in a person's preferences, drives, and behavior which he realizes without thinking (simply because he wants to). Attempts at stifling ancestral memory are equivalent to trying to escape from oneself."[122] In addition to ancestral memory, in Dobroslav's opinion, the range of "keepers" of Slavic worldview sources includes ethnographic material reflected in complex memorial festivals, customs associated with agricultural practices[123], and symbols: "It is known that the Old Russian Pagan Swastika-Kolovrat was widely used in early 20th-century revolutionary symbolism. The classic right-sided swastika decorated the state seal of the Provisional Government and the paper money issued by it... During the Revolution and in the first years after it, swastika-solar signs were

---

120 V.N. Emel'ianov, *Desionizatsiia* (Moscow: 2005), pp.18, 22.
121 Ibid, pp. 14, 20.
122 Dobroslav, *Iazychestvo kak volshebstvo* (Kirov: 2004), p. 30; Dobroslav, *Iazychestvo: Zakat i Rassvet* (Kirov: 2004), p. 20; Dobroslav, *Prirodoliubivaia religiia budushchego* (Kirov: 2004), p. 14.
123 Dobroslav, *Iazychestvo: Zakat i Rassvet*, pp. 30, 40; Dobroslav, *Svetoslavie (ocherki iazycheskogo mirochuvstvovaniia)* (Kirov: 2004), p. 22.

clearly used alongside other revolutionary emblems and were perceived by the people as signs of victory, as the personification of Soviet power."[124] Dobroslav also cited folklore, lullabies, ritual charms (*zagovory*), fairy tales[125], epics akin to the Byliny[126], and the accounts of foreigners.[127] This list of elements allowed Dobroslav to speak of the viability of Russian paganism, of its immortality. As a confirmation of such a conception, this leader of pagan National Socialism identified a number of periods of Russian paganism "in action." It is noteworthy that his classification includes both events associated with "open paganism", i.e. those generally accepted by official science, as well as an "occasional" series, i.e. a list of historical personages who, in Dobrovolsky's opinion, were oriented towards paganism unconsciously, underpinned by genetic memory. Thus, following the first anti-pagan religious reform of Vladimir, which established gods and idols foreign to the Slavs, and the second reform entailing the violent Christianization of Rus in 988, paganism manifested itself in the time of Yaroslav the Wise, who exacted the zabozhnich'e[128] tax for the right to perform services in honor of the goddess Rozhanitsa[129], in the time of Prince Gleb of Novgorod, who suppressed the "revolt of the volkhvs" in the Northern capital[130], in the time of Prince Vsevolod, who continued the work of the inquisition and burned pagan zealots[131], in the condemnation of "possession" (*besnovanie*) by the Stoglavy Council in 1551[132], in the Razin revolt of the 17th century[133], in folk sects and in the "Populism" of the Narodniks. Dobroslav writes: "Not all Russian Narodniks were inveterate nihilists. Of course, as the dominant ideology of the ruling class which was tightly bound up with the autocracy, Orthodoxy, was condemned and rejected by them. But it is known that the Narodniks considered Russian

---

124   Dobroslav, *Prizrak Kudeiara* (Nizhny Novgorod), pp. 68-69.
125   Dobroslav, *Promysel prirody i nerazumnyi homo sapiens* (Kharkov), p. 12.
126   Dobroslav, *Iazychestvo: Zakat i Rassvet*, p. 56.
127   Ibid, p. 6.
128   A term from the Novgorod Chronicle which seems to have been one of the types of princely tribute in the Novgorod land.
129   Dobroslav, *Ob idolakh i idealakh*, p. 24
130   Dobroslav, *"Prirodnye korni Russkogo Natsional'nogo Sotsializma"*.
131   Dobroslav, *Saryn' na kichku!* (Kirov: 2004), p. 96.
132   Dobroslav, *Svetoslavie*, p. 23.
133   Dobroslav, *Prizrak*, pp. 4-5

folk sects, which had preserved a significant lot of Paganism, to be potential allies, even though they themselves did not engage in any neo-pagan constructions."[134] The revolutionary events of 1917, the Civil War and then the Second World War were also, in Dobroslav's opinion, riddled with elements of paganism and linked to the "awakening of the truly Russian, unconscious Pagan Spirit."[135] Dobroslav also referred to a number of unconscious Russian pagans as "sun-worshippers who deify Nature", such as Briusov, Tyutchev, Khlebnikov, Blavatsky, Rimsky-Korsakov[136], as well as political leaders such as Herzen, Bakunin, Chernyshevsky, and Makhno.[137] Dobrovolsky believed the most powerful stage that accelerated the manifestation of Russian paganism in its current form to be the late 19th and early 20th centuries:

> Following the Pagan-inspired tales of Pushkin and the poems of Fet and Tyutchev, the strongest and most vivid draw towards native roots appeared in Russian culture in the late 19th-early-20th centuries. This time in the development of Russian freedom of thought and enlightenment can rightly be called the era of the Russian Renaissance. National self-consciousness was awakened and the eyes of outstanding poets, writers, artists, scholars, and composers turned in search of the original elements of Rus and consciousness of the everlasting values of true Folk Culture.[138]

Thus, according to the conceptualization of this pagan author, the alternative religiosity of paganism has always existed and has manifested itself in the most important events of history, in the activities and works of the Russian intellectual elite. It bears noting that in his reflections on the question of chronology Dobroslav does not stop at the early 20th century. In one of his numerous pamphlets, *The Call of Thule*, this elder of the movement offers a small autobiographical reference that sheds light on the roots of

---

134 Ibid, p. 70
135 Dobroslav, *Iazychestvo: Zakat i Rassvet*, p. 17; Dobroslav, *Prizrak*, p. 14.
136 Dobroslav, *Iazychestvo: Zakat i Rassvet*, pp. 13, 22; Dobroslav, *Mat'-Zemlia, Chudo-Chudnoe, Divo-Divnoe (vvedenie v geobiologiiu)*, p. 5; Dobroslav, *Promysel prirody*, p. 3.
137 Dobroslav, *Prizrak*, pp. 49, 69-70.
138 Dobroslav, *Promysel prirody*, p. 3; Dobroslav, *Prirodoliubivaia religiia budushchego*, pp. 12, 17.

his pagan worldview. Dobrovolsky writes that the person who had already become the "living source" for many of the movement's adherents (Dobrovolsky was born in 1938), who "exerted the greatest impression on the affirmation of my worldview", was Stanislav Rudolfovich Arsenyev-Hoffman.[139] Dobroslav made acquaintance with this person, who hailed from a Russian-German family, in 1958 while serving his sentence in the Temnik camps. Arsenyev, born in the 1880s, received a philological education in Moscow and continued his studies at the University of Göttingen. During the First World War, he was a member of a secret Russian-German officers society known as "Balticum." After the Bolsheviks came to power, Arsenyev joined the volunteers corps of General von Der Goltz and fought against them in the Baltic states. He then emigrated to Germany and joined emigrant organizations which collaborated with the NSDAP. From conversations with Stanislav Arsenyev, Alexey Dobrovolsky learned of the "Russian Squad" club established in 1924 in Germany for Russian youth, of the Hitlerjugend, the mysticism of Eckart, and more broadly the spiritual seeking among the Russian and German intelligentsias in the 1920s-30s. Dobroslav recounts: "My elder '*Parteigenosse*' combined in the most natural way archaic Pagan spiritual culture and refined university education, romantic fantasy and a sober appraisal of modernity. Eternal and present..."[140]

Thus, in his narratives Dobrovolsky insists on the thesis of the immortality of Russian paganism, citing as evidence a definite sum of actual and hypothetical material. Dobrovolsky holds the period of the awakening of the religious movement in its present form to be the late 19th and early 20th centuries, a time when paganism "greened again."[141] It is in this period that the avant-garde Russian public turned to paganism in both culture and politics.

Rodoslav (A.A. Zinchenko), meanwhile, designates the elements of his pagan chronology in his work *The Winding Paths of Tradition*. Not deviating from the common thesis of contemporary nativists that the traditional Slavic faith has

---
139 Dobroslav, *Zov Tule* (2006), p. 4.
140 Ibid, 4-8.
141 Dobroslav, *Prirodoliubivaia religiia budushchego*, p. 17.

been preserved, Rodoslav, following his associates, holds the main "source-transmission" of knowledge to be ethnographic material, i.e. traditional shirts, *rushnik* towels abounding in sacred patterns, the bylichki collected by ethnographers in the 19th century, and the whole array of all kinds of superstitions.[142] Zinchenko considered the 19th century to be a time of religious seeking among the national intelligentsia.[143] In terms of the periodization of Native Faith in the previous century, this academician of the International Academy of the Spiritual Unity of the World's Peoples singles out 1979 (perhaps as the first year of 20th century Muscovite paganism?). He writes: "In 1979, he [Sergey Novikov (Svetoyar)] along with like-minded associates organized the first pagan pagan rite in honor of the winter sun, Khors, in Bitsa Forest."[144] Furthermore, Rodoslav's work contains information about other pioneers of the new paganism, particularly V.N. Emelianov, who saw paganism exclusively as a worldview for Russians in contrast to S.A. Novikov, the leader of the Moscow Pagan Community who proposed that paganism "will be an instrument of propaganda for our country in the world."[145] The author of *The Winding Paths of Tradition* is critical of one of the "veterans" of the movement, A. Belov (Selidor), who held the beginning of the contemporary variant of Russian paganism to be not 1979 but 1987.[146] Thus, beyond conventional Russian nativist declarations of the continuity of tradition and focusing on source basis, Zinchenko's work, firstly, distinguishes what he sees as the most important chronological periods in the formation of Russian Native Faith, i.e., the 19th century and 1979, and, secondly, he deems S.A. Novikov and V.N. Emlianov to be the "patriarchs" of this current in the 20th century.

Keeping to this method of retrospection in analyzing the monograph *The Strike of the Russian Gods* by the "academician" of the Aryo-Russo-Slavic Academy, V.A. Istarkhov, it bears noting that in this work V.N. Emelianov and the Memory society he

---
142 Rodoslav, *Izvilistye puti Traditsii* (Moscow: 2006), pp. 19, 37.
143 Ibid, p. 25.
144 Ibid, p. 117.
145 Ibid.
146 Ibid, 116.

headed are taken to be the main mouthpieces of the promotion of paganism in the 20th century. Istarkhov writes: "There arose the society of Memory, at the origins of which stood the great pagan V.N. Emlianov. The society began to restore Russian history and, first and foremost, pre-Christian history."[147] As for the 19th century, Istarkhov highlights Alexander Sergeyevich Pushkin as raised by the "descendant of Russian pagan priests" Arina Rodionovna. In this author's opinion, the influence of the latter was decisive on the formation of the poet Pushkin's works, which are "saturated with pagan images and the pagan world-feeling."[148] According to this account, having dealt a blow to the national religion Christianity was compelled to adopt into its arsenal the ideas and symbols of defeated paganism, such as the very name and figure of a triune God, the image of the double-headed eagle (the unity of the two branches of power - spiritual and secular), and phallic symbolism (e.g. the wedding ring and architectural forms of the domes of Christian churches).[149] The set of preserved sources on this matter is the conventional one: Russian legends, myths, fairy tales, proverbs, and sayings. Moreover, this academician claims that the ancient tradition is best of all guarded by the descendants of the Berendei, one of the Russian and Cossack clans.[150]

The arguments of another adherent of the pagan worldview, V.B. Avdeev, on the chronology of the phenomenon under study, boil down to a list of the heretical currents (and their leaders) which have opposed the official state church since the baptism of Rus and up to the 20th century.[151] This author of the work Overcoming Christianity ascribes particular significance to the 16th century, to the reign of Ivan the Terrible, as a time when pagan rites were officially held in honor of the god Dionysus and the tsar's entourage included volkhvs.[152]

The idea of a continuity of tradition is also dear to Volkhv Vadim (V.S. Kazakov), the head of the Union of Slavic Communities

---

147 V.A. Istarkhov, *Udar Russkikh Bogov* (Moscow/Kaluga: 2006), p. 329.
148 Ibid, pp. 130, 245.
149 Ibid, p. 147.
150 Ibid, pp. 242-243.
151 V.B. Avdeev, *Preodolenie khristianstva (opyt adogmaticheskoi propovedi)* (Moscow: 2006), pp. 7-9.
152 Ibid, pp. 18-19.

of Slavic Native Faith. In his book The World of the Slavic Gods, this leader of Kaluga Rodnovery produces a base of evidence for the transmission of pagan knowledge over the centuries through the prism of festival-ritual practice. Among the rites with pagan roots Volkhv Vadim counts birthdays, name days, tonsure, weddings, housewarmings, funerals, and wakes. Despite the centuries-long domination of Christianity, Kazakov holds that the majority of these rites (with the exception of tonsure, which disappeared in the Middle Ages) managed to preserve their pagan foundations. As for pagan festival-holidays, in Kazakov's opinion the situation is much worse: "By festivals are meant annual celebrations with a fixed time. Out of all the abundance of colorful Slavic folk festivals, in the late 20th century we have but two: winter tides and Maslenitsa."[153] In his survey of East-Slavic "pagan chronology", Volkhv Vadim restricts himself to listing the volkhv uprisings in Rus in 1024, 1071, 1091, and 1227, the 16th century sermons condemning Kupala games, and the decree of 1648 which prohibited folk games.[154] Overall, the head of the Union of Slavic Communities of Slavic Native Faith issues the observation that the relics of the Slavic cultural heritage are disappearing, and therefore the task of contemporary Rodnovery consists of reanimating and reconstructing old festivals and rites "in relation to new conditions."[155]

In the pamphlet To Rodoslav by the Pechenev family (?), the authors attach particular importance to the 1990s:

> The '90s were marked by substantial, rapid, turbulent shifts in the consciousness of millions of our compatriots. Those who were baptized quite naturally became cold to Christianity after two to three years. And now, all over the country, in numerous pagan communities, thousands of enlightened and joyful people, young and old, are undergoing the rite of de-baptism and are casting off their Christian yoke.[156]

At this time (in 1991), the first book by the head of the Pechenev family appeared, Native, Good, Strong, which was

---

[153] V.S. Kazakov, *Mir Slavianskikh Bogov* (Moscow/Kaluga: 2006), pp. 177-182.
[154] V.S. Kazakov, *Imenoslov* (Moscow/Kaluga: 2005), pp. 212-214, 217-218.
[155] Ibid, p. 182.
[156] *Rodoslavnomu* (Moscow: 2007), p. 8.

devoted to critiquing Christianity and inquiring as to the native gods and like-minded believers. It should be noted that Pechenev does not consider himself to be a pioneer of Russian pagan literature, but rather concedes this title to Alexey Dobrovolsky (Dobroslav) and his work *The Arrows of Perun*. The heyday of the new paganism, in the opinion of the Pechenevs, was 2005-2007. It is during this time that in many regions across Russia pagan association emerged en masse, the number of which the authors set (with reference to the Internet) at 150.[157]

Another advocate of the idea that the new paganism (or new stage in the life of tradition) emerged in Russia in the late 1980s-early '90s is D.A. Gavrilov (Yggeld), one of the founders of the international social movement, the Circle of Pagan Tradition.[158] In an interview with the editor-in-chief of the official newsletter of the American Alternative Religions Educational Network, Christopher Blackwell, Volkhv Yggeld listed the main sources of contemporary polytheists as medieval Christian sermons against paganism in the 12th-17th centuries, fragments of the Russian chronicles, epics, the *Byliny* ballads, magical ritual discourses (*zagovory*), and ethnographic materials, and pointed out that paganism existed freely during the years of Soviet power as well. In the opinion of Gavrilov, who joined this seeking in 1986, Soviet paganism existed in the form of one current: Cosmism.[159] Among the representatives of paganism in the Soviet era, Yggeld counts Vladimir Vernadsky, Konstantin Tsiolkovsky, and Ivan Efremov. Since the 1990s, Russian nativism has changed form, as the ideas declared by the "Cosmists" were complemented by the cult of ancestors:

> In the early 1990's many people from my generation also came to understand paganism as venerating ancestors. After leaving this life, the ancestors become a spiritual part of Creation and Nature. Together with the High Gods – cosmic super-persons – they are an integral part of this Universe, and they are watching us from other dimensions, from

---

157 Ibid, p. 11.
158 Yggeld, "O permskom S'ezde Kruga Iazycheskoi Traditsii i priniatom na nem manifeste", *Drevo Zhizni: Gazeta etnicheskogo vozrozhdeniia* 28 (2007).
159 Blackwell, "Russian Paganism: Interview with Yggeld."

the Other World, the World to Come, lending us their help and support if we turn to them correctly.[160]

In addition to this work, a whole series of publications on contemporary paganism in Russia of both scholarly and popular character is owed to Gavrilov's pen. Significant additions to solving the problem of the chronology of Russian nativism are contained in a collective work by Gavrilov and A.E. Nagovitsyn's (Velemudr) social association, the Ber Circle, entitled *On Contemporary Tendencies in the Revival of Traditional Polytheistic Beliefs*. In the opinion of these volkhvs, the roots of the pagan revival go back to pre-revolutionary Russia and are associated with such names as A.K. Tolstoy, N.A. Rimsky-Korsakov, V. Vasnetsov, K. Reorich, I. Bilibin, A. Afanasyev, I. Sreznevsky, N. Galkovsky, E. Anichkov, D. Zelenina, and others. The subsequent change in political course did not affect the preservation of interest in the pagan past, as is evidenced by the numerous ethnographic expeditions organized during the first decades of Soviet power. The ensuing era not only did not abandon but, on the contrary, actively employed the traditional Slavic worldview: "From the late 1930s to the '50s, the highest governmental level in the USSR came to realize the feasibility of employing archetypal pagan symbols for counter-propaganda purposes (such as against the Orthodox Church and German occultism)."[161] Together with the above, in the opinion of these authors, the mass publication of texts on Indo-European mythology in the 1960s-'80s and the republication of complete collections of the Russian chronicles contributed to the emergence of the first urban polytheistic groups in the late 1980s.[162]

Also citing the "usual" set of sources[163], the ideologist of the Koliada of the Vyatichi community, Volkhv Velimir (N.N.

---

160 Christopher Blackwell, "Russian Paganism: Interview with Yggeld", *Alternative Religions Education Network* [http://aren.org/newsletter/2009-mabon/action.php?num=4].

161 A.E. Nagovitsyn and D.A. Gavrilov, *"O sovremennykh tendentsiiakh vozrozhdenia traditsionnykh politeisticheskikh verovaniy"*, Schola-2004, *Sbornik nauchnykh statei filosofskogo fakul'teta MGU* (Moscow: 2004), p. 180; *"O proshlom i nastoiashchem iazycheskogo dvizheniia. Manifest iazycheskoi Traditsii* (Moscow: 2007), pp. 28-29.

162 Nagovitsyn and Gavrilov, *"O sovremennykh tendentsiiakh"*, p. 181.

163 Velimir, *Simvolika Drevnei Rusi* (2008); Mezgir, Velimir, Peresvet, *Sut' iazycheskoi very* (2008), pp. 3-6.

Speransky), shares the opinion of most contemporary pagans that the pre-Christian worldview has been in continuous functioning: "Russian pagans are the successors of a long historical process. The contemporary pagan movement in Russia should not be seen as "neo-paganism"... an historical excursus allows us to more clearly understand what was lost in Russian paganism as a result of Christianization and what needs to be sought out."[164] In his monograph *Russian Paganism and Shamanism*, Volkhv Velimir offers a brief history of pagan Rus under the reign of Christianity. According to Speransky, the most important events of Russian paganism over the past 10 centuries should be attributed to: (1) the performances and speeches of the volkhvs over the three centuries following the official baptism of Rus; (2) the symbiosis of paganism and Christianity in the Vladimir principality; (3) the decline of Russian paganism in the 13th century with the loss of the integral pagan worldview as a result of the Mongol-Tatar yoke and the strengthening of the political influence and enrichment of the Orthodox Church; (4) the transformation of the image of volkhvs in the 14th-15th centuries from that of bearers of sacred knowledge to wizards; (5) the continued life of paganism in funeral rites (such as burying the dead in kurgans in 15th century Novgorod); (6) the preservation of the relics of polytheistic faith in the 17th century (such as the Pskov stone idols); (7) the complete loss of conscious understanding of the pagan faith in the 16th-17th centuries; (8) the pagan revival in the form of research by historians and writers starting in the 18th century with the rule of Peter I; and (9) the spike in interest in the pagan past in the 19th and early 20th centuries. Important contributions to the restoration of the traditional worldview are seen in the works of A. Kaisarov, G. Glinka, A. Afanasyev, Reorich, Vrubel, Stravinsky, Vasnetsov, Blok, and Velimir Khlebnikov.[165]

The volkhv of Koliada of the Vyatichi's view of the beginning of the contemporary stage in Russian paganism largely coincides with the chronological periodization of his like-minded associates from the Circle of Pagan Tradition, but with important additions. As the

---

164 Volkhv Velimir, *Russkoe iazychestvo i shamanizm* (Moscow: 2006), p. 329.
165 Ibid, pp. 21-22, 330-332; Volkhv Velimir, *Kniga prirodnoi very* (Moscow: 2009), p. 29.

volkhv remarks: "The current interest in paganism is rather not religious, but political, having arisen with the ideas of Emelianov and the ideas of *De-Zionization*."[166] However, the "Emelianov group's" attempts at reviving the faith of their ancestors in the 1970s were not met with support in society and did not come into demand. The new splash of interest in the pagan heritage began in the mid-1980s. The reason: the brewing crisis situation that ended with the collapse of the economy, culture, and political system of the Soviet Union.[167] It was at this time that Velimir himself came to paganism, as he recalls: "The author of these lines realized he was a pagan in 1984-1985, and the rite of initiation took place under Dobroslav in 1993, when I already felt the volkhv calling within me."[168] It seems that this fairly precise periodization proposed by Speransky fully deserves critical consideration.

The era of the 1990s has been spoken of as a special time in the history of Russian neo-paganism by the founder of the Slavic-Goritsky Wrestling School, A. Belov. As the latter author of the online article "Paganism as a Phenomenon of Contemporary Russian Religiosity" notes, the key "epochal date in the history of contemporary paganism is considered to be 24 June 1990. On this day, Dobroslav held a Kupala-Solstice festival which gathered, for the first time in several hundred years, more than a hundred pagans."[169] Within three years, in 1993, according to Belov, one of what is now the oldest pagan associations in Russia, the Triglav community in Obninsk, was founded.

In her seminal work on the rebirth of ethnic religiosity in contemporary Europe, *Aeneas Awakened*, the volkhvess-leader of Ukrainian Native Faith, Zoreslava (G.S. Lozko) also considers the 1990s to be the formative time of the emergence of Russian paganism: "The first organizations of a pagan orientation emerged in former Leningrad (now Saint Petersburg) in the early 1990s under the names 'Union of the Venedy' and 'Federation

---

166 This remark by Speransky was recorded in an interview with the author on 22 February 2010 in Troitsk as part of field materials.
167 Velimir, *Kniga prirodnoi very*, pp. 29-30; Velimir, *Russkoe iazychestvo i shamanizm*, p. 340; Mezgir, Velimir, Peresvet, *Sut' iazycheskoi very*, p. 3.
168 Velimir, *Kniga prirodnoi very*, p. 95.
169 A. Belov, *Iazychestvo kak fenomen sovremennoi rossiiskoi religioznosti. Chast' 2* [http://www.portal-credo.ru/site/?act=fresh&id=458].

of Slavic-Goritsky Wrestling', which were not initially religious associations."[170] Unlike the Venedy and "Slavic-Goritsky wrestlers", the first religious organization of Rodnovery in Russia was the Nizhny Novgorod Regional Pagan Community which announced itself in 1992. In Zoreslava-Lozko's opinion, however, this association could not be called ethnically homogenous (Russian). The Nizhny Novgorod community's banner came to unite not as many Russian pagans as it did representatives of the Volga region's indigenous *ethnoi*. Instead, the author of *Aeneas Awakened* holds the "pagan enlightener" Dobroslav to have been the first Russian Rodnover, who succeeded in holding the first congress of nativist adepts in 1993.[171]

In our survey, the socio-religious current of Russian polytheists is represented by a significant number of authors, each of which has their own individual approach to determining the starting point and historical development of the chronology of the movement propagated by them. Without a doubt, the lack of a unified point of view on the "time question", along with the uncertainty in designating the first pioneers of 20th century Russian paganism, cannot be counted among those factors which unify these representatives of Russian "*ethnica*." According to the hypotheses considered here, the most important chronological periods in the formation of Russian paganism within the past century are the first decade of the 20th century, the 1970s, and the mid-1980s-early 1990s. The question of determining the first 20th century pagan leader is complicated by a number of circumstances, the most substantial of which is the presence of diverse trends within Russian polytheism which, without a doubt, affects preferences in the "choice of leader." Hence also the search for forerunners of contemporary paganism in opposing vectors of development in Russian society, politics, culture, etc. Moreover, at the present time, the Russian variant of this socio-religious phenomenon is already represented by several generations, each of which has nominated their own contender for the role of "founding father", which greatly complicates the search for the

---

170 G. Lozko, *Probudzhena Eneia* (Kharkov: 2006), p. 146.
171 Ibid.

first "pagan figure." Despite this "leadership inconsistency", the majority of "second-wave" Rodnovery, i.e. the generations that came to paganism in the 1980s, highlight V.N. Emelianov and A.A. Dobrovolsky among the mass of 20th century social and political figures in one way or another associated with their ideal. However, the works of these generally recognized propagandists of paganism contain both the names of their associates, as in the first case, and the names of their teachers, as in the second case, which significantly expands the list of Russian pagans in the 20th century, thereby pushing the chronological boundary of this phenomenon further back. All of the above does not allow us to speak of any integral, complete, properly pagan historiography in the present time.

***

ASPECTS OF THE CODIFICATION OF CONTEMPORARY SLAVIC PAGANISM: THE DATA OF FIELD STUDIES[172]

Since the emergence of the first adepts of "reborn" indigenous Slavic religiosity in the USSR (in the mid-late 1970s) up to the present era of the functioning of both individual, national-oriented pagan gurus as well as entire communities and associations of a polytheistic orientation, two questions that have remained relevant are the place of the ordinary proselyte within the constructed "tradition" and the worldview basis of the ordinary participant in the ritual-festival "cycle." With respect to contemporary methodologies applied in the analysis of the phenomenon of Russian paganism in the 20th-21st centuries, we can note a number of peculiarities which hinder the scholarly community from achieving the desired "research synesthesia" of bringing the new Rodnoverie ("Native Faith") under a single classifier. First and foremost, attention should be paid to the dominance of the "desk approach" to studying the subject under consideration, an approach which, in turn, narrows the source base (in terms of both chronology and content) and minimizes the level of objectivity of the specialist's data. The "desk view" of contemporary paganism also entails the hidden danger of ignoring "mass material." Hence the most common mistake of convinced theoreticians: referring to the narratives, network statements, etc. of individual representatives of the pagan diaspora (most often leaders) and passing off the latter's personal opinions as the ideological mode of the entire community or even the whole movement. Moreover, in the vast majority of cases, scholars not only neglect to analyze the views of the pagan masses, they also cover the complex worldview of the leader of a group altogether superficially. As a result, scholars become even further removed from the objective and comprehensive study of this type of religiosity, and the interested audience receives an inverted and eclectic "scientific product."

---

172 Article previously published in *Acta Baltico-Slavica 38* (2014).

In our opinion, the way out of this established impasse can be found by taking into account and implementing two research concepts. The first proposes that contemporary Slavic paganism be examined from the position of personalism, i.e. comprehensively analyzing the personalities of the leaders of the concrete socio-economic and religio-political cells (communities, associations) of the zealots of pre-Abrahamic religiosity. Pursuing the path set by this discourse allows for the determining of the major, mainstream trends of this phenomenon as such are formulated by specific pagan didaskals with emphasis on the the latters' author-specific ideological systems.[173] The second concept aims to unveil the Slavic variations of 21st century nativism from within. This concerns the determination of the symbol of faith in the views of the ordinary pagan congregation. The present article is devoted to pursuing precisely such an analysis of the individual components of "popular paganism."

In connection with the peculiarities of the topic under consideration, the main method of research employed here is participant observation[174], and the main source is the author's field materials in the form of a questionnaire as well as free-flowing interviews with members of pagan associations.

The author's questionnaire survey included 20 questions divided into four semantic groups. The first five questions concerned respondents' personal information. The sixth through ninth questions aimed to determine the source basis of contemporary pagans. The third bloc of questions, numbers 10 to 13, directly concerned pagan faith, such as the pantheon and ritual-holiday practice of communities. The concluding question

---

[173] An attempt to highlight one of these trends in the Russian paganism of the last two centuries, with an emphasis on the role of the individual in this religious phenomenon, was undertaken in our monograph on the worldview of A.A. Dobrovolsky: R.V. Shizhensky, *Filosofiia dobroi sily: zhizn' i tvorchestvo Dobroslava (A.A. Dobrovol'skogo)* (Moscow: Orbita-m, 2013).

[174] The authors of the monograph *New Religiosity in Contemporary Russia* hold participant observation to be the only possible methodology applicable to working with small religious groups. See: A.A. Ozhiganova and Iu.V. Filippov, *Novaia religioznost' v sovermennoi Rossii: uchenia, formy i praktiki* (Moscow: Institute of Ethnology and Anthropology of the Russian Academy of Sciences, 2006), pp. 12-13.

inquired into the peculiarities of the worldview of the "ordinary" adepts of this religious current. The material presented in this study relates to the second (partially) and third blocs of questions and is based on two responses by nativists to questions concerning identificational characteristics as well as two key questions disclosing the religious predilections of the diaspora. The latter were "List the most revered deities of your community" and "List the deities which you personally most revere."

In order to maximize the anticipated results and obtain reliable information, the survey involved three multi-level associations: the community, fellowship (union), and confederation.[175] Accordingly, the first form of organization, the community, was represented in the survey by the Yaroslavl community Landmark of Veles, the union form was represented by the Fellowship of Kin of White Rus, and the confederation type by the Veles Circle and Union of Slavic Communities of Slavic Native Faith, the latter of which have previously managed to organize and hold a joint holiday festival (*sviato*). During the survey, the author tried to preserve the individuality of the data, which meant being directly present with interviewees and, as far as such was possible, not allowing for communication within the group on the questions. The latter condition, along with the specificity of the location of the "experiment" (a forest area in the first and third cases, and a closed room in the second) conditioned the specifics of the data obtained in terms of the actual population surveyed but, in our opinion, did not radically affect their content.

One common feature of the surveyed groups is their organizational youth. The chronology of these associations' establishment in their current form ran between 2009 and 2013. The Landmark of Veles Native Faith Community of Slavs from

---

175 In this case, the pagan confederation is considered a short-term association of autonomous "Native Faith" unions with the goal of holding a joint festival or preparing common documents whose subsequent publication automatically entails a higher status in the spaces of alternative religiosity in the Russian Federation, etc. One striking example of the practical activity of such a "super-union" can be seen in the general activity of the Union of Slavic Communities of Slavic Native Faith and the Veles Circle in their traditional annual ("year-circle") festivals Kupala and Perun Day in 2013.

Yaroslavl was formed on 11 December 2003 on the initiative of V. Khabarov (known as "Rian").[176] In 2009, this "religiously-based public association" (from the "Community Charter"[177]) was relocated with a new community "high-leader" (*verkhovod*), E. Torgovanov (Targitai). Since 2010, the center of the ritual-holiday life of Landmark of Veles has been the city of Rybinsk. The relocation of their "pagan capital" from Yaroslavl to Rybinsk was dictated exclusively by the role of the leader in the community's functioning. Despite the group's legal recognition of higher authority to be the Veche assembly of all Rodnovery[178], as enumerated in its charter, in practice the only "reaffirming" element of Landmark of Veles that is responsible for the whole complex array of the community's practical life, from updating the organization's site to designing scenarios for festival-ritual holidays and their hosting, is the high-leader. Another specificity of this organization enshrined in its charter is the clearly defined syncretism of the religious and the national, i.e. the "Native Faith" (pagan) and the Slavic (Russian). Worthy of special attention is the declared autonomy of the organization and its lack of membership in other domestic and foreign nativist unions.

The author's survey was conducted among Landmark of Veles community members on 23 February 2013 during the group's

---

176 At the moment of its establishment, this organization consisted of four people. The number of community members increased in 2004 (according to Targitai, by 6-8 people). The main festivals of the Yaroslavl community mentioned on the old website of Landmark of Veles are Yarila-Veshniy (April), Earth Day (May), Perun day (July), Roda and Rozhanits (September), Maslenitsa and Morena-Winter (March). The previous leadership of these Yaroslavl pagans actively developed the association's external ties. By 2005, the Landmark of Veles had collaborated with the Khorovod community in Kostroma, the Triglav community in Obninsk, Rodoliubie in Moscow, and the Arkona community in Kaluga. Data from personal correspondence between R.V. Shizhensky and E.A. Torgovanov (location: Rybinsk), 13/5/2013.

177 *Ustav Obshchiny - Ustav Iaroslavskoi Rodnovercheskoi Obshchiny Slavian "Velesovo Urochishche."*

178 The community's charter reads: "The Veche is convened no fewer than four times a year and is authorized to adopt decisions given the presence of 75% of the Community's members. The Veche elects the high-leader, the bookkeeper, the military leader, and treasurer. The Veche adopts the Order of the Community and amends and appends it. The Veche terminates the activity of the Community. The Veche accepts and excludes members of the Community. The Veche decides on matters pertaining to the targeted spending of Community resources. The Veche decides on all other important aspects of the life of the community. All matters are resolved in the presence of 75% of votes for or against."

festival in honor of the god Veles.[179] Present at the community's shrine complex, which is located in a forest thirty kilometers from Rybinsk, were 36 people representing three of the region's cities: Yaroslavl, Rybinsk, and Uglich. Seventeen of those present were respondents. Based on the responses to the question "What pagan community do you belong to and what is its name?", it turned out that 53% or nine respondents belonged to the community that organized the festival, Landmark of Veles, while the other eight (47%) did not belong to any pagan association. Let us note that only one respondent offered an explanation of their community status: "I am not a member, but I am interested in the culture of my state and I am for the rebirth of ancient traditions."

According to the leader of the Belarusian organization Fellowship of Kin of White Rus, M. Prokopenko (Vezemar), the association was organized in Minsk in 2012. The core of the union is constituted by five active members, and festival-ritual events are attended by 15-18 people.[180] Similar to the Yaroslavl community, these Minsk nativists adhere to the Veche principle

[179] At the present time, a certain portion of representatives of the nationally-oriented pagan worldview have not developed a strict chronological periodization for the holding of holidays both on the internal (individual-communal) and the inter-community level of the diaspora. The motivation for shifting the dates of festivals can be based on a whole series of extremely diverse reasons, from the illness of the *volkhv* (priest) who conducts the holiday to the coincidence of the ritual day with workdays. On the whole, the practice of "moving festivals" once again emphasizes the modernity of this paganism in practice. For example, unlike Landmark of Veles, one of the leaders of the Kaluga Rodnovery, V.S. Kazakov, holds Veles Day to be 12 February, while Volkhv Veleslav, who heads the Rodoliubie community, adhere to a different date: 11 February, etc. V.S. Kazakov, *Imenoslov* (Moscow/Kaluga: Russkaia Pravda, 2005), p. 133; Volkhv Veleslav, *Osnovy Rodnoveriia. Obriadnik. Kologod* (Saint Petersburg: Vedicheskoe Nasledie, 2010), p. 276.

[180] Personal correspondence between R.V. Shizhensky and Vezemar (location: Minsk), 2/8/2013. At present, there are very few specialized studies devoted to the urban variation of contemporary Belarusian paganism. Existing articles and essays are often uninformative. This situation can be explained by the isolation and externally closed-off character of Belarusian pagan groups, who do not wish to make their activities public due to the political, social, and religious situation in the republic, as well as the elementary underdevelopment of this nationally-oriented institution in the conditions of contemporary urbanization. On some peculiarities of the development of paganism in the Republic of Belarus, see: A.V. Gurko, *Neoiazychestvo v Belarusi: predposylki i usloviia vozniknoveniia, organizatsionnye formy, perspektivy. Neoiazychestvo na prostorakh Evrazii. Prilozhenie k zhurnalu "Stranitsy"* (Moscow: St. Apostle Andrey Biblical-Theological Institute: 2001), pp. 68-79; T.V. Shelbanova and Iu.G. Bolotova, *Iazycheskoe nasledie v sovremennoi dukhuvnoi kul'ture*, in *Sbornik nauchnykh rabot studentov vysshikh uchebnykh zavedeniy Respubliki*, NIRS 2004 Belarus (Minsk: 2005), pp. 235-238.

of administration, the so-called "Veche circle" being the basis of the organization. Once again in parallel with Landmark of Veles, the most important practical function is assigned to the community leader, the "elder" or "head": "The Veche circle includes active people (comrades) who practically and in deeds participate in the rebirth of tradition. They take an active part in the discussion of issues concerning the fellowship's activities, perform various types of work related to the interests and activities of the fellowship... The leader (elder) makes the final decisions and bears full responsibility for them." Despite the organization's young age, the fellowship is actively developing in the information sector, especially on the Internet. A central coordination site of the association and four thematic sites are currently active in virtual space. The first of the latter projects, the website Sventovit, is dedicated to warrior culture, the second is an electronic version of the samizdat journals Living Water and Fellowship Bulletin, and the third is aimed at covering Native Faith and tradition in Belarus. In addition, members of the fellowship periodically organize and participate in thematic meetings (seminars, lectures) and maintain practical religious activities which consist of regularly holding such holiday-festivals of the annual pagan cycle as Koliada, Gromnitsa, Maslenitsa, etc.

The survey was conducted among the pagans of the Fellowship of Kin of White Rus in Minsk on 5 May 2013 during one of the thematic meetings of these Rodnovery. The meeting was attended by 22 people, of which 19 residents of Minsk answered the questionnaire. Out of the total 90 people interviewed from this milieu, 74% or 67 people did not belong to any pagan association but attended holiday-festival and educational events, while 13 or 69% marked the box or left it empty. Three respondents (16%) were members of the Fellowship of Kin of White Rus.

Turning to analyze the questionnaire material obtained from the pagan confederation, attention should be paid to the uniqueness of this projection itself, i.e. the unification of two unions of contemporary bearers of alternative worldview. While pagan collaboration has already had successful experiences in the

Russian Federation[181], the task authorities of community gatherings have been of an advisory character and have not concentrated on the ritual aspect as an important component of their religious system. In this regard, the Kupala festival organized by the confederation of the Veles Circle (founded in 1999) and the Union of Slavic Communities of Slavic Native Faith (founded in 1997) should, without a doubt, be considered a unique phenomenon in the development of the contemporary Slavic variant of paganism. The joint Kupala was held at Krasny Lug near Maloyaroslavets in the Kaluga region on 21-23 June 2013.[182] The festival event was attended by 1500-1800 people (their first Kupala in 1998 was held with 20 community members). In addition to the direct participation in the Kupala mystery, the ritual component of the holiday festival included pagan weddings, rites of purification, naming rites, etc. The questionnaire survey conducted on 18-22 June was participated in by 91 people.[183] Out of 90 respondents to the question, 76% or 68 people did not belong to any pagan associations. Among them, one respondent shared their plan to join a certain organization, while another was visiting the holiday-festival events of different communities. According to the survey data, the Kupala festival was participated in by 13 communities, nine of which were represented in the questionnaires once. The organizations named included Landmark of Veles, the Kursk Northern Slavic Community, Khodor (?) the historical-

---

181 One example of such cooperation was the assembly of pagan organizations on the desecration of the shrine complex in Tsaritsyno Park. The meeting took place on 27 July 2008 with approximately 40 Rodnovery, including representatives of the Circle of Pagan Tradition, the Veles Circle, the Union of Slavic Communities of Slavic Native Faith, and the religious group Slaviia. Lone-pagans were also present, and a representative of the Skhron Ezh Sloven community spoke to the gathering via telephone. Yggeld, *"Soveshchanie na 'Baran'em Lbu'", Derevo Zhizni: Gazeta etnicheskogo vozrozhdeniia 23* (Troitsk: 2008), p. 2.

182 The leaders of the Veles Circle have traditionally held Kupala festivals at this location since 1998.

183 This surveying confronted the research team with the specific peculiarities of working in the "large-scale pagan field." These include, firstly, a significant percentage of refusals to fill out the questionnaires due to potential respondents' engagements (preparing camp, participating in organizational events, etc.) as well distrust of the interviewers, and, secondly, as noted by the Kupala organizers themselves, the presence at the festival of a huge number of mummers (people who come for regular outdoor recreation, dressing up in costume, and religious components with the prefix "ethno-").

reconstruction club Kelaz (presented by one respondent as a community institution), the Rodolad Native Faith community of Astrakhan, Thule, the Union of Slavic Communities of Slavic Native Faith, Skhoron Ezh Sloven, and the Veles Circle. Let us note that the latter three associations are not communities but unions. In addition, one respondent indicated that they were present with their community, which was unspecified. The largest number of surveyed pagans belonging to one association was the case of the Veles Circle, which counted seven participants. Two of the respondents who called themselves adepts of this organization specified their community affiliation as belonging to the Troesvet and Kolo Roda associations. The White Stone historical-ethnographic club (stated in the questionnaire as a community) was represented by two members. The communities Troesvet and Rodoliubie were respected by three respondents each.

Out of the 90 respondents, only 24% were members of pagan associations. Thus, the number of proselytes of the most widely represented organization, the Veles Circle, comprised only 8% of the total participants. It is also worth noting that, according to the survey data, out of 13 communities only nine were represented at the festival by more than one adept. Out of 22 community members, nine were there alone. This state of affairs is typical not only for Russia-wide pagan events but also local events, such as the festivals of one community alone, where the number of non-community-members often exceeds the number of community members. For example, 69% of participants of the above-mentioned event in Minsk did not associate themselves with any specific association. This trend can also be seen in the Rybinsk material, where 53% of those present at the festival were from outside of the community framework.

Based on the data of the questionnaire surveys, it can be said that the institutionalization of Russian adherents of polytheism is fairly weak and undeveloped. The represented associations are too small to position themselves on any scale beyond the local (urban) and regional. Even "on the ground", more than half of respondents who participated in the rites of one or another community were not members of an organization.

The second question of the bloc touched on "pagan chronology" and aimed to determine the degree of adepts' immersion into the identified worldview as well as to identify the pagan "seniority" of respondents. Out of the 17 pagans surveyed at the festival of Veles near Rybinsk, two people (12%) did not respond to the question. Twelve percent of respondents had less than a year of pagan experience, while 59% or 10 respondents had one to three years. One nativist had been a "follower of tradition" for eight years, and another for 16. The average standing of a community members' "being in paganism" was 4.2 years, while the average of a non-community-member is 1.5 years. In the Fellowship of Kin of White Rus, out of 17 respondents, only one had less than a year of experience, 47% (nine people) had one to three years, three people indicated more than three years of standing, while two counted more than 10 years of identification with this worldview phenomenon (one of whom has been a pagan their entire life). Five respondents (26%) did not respond to the question. Noteworthy here is that if the average pagan standing of community members is six years, then the average for a non-community-member is approximately 2.5 years.

According to the data obtained during the pagan-confederative Kupala, the second question was not responded to by three people. One respondent did not identify themselves as a pagan. Three respondents had less than one year of experience, while 21 people had from one to three. Thirty-six people claimed up to 10 years of standing, while 16 respondents indicated more than 10 years of "following tradition." Nine respondents answered that they had been involved "their whole life", "since childhood", "since a past life", etc. The average length of community members' involvement was approximately 7.8 years (not counting the responses "from birth", "their whole life", etc.). The distribution of "pagan age" across organizations is the following: Veles Circle - 4.8 years, White Stone - 8, Rodoliubie - 6, Troesvet - 4.8 years. The average pagan experience of non-community-members was 6.6 years. For visual clarification, the summarized data on respondents' pagan standing is presented in Table 1:

Table 1

	Minsk	Rybinsk	Maloyaroslavets
Less than one year	5%	12%	3%
1-3 years	47%	59%	23%
3-10 years	16%	6%	40%
More than 10 years	10%	6%	18%
Not pagan			1%
No response	26%	12%	3%
Standing of community member	6 years	4.2 years	7.8 years
Standing of non-community participant	2.5 years	1.5 years	6.6 years

We can conclude from the data of this table that the overwhelming majority of participants in community events have a pagan standing of up to three years (59% in Rybinsk and 47% in Belarus). At the Russia-wide event, on the contrary, the majority of adepts (40%) had been followers of the contemporary pagan tradition for more than three years. It is also worth noting that in all three of the organizational variations considered, i.e., community, union, and confederation, the average experience of a community member is substantially higher than that of a "free listener", which indicates that core of these designated young pagan associations has been increasingly established.

As for the question "List the most revered deities of your community", three respondents (18%) from Landmark of Veles did not respond. One pagan worshipped only his ancestors, while another took the position of a "true polytheist": "Every deity is to be worshipped at its time in the calendric cycle." Two people indicated Veles to be the only god they worship. In total, this deity was listed on questionnaires by 11 respondents or 65% (one of whom called the god Volos). Perun was preferred by 53% or nine respondents, and Lada and Svarog in turn by 30%. Mara, Makosh, and Dazhdbog were worshipped by four people (24%), while two adepts worshipped Stribog and Rod. Chernobog, Belobog, Mokus, Koliada, Kupala, Lel, Zmeiulan, and Yarilo were each mentioned once. In total, 16 deities were named by the pagans.

Ten respondents (53%) from the Fellowship of Kin of White Rus did not respond to this question. In total, the Belarusian nativists cited 15 deities. Among them, Perun was preferred by 37% or seven community members, Veles 32% (six people), and an equal number of pagan worshipped Svetovit. Next in the rating came Rod at 26% (five people) and Svarog at 21% (4 respondents). Odin and Semargl were revered by 16% of respondents (three respectively). Yarilo, Dazhdbog, and Damp Mother-Earth were indicated once. Furthermore, nature was indicated as the divine essence by one respondent.

The question about the most revered personages of the pantheon was ignored by 42% or 38 of the pagans surveyed at Kupala. Responses in the form of "I worship all of them" were formulated in the following variations: "I worship native gods", "everything is god", "god is everything", "there are none more worshipped than others, each of them bears their own knowledge", "all the gods are equally worshipped", and "one in many and many in one." These were the answers of six people or 7%. In total, 16 different deities were mentioned by adepts. Thirteen percent indicated one deity, seven of them indicating Veles as the "one god" (one respondent also indicated: "he is Shiva"). Two people indicated Rod, while Stribog, Perun, and "Tartra" (?) each had one. The rating of gods presented by the pagans gathered near Maloyaroslavets was the following: Veles was mentioned by 41% of respondents, and out of the total 45 who answered this question positively, only eight did not indicate this deity. In second place in popularity among respondents was Perun, who was indicated by 27% or 24 respondents, followed by Makosh with 25% or 22 respondents and Svarog with 22% or 20 people. The top five was closed with Rod with 18% or 16 people. Lada was indicated by 17% or 15 pagans, Dzahdbog by 11%, and Yarilo by 9%. Moreover, the new pagan Slavic pantheon featured Mara with 6% or five respondents, Troyan with 3%, and "Tartra", Belobog, Chernobog, and Lel were each mentioned once. It is also worth noting that the chronicle entities Semargl, Khors, and Stribog were mentioned only once.

Table 2

	Maloyaroslavets	Minsk	Rybinsk	Average
No response	42%	53%	18%	38%
"Monotheism"	13%	0%	12%	8%
Veles	41%	37%	65%	48%
Perun	27%	32%	53%	37%
Makosh	25%	11%	24%	20%
Svarog	22%	21%	40%	24%
Rod	18%	26%	12%	19%
Lada	17%	11%	30%	19%
Dazhdbog	11%		24%	12%
Yarilo	9%			3%
Svetovit		32%		11%
Stribog		11%	12%	8%
Mara	6%		24%	10%
Odin		16%		5%
Semargl		16%		5%
Troyan	3%			1%
Number of deities	16	15	16	15

Table 3: Rating of "Mono-Religiosity"

	Maloyaroslavets	Minsk	Rybinsk	Average
Veles	58%		100%	53%
Rod	17%			6%
Stribog	8%			3%
Perun	8%			3%

The data of these tables suggests a sufficient motleyness of views among adepts of the contemporary pagan movement with respect to the divine realm. The total number of gods worshipped in the associations under consideration varied from 15 to 29, and the lists of worshipped mythological entities often included deities of non-Slavic origin. For instance, 16% of pagan surveyed in Belarus preferred Odin. However, alongside the polytheistic orientation of these associations, traits of henotheism are also characteristic. In Rybinsk and Maloyaroslavets, 12% and 13% of respondents respectively attached priority to one community deity. From the pantheon established by Vladimir in 980, Perun, Makosh, and Dazhdbog enjoyed the greatest popularity among young pagans (except in Belarus). Semargl, meanwhile, was mentioned only by nativists from abroad. The veneration of Khors did not exceed the 1% threshold in any of the communities. Also of no small interest is the fact that lesser-known deities are represented in the contemporary pagan pantheons. Mokus and Zmeiulan can be considered among such deities.

The final question concerned the definition of respondents' personal religious predilections, i.e., the deities which individual adherents of the contemporary pre-Abrahamic worldview worship the most.

Among the pagans in attendance at the festival in honor of the god Veles, four people did not respond to the question, and another four indicated that they worshipped only one deity. Among the latter, Perun, Rod, Odin, and Veles each had one vote. The majority of adepts (47%) indicated Perun. Rod, Svarog, and Lada received 24%, Dazhdbog 18% and Veles 12%. Stribog, Kryshen, Rod, Rozhana, Odin, Koliada, and Kupala each received one vote. Thirteen deities were named in total.

Among the representatives of the Belarusian variation of the movement, six people (32%) did not respond to the question. Four respondents indicated only one deity, Perun and Rod receiving two votes each (11%). The sum of responses which mentioned the latter two gods was 26% or five people, while 21% or four people indicated Veles, Stribog, and Odin. Svarog, Lada, and Makosh received three votes (16%). Yarilo, Semargl, and Thor had 11%, while Dazhdbog and Baldr were mentioned once. In total, 20 deities were registered, the majority of which (around 10) were mentioned on the questionnaire of one respondent.

Among respondents at the Kupala festival, five people did not answer the question. One pagan worshipped their ancestors as deities, while four respondents (5%) worshipped all of the gods. Nineteen percent of those surveyed indicated one deity as the main one. Among them, five respondents (6%) named Veles. Rod and Svarog received 3%. Makosh, Lada, Perun, Nav, Mara, and the Sun (*Solntse*) were mentioned once.

Thus, out of 90 people surveyed, 47% or 42 pagans worshipped Veles, Perun was chosen by 40% or 36 people, and in third place was Svarog with 32% or 29 people. Twenty-three percent or 21 respondents named Rod, and almost the same number (22%) Makosh. Dazhdbog was singled out by 12% of respondents. Next came Lada with 11%, Mara and Yarilo with 7% (6 respondents), Stribog with 4%, and Lel and Semargl with 2%. The following deities received one vote: Svetovit, Troyan, Khodor, Kryshen, Dzha, Buddha, Thor, Odin, Njörðr, Radegas, Shiva, Rozhanitsa, etc. In total, about 29 different deities were named by adepts.

Table 4

	Maloyaroslavets	Minsk	Rybinsk	Average
No response	6%	32%	24%	21%
"Monotheism"	19%	21%	24%	21%
Veles	47%	21%	12%	27%
Perun	40%	26%	47%	38%
Makosh	22%	16%	6%	12%
Svarog	32%	16%	24%	24%
Rod	23%	26%	24%	24%
Lada	11%	16%	24%	17%
Dazhdbog	12%		18%	10%
Yarilo	7%	11%		6%
Stribog	4%	21%	6%	8%
Mara	7%		6%	2%
Odin		21%	6%	8%
Semargl	2%	11%		4%
Thor		11%		4%
Number of deities	29	20	13	21

Table 5: Rating of "Mono-Religiosity"

	Maloyaroslavets	Minsk	Rybinsk	Average
Veles	30%		25%	18%
Perun	6%	50%	25%	27%
Svarog	15%			5%
Rod	15%	50%	25%	30%
Odin			25%	8%

First of all, on the individual level, the number of adepts who indicated only one deity as their most revered significantly exceeded the number of those who belonged to a community (average 8 and 21% respectively). This suggests much more developed monotheistic (or henotheistic) elements among individual adepts of the movement and a leveling of this trend on the community level. Moreover, a community can be constituted by uniting associations adhering to different deities, as a result of which the community pantheon is only a total indicator of the divine propensities of its adepts. Secondly, if on the community level the most popular god is Veles with 48%, then on the level of individual worship Perun leads with 38%, with Veles in second place with 27%. It is noteworthy that according to the data obtained from responses to the question of personal patron-gods, the percentage of Veles' worshippers was low in Landmark of Veles. According to the rating of mono-religiosity, Rod leads with 30% despite the fact that on the community level he claimed only 6%. Next after Rod is Perun, who in the individual count had 27% and on the community level 3%. The situation is different with Veles, who, on the contrary, accrued 18% in individual indices and 53% in the collective count. The latter speaks in favor of a certain deliberately constructed pantheon existing even within associations. It bears noting that the representatives of the Belarusian fellowship were not inclined to single out a main, supreme deity on the collective level. At the same time, one in five respondents indicated such a personage in their individual preferences.

***

PARTICULARITIES OF STUDYING CONTEMPORARY SLAVIC PAGANISM: HISTORIOGRAPHICAL ANALYSIS OF THE LEADER OF THE KOLIADA OF THE VYATICHI COMMUNITY, NIKOLAI SPERANSKY (VELIMIR)[184]

The Russian variations of the revived pagan worldview have already been the subject of reflection and reaction for a significant number of sciences in the Humanities for more than a decade. Dozens of notes, articles, and monographs have been dedicated to considering the genesis and source basis of the 20th and 21st-century Russian pagan movement. Scholars have been particularly interested in analyzing certain trends within this pagan construct. The resulting classification of conclusions has covered both the structural field of *Rodnoverie* ("Native Faith")[185]

---

184 First published in *Sektovedenie [Sect Studies]* 5 (2016).
185 The term *rodnoverie* and the derivative self-designation of a portion of contemporary pagans, *rodnovery*, have an altogether ambiguous history of origin. According to the point of view of the leader of the Association of Ukrainian Native Faith, G.S. Lozko (Volkhvess Zoreslava), "*rodnoverie*" is only an abstraction, a scientific form of the term *rodnaia vera*. The notion of "ridna vira" was first used by the founder of modern Ukrainian paganism, V. Shayan, in his religious seeking at the beginning of the previous century. At virtually the same time, through the efforts of Jan Stachniuk "*rodzima wiara*" entered the Polish "pagan lexicon" (- online interview with G.S. Lozko, 5/10/2010, author's personal archive). A different version of the origin of this term is presented by the volkhv of the Ryazan-based Troesvet pagan community, Bogumil (B.A. Gasanov), who believes that Rodnoverie began in 1997 with the establishment of the Union of Slavic Communities. Thanks to Bogumila's active position, this name has been appended with another part: "Slavic", hence "Slavic Native Faith" (*Slavianskaia Rodnaia Vera*). The spiritual head of Troesvet has remarked that this step was taken to specify the ethnic and religious component of the future union. B.A. Gasanov, however, admits that when he created this term he was oriented towards the Polish tradition. The transformation of *rodnaia vera* into the definitional *rodnoverie*, in Bogumil's opinion, took place at the turn of the millennium. The term was introduced into the contemporary Russian pagan milieu by the volkhv of the Rodoliubie community, Veleslav (I.G. Cherkasov) (-audio interview with Bogumil in Ryazan, 13/8/2011, author's personal archive). See "The Slavic Religious Alternative: The Slovenian Variant" in this volume. A definite victory of these adherents of pre-Abrahamic religiosity is the use (and recognition) of this definition by the scholarly community. See, for example, I.A. Bessonov, *"Kalendarnye prazdniki sovremennykh ekoposelenii (na materiale subkul'tury 'anastasievtsev')"* in *Kompleksnye issledovaniia traditsionnoi kul'tury v postsovetskii period 14* (Moscow: State Republican Center of Russian Folklore, 2011), p. 405.

and the whole spectrum and spheres of this social unit's being, from ideological explorations to ecological problems. With few exceptions, at the center of attention of scholarly studies have been the concrete associations of this alternative religiosity's adepts, e.g. the community, union, etc., as having an established, shaped, and pronounced arrangement of self-determination. The latter encompasses the mass of narratives of community representatives, video and Internet data, and, finally, the "material" (cult-ritual) "archive" of such associations. Based mainly on these sources and, to a lesser extent, field materials, contemporary scholars of this diasporic religiosity have drawn their own conclusions.

Yet another particularity ought to be recognized in the practically total absence of works dedicated to analyzing the worldviews of specific leaders, those "enlightening educators of paganism." Without a doubt, in examining particular communities scholars have referred to the statements and described the array of actions of the leading proselytes of associations, only to stop here before deepening immersion into the worldview basis of individual pagan personalities. The main conclusions that follow suggest a certain inaccuracy: references to the statements of one or several people are passed off as the general opinion of all members of a community or union. Unfortunately, to this day the arsenal of tools for collecting primary data (which, let us repeat, is done super-minimally in any case) has not come to include mass surveying and interviewing the ordinary members of contemporary Russian pagan groups. Such a practice would allow the scholarly world to see the "ordinary", popular "Native Faith" without mediators and the direct creators and propagandists of this phenomenon. Despite persistent attempts to reduce the Russian pagan movement to the emergence of impersonal, "gray", aggressive, marginal elements[186], there can

---

[186] Let us cite a typical example: "As Dmitry Dobrykh has said, there are groups which do not gravitate towards any of the radical movements, but exist on their own and interact exclusively within their circle. It is very difficult to implant an agent in such a structure, because people don't just come in from the outside. Every 'recruit' is recommended by the group's members who personally know them for more than a year. One example of such a group are the Rodnovery, the followers of the ancient Slavic pagan cult of fire-worshippers. Madly cruel and bloodthirsty, they've cracked down on all infidels and foreigners. The bloodiest and most cruel murders of recent years are on the consciousness of their contemporary followers" - M. Burdakov, *"Ubit' po-russki"*, *Profil'* (27/12/2010) [http://www.profile.ru/politics/item/59381-ubit-po-russki-59381].

be no doubt that the basic canvas of the paganism of the last two centuries has been shaped by precisely these individual adepts. All the more strange is the absence of specialized studies dedicated to the new volkhvs and, accordingly, the role of the pagan personality in the historical locus of the new Russia.

One of the leaders of the "religious traditionalist" camp to have colorfully announced themselves in the last decades of the 20th century was the leader of the Koliada of the Vyatichi community of Moscow, Velimir (N.N. Speransky). Overall, the information directly pertaining to Speransky's worldview path is quite "dosed", as interest does not extend beyond that certain set of "nodal", classical themes developed by the Russian scholarly community in its analyses of the phenomenon of contemporary Russian paganism. In particular, this person of interest to us has been mentioned in connection with the construction of the classifier of "domestic young paganism" by one or another specialist. In such cases, the fundamental principle, for all the paradox of such a "union", is the product of a mixing of incomplete inductive and deductive methods.

The basis for this systematization can be the search for the sources of the very subject under study. The ethnologist V.A. Schnirelmann classifies the cultural center led by Velimir, the Vyatichi community, as one among "neo-pagan groups that focus on Slavic uniqueness and which strive to restore the ancient Slavic pagan cultures and rituals in the 'purest' form, distancing themselves from any external influences and avoiding foreign borrowings."[187] A similar position is taken by the expert on religious sectarianism, A.L. Dvorkin, who designates this community as "nativist."[188] In his considerations on the characteristics of Koliada of the Vyatichi doctrine, A.B. Yartsev believes that Speransky is influenced

---

187 *"Perun, Svarog i drugie: russkoi neoiazychestvo v poiskakh sebia"* in *Neoiazychestvo na prostorakh Evrazii* (Moscow: Biblical-Theological Institute of St. Apostle Andrey, 2001), p. 21

188 A.L. Dvorkin, *Neoiazychestvo v Rossii: nativistskie sekty* in *Sektovedenie. Totalitarnye sekty. Opyt sistematicheskogo issledovaniia* (3rd edition) (Nizhny Novgorod: Izdatel'stvo bratstva vo ima sv. kniazia Aleksandra Nevskogo, 2002), p. 539.

by shamanistic ideas.[189] The source of Velimir's shamanic practice has also been revealed by the journalist A. Belov in the online article "Paganism as a Phenomenon of Contemporary Russian Religiosity." In the opinion of the latter author, Nikolai Nikolaevich Speransky received shamanic initiation during one of his trips in Siberia.[190] Belov's conclusions directly contradict the "Slavic uniqueness" of the head of the Vyatichi noted by Schnirelmann.[191] A.V. Prokofyev adds to Speransky's shamanism that he has pioneered the latter in the articulation of Slavic mystical practice.[192] The scholar of religion A.V. Gaydukov deems "Vedism" to be another source at the heart of the worldview of this community and the leader of the center.[193]

The core of the ensuing principle of classification is a cumulative sample from the chronological history of this organization (including quantitative characteristics) and some aspects of the "pagan and secular biography" of Speransky, assessing his role and personality in the community and movement as a whole. In his monographic work, *The Resurrection of Perun: Towards Reconstructing East-Slavic Paganism*, L.S. Klein, although regarding Speransky as one of the intellectual leaders of the "current formalized pagan movement", altogether arbitrarily "scrolls through" the data of Velimir's life and works. According to the information presented in this work, Speransky is a physicist by education, the author of the *Russian Pagan Manifesto* (1997), and an active Internet user. Klein also particularly dwells in his characterization of this volkhv on what is one of the most popular plots in both scholarly and subject milieux, namely, the infamous hoax narrative, *The Book of Veles*. Klein emphasizes: *"The Book*

---

[189] A.B. Yartsev, *Antropologicheskie aspekty politicheskikh i sotsial'nykh uchenii v sovremennom neoiazychestve v Rossii* (Moscow: BBI, 2012), p. 5.

[190] Speransky himself denies this statement in his online correspondence with the present author from 11/12/2012 (author's personal archive).

[191] A. Belov, "*Iazychestvo kak fenomen sovremennoi rossiiskoi religioznosti, Chast' 3*", LiveJournal (27/92007) [https://mahiravana.livejournal.com/9006.html].

[192] A.V. Prokof'ev, "*Sovremennoe slavianskoe neoiazychestvo (obzor)*".

[193] A.V. Gaidukov, "*Politicheskie aspect vozniknoveniia neoiazychestva v Rossii*", in *Gertsenovskie chteniia 1997: Aktual'nye problemy sotsial'nykh nauk* (Saint Petersburg: Faculty of Sociological Sciences of Herzen State Pedagogical University of Russia, 2004), p. 160.

of Veles by Miroliubov-Kura-Lesnogo and the *Veles Book of Bus Kresen* (Asov-Barashkov) were not written by ancient volkhvs, but by modern volkhvs and, in this sense, are forgeries. But he [Speransky] does not consider such to be any less interesting and less pagan because of this. Does it really matter when they were made? What is important is what they teach."[194] Velimir is also recorded among the "patriarchs of paganism" by G. Gomenyuk, S. Tereshchenko[195], M. Doroshenko[196], and others. Speransky's intellectuality and research talent in the field of Russian folklore and craft has been written about by V. Prokofyev and the authors of *The Religious Organizations of Russia*.[197] The history of Velimir's community is quite arbitrarily outlined in the work of the president of the Panorama Information-Research Center, V.V. Pribylovsky. The latter author fixates on the creation of the Koliada of the Vyatichi as the result of the merging of the group and center bearing the same name.[198] Furthermore, Pribylovsky expands the range of Velimir's works. Alongside the *Russian Pagan Manifesto* noted by Klein, the leader of Panorama refers to the book *A Word to Venerators of Ancient Culture*, released in 1996, and *Summoning the Gods: A Word to Russian Pagans*,

194 L.S. Klein, *Voskreshenie Peruna. K rekonstruktsii vostochno-slavianskogo iazychestva* (Saint Petersburg: Evraziia, 2004), p. 123.
195 G. Gomeniuk and S. Tereshchenko, *"Russkoe i ukrainskoe neoiazychestvo"* (Center for Apologetic Studies), p. 2.
196 M. Doroshenko, *"Slavianskoe neoiazychestvo" in XI Rozhdestvenskie obrazovatel'nye chteniia. Informatsionno-konsul'tatsionnyi tsentr sv. Irineia Lionskogo* [http://www.iriney.ru/sects/heathen/news009.htm].
197 Prokof'ev, *"Sovremennoe slavianskoe iazychestvo"*; A. Bundina, P. Kozlov, A. Mukhin, *Religioznye organizatsii Rossii* (Moscow: TsPI, 2001), p. 102. More detailed information shedding light on both the basic "pagan occupations" of Speransky and the stages of the biography of this volkhv of the Vyatichi in A. Belov's article: "Born in Moscow on Kutuzovsky prospect, Speransky moved to Vitebsk. Upon graduating from Moscow State University's Faculty of Physics, Speransky joined the Kurchatov Institute (Troitsk), where he has worked to this day as a senior research fellow. Fascinated with painting and then traveling, Speransky went around the Caucasus, the Kola Peninsula, the Urals, Altai, Pamir, Central Asia, and the forests and taiga of Siberia...He continues to carve, paint and write books, give lectures, hold community festivals, and publishes the newspaper *Tree of Life*."
198 The respondent commented on this historiographical survey concerning the history of the community's founding and the "status" of his person in the following away: "Authors often, out of an unscrupulous economy of efforts, don't engage in searching for any new information, but only rewrite the references of a previous author or the fragment of another, often coincidental textual source without thinking about its degree of credibility" - online correspondence with N.N. Speransky (11/12/2012) from the author's personal archive.

published in 1999.[199] While avoiding specifics on questions of the pagan bibliography associated with this volkhv, A.V. Prokofvyev is content with counting Velimir in the ranks of the pagan camp's popular ideologues.[200] A.N. Agaltsov has approached analyzing Speransky's "nominal sources" in more detail. Using as a case study Speransky's *Book of Natural Faith*, this scholar discusses the topic of pagan asceticism and concludes that the transformation of the metaphysics of asceticism into a religious principle "determines the content and meaning of neo-pagan ritual actions and rites in accordance with this style and way of life."[201]

With regards to the time of birth and activation of the trend to which Speransky belongs, the scholarly world expresses different points of views. According to some, the time period of the "genesis of Velimir" straddles the clearly fixed '70s-'80s of the past century, and this contemporary volkhv is thus counted among the "first-wave" pagans. Others are inclined to move this volkhv's activism into the 1990s and into the "extra-chronological" present. In terms of the quantitative population of this group to have emerged, the "first pagans" are automatically appraised as few in number.[202]

In contrast to the preceding gradation-overviews which only somewhat touch upon certain spectra of Speransky's life, activities, and worldview, a third classification which is most popular in the scholarly world is a kind of conclusive evaluation module whose backbone is formed exclusively out of the intellectual, ideological, and other motivations of the author. Thus, the very principle of scholarly research is violated. Whether turning to a bare minimum of sources or completely neglecting them, the specialist issues their own verdict and writes the personality under investigation

---

199 V. Pribylovskii, *"Ideinye tsentry politicheskikh neoiazychnikov"*, RELIGARE: *Pravoslavnyi pravozashchitnyi tsentr 'Territoriia tserkvi'* (2004) [http://www.religare.ru/2_9726.html]; Velimir, *"Vozzvanie bogov. Slovo k russkim iazychnikam"*, Nasledie predkov: zhurnal pravoi perspektivy 6 (Moscow: OOO RUSPECHAT', 1998), pp. 51-52.

200 Prokof'ev, *"Sovremennoe slavianskoe iazychestvo."*

201 A.N. Agal'tsov, *Rossiiskoe neoiazychestvo kak religiozno-nravstvennyi fenomen* (dissertation for Candidate of Philosophical Sciences, Tula: Tolstoy Tula State Pedagogical University), pp. 17-18.

202 Prokof'ev, *"Sovremennoe slavianskoe iazychestvo"*; Gomeniuk and Tereshchenko, *"Russkoe i ukrainskoe neoiazychestvo"*; Klein, *Voskreshenie Peruna*, p. 112; Pribylovskii, *"Ideinye tsentry."*

off under one or another camp and correlates him with one or another trend in the pagan movement. For instance, in his underscoring of "four interlaced currents in contemporary neo-paganism", Doroshenko associates the Circle of Pagan Tradition, and therefore Velimir as one of this organization's members, with the ecological trend.[203] Pribylovsky, meanwhile, fixating on the existence of two ideological poles in the Russian Rodnovery milieu, considers the Circle of Pagan Tradition to represent a folkloric-playful paganism that is weakly politicized and is largely similar to the fans of J.R.R. Tolkien's work and the role-players of military-historical clubs. Moreover, in characterizing the views of these folklorists as "national-patriotic", this scholar directs attention to this pole's leaders' deliberate departure from radical currents adhering to positions of Nazism and national-chauvinism.[204] E.K. Ageenkova, a member of the Expert Council for Religious and Ethnic Affairs of the Republic of Belarus is inclined from analyzing the content of ten issues of Speransky's newspaper, *Tree of Life*, to classify the ideological arrangements of the Koliada of the Vyatichi and the Circle of Pagan Tradition as moderately nationalistic and anti-Christian.[205] Gaydukov, who uses the activity trends of neo-pagan associations in Russia as a universal classifier, relates the Vyatichi cultural center to "Vedic communities of a health-lifestyle and religious character whose activities are aimed at harmonious coexistence with nature."[206] In an appendix to his dissertation (the table "Classification of neo-pagan groups by ideology"), this scholar classifies Velimir's Vyatichi as "a strong version of national-patriotic groups" alongside Dobroslav, the Kaluga Slavic Community of Kazakov, the Moscow Slavic Pagan Community, Skhoron Ezh Sloven, and others.[207]

Dividing contemporary pagan organizations into religiously-tinted political parties and politically indifferent, quasi-religious

---

203 Doroshenko, *"Slavianskoe iazychestvo."*
204 Pribylovskii, *"Ideinye tsentry."*
205 E.L. Ageenkova, *Nekotorye aspekty slavianskogo neoiazychestva - t. II* (Zhirovichi: Minsk Spiritual Seminary), p. 16.
206 Gaidukov, *"Politicheskie aspekty"*, p. 160
207 Gaidukov, *"Ideologiia i praktika sovremennogo slavianskogo neoiazychestva"* (dissertation for Candidate of Philosophical Sciences; Saint Petersburg: Herzen Russian State Pedagogical University, 2000), p. 150.

cultural formations, V.M. Storchak believes that the Vyatichi center which Speransky heads belongs to the second category. Prokofyev bases his "double" classification on the principle of distinguishing between Russian nativists in terms of residence and directionality of worldview seeking. According to the "filiation" data, the Koliada of the Vyatichi is a metropolitan (urban) folkloric community.[208] V.B. Meranvild emphasizes the structural erudition of the Vyatichi and notes a predominance of moral-ethical attitudes in the worldview of this organization's community members.[209]

For all of its "multipolarity", the existing historiography on this subject has a pronouncedly thematic focus. On the one hand, the epicenter of scholarly coverage of the "pagan question" has remained on the same level as before, only the subjects of analysis have changed. If previously the central place in specialist works was occupied by detailed analyses of history pertaining to the Book of Veles, then since 1997 (the time of the Vyatichis' publication of the *Russian Pagan Manifesto*) the list of narratives most often found in the research field are the "Bittsevsk Agreement" and "Bittsevsk Appeal" of 2002, documents which laid the foundation for the official history of the Circle of Pagan Tradition, an organization directly tied to Speransky's activism.[210] On the other hand, in its elaboration of a "pagan classifier" the scholarly world has honed its attention towards two "competing" unions, the Union of Slavic Communities of Slavic Native Faith and the Circle of Pagan Tradition as representing an ethno-oriented trend among 20th-21st century zealots of national archaism. Regarding the ideological contrast of these organizations, scholars of the Humanities have naturally drawn attention to the collective leaderships of these associations in the format of simply listing their participants as well as in the form of citing pagan ideologists who have highlighted their different approaches to restoring their sought-for original "tradition."[211]

---
208 Prokof'ev, *"Sovremennoe slavianksoe neoiazychestvo."*
209 V.B. Meranvil'd, *Slaviano-goritskoe dvizhenie kak odna iz form vozrozhdeniia russkoi natsional'noi kul'tury* (Yoshkar-Ola: Mari State University, 2004), pp. 21, 24.
210 V. Chudinov, *"Kul'turno-mifologicheskoe nasledie slavian i neoiazychestva"*, Institute of Ancient Slavic Literature and Ancient Eurasian Civilization [https://www.runitsa.ru/index.php#36191].
211 Pribylovskii, *"Ideinye tsentry."*

Unlike these cases of episodic testimonies on Speransky, the works of O.I. Kavykin and V.A. Schnirelmann contain more detailed descriptions of the worldview basis of Volkhv Velimir. Among the undoubted pluses of Candidate of Historical Sciences Kavykin's monograph *Rodnovery: The Self-Identification of Neo-Pagans in Contemporary Russia* we should identify the use of a significant number of sources, including those by Speransky and narrative sources of which Velimir was one of the team of authors.[212] Turning to analyze the worldview of the leader of the Koliada of the Vyatichi, Kavykin establishes Speransky's place in the contemporary Russian [pagan] movement as a figure among the leaders and popular ideologues of paganism.[213] This author draws attention to Velimir's intellectual stock, noting his use of the conceptual apparatus of scholarship, particularly his "appeal to such conceptualizations of myth as those of Grimm, Taylor, Frazer, Freud, Afanasyev, and Losev."[214] This scholar holds the most important loci of Speransky's worldview to be: firstly, an idealized "folk idea" which brings this volkhv close to Russian Narodnichestvo; secondly, assigning nature an hierophantic status and automatically (by definition) counting the state as a negative force "striving to destroy Nature so sacred to pagans."[215] Thirdly, religious practice (particularly the rite of initiation) is seen as occupying one of the central places in the worldview propagated by Velimir, wherein the emphasis falls on the sacralization and syncretism of the latter and moral ideals.[216] Fourthly, the term *Darna*, borrowed by Velimir from Lithuanian tradition, is a most important notion which characterizes this pagan's notion of harmony, as it is with this definition and by following "the concept of harmonizing the rhythms of man and nature" that the Golden Age is associated.[217] Fifthly, Speransky is inclined to endow mythology with the function of regulating relations within society and resolving a person's spiritual problems. The

---

212 O.I. Kavykin, *"Rodnovery": Samoidentifikatsiia neoiazychnikov v sovremennoi Rossii* (Moscow: Institute of Africa of the Russian Academy of Sciences, 2007).
213 Ibid, pp. 11, 57
214 Ibid, p. 97.
215 Ibid, pp. 93, 133.
216 Ibid, pp. 94-96.
217 Ibid, p. 134.

source of myths, according to the views of this pagan leader, is nature.[218] Sixthly, characteristic of Velimir's ideology is his view of monotheism from the standpoint of its current relevance: "the Abrahamic religions are not adequate for the tasks facing modern mankind."[219] Seventhly, this pagan's texts present nationalism (as a movement aimed at the revival of folk culture) in the form of a mutual-exclusion: it can be either constructive or destructive (aggressive).[220] Based on this sum of conclusions and guided by his research tasks, this historian counts Velimir in the camp of those Rodnovery whom he identifies as "tolerant."[221]

In his recent monograph *Russian Native Faith: Neo-Paganism and Nationalism in Contemporary Russia*, Doctor of Historical Sciences Viktor Schnirelmann deems one of the goals of his work to be "analyzing the question of tolerance or intolerance in the ranks of the Russian neo-pagan movement."[222] It seems only natural that in his disclosure of this goal as well as his first-rank task, i.e. "offering a general presentation of the history of the contemporary Russian neo-pagan movement", this author touches upon a range of issues associated with the personality of interest to us among the camp of contemporary "traditionalists."[223] Like the bibliographical array of Kavykin's work, Schnirelmann uses both "pagan documentation" (e.g. the Bittsevsk Appeal, the Manifesto of Pagan Tradition, the Russian Pagan Manifesto, the Kolomensk Appeal) as well as personal narratives (this ethnologist cites five of Velimir's works). Keeping with the tradition of characterizing Speransky as a representative of the leadership cohort of Russian nativists, this ethnologist draws attention to the specifics of Velimir's passion for the visual arts and presents some data from this pagan's life "in the world."[224] Schnirelmann dwells in considerable detail on the history of Speransky's participation

---

218 Ibid, p. 149.
219 Ibid, pp. 135-136.
220 Ibid, p. 131.
221 O.I. Kavykin, *Konstruirovanie etnicheskoi identichnosti v srede russkikh neoiazychnikov* (dissertation for Candidate of Historical Sciences; Moscow: Institute of Africa of the Russian Academy of Sciences, 2006), p. 20-21.
222 V.A. Schnirelmann, *Russkoe rodnovere: neoiazychestvo i natsionalizm v sovremennoi Rossii* (Moscow: BBI, 2012), p. XIII.
223 Ibid.
224 Ibid, pp. 177, 193.

in different Native Faith associations in Russia. The beginning of this chronology in Schnirelmann's monograph is a series of "research strokes" on Velimir's Vyatichi center. The author sees the beginning of this organization, which was founded on 14 June 1995, in the activities of the Tsaritsyno Ecological-Cultural Center (1983-2001). Schnirelmann writes: "In late 1997 the Vyatichi merged with the equally small Koliada group previously headed by Velemudr and Mezgir. Mezgir and Velimir founded a new community which acquired the name Koliada of the Vyatichi. In 2001, the Slavia Fellowship of Natural Faith spun off from it."[225] According to his own classifier of Russian pagans featured in a 2001 work, Schnirelmann identifies this volkhv's community as a group of the urban intelligentsia that brought together several dozen people.[226] This historian draws attention to the official side of "Velimir's project", noting that the Koliada of the Vyatichi community was registered by the authorized committee of the Government of Moscow on 20 November 1998. A natural continuation of this organizational evolution and description of Speransky's worldview map is this ethnologist's reference to "one of the most authoritative community associations", the Circle of Pagan Tradition.[227] Upon mentioning the leaders of the Circle of Pagan Tradition, which in scholarly milieux is standardized in the procedure of enumerating pagan cells belonging to the organization and its associated union relations, Schnirelmann dwells on the internal arrangements of these proselytes of the pagan worldview. Analyzing two of the Circle's documents, the Bittsevsk Appeal and the *Manifesto of Pagan Tradition*, Schnirelmann concludes that the Appeal incited a split in the Russian nativist movement over questions of relations with the world religions, racism, and neo-Nazism. An examination of the provisions of the *Manifesto of Pagan Tradition* led this historian to take note of Circle members' interest in social issues and a certain agreement with the authors in their critique of modern civilization. Schnirelmann considers the minuses of the document to be: Rodnovery's idealization of primitive antiquity (recognizing it to be a problem-free Golden

---

225 Ibid, pp. 193-197.
226 Schnirelmann, *"Perun, Svarog, i drugie"*, pp. 29-30.
227 Schnirelmann, *Russkoe rodnoverie*, p. 17.

Age) based on zero knowledge of it, a lack of definition for their propagated "natural way of life", and their attacks on science and construction of their own "scientific knowledge." Furthermore, in terms of his established aims, one of the author's main conclusions arising from the examination of this document is his recognition of both it, and therefore Velimir (Speransky), to be intolerant pagans: "[the manifesto] incites xenophobia and is fraught with aggravating interethnic relations in Russia."[228] Previously, and again keeping with tradition, in his comparison and contrasting of the Circle of Pagan Tradition and the Union of Slavic Communities Schnirelmann cites Speransky's statements to conclude that the teachings of the Circle are predominated by a "Pochvennist point" in contrast to an "SS-ish" absolutization of the role of blood.[229] Without dwelling on this specialist's conclusions on nationalism and racism directly in relation to the leader under study (we will move on to these later), let us note that in his monograph Schnirelmann does not stop at discerning "turmoil" in the pagan camp. The very basis of the functioning of the Circle and the Union allows this ethnologist to propose his own chronology for the development of the movement. Highlighting these major organizations as the driving forces of the pagan "third stage" (the turn of the 20th-21st centuries), Viktor Schnirelmann discerns a reason for the restoration of relations between the latter: common concern over the destruction of sacred communal sites.[230] In addition, Russian Native Faith presents cases of public actions by the Circle of Pagan Tradition, such as picketing, letters to authorities (mayors, prosecutor's office, and the patriarchate), and an array of communications and discussions which, without a doubt, broaden horizons for the reader and to a certain extent contribute to the construction of an objective picture of the activist orientation of these pagans, as well as testifies to the author's extensive engagement of Internet sources.

Besides such descriptions of the Koliada of the Vyatichi, the Circle of Pagan Tradition, and other associations led by or associated with Speransky, the works of this chief research fellow

---

228 Ibid, p. 230.
229 Ibid, p. 196.
230 Ibid, pp. 234-235.

of the Institute of Ethnology and Anthropology of the Russian Academy of Sciences contain information directly pertaining to the worldview aspirations of Volkhv Velimir. A kind of preamble of evaluative constructs contained both in earlier texts and in the above-discussed monograph ought to be recognized in Schnirelmann's extremely interesting comparison of one of the axiomatic positions of contemporary pagans (Speransky in particular) with a slogan of the Third Reich: "It should not be forgotten that in the recent past the slogan 'live in harmony with nature' was most popular in none other than Nazi Germany, which was the first in Europe to adopt detailed environmental conservation laws."[231] Taking this message into account, let us examine the "pagan Velimir in the eyes of the scholar Schnirelmann." In the collective monograph *Neo-Paganism in the Expanses of Eurasia*, this historian identifies two problematic zones associated with the leader of Koliada of the Vyatichi: Speransky's own notion of paganism and religious systems in general, and the peculiarities of this community leader's doctrine. In the first case, in the opinion of this scholar, Velimir applies cyclical theory to Russian paganism. In his striving to substantiate Slavic paganism, Speransky limits the "Indo-European element" to the European component while recognizing the kinship of Russian paganism with the ideas of the Rigveda. Moreover, he sympathizes with the folk manifestation of this religiosity while rejecting Christianity.[232] Secondly, this volkhv's doctrine features pronounced Manichaean ideas of an eternal struggle between the forces of good and evil embodied in Belbog/Rod and Chernobog. However, this ethnologist notes, "Speransky's system preserves the Christian principle of retribution, which no pagan religion knew: a person who commits evil will suffer a sad fate in the next world. It is also hardly doubtable that the depiction of Chernobog as a bearer of Absolute Evil is inspired by the Christian teaching on Satan."[233] In his examination of Velimir's pantheon, Schnirelmann sees characters from Russian folk tales that are atypical of pre-Christian Slavic beliefs. The historian also does not agree with the

---
231 Ibid, p. X.
232 Schnirelmann, *"Perun, Svarog i drugie"*, pp. 22-24.
233 Ibid, p. 23.

pagan author's interpretation of one specific deity. Emphasizing in particular his image of Mother Earth, this scholar holds the main motivation for the appearance of the Great Goddess of Russia to be "a highly emotional attitude towards the territory of his people and a readiness to defend it to the last drop of blood."[234] In summating and characterizing Velimir's religion as a "religion of salvation" built on the principles of a gentle respect for nature and preserving ancestral cultural heritage, this author of a chapter in the above-cited collective monograph draws parallels between a "pronounced cultural accent" in Speransky's doctrine and "the old German idea of contrasting culture and civilization."[235] In the above-cited work from 2012, alongside repeating that the head of the Koliada of the Vyatichi's "Slavo-Aryanism" is based on sources from 1996-1997, Schnirelmann adds to this basis of theses on the subject's worldview the following obtained from an analysis of Velimir's book, *Volkhvs against Globalism*: (1.) Speransky's ideology includes racial theories and global conspiracy theories; (2.) Velimir predicts a pagan revolution (through appealing to a utopia of traditional communal life) and acts as the initiator of creating a "pagan socialist party"; (3.) the volkhv constructs a "Russian pagan idea" in a populist myth about the Russian people; (4.) In Speransky's view, the Russian people are anti-democratic, and this pagan's concept does not accept human individuality, but is based exclusively on peoples-ethnoi; (5.) the author of *Volkhvs against Globalism* has a pronouncedly essentialist approach to ethnicity up to the point of racialization (ethnos = a biological unity), as Speransky is against the mixing of folk cultures; and (6.) the volkhv manifests a clear phobia of migrants and dreams of a "Russia for Russians." Besides his "exposure" of Speransky's worldview through the prism of determining this pagan's degree of tolerance, this scholar also touches on "private issues." For instance, Schnirelmann draws attention to a series of definitions of "acceptable" and "unacceptable" for the volkhv of the Koliada of the Vyatichi[236], indirectly referring to "scholars" and Velimir's

---

234 Ibid.
235 Ibid, p. 24.
236 The term "pagans" (*iazychniki*) remains acceptable for Speransky, but not "neo-pagans" (*neoiazychniki*).

negative attitude towards professional humanities-scholars and others.

It is particularly worth emphasizing this ethnologist's position with regards to the participation of Russian pagans in the First World Congress of Ethnic Religions held on 20-24 June 1998 in Vilnius. Speransky was among the delegates from the Russian Federation. Despite Schnirelmann's detection of a "spirit of resurgent ethnic nationalism"[237], the form of European paganism represented by the participants of this event is classified by this Doctor of Historical Sciences as moderate. Moreover, recognizing the concluding declaration of the congress to be void of any spirit of racism and xenophobia, the author of the monograph Russian Native Faith literally regrets the absence of the "ethnophones" Kazakov (the head of the Union of Slavic Communities of Slavic Native Faith) and Speransky at ensuing congresses. In Schnirelmann's point of view, the "expansion and deepening of contacts with Western neo-pagans would help their East-Slavic counterparts overcome their overwhelming ultranationalist passions."[238]

Thus, two of the most important of Viktor Schnirelmann's conclusions on Velimir's "pagan cause" should be recognized as the reduction of the latter's worldview to terms of "cultural racism" and, most interestingly, counting Speransky among the members (and leaders) of "Russian political neo-paganism."[239]

Besides Russian scholars of the Humanities, attention has also been drawn to the "Velimir phenomenon" and Speransky's personality by representatives of the Western scholarly community, such as the Finnish scholar Kaarina Aitamurto, whose has presented her own views on contemporary Russian paganism in the dissertation *Paganism, Traditionalism, Nationalism: Narratives of Russian Rodnoverie*. Despite the absence of interview materials in this work - which, according to Aitamurto, was due to subjective reasons - the bibliographical list features materials both directly and indirectly pertaining to Velimir and, overall, is not inferior to the source base of Russian specialists (for

---
[237] Ibid, p. 238
[238] Ibid.
[239] Ibid, p. 197.

instance, the author of this dissertation cites six of Speransky's works).[240] Adhering to international scholarly solidarity, this Finnish scholar considers Velimir a representative of the technical intelligentsia and one of the pioneers of today's variant of Russian paganism. In Aitamurto's opinion, Soviet physicists, of which Speransky was one, constituted an "island of intellectual integrity" which gave birth to Russian Rodnoverie thanks to certain privileges such as the freedom and objectivity of this science itself (which was less exposed to the influence of Marxist-Leninist ideology).[241] Similar to the line of Russian specialists on 20th-21st century paganism, Aitamurto defines the territorial framework of Velimir's pagan variant as a phenomenon peculiar to the capital city. In her analysis of the worldview "options" of the leader of the Koliada of the Vyatichi, this foreign scholar devotes considerable attention to Speransky's relation to the most popular political system in Europe - democracy. Using the *Russian Pagan Manifesto* and this pagan's *Volkhvs against Globalism*, as well as others, Aitamurto draws a number of conclusions according to which Velimir's views of European democratism should be characterized as categorically anti-Western. In the opinion of this Finnish scholar, Speransky does not accept the unipolar world system, and recognizes democracy to be equivalent to feudalism.[242] Moreover, as Aitamurto writes, Velimir's anti-democratism raises a whole mass of questions for Western scholars pertaining to his argumentation, or rather absence of such.[243] Yet this scholar sees in this volkhv's works the results of a life spent under the conditions of democracy. Egoism and the overwhelming predominance of a materialistic component of social life are identified as negative consequences of the Western path of development. Moreover, in this dissertation study it is not only democracy as a form of governance that is examined as not suiting this pagan ideologist -

---

240 Ibid, pp. 293-294, 310.
241 Ibid, p. 64.
242 Kaarina Aitamurto, *Paganism, Traditionalism, Nationalism: Narratives of Russian Rodnoverie* (London: Routledge, 2016), pp. 53, 251; Ibidem, "The liaison of nationalism, conservatism and leftist ideology within Rodnoverie - approaching the paradox", paper presented at the annual conference of the American Academy of Religion (2010), p. 7.
243 Aitamurto, *Paganism, Traditionalism, Nationalism*, p. 251.

the head of the Troitsk community rejects the institution of the state as such. Velimir sees the fundamental cell of political systems as a tool for the destruction of both nature and humanity. Moreover, Speransky's "black list" includes civilization itself, which "has cut people off from the natural environment, weakened their physical condition and tries to compensate for this with its own goods, with technical means."[244] In parallel to Schnirelmann's opinion, Aitamurto is also inclined to consider part of the worldview of this volkhv of the Koliada of the Vyatichi to be conspiracy theory presuming a concentration of control of global political and economic life in the hands of a closed elite. As this scholar notes, such a theory is tied to a critique of globalization processes, the Western path of development, and Russians' bet on a multipolar world. Turning to the results of this analysis of such a "personal paganism", Kaarina Aitamurto goes against Kavykin's theory on the existence in Russian Native Faith of clearly fixed pagan "camps" tied to criteria of "tolerance" and "intolerance", and instead suggests that Velimir's views be classified as a mid-range variation.[245] The Finnish scholar includes in the definitional range characterizing the views of this pagan ideologist the following: ethnic nationalism, conservative collectivism, and Western-oriented xenophobia.[246]

The preceding historiographical overview allows us to draw a number of conclusions. Firstly, at the present time there is no specialized study, in either Russian or foreign Humanities scholarship, devoted to a detailed, "step-by-step" analysis of the worldview of Velimir (Speransky) as one of the ideologists of Russian paganism in the late 20th and early 21st century. Secondly, with few exceptions the whole spectrum of the few studies that touch upon this contemporary volkhv reify this figure in terms of a definite organization, whether the Koliada of the Vyatichi community or the Circle of Pagan Tradition union, and devalue and reduce the "personal pagan phenomenon" of Velimir

---

244 Ibid, p. 157.
245 Ibid, p. 148.
246 Ibid, p. 148; Ibidem, "The liaison of nationalism", p. 7. "I believe that the Circle of Pagan Tradition represents the liberal wing, but within it Velimir is probably the most conservative and nationalistic thinker" - online correspondence with Kaarina Aitamurto (4/12/2012) from the author's personal archive.

to the latter. Thirdly, despite the fixation on and determination of the major components of the Native Faith discursive field of Speransky, both Schnirelmann and Kavykin, significant parts of whose works are dedicated to analyzing the views of this leader of urban nativists, are inclined towards a reductionism of the question of this individual pagan. The latter finds expression in the approach and position established by these scholars in which the categories of "tolerance" and "intolerance" constitute the central analytical discourse, an approach which significantly narrows the framework for analyzing the phenomenon in question and deprives both "young pagans" and the interested audience (readership) of the right to the "genetic diversity" of this religious and socio-political movement. Fourthly, this "mainstream" of part of the scholarly community engaged in investigating contemporary Russian alternative religiosity either fully or partially ignores field materials.[247] Hence the whole array of problems facing scholarship such as references to outdated and often irrelevant publications, the absence of necessary and diverse "maximums" in the use of groups sources (such as, in the case under consideration, ignoring the pagan periodical largely of Speransky's individual "printed voice"), etc.

***

---

[247] The present author has repeatedly drawn attention to this fact. See, for example: R.V. Shizhensky, *Filosofiia dobroi sily: zhizn' i tvorchestvo Dobroslava (A.A. Dobrovol'skogo)* (Moscow: Orbita-m, 2013), p. 6.

II. LANDMARKS OF CONTEMPORARY PAGAN FAITH

YAV', PRAV', AND NAV' AS RELIGIO-PHILOSOPHICAL FOUNDATIONS OF SLAVIC NEO-PAGANISM[248]

The emergence of the religious phenomenon known as Slavic neo-paganism ("Native Faith", "traditionalism", etc.) in Ukraine in the 1930s and in Russia in the late 1970s predetermined the formation of a religio-philosophical basis for the milieu of followers of contemporary nativism.[249] One most important element of the new pagan worldview is a kind of "conceptual bloc" encompassing three categories: *Yav', Nav',* and *Prav'*. In the opinion of those few scholars who have dealt with this question[250] and according to our own observations, these philosophico-theological notions have found fertile soil among virtually all of the major neo-pagan religious organizations and associations of Russia and Ukraine. Despite their general recognition and popularity, however, Yav, Prav, and Nav do not have a single explanation among the whole neo-pagan world. These terms are understood and interpreted in different ways by the ideologists of the new constructed paganism. A review of Native Faith narrative sources allows us to highlight a number of versions disclosing the various respective meanings of these concepts.

The most widespread interpretation of these religio-philosophical (or quasi-philosophical[251]) notions is the idea that Yav, Prav, and Nav are the three worlds of the Slavic mythological worldview. In this projected mythological "triworld", Prav is the world of the celestial gods, Nav is the abode of dark deities, and Yav is the earthly world, the world

---

248 Article first published in *Nauchno-tekhnicheskie vedomosti Sankt-Peterburgskogo gosudarstvennogo politekhnicheskogo universiteta. Gumanitarnye i obshchestvennyi nauki [Scientific-Technical Publications of Saint Petersburg State Polytechnic University: Humanitarian and Social Sciences]* 1:118 (2011).
249 G. Gomeniuk, S. Tereshchenko, *Russkoe i ukrainskoe neoiazychestvo* (Saint Petersburg/Kiev: Center for Apologetic Studies), pp. 2-3.
250 See A.M. Cherniy, *Religieznavstvo. Posibnik* (Kiev: Akademvidav, 2003); V.A. Schnirelmann, *"Russkoe neoiazychestvo: kvazireligiia natsionalizma i ksenofobii"* [http://www.religio/ru/relisoc/27_print.html].
251 Schnirelmann, ibid.

of people.[252] In addition to such mythological worlds, these sought-after notions are also identified as categories of the emerging neo-pagan philosophy, in which Prav is allotted the role of divine law[253], Yav is presented as the sensible world of "everything manifest", and Nav exists as a world that represents the "whole totality of the subtle planes of Being"[254] inaccessible to our understanding.

These terms also figure as the most important components of the human individual. According to the compilers of the *Calendar of the Most Important Ukrainian Folk Holidays of 2006-2007*, Prav accounts for the moral condition of a person, Yav for their material prosperity, and Nav for culture and knowledge.[255] Volkhv Veleslav correlates these three neo-pagan concepts with the specifics of the human body's structure: Prav is the forehead, Yav the shoulders, and Nav the stomach.[256]

In the annotations to his translation of the *Book of Veles*, A.I. Asov presents a whole list of possible interpretations of Yav and Nav, such as being the male and female elements, day and night, death and life, the intelligent and the animalistic. At the end of his numerous considerations, the latter author resolves that this "mysterious troika" correlates to the triune god Rod: "Yav is the Father, Nav is the Son, and Prav the Spirit."[257] Some neo-pagan writers substantiate the philosophical component of these concepts by referring to the experiences of the East, where

---

252 Velimir, Veleslav, and Vlasov, *Put' Volkhva* (Donetsk: Kashtan, 2007), pp. 8-9; Veleslav, *Uchenie volkhvov: Belaia kniga* (Moscow: Institut obshchegumanitarnykh issledovanii, 2007), p. 21; A. Belov, *Veles - Bog Rusov. Neizvestnaia istoriia russkogo naroda* (Moscow: Amrita-Rus', 2007), pp. 90, 174; Bogumir, *Rodnaia Vera. Istochnik schast'ia* (Khmelnitsky: Dukhovnoe izdanie Rodovogo Ognishcha Rodnoi Pravoslavnoi Very, 2007), pp. 95-96, 99; G. Lozko, *Kolo Svarozhe* (Kiev: Ukrainskii pis'mennik, 2005), p. 50.

253 The ideologists of Native Ukrainian National Faith, the "RUNIVirs", extend the term "law" (*zakon*) to all three notions. See: *Mudrist' Ukrainskoi Pravdi: Nauka RUNViri, Silenkiyanin, Vira v Dazhboga* (Kiev: OBEREGI, 1996), p. 161.

254 G.Z. Maksimenko, *Velesova kniga. Vedy ob uklade zhizni i istoke very slavian* (Moscow: Academy of Management, 2008), p. 363; Y.V. Gnatiuk, *Dovelesova kniga. Drevneishie skazaniia Rusi* (Moscow: Amrita-Rus', 2007), p. 20. See also the discussions of this topic on Veleslav's *LiveJournal* forum: https://veleslav13.livejournal.com/8905.html.

255 M.I. Polishchuk, *Kalendar viznachnikh ukrainskikh narodnikh sviat* (Lutsk: Tverdinia, 2006), pp. 20-21.

256 Veleslav, *Uchenie volkhvov*, p. 428.

257 A.I. Asov, *Velesova kniga* (Moscow: Manager, 19994), pp. 282-283.

they find analogues to Yav, Prav, and Nav in the Rigveda[258], the doctrine of chakras[259], and so on.

A preliminary critique of these espoused hypotheses leads to the following result: the first theory is the closest to the notions of the cosmos, world order, and tripartite division of space that are widespread throughout the mythological systems of the world's peoples. Fitting into this "historical version" is the view of some Native Faith adepts that Yav, Prav, and Nav are the foundational parts of the World Tree: "The threefold nature of Troyan-Triglav can be explained through the notion of the three spheres of being which have appropriate symbolism reflected in the Tree of Life: the roots are the deceased Ancestors (Nav), the trunk is living people (Yav), and the crown with branches and leaves is the world of the Gods (Prav)."[260] It is noteworthy that only the lower world of Nav becomes the subject of further structuring within the "threefold world." Adherents of modern paganism divide Nav into two parts: "Light Nav" (one variant being the Celestial Iriy, the world of Slava) and "Dark Nav" (Hell). This division of the lower world finds explanation in the new pagan mythology. According to the ideas of Veleslav, the volkhv of the Rodoliubie community, "Dark Nav" is the abode of undeveloped souls, while "Light Nav" is the abode of the holy souls of the ancestors.[261] Volkhv Bogumil offers a different interpretation of the worlds of Nav: "Light Nav is the abode of unborn souls... Dark Nav is the abode of dashing spirits and the souls of abusers (sinners)."[262]

This contemporary gradation of the world beyond might be based on the ancient Scandinavian notion of the cosmos. By virtue of the preservation and relative accessibility of Scandinavian sources, Slavic neo-pagans rather often use the "mythological baggage" of their Northern neighbors for comparison and

---

258 G. Lozko, *Kolo Svarozhe*, p. 198.
259 Velimir, Veleslav, Vlasov, *Put' Volkhva*, pp. 137-139.
260 G. Lozko, *Kolo Svarozhe*, p. 50. See also Bogumir, *Rodnaia vera*, p. 95; Velimir, Veleslav, Vlasov, *Put's Volkhva*, p. 9.
261 Veleslav, *Uchenie volkhvov*, pp. 188, 499.
262 Bogumir, *Rodnaia vera*, p. 95. See also V.A. Istarkhov, *Udar russkikh bogov* (Saint Petersburg: Redaktor, 2001), p. 225.

sometimes full copying. In addition to the primordial World Tree, Ukrainian Rodnovery use the famous Zbruch idol as an example of the tripartite division of the universe.[263]

Other versions and theories represent artificial theologico-philosophical constructs which have no historical or religious basis. Without a doubt, contemporary neo-pagan proselytes face the need to expand the range of content and characteristics of the mythical world order which they claim. Hence the persistent desire and effort on the part of some Rodnovery to introduce a whole array of new religio-mythological constructs and to correlate the notions of Nav, Yav, and Prav with foreign philosophical concepts. Another part of the neo-pagan elite which rejects "outside" influence, the path of borrowing and possible reconstruction, chooses instead the easy path of "mythological composition."

By the will of the Native Faith elite, the Slavic neo-pagan "threefold world" falls under the patronage of a whole pantheon of deities. It bears noting that the "authorities" of the gods in the creation and control of the cosmos as well as the individual links between mythological entities and specific worlds differ greatly between Native Faith communities throughout Ukraine and Russia. The demiurges of Yav, Nav, and Prav are held to be the gods Rod[264] and Svarog.[265] The majority of Rodnovery recognize Perun[266] and Sviatovit[267] to be the defenders and guardians of the threefold world. Veles is the only deity associated by virtually all neo-pagans with the netherworld of Nav.[268] The role of the intermediary between the celestial and earthly worlds is fulfilled

---

263 One of the main ideologues of Ukrainian neo-paganism, G. Lozko, describes this statue as of Svyatovid and considers it to be a pagan monument depicting the three tiers of the universe - Lozko, *Kolo Svarozhe*, p. 133.
264 Bogumir, *Rodnaia vera*, p. 68; Knyaz Svyatobor (compil.), *Russkaia letopis 'Veles kniga': Sviashchennaia kniga slavian* (Kiev: Intertrekhnodruk, 2001), p. 7; Veleslav, *Obriadnik* (Moscow: Institut obshchegumanitarnykh issledovanii, 2003), p. 3.
265 Veleslav, *Uchenie volkhvov*, p. 41; Asov, *Velesova kniga*, pp. 39, 274; Lozko, *Ridna chitanka* (Vinnitsa: Kontinent-Prim, 2007), p. 18.
266 Veleslav, *Uchenie volkhvov*, p. 60; Velimir, Veleslav, Vlasov, *Put' volkhva*, p. 9.
267 Maksimenko, *Velesova kniga*, p. 40; Bogumir, *Rodnaia vera*, p. 68; Asov, *Velesova kniga*, p. 7.
268 Veleslav, *Uchenie volkhvov*, pp. 116, 119; Velimir, Veleslav, Vlasov, *Put' volkhva*, p. 15; V.S. Kazakov, *Mir slavianskikh bogov* (Moscow/Kaluga: Russkaia Pravda, 2006), p. 76; B. Yakovenko, *Religiia solntsa. Koren i drev slavianskoi tsivilizatsii* (Kiev: Intertekhnodruk, 2004), p. 19.

by Simargl[269], and contact between the world of people and the netherworld of the afterlife is performed by birds.[270] One can also encounter a more extensive division of the gods into "kingdoms." According to Yggeld and Velemudr of the Ber Circle Native Faith association, Yav is the dominion of Svetovit, Radegast, and Dazhdbog Svarozhich. Prav, in turn, is assigned to Stribog, Svarog, and Perun.[271] Ukrainian Rodnovery conceive other gods for the upper world: in the opinion of G. Lozko, the realm of Prav is that of Lada, Dazhdbog, Perun, and Makosh.[272] Such discrepancies are very common.

Yet another "know-how" of contemporary followers of paganism is correlating these three terms with the notion of "Triglav." In neo-pagan narratives, Triglav generally appears in two versions: either as a direct incarnation of the three worlds of Yav, Prav, and Nav[273], or as a triune deity of Svarog-Perun-Veles corresponding to Prav-Yav-Nav.[274]

The above-cited materials allow for several conclusions to be drawn. Firstly, to this day neo-pagan associations and individual leaders of the Native Faith current in Ukraine and Russia, both within these republics and on the international (East Slavic) level, have not been able to develop a single concept or common model explaining the religion-philosophical values propagated by them. This statement is based on: (a), the absence of a clear conceptual apparatus revealing the essence of the most important terminology and worldview basis of Yav, Prav, and Nav; and (b.) the futile attempts by the neo-pagan elite between communities in Russia and Ukraine to "populate the neo-mythological worlds" through their own speculations and constructions of an imaginary pantheon encompassing different gods.

Secondly, despite its youth, the neo-pagan current has managed to construct its own religious system in general

---

269 Lozko, *Kolo Svarozhe*, p. 52; Bogumir, *Rodnaia vera*, p. 70.
270 Lozko, *Kolo Svarozhe*, p. 184.
271 Yggeld and Velemudr, *"Krug Bera", Izvednik russkogo iazychestva*.
272 Lozko, *Kolo Svarozhe*, p. 36.
273 Kazakov, *Mir slavianskikh bogov*, p. 26; Bogumir, *Rodnaia vera*, p. 99; Istarkhov, *Udar russkikh bogov*, p. 225.
274 Veleslav, *Obriadnik*, p. 51; Maksimenko, *Velesova kniga*, p. 363. Other hypostases of Triglav can be encountered throughout Slavic neo-paganism, on which see: Mezgir, *"Koliada Viatichei", Izvednik russkogo iazychestva*.

terms and to successfully manipulate it. The consequences of socially-actualized religious preaching have been reflected in the appearance of new religious holidays (e.g. the Holy Day of Prav[275]), the names of neo-pagan communities (e.g. the Slavic Native Faith Community of the Unity of Prav in the village of Moskovsky[276]), religious schools (the high spiritual educational institution PRAV', or the "Orthodox Native Faith Academy of Faith-Knowing" [*verovedan'ia*] in Khmelnitsky, Ukraine[277]), as well as in healing practices[278] and even the interpretation of state symbols (for instance: "It is no wonder that on the coat of arms of Ukraine, the trident, the symbol of Prav is in the center... On the state coat of arms Nav is on the left, Prav is in the middle, and Yav is on the right"[279]). Their success in implanting these "neo-mythological terms" has been so tangible that even scholarly and journalistic literature has fallen under the influence of Yav, Prav, and Nav, particularly a considerable number of dictionaries and reference books on the beliefs of the ancient Slavs. For example, in E.A. Grushko and Y.M. Medvedev's *Dictionary of Slavic Mythology* - which is advertised as "recommended as a textbook on Russian language, literature, and history in secondary schools, colleges, gymnasiums, and higher educational institutions" - this neo-pagan religious "trinity" is claimed to be "the embodiment of time in Slavic cosmogony."[280] There are dozens of such examples.

The source base of the terms under consideration is extremely weak. If we do not take into account the fantastic theories of Native Faith ideologues on the origin of the notion of "Prav" being the universal law of the Aryan tribes of the Tripolye culture of the sixth to third-millennia BCE, the version that the laws of Nav, Prav, and Yav have been preserved on Ukrainian embroidery

---

275 Lozko, *Ridna chitanka*, pp. 29-30; Polishchuk, *Kalendar*, p. 18.
276 *"Vera Rodnaia"* [http://svetogor.nm.ru/vera.htm].
277 Bogumir, *Rodnaia vera*, pp. 72-75.
278 O.D. Dukhova, *Kamen' Velesa: Zashchita ot zla i zhiznennykh neudach* (Saint Petersburg: Nevsky prospekt, 2005), pp. 148-151.
279 Polishchuk, *Kalendar*, pp. 18-19; Lozko, *Kolo Svarozhe*, p. 150.
280 E.A. Grushko, Y.M. Medvedev, *Slovar' slavianskoi mifologii* (Nizhny Novgorod: Russkii kupets & Bratia Slaviane, 1996), p. 452; L.M. Vagurina (compil.), *Slavianskaia mifologiia. Slovar'-spravochnik* (Moscow: Linor, 1998), pp. 227, 236; A. Chernitsky, *Bolshoi mifologicheskii slovar'* (Moscow: GElios, 2008), p. 48.

cloths[281], or, finally, the equating of the Slavic Yav to the Semitic Yahweh[282], then the most important and virtually only source in which these three terms are attested is the famous mid-20th-century forgery, the *Book of Veles*. The notions of Yav, Prav, and Nav are encountered more than once across the numerous editions and translations of this purported "ancient relic of Slavic writing." Generally speaking, the information which the author of the *Book of Veles* offers on these neo-pagan mythological paradigms consists of small addenda to the main narrative. In most cases, Yav, Nav, and Prav are mentioned by the compiler of the *Book of Veles* during glorifications of a given deity or during the fulfillment of important, pivotal events. Overall, like the entire work, the lines devoted to these notions are extremely uninformative, vague, and factologically poor. As an example we can cite some excerpts from various translations of the *Book of Veles* devoted to this topic:

> "Yav is the current, that which is created by Prav. Nav is after it, and before it is Nav. In Prav there is Yav."[283]

> "So it is said of our Did, death is Yav, because it is current. Creation happens in Prav. The sky of Nav is in Prav. Before it is Nav and after it is Nav. In Prav there is Yav, let us learn the old."[284]

> "Yav is current and created by Prav. For Nav is after: before there is Nav, and after there is Nav, and in Prav there is Yav."[285]

This material not only does not shed any light disclosing the religio-philosophical meaning of Yav, Prav, and Nav, but also allows us to argue that the numerous successors and followers of this forgery's author, in trying to add their own "zest", have even further confused the already complex entanglement of the Book of Veles in general and these terms in particular. It bears particular note that apologists of the *Book of Veles* are not always capable of offering an accurate interpretation of the "mysterious trinity." For instance, B.A. Rebinder, relying on the previous translations of Lazarevich, Sokolov, and Kirpich and analyzing the text of

---

281 Lozko, *Kolo Svarozhe*, pp. 198-199.
282 V. Emelyanov, *Desionizatsiia* (Moscow: Russkaia Pravda, 2002).
283 Asov, *Velesova kniga*, p. 73.
284 Maksimenko, *Velesova kniga*, p. 18.
285 Svyatobor, *Russkaia letopis' 'Veles kniga'*, p. 27.

tablet 6B containing the word "Yav", put a question mark by this unknown term. The very author of this sensational "artifact", Yuri Petrovich Miroliubov[286], writes of Yav, Prav, and Nav in his numerous writings that despite his efforts he could not "discover even traces of such beliefs among the people."[287]

It is also noteworthy that some contemporary advocates of paganism (or people sympathetic to its revival) recognize at least two of these three terms of contemporary religious traditionalists to be artificial and contrived. The compilers of the *Dictionary of the Russian Pagan Worldview* declare that Yav and Prav are "nowhere to be found in 'pure form' in reliable sources."[288] This presumption is confirmed by the absence of any mentions of an "earthly world and divine world" in the studies of Russian scholars of mythology and most reference publications. In fairness, it should be noted that several dictionaries (such as those of Vladimir Dal, S.I Ozhigov, and D.N Ushakov) contain the word *yav'*. However, their treatments of this notion have nothing in common with the religio-philosophical construct of neo-pagans.[289]

The case of the historical fate of Nav, which is for Native Faith the world-beyond of the god Veles, is more complex. The compilers of the above-mentioned Dictionary of the Russian Pagan Worldview consider Nav to be a reliable, "logical notion" of the Russian mythological worldview with historical roots. According to their theory, Nav is the "un-manifest (*neiavlennyi*) world", the invisible "non-reality (*ne-iav'*), often the "world of the dead" or a deceased person themself.[290] Indeed, a word close to the neo-pagan Nav as world of the dead is mentioned both in narrative sources and in Slavic folklore: *nav'e* and *nav'i*. This term is cited by the authors of the *Dictionary of the Russian Pagan Worldview*,

---

286 V.P. Kozlov, "Khlestakov otechestvennoi 'arkheologii', ili tri zhizni A.I. Sudakadzeva" in *Chto dumaiut uchenye o 'Velesovoi knige'* (Saint Petersburg: Science, 2004), p. 235.
287 Quote from O.V. Tvorogov, "Vlesova kniga" in *Trudy otdela drevnerusskoi literatury XLIII* (Leningrad: Science, 1990), p. 245.
288 S. Ermakov (ed.), *Russkoe iazycheskoe mirovozzrenie: prostranstvo smyslov. Opyt slovaria s poiasneniiami* (Moscow: Ladoga-100), 2008), pp. 131, 187.
289 Dal wrote in the fourth volume of his *Tolkovyi slovar' zhivogo velikorusskogo iazyka* (Moscow: Russkii iazyk, 1998): "*Iav'* is a sober, conscious state, not sleepy and without delirium and drowsiness, in full, healthy mind." See D.N. Ushakov (ed.), *Tolkovyi slovar' russkogo iazyka t. IV* (Moscow: Russkie slovari, 1994), p. 1454; S.I. Ozhigov, *Slovar' russkogo iazyka* (Moscow: Russkii iazyk, 1990).
290 *Russkoe iazycheskoe mirovozzrenie*, p. 113.

but for some reason only at the very end of their article without devoting due attention to it.

Nav'i are known from Old Russian chronicles as personified images of death. The Laurentian chronicle mentions *nav'i* twice. In 1089 the arrival of Metropolitan Ioann (John) was associated with "the *nav'e* coming", and in 1902, when mysterious *nav'i* entities beat the inhabitants of Polotsk.[291] Information on *nav'i* is also contained in sermons against paganism, such as those of St. Grigory and St. Ioann Zlatoust. The latter speak of prayers to *nav'i* in the bathhouse.[292] E.V. Anchikov, who recorded this ritual in the early 20th century, suggests that these prayers were accompanied by plentiful feasts.[293] In Bulgarian folklore, *nav'i* are:

> bird-like souls of the dead which fly at night, in storm and rain, on evil winds, and scream like hungry hawks. The cry or song of these birds means death. The *navi* (*navatsi*) attack pregnant women and children, suck their blood, and drink the milk of cows. They are described as assuming the form of enormous naked birds or naked roosters the size of an eagle.[294]

Naviy are attributed the quality of being dangerous to humans by the inhabitants of the Carpathian mountains: "*Navi* are disembodied souls of the dead, they fly on evil winds and can direct these winds to human fields, causing drought...In the Carpathians *navki* are forest spirits which can transform into beautiful girls, reckless youth are lured by their laughter and charming voices into chasms and off cliffs."[295] In Smolensk tradition, one of the names

---

291 *Lavrent'evskaya letopis'* in *Polnoe sbornie russkikh letopisei t. I* (Moscow: Iazyki russkoi kul'tury, 1997), pp. 208, 215.
292 N.M. Gal'kovsky, *Bor'ba khristianstva s ostatkami iazychestva v Drevnei Rusi* (Moscow/Kharkov, 1913/1916).
293 E.V. Anichkov, *Iazychestvo i Drevniaia Rus'* (Moscow: Indrik, 2003), pp. 160-161. The "Word to the Ignorant" (*Slovo k nevezham*), which survived only in lists from the 16th century, contains an account of objects sacrificed to "*nav'i*" - eggs, meat, and milk. See Viljo Johannes Mansikka, *Religiia vostochnykh slavian* (Moscow: Gorky Institute of World Literature of the Russian Academy of Sciences, 2005), pp. 154-155; B.A. Rybakov, *Iazychestvo drevnikh slavian* (Moscow: Science, 1981), pp. 34-35.
294 Rybakov, *Iazychestvo drevnikh slavian*, p. 36.
295 G.O. Berdnik, *Znaki karpatskoi magii: taemnitsa starego mol'fara* (Kiev: Gamazin, 2008), p. 246.

of a far from peaceful mythical water-personage is "*navnoi*."[296] As for analysis of the etymological meaning of *nav'* (*nav'e, navei, navy*), part of the scholarly community holds *nav'* to be, among other meanings (such as a dead man, a grave, a ship, the soul, etc.), the world of the dead.[297] However, the majority of scholars concur that this term was used to refer to mythical entities which sent disease and death upon people.[298] Further specification of this image leads to an interesting dilemma: are "*navs*" to be considered the deceased, the restless dead, disembodied spirits, or ghosts? Following Professor A. Sobolevsky, who put forth his own theory to resolve this question in the late 19th century[299], we believe that originally the Slavs imagined *nav'e* to be malicious spirits (souls)[300] which disturbed people from time to time. In favor of this supposition speaks the Slavic rite of cremation intended to avoid the possibility of a buried corpse turning into a malicious restless ghost. The recognition of *navi* to be mythical beings, and not the netherworld of the Eastern Slavs (as for the West Slavs, the word *nav* is attested in the Czech language as referring to the underworld[301]), puts an end to the question of the "authenticity" of the third, "lower" neo-pagan world.

There is no doubt as to the fact that the ancient Slavs did have a developed mythological system with a fully formed hierarchy of deities, a structured system of the cosmos, etc. Unfortunately, however, a large part of the pagan heritage of the Eastern Slavic

---

[296] N.A. Krinichnaia, *Russkaia narodnaia mifologicheskaia proza: Istoki i polisemantizm obrazov t. I* (Saint Petersburg: Nauka, 2001), p. 455.

[297] M. Fasmer, *Etimologicheskii slovar' russkogo iazyka t. III* (Moscow: Progress, 1987), p. 35; Lubor Niederle, *Slavianskie drevnosti* (Moscow: Aleteia, 2000), p. 231; A.V. Nikitina, *Russkaia demonologiia* (Saint Petersburg: Saint Petersburg University, 2006), p. 383.

[298] Friedrich Arnold Brockhaus and I.A. Efron, *Entsiklopedicheskii slovar' t. XX* (Saint Petersburg, 1897), p. 419; A.S. Famintsyn, *Bozhestva drevnikh slavian* (Saint Petersburg: Aleteia, 1995), p. 319. S.A. Tokarev (ed.), *Mify narodov mira* (Moscow: Bol'shaia Rossiiskaia entsiklopedia, 1997), pp. 195, 452; V.A. Dal, *Tolkovy slovar' zhivogo velikorusskogo iazyka t. 2*, p. 389; D.O. Shepping, *Mify slavianskogo iazychestva* (Moscow: TERRA, 1997), p. 106; M. Vlasova, *Novaia ABEVEGA russkikh sueverii* (Saint Petersburg: Severo-Zapad, 1995), pp. 245-246.

[299] A. Sobolevsky, "Nav'e i Verziulovo kolo", *Russkii filologicheskii vestnik XXIII* (Warsaw, 1890), p. 79.

[300] A.N. Afanasyev, *Poeticheskie vozzreniia slavian na prirodu t. 3* (Moscow: Sovremennyi pisatel', 1995), p. 119.

[301] Ibid, p. 35.

world has been lost. It is being recreated and reconstructed by scholars bit-by-bit with the use of a whole complex array of scientific methods. In most cases, Russian and Ukrainian neo-pagan communities' formulations of their religio-mythological basis, including their construction of the worlds of Yav, Prav, and Nav, do not have any strong historico-cultural foundation, but rather introduce elements of chaos into the most complex process of searching for and restoring the religious foundations of the Eastern Slavic peoples.

***

THE GOLDEN AGE IN THE WORKS AND PREACHINGS OF SLAVIC NEO-PAGANS[302]

In turning to the historical concepts and "chronological *études*" of contemporary pagan organizations in Russia, it bears dwelling in particular on the so-called "Golden Age" so often mentioned in the latter's narratives. As the Moscow scholar Viktor Schnirelmann notes: "This neo-pagan concept proceeds from the notion that the most brilliant pages of Russian history were written long before the 10th century, i.e. in an era that left almost no written testimonies of the history of the Slavs, not to mention of 'Rus.' This opens up considerable scope for the most sophisticated fantasies and for inventing the past."[303]

Unfortunately, the scientific thought of religious scholars in contemporary Russia (except for the works of Schnirelmann) cannot boast anything substantial in the study of this question. Yet the striking fact remains that all neo-pagan currents striving to create their own original mythologies position this theme of the Golden Age as key. For example, in his response to email inquiries, Rodomir (one of the members of the Volkhvs of Rod community) referred to history with the following phrases as chronological determinants: "at the dawn of time", "since those times", "since then", or "once upon a time, long ago", or "in old times."[304] As a general rule, neo-pagan ideologists borrow the foundations for their deliberations on the "prehistory" of humanity as a whole and the Slavs in particular from surviving legends and myths (not necessarily of Russian origin), from their own "developments", as well as from "sacred" texts whose historicity and authenticity are not recognized by official science.

---

302 Article first published in the conference volume *Religii Povolzh'ia: problemy sotsial'nogo sluzheniia [Religions of the Volga Region: Problems of Social Service]* (Nizhny Novgorod: N.I. Lobachevsky Nizhny Novgorod State University, 2009).

303 V.A. Shnirelmann, "Neoiazychestvo i natsionalizm (vostochnoevropeiskii areal)", *Issledovaniia po prikladnoi i neotlozhnoi etnologii 114* [http://www.iea.ras.ru/lib/neotl/07/2002062247.htm].

304 Volkhv Rodomir, *"Otvety Rodicham"* [http://volxv.info/site/artic/es.html]; *"Predposylki k vozniknoveniiu obshchin Volkhvov Roda"* [http://volxv.info/site/artic/es.html].

133

One example of such seeking is the legend of the creation of the world presented by the Koliada of the Vyatichi community. According to this legend, the first beings in the universe were the gods Rod and Chernobog. After the creation of the foundations of the cosmos, the younger gods, and the moral laws, these primal gods turned all of their energies towards the creation of people. With the birth of humanity and the "enlivening" of people by the gods began the era of the Golden Age: "Then Rod and Chernobog taught them their knowledge. Having accepted it, people began to live and be fruitful on Earth, they began to know the earthly Gods. And they accomplished all of those things which we call history."[305]

One of the leading ideologues of Russian neo-paganism, Volkhv Veleslav of the Rodoliubie community, lists four ages of mankind in his "Brief Dictionary of a Rodnover": (1) the Golden Age of Svarog, characterized by this author as the time of the reign of truth, justice, peace, and divine knowledge; (2) the Silver Age of Dazhdbog, the era of the gradual extinguishing of these virtues; (3) the Bronze Age of Perun, the time of the decline of morality and the beginning of power struggles; and (4) the Iron Age of Koshchey, or modernity, the era of godlessness and violence.[306] Listing the commandments of the patron of the Golden Age, Svarog, Veleslav outlines the virtues of the Slavic demiurge. In this volkhv's opinion, Svarog is the creator of light, the ancestor of the Russian people, the one who taught the Slavs' ancestors to forge iron and plow the earth. Svarog shaped the first hearth, created the sun, the stars, and dawn, and compiled instructions for the four "estates" of tillers, artisans, warriors, and volkhvs. He also gave people his son, Svarozhich, or earthly fire.[307] Finally, it is Svarog who is the creator of Yav, Nav, and Prav, the fundamental worldview categories of contemporary pagans.[308] The adepts

---

[305] M.S. Vasil'ev, A.L. Potapov, N.N. Speransky, *Iazychniki otvechaiut 5* (Troitsk: Trovat, 1999), p. 9.
[306] Volkhv Veleslav, *Uchenie volkhvov: Belaia kniga* (Moscow: Nauka, 2007), p. 625.
[307] Ibid, pp. 41, 81.
[308] None of these notions are to be found in historical Russian sources. One attempt at interpreting the "triworld" was undertaken by the compilers of the dictionary *The Russian Pagan Worldview*. See S. Ermakov, D. Gavrilov, *Russkoe iazycheskoe mirovozzrenie: prostranstvo smyslov* (Moscow: Ladoga-100, 2008), pp. 113, 130, 187.

of the Krina community also associate Svarog with an era of universal prosperity.[309] The main shortcoming of Russian neo-pagan conceptions of the "Golden Age of Svarog" remains that very chronological uncertainty originating at the "dawn of time."[310] Unlike Russian polytheists, contemporary pagans in Ukraine are more "detailed" in their determinations of the time of the "Slavic earthly paradise." Volkhv Bogumil presents his own hypothesis of the birth of the universe in his pamphlet *Native Faith: Source of Happiness*. In this author's opinion, the Days of Svarog (lasting 4,320,000,000 years) are divided into four segments: the Night of Svarog, the Dawn of Svarog, the Noon of Svarog, and Twilight. According to this timescale, the Golden Age falls under the Dawn of Svarog, encompassing 1,728,000 earthly years: "This was the time when man manifested his best qualities: creativity, love, justice, and goodness. People communicated with the Gods and lived righteously."[311] The leader of the Native Faith Association of Ukraine, Galina Lozko, recognizes Svarog to be the main cultural hero, the supreme creator-god of the Ukrainian pantheon, and clearly defines the time of his cult's birth: "The cult of Svarog was likely born between the Bronze and Iron Ages."[312]

Yet it is not only the mysterious time of Svarog with which the neo-pagans of Russia and Ukraine associate the dawn of Slavdom. As a general rule, the historical ideal appears to be the time of pagan Kievan Rus. The Rus of the Byliny is depicted as a centralized, ethnically homogenous state.[313] In the opinion

---

309 "According to legend Svarog gave the ancestors a covenant in the form of four golden objects: a plow and yoke to cultivate and eat from the native ancestral land, a cup of life to be constantly full, and an ax to defend against uninvited, hostile guests" - A.G. Rezunkov (ed.), *Kolovorot 2008. Slavianskii solnechno-lunnyi kalendar'-mesiatseslov* (Saint Petersburg: Center for Strategic Studies, 2007), p. 37. Volkhv Bogumil describes this legend in different terms: "Many thousands of years ago, the Forefather Dazhbog bestowed upon the Slavic *rod* a grain of rye and showed how the sown grain sprouts and gives rise to the yield of harvest. Father Veles taught plowing, sowing, and reaping, and Father Svarog forged a plow and taught how to grind grain and bake bread" - Volkhv Bogumil, *Rodnaia Vera. Istochnik schast'ia* (Kmelnitsky, 2007), p. 37.
310 Rezunkov (ed.), *Kolovorot 2008. Slavianskii solnechno-lunnyi kalendar'-mesiatseslov*, p. 37.
311 Volkhv Bogumil, *Rodnaia Vera. Istochnik schast'ia*, p. 20.
312 G. Lozko, *Kolo Svarozhe* (Kiev: Ukrainskii pis'mennik, 2005), p. 32.
313 V.B. Avdeev, *Preodolenie khristianstva* (Moscow: Russkaia Pravda, 2006), p. 6.

of Rodnovery, popular Veche democracy in this era prevailed[314] and there existed a rich, developed, written tradition that was lost with the adoption of Christianity.[315] The Slavs are presented as the bearers of high moral ideals, as guardians and protectors of nature.[316]

The views of the elder of the Russian neo-pagan movement, Dobroslav (Alexey Dobrovolsky), on the era of the superhuman and the time of universal prosperity overall fit into the general outline of neo-pagan explorations. Dobrovolsky's reflections on the Golden Age are based on such elements as the symbiosis of primordial man and the surrounding world, totemism, a "primordial knowledge" intrinsic to ancient people, and matriarchy:

> Primordial man and large carnivores were never sworn enemies, because man was not their constant prey. There is reason to believe that the most "terrifying" of royal predators - the cave lion and the bear - threatened him least of all. The usual relation between man and these beasts was mutual respect: they reckoned with each other, preferred to avoid meeting and, unless absolutely necessary, did not interfere in each other's lives. The real danger posed to man was the attack of herbivores, such as vicious wild bulls, rhinoceros, and boars. The relation of the Stone Age hunter to the most perfect predator, the wolf, was shrouded in strange mystery... The wolf always followed man, as did man the wolf, but, observing an unwritten law, they did not hunt each other. Without a doubt, they experienced a mutual, subconscious attraction. And it was the beast called the Wolf that was the sacred animal of all Northern peoples.[317]
>
> Totem means a patronizing, protecting Progenitor, the First Ancestor. Totemism is confidence in the intimate connection between a tribe and its faithful natural kinsman in animal guise. Totemism is rooted in

---

314 B. Iakovenko, *Iazychestvo slavian Kievskoi Rusi* (Kiev: Poligraf), p. 33.
315 "Not only all written works which recorded the traditions of our ancestors and their religion, but even the writing script itself was destroyed by barbaric methods." - M. Polishchuk, *Kalendar viznachnikh ukrains'kikh narodnykh sviat. Svarozhe kolo* (Lutsk: Tverdinia, 2006), p. 4.
316 Ibid, p. 6; Avdeev, *Preodolenie khristianstva*, pp. 199, 218.
317 Dobroslav, *Svetoslavie (ocherki iazycheskogo mirochuvstvovaniia)* (Kirov: Viatka, 2004), p. 44.

the perception of a man who is not alienated from nature, completely different than ours. He saw living creatures around him as gifted with reason, soul, and will, like himself...It was the hunter who, knowing the life of wild animals, most revered the WOLF... The wolf inspired him with something akin to comradely sympathy: after all, he is also a risky scavenger and hunter! And hunting is not a fun pastime, but someone's death... This made man comprehend the wolf as a kindred spirit, as the creature closest to him... Children raised by wolves are either future ancestors or tribal leaders and heroes.[318]

In the primordial - and that means perfect - pagan worldview, there was no contrived, radical contrast of the natural and the divine, the material and the ideal, the illuminated and the mundane, the ordinary and the majestic, Nature and Man. These notions constituted a single whole which could not possibly be divided without destroying the organic unity of their being...[319]

All the legends and myths of the Golden Age affirm with striking unanimity that in the beginning man had the ability to understand animals and birds... The ability to think without words, in pure sensorial images, allowed them to understand other living beings and to be understandable to them. This is that most ancient and perfect language of feelings that is implied in fairy tales, where birds, animals, plants, and people freely speak with one another in a common language. Intuitive, prophetic knowledge is wordless... All his [primordial man's] feelings, moods, and intentions were eloquently and truthfully manifested in gestures, glances, facial expressions, involuntary exclamations, and hums.[320]

Woman, playing the main role in primordial society, acted as the guardian of the Sacred Fire and, in the opinion of a number of researchers, was the first to discover it... Matriarchy [is associated with] the veneration of Mother-Earth, the pure cult of Nature without faith in higher, supra-natural gods or god, and the absence of a priestly estate. The universal Foremother-Earth herself was the personification and visible hypostasis of the Divine, and Woman was, with her birthing force, the personification of Earth and the Principle of Life... The

318 Ibid, pp. 45-46.
319 Dobroslav, *Mat'-Zemlia. Chudo-Chudnoie. Divo-Divnoe (samizdat)*, p. 54-55.
320 Dobroslav, *Bezbozhnye chudesa zhivoi prirody* (Kharkov: *Sfera*), pp. 43-45.

mother was more of a Deity than a chief... All of family and social life was structured around her. The woman was the head of the rod, the keeper of the hearth, the guardian of the ancestral orders and customs, the performer of rites and sacred acts. She was the heiress of magical knowledge and the intermediary with the world of the Spirits, for genetically intrinsic to her, as a woman, was an acute, intuitive sensitivity to occult influences... Peace-loving, matro-centric culture did not know of castes, slavery, and wars. It was a time of universal equality, including between the sexes.[321]

In Dobroslav's opinion, the ideal world order did not pass over mankind without leaving any trace, but rather left a very noticeable mark manifest in the creative intellectual activity of Stone Age people.[322] These discoveries were facilitated by two factors, particularly the climatic conditions of the ancestral homeland of mankind:

> Man as the bearer of Reason could hardly appear in such warm, fertile lands where the abundant gifts of Nature made improvement unnecessary and hindered the development of mental and spiritual abilities. Man was born in the forests of the North, where harsh climatic conditions did not allow him to relax. To survive, preserve, and continue his rod, he was required to think and invent. To pluck the ripe fruits of trees around the year, a big mind is not needed.[323]

Dobroslav also more than once speaks of a kind of "sleepwalking unconsciousness" of ancient man.

Dobroslav is the only one among the mass of the neo-pagan intellectual elite to single out reasons for the decline of the Golden Era of mankind. These include, first and foremost, mankind's struggle with nature, the development of speech,

---

[321] Dobroslav, *Ob idolakh i idealakh* (Novaia Zemlia, 2007), pp. 15-16.
[322] "By means unknown to us, he straightened mammoth tusks for spears and struck the saber-toothed tiger with such a formidable weapon. He turned a predatory (!) beast into his only friend... The 'illiterate' man of the Stone Age calculated the motion of the celestial bodies and predicted solar eclipses with amazing, incredibly accuracy... He healed with the charm-word (*zagovor*), herbs, and stone needles... In a way that is completely incomprehensible to us, our distant Primogenitor erected enormous stones exceeding any notion of the capabilities of a mere mortal..." - Dobroslav, *Mat'-Zemlia. Chudo-Chudnoe. Divo-Divnoe*, p. 47.
[323] Dobroslav, *Zov Tule* (Khlynovsky ekspress, 2006), p. 20.

the emergence of cattle breeding, patriarchy, the disintegration of the primordial communal system and, as a consequence, the emergence of slave-owning states and the establishment of the monotheistic religions. Like some other representatives of contemporary Russian paganism[324], this elder believes that it is possible to revive this ideal time. From Dobroslav's narratives we get that humanity will be able to come to such cherished times only after the most serious, total renewal and rebirth - after eschatological catastrophe.[325] The new world will be inhabited by a new man. Strange as such may seem, this image of the superman presented by Dobrovolsky does draw from the historical past: in addition to the people of the Paleolithic, the "list of dignified people of the future" includes German youth of the 1930s and the Slavic heroes of Kievan Rus.

There is no doubt that the very idea of the Golden Age has a huge, centuries-old history. Belief in an era of the prime of mankind is reflected in the myths of many peoples of antiquity "dispersed" across all continents. One of the most exemplary descriptions of this "paradisal time" should be recognized in the Greek myth of the five ages of mankind. After setting up hypotheses on the origin of people (whether from the teeth of a dragon, or from Prometheus' intervention, etc.), the compilers of this myth, alternately referring to the five ages of life on earth, present a brief characterization of the human race:

> These [first] men were the so-called golden race, subjects of Cronus, who lived without cares or labour, eating only acorns, wild fruit, and honey that dripped from the trees, drinking the milk of sheep and goats, never growing old, dancing, and laughing much; death, to them, was no more terrible than sleep. They are all gone now, but their spirits

---

324 For example, in the opinion of the volkhv of the Koliada of the Vyatichi Native Faith community, Velimir, the era of supermen and universal prosperity can be restored: "The Golden Age is possible if people en masse return to their primordial ancient faiths and rethink their eternal values in today's impressions. The possibility of the Golden Age boils down to resolving the question: Can humanity somehow appease its consumer urges, solve global ecological problems, and live in a state of stable happiness?" - Volkhv Velimir, *Russkoe iazychestvo i shamanizm* (Moscow, 2006), p. 153.

325 Dobroslav, *Prirodoliubivaia religiia budushchego* (Kirov: Viatka, 2004), pp. 7-8; Ibidem, *Ob idolakh i idealakh*, pp. 45-47.

survive as genii of happy music retreats, givers of good fortune, and upholders of justice.[326]

Such myths describe in great detail all the blessings bestowed upon people by the cultural heroes and demiurges of the Golden Age. For instance, the Roman Saturn rallied the scattered mountain tribes and taught them how to cultivate the land and introduced the first laws[327], the Scandinavian Ynglings (Odin and Njord) granted people the art of war, fruitful annual harvests, and the runes[328], and in the Kalevala the Karelian Väinämäinen figures as the creator of the whole world. It cannot be ruled out that in their deliberations on such an era of universal good, neo-pagan leaders have turned to similar such historical and mythological plots, possibly borrowing, adopting the structure and the "text" of the latter. However, the poverty of new pagan explorations of the Golden Age, their fantasticalness, and frank fable-like character are grounds for doubt. One of the most "lively" Native Faith conceptions of an era of god-men, that of the elder Dobroslav, does not withstand criticism.

Dobrovolsky puts forth that the flourishing heyday of humanity, the greatest concentration of its physical, intellectual, spiritual-mystical forces, pertains to the Paleolithic.[329] However, despite the fact that this period of time was the longest in the history of mankind, the achievements of Paleolithic people were much inferior to the future era deemed the "Neolithic Revolution."[330] A definite "backwardness" of Paleolithic mankind is evidenced, for example, by the fact that the appearance of vocal speech (an unconditional fact of the development of society) is related only to the final period of the Upper Paleolithic (35,000-12,000 years ago).[331] Dobroslav, however, idealizes the Old Stone Age and considers the ensuing periods of human history to be regress, the

---

326 Robert Graves, *The Greek Myths* (New York: Penguin, 2017), p. 76.
327 James George Frazer, *The Golden Bough: A Study of Magic and Religion* (1890).
328 Snorri Sturluson, *Heimskringla*.
329 For example: "Tales of the Golden Age exist among all peoples and their roots go back to the deep layers of human being, the Old Stone Age, the era of matriarchy..." - Dobroslav, *Ob idolakh i idealakh*, p. 15.
330 A.I. Martynov, *Arkheologiia* (Moscow: Vysshaia shkola, 1996); G.N. Matiushin, *Arkheologicheskii slovar'* (Moscow: Prosveshchenie, 1996).
331 P.F. Protasenia, *Problemy obshcheniia i myshleniia pervobytnykh liudei* (Minsk: Izdatel'stvo ministerstva vysshego, srednego spetsial'nogo i professional'nogo obrazovaniia BSSR, 1961), p. 49.

departure of people from their true nature-worship.[332] Dobroslav's primordial socialism has an altogether authoritative opponent in the person of the English ethnographer and scholar of religion, James George Frazer, who not only proved the backwardness and inviability of the primitive communal system but generally called into doubt the very idea of the Golden Age: "From this low and stagnant condition of affairs, which demagogues and dreamers in later times have lauded as the ideal state, the Golden Age, of humanity, everything that helps to raise society by opening a career to talent and proportioning the degrees of authority to men's natural abilities, deserves to be welcomed by all who have the real good of their fellows at heart."[333]

As a general rule, the ideas of paradisal times presented by the ideologists of Russian paganism are extremely vague and their presentation lacks specifics and often logic altogether. Amidst a significant divergence of opinions, pagan apologists of the "Golden myth" nonetheless concur that the development of humankind and its contemporary position constitute intellectual and moral regress, retreat, or, better said, departure from the great, noble ideals of the past. For Russian and Ukrainian pagans, the legend of the Golden Age serves as means for discrediting monotheistic religious conceptions, primarily Christianity. It should be emphasized that this juxtaposition of a pre-Christian Golden Age with a Christian "Iron Age" is driven not by logic, but by vivid, shocking tales and sometimes simply artistic images. Neither are based on historical sources, but rather often contradict the well-known positions of archaeology, ethnography, and other disciplines. The Golden Age is not a subject of historical seeking, but a kind of ideological paradigm which in contemporary paganism serves as a vivid means of political preaching.

***

---

332 "Paganism, as a folk religion, is forgotten and recedes into the unconscious, into the domain of 'superstitions' and 'prejudices'...It is not at all a coincidence that these times coincided with the so-called neolithic revolution, the collapse of the primordial-communal system and the emergence of slave-owning despots." - Dobroslav, *Iazychestvo: zakat i rassvet* (Kirov: Viatka, 2004), p. 28.

333 James George Frazer, *The Golden Bough: A Study of Magic and Religion* (1890). Further, Frazer writes: "No human being is so hide-bound by custom and tradition as your democratic savage; in no state of society consequently is progress so slow and difficult."

A COMPARATIVE ANALYSIS OF THE TEXTS OF ALEXEY DOBROVOLSKY AND HERMAN WIRTH: TOWARD THE QUESTION OF THE SOURCE BASE OF RUSSIAN NEO-PAGANS[334]

The idea of returning to paganism and a unique re-mythologization of worldview was first declared in Germany at the turn of the 15th-16th centuries.[335] By the early 20th century, this idea found support among many representatives of the European intellectual elite. In Russia, the new paganism appeared in the 1970s-80s and openly announced itself amidst the troubled times of the 1990s.[336]

The main typological range of Russian neo-pagan organizations encompasses three mutually-complementary groups: national-patriotic, natural-ecological, and ethnographic-reenacting.[337] From its emergence up to the present, the national-patriotic wing of the movement has been the most vital and active. This position is explainable in terms of the invariance and solid structural organization of communities as well as the articulate historico-historiographical and ideological basis (dating back to the late 1970s) characteristic of this trend. The result is a relatively constant number of proselytes and a mass of "sympathizers."

It bears recognizing that one of the oldest representatives of the national-patriotic current of Russian paganism, the "intellectual

---

334 Article first published in the volume *Rossiiskaia gosudarstvennost' v litsakh i sud'bakh ee sozidatelei: IX-XXI vv. [Russian Statehood in the Persons and Fates of its Founders]* (Lipetsk: Lipetsk State Pedagogical University, 2009).
335 V.A. Schnirelmann, *"Izobretenie religii: neoiazychestvo v sovremennoi Rossii"*, religio.ru (2009).
336 "Since 1990, Russia has seen the organized formation of neo-pagan structures: separate spiritual movements and communities have emerged and political parties placing the neo-pagan worldview at the foundation of their ideologies have arisen." - Ibid.
337 A.V. Gaidukov, *"Neoiazychestvo. Programma kursa po vyboru"*, in *Gertsenovskie chteniia 2004: Aktual'nye problemy sotsial'nykh nauk* (Saint Petersburg: Faculty of Sociological Sciences of Herzen State Pedagogical University of Russia, 2004), pp. 358-362.

author of its ideological projects"[338], is Alexey Alexandrovich Dobrovolsky, better known by his pagan name Dobroslav. Dobroslav's biography has long since become accessible to the broader public. The personality of this neo-pagan leader and the landmarks of his life-path have drawn the attention of both adepts of the pagan tradition and opponents of the reconstruction (or construction) of the mythology of the ancient Slavs.[339] The afterword to many of Dobrovolsky's works contains the following biographical information:

> Born in Moscow in 1938. At the age of 19 he was convicted for the first time under Article 58 for establishing a Russian nationalist youth organization. He spent a total of 13 years incarcerated. In 1989, he left the capital, adopted the name Dobroslav, and settled in the abandoned village of Vasenevo in the Shabalinsk district of the Kirov region. This place has since become the spiritual center of reborn Slavic-Russian Paganism. There, in the bosom of Nature, Dobroslav writes his enlightening works. Each year, on the Kupala holiday on 22 June, his comrades and associates come together there from all over Rus.[340]

On what are Dobroslav's ideological preachings based? What is the reason behind the "vitality" of the movement he created? In our opinion, the twenty-year "project" of this neo-pagan leader owes its existence to several factors: firstly, the personal charisma, the intellectual and spiritual "baggage", and the life experience of this "nature-lover"[341]; secondly, the development of an external

338 Ibid.
339 See, for instance, the account of the Catholic portal *katolik.ru*, "Gruppy slavianskogo iazychestva: gruppa Dobroslava"; V. Terekhov, "Ob aktual'nykh tendentsiiakh v sovremennom russkom nativizme", *Martyr Saint Irenaeus of Lyon Center for Religious Studies* (25/2/2013) [https://iriney.ru/okkultnyie/neoyazyichniki/ob-aktualnyix-tendenczyiax-v-sovremennom-russkom-nativizme.html]; A. Aratov, "Interv'iu s Dobroslavom" [http://rp.kronov.ru/intdobro.htm]; "Dobroslav: Biografiia, Intervalu raznykh let" [https://velesova-sloboda.info/heath/dobroslav.html#02]; "Publichnaia internet-biblioteka Vladimira Pribylovkskogo", *Anticompromat* [http://anticompromat.panchul.com/pribyl/index.html]; "Topor: Kupal'skaia noch' v Shabalinskikh lesakh", *Sechs 2* (Yoshkar-Ola, 2008), pp. 5, 7-9; Dobroslav, "Nabroski moego stanovleniia", *Poslednii rubezh: obshchestvenno-politicheskoe izdanie 1* (Yeysk, 2008).
340 Dobroslav, *Svetoslavie (ocherki iazycheskogo mirochuvstvovaniia)* (Kirov: Viatka, 2004), p. 96.
341 Dobroslav, *Bezbozhnye chudesa zhivoi prirody* (Kharkov: Sfera, 2002), p. 35.

component (attributes) for this movement[342]; thirdly and mainly, a worldview concept consisting of a colorful explication of paradigms and relics disclosed throughout this hermit's numerous narratives (counting more than 20 works). In the opinion of the Moscow scholar of Russian neo-paganism Viktor Schnirelmann, one of the sources of contemporary followers of nativism should be recognized in "ethnological theories popular in Hitler's Germany."[343] Dobroslav's autobiographical essays confirm this supposition. In one of his last pamphlets, *The Call of Thule*, Dobrovolsky spoke of a certain Stanislav Rudolfovich Arsenyev-Hoffman.[344] As Dobroslav himself reports, this man exerted enormous influence on the formation of his worldview.[345] It was from conversations with this Stanislav Rudolfovich Arsenyev that the future neo-pagan leader learned of Russian-German youth unions active in Germany in the 1920s and the synergism of these representatives of the "Nordic race" in the cause of reviving the pagan faith of their ancestors.[346] It is possible that the Kolovorot, the swastika-like symbol which appears in Dobroslav's "intellectual-visual stock", is owed to none other than this Arsenyev. Recognizing this Russian-German emigrant to bear the *de facto* status of being Dobroslav's first teacher, we will attempt to seek out Dobrovolsky's *de jure* didaskalia.

---

[342] "Dobroslav sostavil pervyi kratkii slavianskii imenoslov i iazycheskii mesiatseslov (kalendar'), utverdil KOLOVOROT (vos'mulichevuiu svastiku) kak znak vozrozhdaiushchegosia iazychestva", *Secha 2* (Yoshkar-Ola), p. 5.

[343] Schnirelmann, *"Izobretenie religii"*; Ibidem, *"Mnogolikoe neoiazychestvo"*, *Rodina* 4 (2003).

[344] "Stanislav Arsenyev was born in the 1880s in Riga... He came from a Russian-German family. He studied in Moscow, where he graduated from the Faculty of Philology (in German literature). He then continued his education at the University of Göttingen. During the First World War, he was a military translator. He was a member of the secret Russian-German officers' society "Balticum" founded by General von der Goltz, adjutant to Kaiser Wilhelm II... After the Bolsheviks' usurpation of power, Arsenyev fought them in the Baltics... Then, like many of his comrades, he settled in Germany where he participated in emigrant organizations collaborating with the National Socialist German Workers Party" - Dobroslav, *Zov Tule* (Khlynovskii ekspress, 2006), pp. 4-5.

[345] Ibid, pp. 4, 8.

[346] "Arsenyev confided that he was charged with a primordial energy when meeting the close-knit ranks of marching columns of youth with fluttering banners... The magnetism of this action of many thousands contributed to the emergence of a unanimously pulsating psychic field" - p. 9.

An analysis of the basic elements of the worldview foundation of Dobroslav's doctrine allows us to include in the list of his "ideological teachers" Professor Herman Felix Wirth, who is known to specialists as the head of the Ahnenerbe ("Ancestral Heritage") society. In addition, Wirth was the author of a number of studies, such as *Die Heilige Urschrift der Menschheit* and *Der Aufgang der Menschheit*, as well as a publisher and ardent defender of the Old Frisian runic book whose authenticity is the subject of great doubts, the *Oera Linda Chronicle*.[347] Studying of the latter text (translated into Russian with commentary by A.V. Kondratyev) allows one to determine the commonality and in some places complete equivalence between the concepts of Herman Felix Wirth and Alexey Alexandrovich Dobrovolsky.

Citing the runic of the *Oera Linda Chronicle*, employing the comparative linguistic method, and engaging in the comparative analysis of Indo-European symbols, this Dutch thinker arrived at the conclusion that a spiralic-cyclical notion of time was intrinsic to the Nordic peoples. Wirth deemed the six-spoked wheel (and all of its possible variations) to be their symbol and relic of time and the divine. In particular, Wirth saw one variant of the Northern emblem of infinite rotation in the eight-spoked uleborden.[348] The Nordic tradition's symbol of the reintegration of the world is thus "the turning-cross or gammatic cross (the swastika), which comes from the most ancient sacred symbol of the year and the course of time."[349] Such conceptions of time and its attributes are also characteristic of Dobroslav's historico-mythological concept. According to the Russian neo-pagan leader, nature and the universe more broadly abound with examples of "circling spheres" and "series of ideally coherent cycles." In Dobroslav's words: "Nature is all-perfect. Nature's highest beauty lies in its totality and full completeness. This is the beauty of mature, self-containing being

---

347 Russian edition: Herman Felix Wirth, *Khronika Ura Linda. Drevneishaia istoriia Evropy* (trans. By A.V. Kondrat'ev; Moscow: Veche, 2007).
348 "The six-spoked wheel is the Nordic ideogram of the Year, the ideogram of God, which means the same thing as the eight-spoked wheel, the latter being appended with a line of "middle time" corresponding to the East and West (Spring and Autumn) which was insignificant in the North" - ibid, p. 222.
349 Ibid, p. 224. Herman Wirth attributed the emergence (or update) of the sacred wheel, the swastika, to the late second millennium.

in eternal rotation."³⁵⁰ Dobroslav's ideogram representing the rotation of the universe is also a swastika symbol: the Kolovorot. It bears particular emphasis that what Dobrovolsky held to be the main emblem of resurgent Russian paganism, the eight-pointed gammadion in a circle, is precisely what Herman Wirth proposed (or designed) and interpreted to be the most ancient.³⁵¹

Turning to the prehistory of mankind, Wirth placed the ancestral homeland of the Indo-Germanic race in the Arctic. This harsh Northern region, inhabited in deep antiquity (several million years ago) by the "Arctic-Nordic" peoples, was, in this professor's opinion, a prosperous land. The reason for the migration of the "Nordics" was irreversible climate change.³⁵² The leader of Russian neo-pagans also held the North to be the primordial zone of mankind: "Obscure ideas and archaic legends of a Northern Homeland have been preserved among many Indo-European peoples... All of these legends are genetically linked and descend from a single archetype which, overall, might be called the 'Legend of the Nordic Ancestral Homeland.'"³⁵³ The views of these teachers also coincide in their solving of one of the main "Northern questions", i.e. the location of the mysterious Atlantis and Thule. Following the head of the Ahnenerbe³⁵⁴, Dobroslav believes Atlantis and Thule to be names for one and the same continent or archipelago, the "maternal-ancestral hearth" of the Aryan peoples.³⁵⁵

Both Herman Wirth and Alexey Dobrovolsky associated the era of the mythical "Golden Age" and paradisal times with matriarchal governance. In his commentary on the *Oera Linda Chronicle*, the professor designated this matriarchy to have been a form of governance in which the most important role was concentrated in the hands of the "honorary mother" and "governess-maidens." The main aspect of this system was not

---

350 Dobroslav, *Iazychestvo: zakat i rassvet* (Kirov: Viatka, 2004), pp. 65-65; Ibidem, *Prirodliubivaia religiia budushchego* (Kirov: Viatka, 2004), pp. 14-15; Ibidem, *Svetoslavie*, pp. 32-33.
351 Footnotes to Wirth, *Khronika*, p. 454.
352 Ibid, pp. 37, 84.
353 Dobroslav, *Zov Tule*, p. 21.
354 Wirth, *Khronika*, p. 84
355 Dobroslav, *Zov Tule*, pp. 20-21.

so much the degree of influence of Frisian chosen women on the socio-political development of their people as it was the sacred-cultic function ascribed to these women: "The cult was... a social, state, and state-ordered affair. It was in the hands of women. The woman among them who was called to lead and preserve the cultic order, protect the folk tradition, and so on thus bore the highest responsibility for the administration of the state."[356] Dobroslav also believes women to be the divine chosen ones, the keepers of ancestral memory:

> The mother was more of a Deity than a chief... All of family and social life was structured around her. The woman was the head of the Rod, the keeper of the hearth, the guardian of the ancestral orders and customs, the performer of rites and sacred acts. She was the heiress of magical knowledge and the intermediary with the world of the Spirits, for genetically intrinsic to her, as a woman, was an acute, intuitive sensitivity to occult influences.[357]

In both of these worldview conceptions, the transfer of power from women to men and the ensuing era of patriarchy is conceived as regression, as the end of paradise on earth.

At the heart of Alexey Dobrovolsky's religious doctrine also lies the notion that the Sun, Yarilo, was the most ancient and perhaps originally the only deity of the ancient Slavs.[358] In the opinion of this pagan hermit, the Slavs worshipped the solar disk and the sun itself. The divinities which replaced Yarilo and displaced him into the background already bore altered, unnatural anthropomorphic appearances: "These were already

---

[356] Wirth, *Khronika*, p. 276.
[357] Dobroslav, *Ob idolakh i idealakh* (Novaia Zemlia, 2007), pp. 15-16.
[358] This is confirmed by the calendar compiled by Dobroslav of the most important holiday-festivals associated with light: "According to the pagan worldview, the driving force of the circle for us is Yarilo, the Sun. Yarilo is the ancient name of our Luminary which goes back to the pan-Indo-European designation of the year as the annual turning of the sun. The Sacred Holiday-Festivals and Rites born from praising the Sun were associated with definite solar phases. These Celebrations should be celebrated not according to the Sun, not according to the modern church or civic calendars. For the Slavs the starting point of the annual circle (the turning of the sun) was the New Year, the Birth of the New Sun on 25 December, when daytime beings to increase following the solstice" - [http://dobroslav.onestop.net/works/dobroslav_24.html].

gods of the Sun, not the SUN-GOD."[359] As follows, albeit with a small degree of stretch, it could be argued that at the heart of Dobroslav's doctrine lies belief in a solar monotheism (or, in an extreme case, henotheism). This neo-pagan adept's hypothetical assessment that monotheism was primordial and intrinsic to mankind fully corresponds, or more accurately copies Herman Wirth's idea of a "polar, solar monotheism."[360]

Such comparative analysis of the concepts embedded in the narratives of the 20th century German scholar Herman Wirth and the ideologist of Russian neo-paganism Alexey Dobrovolsky permits the argument to be made that one of the sources of contemporary nativists is the historico-mythological inquiries of the Germanic school of "interdisciplinary synthesis" of Herman Wirth.[361] Contemporary Russian pagans' study and partial copying of the main ideas of German advocates of national, traditional faith brings the former close to the ideas of the pan-European neo-Romantic movement of the late 19th and early 20th centuries, which in turn dates back to the first pagan treatises of the 15th century.

***

---

359 Dobroslav, *Iazychestvo*, p. 25.
360 Wirth, *Khronika*, p. 37.
361 The professor based his research on both traditional disciplines, such as philosophy, archaeology, ethnology, and philology, as well as on teachings not recognized by official science, such as Atlantology, etc. See Wirth, *Khronika*, p. 43.

THE CONTEMPORARY RUSSIAN PRIESTLY-VOLKHV "CASTE" SEEN THROUGH THE PRISM OF THE RELIGIOUS CONCEPTS OF CHRISTOPHER DAWSON[362]

"Religion is the key of history. We cannot understand the inner form of a society unless we understand its religion. We cannot understand its cultural achievements unless we understand the religious beliefs that lie behind them. " - Christopher Henry Dawson

Over the past several decades, the phenomenon of contemporary Russian paganism has become the object of scholarly reaction and reflection. The source basis of the movement, elements of its holiday-ritual arrangement, and the history of various "'young-pagan' associations" have been subjected to analyses. At the present time, however, the Russian scholarly community lacks specialized works on the peculiarities of one of the most important elements of 21st century paganism: the institution of its cult clergy, which is responsible both for its formation and development as well as the whole complex array of the functionality of this social, culturo-political phenomenon. Moreover, the question of the historical legitimacy of the new priestly-volkhv community, and of the possibility of considering this "estate" or "caste" of the pagan world to be a real religious group, remains open.

Of interest in this regard is shedding light on the question of this contemporary pagan spiritual class through the prism of the fundamental religious hypothesis of the great English historian, philosopher, and cultural scholar Christopher Henry Dawson (1889-1970). As the objects of this experimental

---

362 Article first published in R.V. Shizhensky (ed.), *Iazychestvo v sovremennoi Rossii: opyt mezhdistsiplinarnogo issledovaniia [Paganism in Contemporary Russia: The Experience of Interdisciplinary Research]* (Nizhny Novgorod: Nizhny Novgorod State Pedagogical University, 2016). Article prepared with the financial support of the Russian Humanitarian Science Foundation as part of the research project "Comprehensive Historical-Religious Study of the Phenomenon of Russian Neo-Paganism" (Project #15-31-01247).

platform we have resolved to employ narratives and interviews with such pagan ideologues from the last quarter of the 20th and the beginning of the 21st century as Alexey Dobrovolsky (Dobroslav) and Nikolai Speransky (Velimir). This selection of personalities is substantiated by the following reasons. Firstly, according to established studies, Dobrovolsky (1938-2013) should be considered the first pagan of Soviet Russia to articulate an original ideology, mythology, and holiday-ritual complex.[363] Secondly, at the present time Speransky is one of a handful of leaders of the pagan camp who have managed to syncretize a whole spectrum of problematic fields of questions into a unified worldview. Thirdly, these diaspora[364] leaders possess the necessary "pagan ranking" and the most solid basis of published texts.

The subject of cult servants occupies a central place in Christopher Dawson's work *Religion and Culture*, figuring as one of the two elements that constitute religion as such: "For every historic religion from the lowest to the highest agrees on two fundamental points - first in the belief in the existence of divine or supernatural powers, and secondly in the association of these powers with particular men, or things, or places or ceremonies, which act as channels of communication or means of access between the human and the divine worlds."[365] We will examine the topic of sacred objects, places of power and ceremonies as necessary elements of theogamy, according to Dawson's terminology, below. Firstly, it is necessary to turn to the bearers of sacred tradition in accordance with the conceptualization of this English scholar. Engaging in historical retrospection, Dawson established the existence of an institution of spiritual leaders among primitive as well as modern, larger cultures. Accordingly, the priesthood, and with regards to the contemporary variant of Slavic paganism the priestly-volkhv class, is chronologically stagnant. The priesthood is *a priori* one of the strata of society, "religion embodied in a stable

---

363 See: R.V. Shizhensky, *Filosofiia dobroi sily: zhizn' i tvorchestvo Dobroslava (A.A. Dobrovol'skogo)* (Nizhny Novgorod: Povolzh'e, 2014).
364 On the definition of diaspora see Roman Shizhensky, "The Russian Pagan Diaspora: Definitions of Neo-Paganism in Contemporary Russia" in this volume.
365 Dawson, *Religion and Culture*.

institution."[366] Recognizing the inherent differences between the numerous systems of "spiritual orders", this philosopher deduced a number of original archetypes that are characteristic of all cultures. Dawson refers to three types: the priest (brought up and separated from society to perform rituals and ceremonies that shape an essential link between society and its gods), the king or lawgiver (personal representatives or incarnations of divine power); and the prophet or seer (the pronouncer of the divine will, the interpreter of dreams and prophecies). The author emphasizes that these categories do not exclude one another, as each of them can encompass several functions.

This typology proposed by the English specialist finds fertile soil in Russian new-pagan material. It bears taking note of the fact that both Dobrovolsky and Speransky, as representatives of the first two generations, as the pioneers of constructing the contemporary polytheistic worldview, were compelled, first and foremost by virtue of their "pioneering", to combine the "duties" of priest, leader (lawgiver), and prophet. At the same time, the works of these pagan ideologists are an eclectic conglomerate of utopias, from ecological to political projects, reflecting these contemporary volkhvs' views of an ideal world and the role of their "colleagues' in the pagan *terra incognita*. The resulting autopoesis allows us to comprehensively examine such pagan sources of both primary and secondary origin.

Dawson's priest in Dobrovolsky's variation performs the rites of naming and de-baptizing and holds the annual holiday-festival of Kupala that is so fundamental for contemporary pagan proselytes. Finally, he is one of the first to develop and use sacred texts, such as prayers, invocations, spells, charms, and confessions. "Dobroslav the lawgiver" appeared in the period between 1990 and 1995, when the pagan gave educational lectures. Taking the ideology of this Vasenevo hermit as their basis, the admirers of Dobrovolsky's creative work established the Arrows of Yarilo Society for the Protection of Nature. The culmination of Dobroslav's lawgiving-governing function was

---

366 Ibid, p. 87. Note should also be made of this historian's call to study the specific forms of this class across different cultures and that such studies should precede the process of conceptualizing it as a social institution.

his recognition as leader of the Russian Liberation Movement at a constituent Veche of communities on 22 June 1997.[367]

The third archetype, that of the seer, is most fully revealed in Dobrovolsky's apocalyptic musings on the future of humanity. For a number of reasons, Dobroslav's imminent decline of mankind is marked by a distinctive axis of evil, the cornerstone of which is fulfilled by mono-religiosity. According to this elder of the Russian Liberation Movement, it is the centuries-long rule of monotheism that has led humanity into an all-around crisis in the spiritual state of society.[368] Dobroslav deems one of the main horses of the apocalypse of contemporary religiosity to be the proclamation of man as the crown of creation, as the highest, God-chosen race ruling over nature.[369] It is the Abrahamic religions that led the cohort of evil of capitalism and its derivatives, the market economy and race for consumption. The pagan leader also attributes the unacceptable technocratic path of human development to this range of evils. Dobroslav thus considers the spiritual degradation of *Homo sapiens* and the current ecological crisis to be the result of society's wrong choice of worldview path.[370] According to Dobroslav's theory, with the cleansing of the earth will "appear in the blood and tears of birth pagans" a new man of new constitution with a new thinking and new outlook on the surrounding world.[371] The Vasenevo hermit puts the old, primordial experience in synthesis with a triumphant "love of nature" at the core of the worldview of the people of the near future.[372]

---

367 "The bulk of Dobroslav's work on the stage of the Russian Liberation Movement consisted of educational-agitational activities through the dissemination of proclamations (on which first appeared the signature 'Dobroslav, elder of the Russian Liberation Movement' [ROD]), correspondences with like-minded associates, and the publication of books." - Shizhensky, *Filosofiia dobroi sily*, p. 36.
368 Dobroslav, *Prirodoliubivaia religiia budushchego* (Kirov: Viatka, 2004), p. 20.
369 Dobroslav, *Skazanie of Tsvetakh* (Khlynov, 2005), p. 85.
370 Dobroslav, *Iazychestvo: Zakat i rassvet* (Kirov: Viatka, 2004), p. 76.
371 Dobroslav, *Ob idolakh i idealakh* (Novaia Zemlia, 2007), p. 47.
372 "Returning to our Ancestors' understanding of the World should not be understood as a complete, literal, and mechanical carrying over to our time. The paganism of the dawn cannot be taken as recreated one-to-one... It follows that we should take only their approach, their very principle and basic conviction which has been picked up by modern ecologists: NATURE IS WISE AND ALWAYS RIGHT. It is necessary return to the most important aspect: viewing Nature as ONE WITH MAN, LIVING AND INTELLIGENT BEING." - Dobroslav, *Prirodoliubivaia religiia budushchego*, pp. 15-16.

Dawson's thesis that the functionalities of religious archetypes can be synthesized can also be traced in Dobrovolsky's works. In the latter, priests (volkhvs) act both as intermediaries between worlds and as "kings" dictating their will to and leading society. The image of the ancient sorcerer is thus crowned with a halo of mystery and holiness. In singling out the volkhvs from the possible hierarchy of servants and guardians of pagan cult, this author is inclined towards Nietzschean ideals which hyperbolize the volkhv to the point of being an *Übermensch*.[373] The scope of activities of the latter is all-embracing: Dobroslav's volkhvs are responsible for the birth of a new, healthy generation (through the organization of wedding rites in proper places of power)[374]; it is to them that originally belonged the prerogative of keeping and transmitting sacred tales (with the adoption of Christianity, this function passed to the fathers of families)[375]; and it is they who are responsible for raising and training the Slavic *ethnos*.[376] Of fundamental importance is that beyond traditional everyday religious functions, Dobrovolsky endows volkhvs with the function of socio-political institutionalization. In the works of this hermit, the Slavic "pagan mentors" are the spiritual leaders of the nation, the main leaders of the Veche assemblies. Upon the adoption of the new faith, they were the ones to become the first fighters and initiators of popular uprisings.[377] Dobroslav remarks that the volkhvs, elders, and fathers of families are representatives of the religious nobility, whose status and position within society encompassed all the possible claims to leadership of secular entities.[378] No less significant is that Dobrovolsky's constructed theocratism is militant: volkhvs are not only shepherds but warriors who carry and, if necessary, defend and propagate "Militant Good Will."

---

373 "Priests are simply cult officials administering sacrifices and deities. The Volkhvs are a qualitatively different notion. During the Christianization of Rus, the Volkhvs were already a relic of the communal-Veche system, hermits, sorcerers, wizards, and sages." - Letter from A.A. Dobrovolsky to R.V. Shizhensky (6/12/2007), p. 2., author's personal archive.
374 Dobroslav, *Mat'-Zemlia. Chudo-chudnoe. Divo-divnoe*, p. 50.
375 Dobroslav, *Iazychestvo kak volshebstvo* (Kirov: Viatka, 2004), p. 10.
376 Dobroslav, *Iazychestvo: zakat i rassvet*, p. 10.
377 Dobroslav, *Volkhvy*, p. 13.
378 Ibid.

Dawson's typology in Speransky's interpretation also reveals these three archetypes. Velimir fulfills the role of intermediary between society and the gods both directly through organizing and holding festival-ritual events as well as through the mass manufacturing (a "sacred-act" in Speransky's words) of idols (*chury*) and inscription-posts (*stolba-zapisi*).[379] In this volkhv's opinion, while working, the master-craftsman should only communicate with the members of his workshop, should not swear or remember insults, and "his underlying spiritual work should be pure."[380] This individual mystical practice also includes a certain attitude on the part of the craftsman during his creation:

> The master should mentally maintain his connection with the god for whom he is preparing to carve an idol for several days. In this case, connection means internal dialogue, attention to behavior, thoughts, readiness to work, and the ability to preserve and refine the future image within him... Passing into a state in which the master finds in his hands not a hewn log but already the embodiment of a god can happen very fast. Five or ten second ago everything could have seemed ordinary, but now suddenly... the master is not alone, the image he is sculpting bears resemblance. It not only looks but speaks with him. The master feels this. His thoughts change. Sometimes, his hands start to shake, consciousness floats, and he doesn't have enough air...[381]

Not counting the idols crafted by Speransky before his conversion to paganism, according to this respondent's recollections the total number of this contemporary volkhv-carver's idols and engravings currently exceeds 30. The Slavic pantheon is represented in the spiritual leader of the Koliada of the Vyatichi's wooden sculpting by carvings of the goddesses Lada and Mokosh and the gods Sviatovit, Yarilo, Dazhdbog,

---

[379] "A typical symbol designating the place of the gods' presence is the inscribed post (*Zapis*). This is a column of phallic contour whose four sides depict the symbols of the pagan faith. It is set up in orientation to the cardinal directions and the ascent and descent of the luminary." - N. Speransky and S. Ermakov, *Mesto. Bogovy stolpy. O sviashchennom meste v russkoi iazycheskoi traditsii* (Moscow: ITs Slava!, 2009), p. 83.
[380] Ibid, pp. 92-93, passim.
[381] Ibid, pp. 88-89, 95-96.

Veles, and Chernobog. In addition, a central place in Velimir's priestly depiction is occupied by religious ecstasy, which is terminologically characterized in the 21st-century pagan community as "rejoicing" (*radenie*). One of the sought-after results of immersion into altered states of consciousness is direct communication with divine beings:

> It is as if water runs down your hands, flowing down the fingers to the ground and making one's cold hands shiver. The water gradually weakens me, loosens my connection with this world, and calls me both towards movement and towards slumber. It is time. I put on the mask. I bang, roar, and call upon all. I don't regret the drum...Out of oneself emerges a feeling like a rocket launching... We are not on earth, but we are not above the trees. We are somewhere in-between. I examine my spirits. First there's complete darkness and then they are in full sight. I call them all by name and ask them for health...We need to enter Nav. To see the ancestors. To send our greetings and ask about the mysteries of being... Soaring over the shrine is already easy to do...[382]

The second archetype is realized by Speransky through his periodical *Tree of Life: Newspaper of Ethnic Renaissance* (published since 2003), through his leadership of the Koliada of the Vyatichi pagan group since 1998, through his public speaking (since 1992), and through his work on programmatic pagan documents, particularly the *Russian Pagan Manifesto*[383], etc.

Deserving of separate attention is the prophetic ("seer") component of Velimir's worldview. One of the component manifestations of the pagan mentality proper to this group led by Volkhv Velimir is reflected in a symbolistic fixation on all kinds of signs, instances, omens, and miracles. Based on the texts describing such phenomena, pagan signs fulfill several functions. These include a directly mythological role or mythmaking function in which signs represent the visible will

---

382 Volkhv Velimir, *Dar shamanizma - dar volkhovaniia* (Moscow: Veligor, 2012), pp. 314-315.
383 For more detail see R.V. Shizhensky, *Pochvennik to iazychestva: mirovozzrencheskie diskursy volkhva Velimira (N.N. Speranskogo)* (Nizhny Novgorod: Povolzh'e, 2015), pp. 38, 42, *passim*.

of a deity and embody the actual presence of higher forces in a ritual. Their religio-practical function can consist in selecting a site for establishing a cult structure (a shrine)[384], in supplying additional incentive to heightening the general mood for a ritual act, in "immersion" into myth, in disarming uncomfortable psychological and spiritual barriers for neophytes, and in creating a new-pagan compilation of sacred wonders[385], possibly with the aim of affirming and confirming the truth of worldview choice. The community members of the Koliada of the Vyatichi associate another group of pagan signs with the appearance of living creatures, such as birds and other animals, at shrines. In his "Word on Idols", Velimir turned to the historiography of this question in search of recommendations on how to relate to such "guests" in sacred places. Despite the failure of his search for sources, the pagan ideologue issued the following verdict: "In our time, the presence of birds at shrines is held to be a natural phenomenon. Birds are not barred from feeding at the altars of the gods."[386] Randomly discovered objects also act as positive signs. As Speransky writes, unusual objects found on the territory chosen for a shrine complex during its preparation are automatically included in the sacred space.[387] Naturally, in the field of pagan signs also figures the "house of a deity" - its man made depiction. Velimir's narratives and those of this volkhv's associates testify to an absence of chronological limitations in the manifestation of "idol signs." Such are not connected with any clearly recorded "stages" of the "life" of an established idol. A miracle can accompany the very moment of placing the symbol of a deity and can consist of a higher power assisting in the process. This is also fixed in the destruction

384 "For a rite is chosen a place which can subsequently become permanent. If we feel blessing from the rites held at a new place, then in time a shrine will arise there" - Velimir, *Nravstvennaia kniga: hakim rodnoveru byt' i pochemu* (Pamphlet #11, Troitsk, 2012), p. 72.
385 Speransky emphasizes the significance of passing onto youth both orally and in writing everything extraordinary and related to existing, active shrine complexes to youth. See Velimir, *Slovo ob idolakh i sviatykh mestakh iazycheskoi very* (Pamphlet #12, Troitsk: Koliada Vyatichei, 2013), p. 30.
386 Ibid, p. 29.
387 One such find during the construction of the shrine in Bitsevsk park in September 1999 was the skull of a dog. See Volkhv Velimir, *Russkoe iazychestvo i shamanizm* (Moscow: Institut obshchegumanitarnykh issledovanii, 2006), p. 468.

of pagan shrines, such as in instances of an idol (or part of it) surviving fire damage.[388]

Speransky's "prophetic" visions of the future and the place occupied by the volkhv case in the constructed pagan utopia are largely identical to Dobrovolsky's. In the works of this contemporary volkhv, the future is portrayed exclusively in the form of a negative eschatology. Future changes will be caused by a number of catastrophes: ecological, civilizational, national, and racial. A natural cataclysm[389] will provoke a resource deficit, first and foremost of oil, and, according to one of the scenarios of the Koliada of the Vyatichi, will bring modern state entities, and following them civilization as a whole, to natural collapse. The place of existing governing institutions will be taken by small local authorities, such as new feudal lords collecting taxes in kind from a demoralized population.[390] Accordingly, Velimir places at the head of the contemporary pagan clergy the volkhvs, the strongest of the priesthood who, in his views, are in possession of a number of specific traits. Firstly, according to the narratives of this author and his associates, this institution is characterized by features of sacralization and mythologization. Volkhvs possess elements of shamanic techniques (they can travel between worlds), they pray to the god Veles, and they are revered by ordinary people on par with the gods.[391] Secondly, the religious primacy of the volkhvs in the preservation and proliferation of experience

---

[388] "When the sculpture [of Lada] was raised to be set into the pit, it miraculously rose upright on its own, with minimal effort on our part, and immediately faced the direction in which we wanted" - Velimir, *"Boginia Lada v Doline Vodopadov", Derevo Zhizni. Gazeta etnicheskogo vozrozhdeniia 50* (Troitsk, 2010). During the installation of an idol of Veles in Losiny Ostrov in 2011, according to pagans, a certain force emanated from the altar stones, which moved in the direction of the shrine virtually on their own" - see: *Derevo Zhizni. Gazeta etnicheskogo vozrozhdeniia 52* (Troitsk, 2012). The head of an idol of Dazdhbog was also found to have survived the hands of arsonists - see *"Vosstanovleno kapishche v Tsaritsyno!", Derevo Zhizhni. Gazeta etnicheskogo soprotivleniia* (Troitsk, 2004).

[389] "The ocean will overflow its shores. Droughts will dry up tropical vegetation, and in Serbia the permafrost will melt by the outpour of the great sea. Storms and tornadoes will be as frequent as rain today." - Volkhv Velimir, *Dar shamanizma*, p. 365. Confidence in the end of this world can be found throughout the texts of Koliada of the Vyatichi practically since the community's founding. See, for instance, M.S. Vasil'ev, A.L. Potapov, N.N. Speransky, *Iazychniki otvechaiut* (Troitsk: Trovant, 1999), p. 7.

[390] Mezgir, Velimir, and Peresvet, *Sut' iazycheskoi very* (Pamphlet #8, 2008), p. 31-32.

[391] Ibid, p. 11.

and knowledge is appended by Speransky with a national (ethnic) orientation for this high pagan clergy. Moreover, the volkhvs have been independent from both the official state-administrative regime in both past and contemporary Russia. Thus, according to Velimir's texts, having been in opposition for more than a thousand years, they can possess fully tangible economic and political power and can even claim the title of people's leaders. The pagan way of life in line with this "volkhv-leaderism", according to Velimir, entails following the principles of a structured group (a pack) with the active participation of ordinary members under the authority of the leader as an open example for all others. At the same time, Speransky conceptualizes the political role of volkhvs in the state pagan system of the future in a somewhat different spirit: imagining the "next" Russia as an independent socialist state with a duumvirate in the form of a people's assembly and monarchy, this young-pagan leader assigns a priestly function to the monarch. In this system, the volkhvs should represent a separate humanitarian institution that is not directly connected to state authority.[392] It is the spiritual chosenness of the priests and volkhvs that allows them to position themselves not only as political leaders of the nation, but as its teachers. Thus, in the point of view of the Koliada of the Vyatichi leadership, the pagan religious caste is responsible for determining the measures of a human's immersion in civilization. To this should be added Velimir's personal opinion that the cultural values of pagan tradition are accumulated by "ordinary nativists" through the conceptual and practical realization of the mystical experience of the volkhv caste.[393] In the forecasted future, such a pagan elite is positioned as a universal messiah called upon to shape the spirituality of subsequent generations.[394]

---

392 Volkhv Velimir, *Rodnoverie* (Moscow: Samoteka, 2012), p. 94.
393 Mezgir, Velimir, *Peresvet, Sut' iazycheskoi very*, p. 14; Velimir, *Darna - uchenie o zhizni v Prirode i obshchestve* (Troitsk: Trovant, 2009), p. 49.
394 "As is evident, we are called upon to formulate the spirituality of the future civilization, whose essence is partially in returning to traditional society and balancing between traditional society and the state" - Mezgir, Velimir, *Peresvet, Sut' iazycheskoi very*, p. 31.

The minor differences between Dobroslav and Velimir's respective "percentages" of the significance of the priest and ruler can find explanation in the pagan diaspora's recognition of these leaders and their specialization. If Dobrovolsky was in many cases a universally recognized leader, "Russian pagan #1", who stood at the origins of the movement and, as follows, largely shaped it into a definite, organized system, then Speransky's religio-political career has been limited to being the spiritual leader of one community. More recently, he has passed into that category of individual pagans so widespread in the young-pagan milieu.[395] However, the categories of priest and prophet are much more fully represented in Velimir's worldview. The latter in particular might suggest a transformation, a kind of "upgrade" of paganism undertaken by the leaders of the second wave. Having more or less developed and adopted a set of symbols, structure, source basis, and other elements, Velimir's nativist generation has focused its attention on "inner paganism": on an active system of ritual and holiday-festival practices.

Thus, Dawson's conceptualization of the primordial sacred archetypes of priest, ruler, and prophet finds expression in the biographies of these first representatives of the leadership stratum of contemporary Russian paganism. In addition, the archaic bearers of religious knowledge present in Dobrovolsky and Speransky's utopias acquire in their texts an idealized status which they have not brought to life. In both cases, in both first and second-rate sources, we can see a functional syncretism of the new priest-ruler-prophet.

Detailing his "portrait" of religious classes, Dawson identifies the following elements as under the authority of the priesthood: maintaining ties between society and divine forces, community education, scholarship, and preserving sacred tradition. The latter

---

395 For example, according to a survey of pagans gathered at the Kupala festival in 2015, the vast majority of polytheists, 321 out of 429 people (74.5%) were not members of a community structure. Correspondingly, only 61 respondents (14.2%) belonged to one or another pagan organization. See: R.V. Shizhensky and O.S. Tiutina, "*Samoidentifikatsiia slavianskikh iazychnikov: sotsial'nyi portret, gosudarstvo i obraz lidera (po dannym polevykh issledovanii)*", Noveishaia istoriia Rossii 1 (Saint Petersburg, 2016), p. 202.

includes sacred literature, philosophy, and ritual and ceremonial codes. The pagan basis of the ideologists under examination here certainly includes all of these listed categories except for the latter one concerning preservation. After all, not only scholars of contemporary polytheism but also the bearers of this worldview themselves often recognize the novelty of 20th-21st century paganism.[396] Dobrovolsky and his entourage attempted to practically implement the idea of a pagan community and tried to distance themselves as much as possible from the prevailing framework of urban civilization. Speransky's group, meanwhile, despite its projections for closed pagan monasteries, has since its founding chosen and actively developed (as is evidenced, among other things, by the certain "pedantry" in their annual celebrations of calendric "holy days" and festivals) precisely the urban variant of paganism. Urban Russian paganism is still the dominant organizational form today.[397]

In the section "Prophets and Divination", our English thinker deduces two more important components of the priestly figure. The first of them is the interdependence of the order of cult attendants and religious tradition: "In all these ways, and many more, the spiritual class forms and is formed by the sacred tradition which binds the whole culture together and imprints its character upon it."[398] In the case of the pioneers of contemporary Russian paganism, the principle of "When you look into the abyss for a long time, the abyss beings to look back into you" manifests itself in the degree to which the ideas of the "first pagan", Dobroslav, have been reflected in the creative works and life position of Velimir. Velimir attended Dobrovolsky's Kupala festival and received his pagan name from him. The former neophyte explained his choice of candidate for one of the most important acts of contemporary paganism in terms of Dobrovolsky's venerable age (55 years) and his desire to not be a "self-proclaimer": "Dobroslav named everyone,

---

[396] Dobroslav, *Prirodoliubivaia religiia budushchego*, p. 15; A.M. Shcheglov, *Vozvrashchenie bogov* (Moscow, 1999); See also: Alain de Benoist, *On Being a Pagan* (North Augusta: Arcana Europa, 2018).

[397] See Roman Shizhensky, "Contemporary Pagan Ratings of Russian Historical Figures: The Data of Field Studies" in this volume.

[398] Dawson, *Religion and Culture*, p. 65.

uniting all into a single Circle, and I took advantage of this to be granted the name of Velimir by him. Afterwards, many years later, it became clear that there are 'self-proclaimers' and there are those who have been granted names. Those who have been granted names have some kind of invisible support in their soul which self-proclaimers do not, regardless of their 'greatness' or contributions to Native Faith."[399] Overall, Speransky's attitude towards the elder of Russian "nature-loving religion" can be assessed as twofold. Velimir believes the positive side of Dobroslav to be his propagation of the cult of vegetation, his "sublime contemplation", and his view that paganism is the "natural spirituality of the Russian people."[400] Of no small significance to the Koliada of the Vyatichi volkhv is Dobroslav's hermit experience, his rejection of materialistic-consumer life in the capital.[401] Velimir also remarks on this pagan elder's cause of improving modern youth.[402]

Without a doubt, Speransky's complex attitude towards Dobrovolsky is accented by yet another side of Dobroslav's worldview which, in Velimir's opinion, is its main foundation. Emphasizing that the "first face" of this Vasenevo recluse, the "nature-loving side" was not a mask but part of his essence, the ideologue of the Koliada of the Vyatichi goes on to criticize

---

399 R.V. Shizhensky, *Pochvennik ot iazychestva*, p. 39; "My attitude towards Dobroslav is complex...And yet I still asked him to grant me my name. Well, there was simply no-one of age who could have done this. I did not want to be a self-proclaimer like Selidor, Veleslav, Vseslav-Charodei, the late Ostromysl, and others today" - online correspondence with Nikolai Speransky from 23/12/2010, author's personal archive. Velimir's journal also contains a description of the rite as including the following elements: purification, initiation, adoption into the rod, and naming. See: Volkhv Velimir, *Russkoi iazychestvo i shamanizm*, pp. 523-524. On the peculiarities of this rite as a religious construct by 20th-21st century pagan leaders, see Roman Shizhensky, "Christian Mystery and Neo-Pagan Ritual Practice: The Question of the Rite of 'De-Baptizing' and 'Naming' in Russian Native Faith Organizations" in this volume.

400 "On the one hand, Dobroslav is the creator of Aroma-Yoga... where a person is suggested to bring themselves close to the intimate world of plants, their scents and life. As a result emerges a veneration of plants which leads a person to perfection" - "*Patriotizm i lichnostnoe sovershenstvo*", *Derevo Zhizni 34* (Troitsk, 2008); Velimir, "*Smysl i perspektivy iazycheskogo dvizheniia*", *Derevo Zhizni 44* (Troitsk, 2009).

401 Online correspondence with Nikolai Speransky from 30/12/2010, author's personal archive.

402 Online correspondence with Nikolai Speransky from 23/12/2010, author's personal archive.

the founder of the Russian Liberation Movement's reverse concept: Velimir considers Dobroslav's idea of a National-Socialist revolution involving the overthrow of everything extant and the establishment of a racial dictatorship to be unacceptable.[403] The volkhv also holds Dobrovolsky's attitude towards the human individual to be unsatisfactory: "...to this day our paganism has not shown interest in the individual personality of the Russian human. Dobroslav became the apostle of pagan socialism, i.e. a paganism that ignores the individual personality."[404] Without a doubt, the Kirov hermit would not consider Velimir a colleague nor a student. However, both the Kupala name-granting of 1993, their correspondence's continuation until 2008, Speransky's attendance of Dobrovolsky's Moscow lectures in the early 2000s[405], as well as, finally, the very fact of Velimir's ambivalent attitude towards the worldview of the pagan ideologist from Vyatka suggests a definite degree of ideological influence by Dobroslav on Velimir's paganism. Moreover, Speransky uses Dobroslav's slogan "Nature, Homeland, Folk" [*Priroda, Rodina, Rod*] which was established in the first published work of the Kirov pantheist's Arrows of Yarilo society.[406] The first generation of 20th century paganism which Dobrovolsky embodied shaped the tradition of Speransky's paganism. At the same time, the "ladder" that emerged continues to function in the present time: for instance, practically all Slavic pagan communities in Russia actively use

---

403 Volkhv Velimir, "*V gostiakh u Dobroslava*" in *Russkoe iazychestvo i shamanizm*, p. 517. This claim was contested by Dobrovolsky in his letter "*Slava Yarile!*", *Derevo Zhizni 38* (Troitsk, 2008).
404 "*Patriotizm i lichnostnoe sovershenstvo.*"
405 "There was one such occasion. Dobroslav came to Konstantin Vasilyev Museum to deliver a lecture 10 years ago... I squeezed between people and hung from a railing in the hall to see him. He suddenly laid eyes on me, almost pointed his finger at me, and suddenly spoke confidently and strongly. That is to say my presence freed him from that massive distaste that peered at him from all sides in the eyes of spoiled Muscovite girls and rotten intellectuals. He needed at least one of his own people, FOR WHOM HE SPEAKS, and who understands him and shares his ideas" - online correspondence with Nikolai Speransky from 23/12/2010, author's personal archive.
406 Compare Dobrovolsky's phrase "The Folk, Homeland, and Nature are one, for their root is one: the ancient pagan Rod" (Dobrovolsky, *Strely Yarila* (Pushchino, 1989, p. 19)" and Velimir's "Russian pagans put three words together: Nature, Homeland, Folk. These words have the same root, the name of the deity Rod." (Velimir, "*Russkoe iazychestvo vchera i segodnya*", talk given at the World Congress of Ethnic Religions in Vilnius, June 1998, published in *Russkoe iazychestvo i shamanizm*, pp. 334-335).

the drum, an instrument which Velimir first introduced into the practical paganism of organizations in central Russia.[407]

The second component directly pertaining to the priesthood is formulated by Dawson thusly: "in each culture this class defines and canonizes the human types which are regarded as spiritual norms or ideals of moral excellence by that culture."[408] The topic of "pagan saints" arose with the very emergence of Russian paganism, especially in relation to its ideology of the past and future "Golden Age" and its dominant conspirological concepts. The whole galaxy of anti-heroes fulfilling the roles of natural antagonists of "pagan saints" should be considered a direct product of the young-pagan conspirology. Images of heroes figure vividly as an integral part of the new-pagan mythologem and emergent worldview across the pages of Dobroslav's works. To dwell on the personalities whom Dobrovolsky highlights from Russian history, first and foremost note should be taken of Kievan Prince Svyatoslav Igorevich. Along with the majority of ideological leaders of the Russian variant of this movement, Dobroslav assigns a peculiar exceptionalism to the Svyatoslav era and even considers Rus in the time of the reign of his son, Igor, a "pagan Power." Svyatoslav's murder is construed not as a political move by the upper echelon of the Byzantine Empire afraid of the growing power of its neighbor, but as the reaction of a Christian state incapable of subduing a free people by force of arms and compelled to destroy the main defender of pagan faith in order to enslave Rus. Besides individuals, Dobrovolsky's narratives also contain a whole list of tribes and social groups which, in his opinion, played an important role in Russian pagan history. One of the central places on this list, without a doubt, is occupied by the Baltic tribe of the Rujani, who inhabited the medieval island of Rujania (modern Rügen): "In 1168 the Danish King Valdemar I, encouraged by Bishop Absalon, took the fortress by storm and burned it to the ground along with the Sanctuary.

---

407 "I first started working with a drum in Lugovaya in 1998. I bought leather for the drum at the market in Izmailovo in a shop with musical instruments. I twisted the hoop from plywood. I moistened the skin and stretched and nailed it. That I was the first to use the drum in rituals was later pointed out to me by Veleslav [Ilya Cherkasov, the volkhv of the Rodoliubie community - R.S.]" - online correspondence with Nikolai Speransky from 18/8/2016, author's personal archive.

408 Dawson, *Religion and Culture*, p. 65.

The last defenders of the temple were burned alive. BUT THE ASHES OF THIS FIRE STILL BEAT IN OUR HEARTS!"[409] The list of heroic tribes also includes the East-Slavic Vyatichi and the Baltic Lutici (the Wiltzi). Following these tribes who tried to resist Christianity openly, by force of arms, the historical arena is opened to clandestine fighters against the foreign religion, such as the *skomorokhi,* heretics, the rebellious common folk of the 17th century, and even the Cossacks. Without a doubt, it should be recognized that the main idea unifying these Slavic tribes is the degree of their resistance to incoming Christianization and their degree of self-sacrifice in the name of preserving the old world order.

Velimir, in turn, analogously finds heroes in the historical past (shamans, *strigolniki, pryguny,* and *khlysty*) as well as highlights moderns worthy of heroic representation. As an example of society living in accord with traditional communal rules, the author cites the experiences of Northern Russia's outlying territories living in a certain isolation from government. To the pluses of the autonomous existence of Northerners and living "according to tradition" Speransky attributes the Veche method of governance involving the consideration of cases at community meetings amidst the de facto absence of control by official authorities, i.e. "priests, police, and officials."[410] This communal form of self-governance, an original achievement of the ancestral archaic system extolled by the volkhv, finds its continuation in the moral ideas of socialism. According to Velimir, with the collapse of the Communist regime, which had "misunderstood" the essence of social justice, "correct socialism" has survived in the ideological programs of Russian young-paganism. It is particularly worth emphasizing that paganism as such is *a priori* presented by this community leader as a popular, primordial, and the only true

---

409 Dobroslav, *Zov Tule* (Khlynovskii ekspress, 2006), pp. 26-27. The historical fate of the Rujani and their main religious center, the temple-city of Arkona, has been central to the contemporary Russian pagan movement for some years already. For instance, the participants of the Bitsevsk appeal (adopted on 17/3/2002 by Rodnovery gathered at the Chertanovsk shrine complex in Moscow, the main goal of which was to unify the cooperation of pagan communities in Russia and abroad) made the fall of Arkona the beginning of its calendar dating.

410 Velimir, *Darna - uchenie o zhizni v Prirode i obshchestve,* p. 52.

worldview, thus turning out to be in "eternal connection" with the Veche institution chronologically passing through one historical epoch to another.

In the chapter "The Elements of Religion: God and the Supernatural" Dawson analyzes the category of the transcendent and comes to the conclusion that there is a close connection between religion and the otherworldly that is inaccessible to knowledge through traditional experience. In the opinion of this philosopher, transcendence is characteristic of all religious communities, from primitive groups to associations of mystics. Dawson considers the transcendent to be the "blue blood of religion", the "residual element of genuine religious experience."[411] Individuals in possession of impersonal power become the religious leaders and intellectual teachers of the community. In the work of this English scholar, examples of entering into revelation (the primary source of religious truth preceding, according to the author's hypothesis, intuition and reason) include mime (dance), trance, fasting, music, and chanting. The religious concepts of Dobrovolsky and Spransky pose vivid examples illustrating current pagan transcendence. By analogy with the historical Manitou, Yok, and Wakanda cited by Dawson, the first pagans of contemporary Russia confer the experience practiced beyond the present world upon certain terms: in the narratives of these polytheists, the transcendent is designated as *"darna"* and *"sila"* ("power" or "force").

"Darna" is a set of fundamental propositions of Nikolai Speransky's pagan philosophy which are attested in the majority of his works over the past 14 years and represent a definite invariant of Velimir's worldview.[412] The very term *"darna"* (meaning "harmony") was borrowed by Velimir from Lithuanian tradition.[413] In its "Russian" usage, however, darna significantly surpasses the "limit" of its original Lithuanian variation of harmony. People

---
411 Dawson, *Religion and Culture*, p. 38.
412 The first mention of this term (not counting journal entries) is to be found in the 1998 pamphlet *Mezhdunarodnye otnosheniia obshchestva 'Viatichi'* and more recently in Velimir's *Nravstvennaia kniga* (Troitsk, 2012).
413 In his "Harmony and Morality" the Lithuanian pagan leader and coiner of this term, Jonas Trinkūnas, associates this term with the following notional series: *daryti, darbas, derlius, derėjimas, dermė, dora* ("to do, work, harvest, to go together, concord, morality"). See Jonas Trinkūnas, *Baltic Religions Today* (Vilnius: Senovės baltų religinė bendrija, 2011), p. 23.

are capable of partaking in darna as a permanent, timeless state through a set of actions which the volkhv characterizes with the notion of ascesis. The aim of pagan spiritual practice is to reveal a person's communion with nature (to feel nature within him).[414] According to Velimir's pamphlet *Darna*, person's proper temporal return to dwelling within the natural environment is based on an inner mystical state encompassing (1) the search for a place to set up camp that is suitable for establishing contact with spirits (whether one's ancestral homeland, the outskirts of one's native village, a spiritually dear place), and (2) the step-by-step implementation of three levels of pagan ascesis. The first is individual "work with fire." This rite contains a direct set of sacrificial acts and a tradition of prayer in the form of petitions and praises. Obtaining darna in the everyday world becomes possible through a mental disposition of peace that can be felt in a burning fire. Second is individual "work with the nighttime forest." This rite includes determining one's fear of nature and independently getting rid of it, achieving an inner state through analyzing what one hears, through breathing techniques, and a prayer tradition consisting of appealing to the goddess Lada. Third is individual "work with the natural environment of water." This rite includes submersion into a pond at nighttime, thus facing the primal fear of communing with "otherworldly nothingness." In addition to individual practices, Speransky's ascesis also involves collective work to acquire *darna*. The desired state is achieved through praising the gods, walking or dancing around a fire together, clapping hands, and singing songs:

> Overall, you need to behave in such a way so as to, without losing the ritual state, bring your imagination into the inner vision of images and the free birth of words... Participants merge with their higher deity and form a single whole in a chain that connects this world with the world of the gods. This gives rise to a sense of inner light and warmth. The deity which appears above each person corresponds to their inner essence. Therefore, it is important for the participants' characters and their dignity to correspond to the chosen divine image... To participate

---

414   Velimir, *Darna*, p. 36.

in such a mystery, participants must spend at least three days in the forest without contact with home and the human world. Afterwards, at least one more night must be spent in the forest.[415]

The corresponding definition and designation of the transcendent in Dobroslav's paganism acquired the name "force" or "power" (*sila*). In his work *The Providence of Nature and Unintelligent Homo sapiens*, this ideologist asserts a certain absence of spiritual and material elements: "By and large, in Nature there is neither spirit nor matter as such - both of these notions have been distorted by idealists and materialists. There is only one fundamental SUBSTANCE - FORCE, which manifests itself at once in the form of matter and in the form of the spirit, possessing all the qualities attributed to matter and spirit."[416] Absolutizing force and placing it above such categories, Dobrovolsky thus focuses on the inhuman, other origin of this substance, which goes back to this pagan leader's main world-shaping source: Nature. The manifestation of this force or power in this new mythological perspective can be seen in certain lines of Dobroslav's works which equate force with spirits and the figure of Rod so popular in contemporary Slavic paganism.[417] This Kirov nature-worshipper knows yet another means by which man can achieve the spirit-forces of the world: Dobroslav holds that the only means of knowing the "Slavic Manitou" to be the heart and, more broadly, the unconscious.[418] In parallel to Speransky's fasting, singing, and other elements contributing to the individual's entry into the world of the unconscious, Dobrovolsky attaches special importance to the practice of the *khorovod*, i.e. singing and dancing in a circle. The cyclical, spiral, circular, *khorovod*-like development of the life path of humanity, and more broadly the universe, is Dobrovolsky's ideal of historical development, reflections of which he sees in the

---

415 Ibid, pp. 64-65.
416 Dobroslav, *Promysel prirody i nerazumnyi homo sapiens* (Kharkov: Sfera), p. 13.
417 Among such "spiritual beings", Dobrovolsky singles out those which are "divine", "semi-divine", "demonic", "ethereal", and "astral." See Dobroslav, *Ob idolakh i idealakh*, p. 12. Further: "The Slavs called this primordial life FORCE awakening NATURE to self-unfolding 'within' ROD. ALL OF NATURE IS THE SELF-MANIFESTATION OF ROD" - Dobroslav, *Svetoslavie (ocherki iazycheskogo mirochuvstvovaniia)* (Kirov: Viatka, 2004), p. 37.
418 Dobroslav, *Liubov' i Smert'*, p. 6.

creations of nature, as embodying the circular movement of the sun, a protective magic circle. This elder of the Russian Liberation Movement remarks that it is by way of the khorovod rite that man has had direct communication with "Native Luminous Forces."[419] This pagan ideologue's books lead us to distinguish three necessary conditions for such connection: (1) the rotation of the khorovod "around the sun" (*posolon'*, from left to right), (2) the inclusion of several *khorovod* circles[420], and (3) a corresponding inner state of participants forming a psycho-energetic chain. The expected result of the *khorovod* mystery should be participants' entry into a "circle" state of ecstasy, "possessed by spirits."[421]

In the worldview conceptions of Alexey Dobrovolsky and Nikolai Speransky, the above-designated definitions of *sila* and *darna* serve as a kind of bridge to pagan ethics. Here we arrive at yet another primary element of Dawson's religion-cultural concept: divine law (cosmic order).[422] Like in Taoism and Confucianism, as highlighted by this English scholar, contemporary Russia's pagan ideologists have articulated their own conception of the "mandate of Heaven." Dobrovolsky introduces the special term "righteous moral law" to mean service to the good: "The highest Ideal accessible to us is, in essence, nothing other than selfless service to the Good. The doer of Good receives, as it were, the reward of meaningfulness and joy of being. Thus is fulfilled the MORAL LAW OF NATURE." Dobroslav places the historical origin of this "law" in the "Golden Age of mankind", the era of the primitive-communal system. This pagan mystic also sees the prototype of the main universal regulator in the moral precepts of the animal world (the law of the jungle): "Moral is that which serves the flourishing of the Rod; immoral is that which is harmful

---

419 Dobroslav, *Radost' Solntsepoklonnika* (Sfera Internet, 2003), p. 23.
420 "At this time the *khorovod* is not formed correctly. There should be three circles: the first of virgins, the second of married women, and the third of all the rest. The circles turn in different directions." - Dobroslav, recorded lecture, Moscow, September 2006.
421 Dobroslav, *Radost' Solntsepoklonnika*, pp. 22-23.
422 "The social way of life is founded on a religious law of life, and this law in turn depends on non-human powers towards which man looks with hope and fear, powers which can be known in some fashion but which remain essentially mysterious, since they are superhuman and supernatural." - Dawson, *Religion and Culture*, p. 56. See also Dawson's cases of "moral reformation."

to it." The logical development of this gospel is a series of theses on the natural, ur-religious origin of morality and the primordial oneness of morality in the culture of classless society. To prove the pre-human origin of moral categories (such as justice and altruism), Dobroslav resorts not so much to his own experience as to the evidence bases of past enlighteners, such as the *Code of Nature, or the True Spirit of its Laws* by the 18th century French utopian communist Abbot Morelly, and the book *Mutual Aid as a Factor of Evolution* by the anarchist theorist and historian of the 19th-20th centuries, Prince Peter Kropotkin. What lies at the basis of moral law in the point of view of this pagan ideologist? Based on his own sensory experience, Dobroslav states: "True morality is sympathizing with and helping disenfranchised beings as much as possible. This is what brings a sense of self-importance. This does not require any special talent or exceptional intellect. Man thus becomes more and more sensitive and responsive. HE BECOMES MORE GOOD." Thus, at the core of the "righteous law" of this pagan from Vyatka is the idea of compassion for all living beings and a codex of serving the good.

Speransky's bank of categories of "pagan righteousness", in turn, is the so-called "Moral Law of Rod." This enlightener of alternative religiosity finds the origins of this law in the mythology of the Slavs and a practice of legal relations dating back into historical timelessness, the era of prehistory. In the first case, the volkhv uses the "Myth of Creation" reconstructed by the Koliada of the Vyatichi on the basis of the works of A.N. Afanasyev, N.M. Galkovsky, D.M. Dudko, a passage from the *Tale of Bygone Years*, apocryphal tales, and anonymous ethnographic materials collected throughout Northern Russia, Ukraine, and Belarus. In the second case, the author deduces that the moral Law emerged out of the trial-and-error life practice of mankind.[423] If the chronology of the Moral Law's emergence is lost in the mythologems of constructed cosmogonic myth, then

---

[423] "All of mankind's life experience shows that the future must be approached by grasping, each time trying and refining one's deeds... And in the very same way, by trying and refining deeds, people have come to the conclusion that there is a Moral Law established in the cosmos, which folk tradition and pagan faith teach to follow at all times." - Velimir, *Kniga prirodnoi very* (Moscow: Veligor, 2009), pp. 268-269.

the end of the order of Rod has historical certainty: Speransky associates the time of deviation from this law with the era of Brezhnev's stagnation, the time of "Soviet relaxation."[424] Velimir deems Russian folk fairy tales to be an historical transmitter and translator of knowledge preserving the principles of the law of Rod. Among the classics subjected to analysis to illustrate the operation of this law, Speransky singles out the novel of M.A. Bulgakov, *The Master and Margarita*. Subjecting such texts to his own "transcription", this pagan enlightener formulates the main provisions of pagan moral legislation, according to which man should: (1) respect the spirits of nature, (2) have a high moral constitution, (3) possess an intimate sense of tact, (4) observe ethical behavior, (5) practice self-restraint, (6) be ready to endure hardships for the sake of friends and high principles, (7) be able to maintain dignity and tradition amidst harsh conditions, (8) work hard, (9) respect elders, (10) be honest, (11) understand that power is not a self-evident attribute of good, (12) recognize that earthly life is equivalent to life in Iriy (the pagan paradise), and (13) recognize the prevalence of spiritual over material values.

To summate our examination of the worldviews of these first- and second-wave Russian pagan ideologists from the perspective of Christopher Dawson's concept, the key discourses which shape this "new volkhv paganism from within" ought to be highlighted. First and foremost, the contemporary spiritual leaders of reborn polytheism, whether consciously or not, have been compelled to syncretize in their persons the three primordial religious archetypes of the priest, the ruler (lawgiver), and prophet (seer). As follows, the leadership of communities, the leading of rites (naming, de-baptizing, etc.), the organization of educational lectures and festivals (Kupala and an overall the celebration of the year-circle), the introduction of sacred texts and symbols into practice, the creation of the figures of the pantheon, and, finally, the articulation of apocalyptic and post-apocalyptic projections, fall under their "jurisdiction." Moreover, it is this emerging

---

424 Velimir, Veleslav, and Vlasov, *Put' volkhva* (Donetsk: Kashtan, 2007), p. 797. In this work, the pagan leaders cite two more examples of world evil. One of them, which was unsuccessful, was German Fascism. The second, which turned out to be more successful, was Christianity's transformation into a state religion. .

priestly-volkhv caste that is the de facto illustration and visible, promulgated example of today's paganism, constructing its future and assigning itself the role of the leaders of a theocratic society.

The singularly defining trait of the new pagan prophets should be recognized not only in their shaping of sacred tradition, expressed in the cult of "pagan saints", but also the intra-caste transmission of tradition, the transfer of ideological stock to the receivers of a sort of pagan "guild association." The manifestations of the "volkhv minimum" and the pagan didaskals of the future leading society ahead to prosperity include the ability to look into and enter the world beyond through the transcendent (*darna, sila*), and their realization of divine law.

***

THE CONCEPT OF PAGAN RE-MYTHOLOGIZATION: THE CASE OF THE 'SIGNS' OF THE COMMUNITY OF NIKOLAI SPERANSKY[425]

One of the paradoxes in the thematic field of the vast number of research works partially touching upon or directly focusing on contemporary Russian pagan "world-building" consists in mixing the theoretico-practical component of creed with general descriptions of the organization (or personality) under study along with the source base of the community and its politico-ideological system. Naturally, as a result of the preparation of such "Native Faith cocktails", mythological and ritual principles are completely dissolved or relegated to the background under the pressure of "exposing" the "young pagans" as is so in demand in some circles in contemporary Russia. Because of this, the phenomenon of today's pagan worldview loses one of its systematic components, its religious specificity, and is thereby turned into an oppositional conglomerate out of "skinning", rallying, criticizing, "Interneting", degrading, etc.

Without a doubt, such exaggerated categories do exist. However, one distinctive trait of Volkhv Velimir (Speransky), as one of the active figures, authors, and leaders of the camp of contemporary adherents of ethnic-colored pre-Abrahamic beliefs, is the author's own complex pagan faith. One of the components of the particular (and step-by-step) manifestations of the pagan mentality of Velimir's group is reflected in a symbolic fixation on all possible kinds of signs, instances, symbols, miracles, and wonders. According to the texts describing such phenomena, pagan signs fulfill multiple functions. These include directly mythological (or mythmaking) functions: signs are the visible will of a deity and personify the actual presence of higher forces in a rite. The realization of this religio-practical function lies in the choice of place for creating

---
425 Article first published in *Colloquium Heptaplomeres* 1 (2014).

a cult structure (a shrine)[426], the introduction of an additional stimulus for developing the general mood for ritual action, "immersion" in myth, removing uncomfortable psychological and spiritual barriers for neophytes, and the creation of a new pagan anthology of sacred wonders[427], possibly with the purpose of affirming and confirming the truth of their choice of worldview.

It is rather difficult to determine the strict, delineated classification framework of "wonders." For the most part, they are non-systematic, random, associated with a specific community event, an expedition trip, or even with a set of direct actions on the part of an individual adept. At the same time, certain regularities can be traced which in one case or another characterize the emergence, course, or results of such signs.

Assigning the contemplation of nature the status of one of the most ancient and foundational sources of pagan knowledge, Velimir sees the active existence of the gods through the prism of natural anomalies.[428] In support of this thesis, the volkhv refers to the destruction caused by the storm on 20-21 July 1998 in the capital: "Tornadoes toppled the crosses on the domes of the Novodevichy Monastery and tore the democratic banner over the Kremlin to shreds. On the riverside, fallen trees damaged the Kremlin wall. Amidst an enormous number of torn-down billboards and fallen trees, only two people were killed, but a mass of cars were damaged."[429] It is more than clear here what set of modern components of Russian society are negative and objectionable to the natural elements (i.e., by extension, the volkhv himself). For Speransky, the storm "punished" an unacceptable religious system, a foreign political system, and all the attributes of "Western" life. Against the backdrop of the destructive consequences of the tornadoes, the contemporary

---

426 "For a rite is chosen a place which can subsequently become permanent. If we feel blessing from the rites held at a new place, then in time a shrine will arise there" - Velimir, *Nravstvennaia kniga: hakim rodnoveru byt' i pochemu* (Pamphlet #11, Troitsk, 2012), p. 72.
427 Speransky emphasizes the significance of passing onto youth both orally and in writing everything extraordinary and related to existing, active shrine complexes to youth. See Velimir, *Slovo ob idolakh i sviatykh mestakh iazycheskoi very* (Pamphlet #12, Troitsk: Koliada Vyatichei, 2013), p. 30.
428 Velimir, *Kniga prirodnoi very* (Moscow: Veligor, 2009), pp. 36, 43.
429 Ibid, p. 37.

volkhv turns to the pagan (positive) side of this act of natural elements. Firstly, the storm acted as a kind of omen, a heavenly sign. As Speransky writes, the first world pagan congress was held in Vilnius during those very days. Secondly, the storm fulfilled the function of a silent oracle confirming the rightness of the paganism practiced by the Koliada of the Vyatichi community. In this pagan leader's description, the association celebrated Kupala during the storm. Thanks to the collective glorification of Perun, a miracle happened: "Not a single lightning bolt hit them, nor were they hit by a tornado, and no trees fell on them. Their fire continued to burn calmly, as if nothing happened at all."[430]

Examples of the manifestation of the divine through natural phenomena can also be found in the periodical of the community. Anomalies happen at pagan places of force: shrines. For instance, upon the installation of an idol of Dazhdbog on 11 January 2004 in Tsaritsyno, Velimir saw the sun rise. A similar natural phenomena was recorded by Velimir on 20 July 2013 at the Zhivitsa shrine and cult center, when a statue of Perun was installed and a festival was held in his honor.[431] Another summertime "natural incident" was associated with the transportation of an image of the goddess Lelia: a sandstorm which occurred during the transfer of the idol acquired a mythological ring in the explanation of the volkhv. Speransky saw in this momentary gust of strong wind the direct divine influence of Perun not wishing to part with Lelia.[432]

The community members of Koliada of the Vyatichi associate another group of pagan signs with the appearance of living creatures, such as birds and other animals, in the space of shrines. In his "Word on Idols", Velimir turned to the historiography of this question in search of recommendations on how to relate to such "guests" in sacred places. Despite the failure of his search for sources, the pagan ideologue issued the following verdict: "In our time, the presence of birds at shrines is held to be a natural

---

[430] Ibid.
[431] *"Vosstanovleno kapishche v Tsaritsyno!"*, Derevo Zhizhni. Gazeta etnicheskogo soprotivleniia (Troitsk, 2004); *"Khronika 2013 - Khronika postanovki idolov v tsentre 'Zhivitsa'"*, Derevo Zhizni. Gazeta etnicheskogo vozrozhdeniia 57 (2013).
[432] Ibid.

phenomenon. Birds are not barred from feeding at the altars of the gods."[433] There does not seem to be any general, constant criteria (or even proposals) for evaluating the appearance and actions of fauna on the sacred territory of a community. Negative, positive, or neutral relations to violators or guests of a sacred space depend on the concrete case and the atmosphere prevailing among those present. For example, the above-mentioned restoration of the shrine complex in Tsaritsyno was marked by the appearance of a forest mouse during the sacrifice of bread to the goddess Lada. Meanwhile, the pagans decided to officially not allow a cat which visited a domestic shrine in the courtyard of a wooden home in Tsaritsyno to eat the altar food, although it remained unspoken that the sacrifice could be left to be taken if unnoticed.[434]

In a certain sense, the community members and volkhv of Koliada of the Vyatichi continue the pagan practice of "zoological signs" of the past, which does have source evidence. The scholar Sreznevsky, for instance, has found this type of Slavic omen in the works of Saxo Grammaticus, Thietmar von Merseburg, Gregory of Nazianzus, and Bishop Kirill of Rostov.[435] Let us repeat, however, that such analogues can be cited only as figurative and nominal. What semantic charge such animal signs bore in the past and, moreover, what they mean in contemporary paganism, seems to be yet another historical and religious mystery. Accordingly, in thinking about the animal signs of Koliada of the Vyatichi, we should take note of the fact that there are no canonical prescriptions for the animal world nor a developed systematization of such signs recorded in the pagan codex of this group.

As for positive signs, such are often randomly discovered objects. As Speransky writes, during the preparation of a shrine items which were found on the chosen territory of the complex were automatically included into the sacred space.[436] Naturally, the

---

433 Velimir, *Slovo ob idolakh i sviatykh mestakh iazycheskoi very* (Pamphlet #12; Troitsk: Koliada Viatichey, 2013), p. 29.
434 "Vosstanovleno kapishche v Tsaritsyno!", *Derevo Zhizhni. Gazeta etnicheskogo soprotivleniia* (Troitsk, 2004); Velimir, *Slovo ob idolakh*, p. 29.
435 I.I. Sreznevsky, *Issledovaniia o iazycheskom bogosluzhenii drevnikh slavian* (Moscow: Knizhnyi dom LIBROKOM, 2013), p. 9.
436 One such find during the construction of the shrine in Bitsevsk park in September 1999 was the skull of a dog. See Volkhv Velimir, *Russkoe iazychestvo i shamanizm* (Moscow: Institut obshchegumanitarnykh issledovanii, 2006), p. 468.

"house of the deity", or the deity's man-made depiction, falls into this field of pagan signs. The narratives of Velimir and this volkhv's associates testify to an absence of chronological restrictions for the appearance of "idol signs." Such are not connected with any clearly recorded "stages" of the "life" of an established idol. A miracle can accompany the very moment of placing the symbol of a deity and can consist of a higher power assisting in the process. This is also fixed in the destruction of pagan shrines, such as an idol's protection from fire damage.[437]

In addition, non-verbal appeals to natural objects and the gods of the pantheon can have magical effects. As an example of this we can cite two letters of Kseniya in the 25th issue of the Tree of Life newspaper, in which the conceptual link with the village birch tree and gifts to the tree are said to bring a positive dynamic to the author's life-path. In the 38th issue of the publication, this pagan attributed unusually benevolent behavior on the part of passengers in the metro at rush hour to the effective intervention of the goddess Makosh.[438] In her article on an expedition to Seydozero[439], the volkhvess, author, and active member of Koliada of the Vyatichi, Arena Vesta (Galina Ponomareva), also cites an instance of assistance afforded by higher powers: after silently praising "Mother Tundra", this nature deity fulfilled Vesta's childhood dream by granting her a deer horn.[440]

---

[437] "When the sculpture [of Lada] was raised to be set into the pit, it miraculously rose upright on its own, with minimal effort on our part, and immediately faced the direction in which we wanted" - Velimir, *"Boginia Lada v Doline Vodopadov", Derevo Zhizni. Gazeta etnicheskogo vozrozhdeniia 50* (Troitsk, 2010). During the installation of an idol of Veles in Losiny Ostrov in 2011, according to pagans, a certain force emanated from the altar stones, which moved in the direction of the shrine virtually on their own" - see: *Derevo Zhizni. Gazeta etnicheskogo vozrozhdeniia 52* (Troitsk, 2012). The head of an idol of Dazdhbog was also found to have survived the hands of arsonists - see *"Vosstanovleno kapishche v Tsaritsyno!", Derevo Zhizhni. Gazeta etnicheskogo soprotivleniia* (Troitsk, 2004).

[438] Kseniia, *"Moia berezka", Derevo Zhizni. Gazeta etnicheskogo vozrozhdeniia 25* (Troitsk, 2007); Ibidem, *"Makosh'", Derevo Zhizni. Gazeta etnicheskogo vozrozhdeniia 38* (Troitsk, 2008).

[439] Seydozero is also held to be a sacred site by Russian Asatru, i.e. adherents of the Northern (Scandinavian) pagan tradition. See NordicRunes, *"Seidozero - Mesto Sily", Severnyi Veter 3* (Prostobuk, 2013).

[440] *"Vtoraia ekspeditsiia na Seid-Ozero", Derevo Zhizni. Gazeta etnicheskogo vozrozhdeniia 54* (2012).

Sacralization and the "signification" or "symbolization" of "tradition" is manifested directly through the social sphere of people involved in contemporary paganism as well as outsiders and random persons who find themselves in a "place of power." We can relate to this type of pagan signs Velimir's report on the magical influence of the Ukrainian pagan G.S. Lozko (Volkhvess Zoreslava) on Lithuanian tour guides who refused to allow the pagan delegation onto the grounds of a cathedral archeological site where an altar to the god Perkunas had been preserved. Thanks to the influence of this leader of the Association of Rodnovery of Ukraine as well as the will of the god Perun, the delegates of the first Congress of Ethnic Religions succeeded in being able to visit the shrine. Another report by the volkhv on an expedition to Arkaim contains an account of pagans' ascending up Mount Shamanka: during the expedition up this holy site, a sign appeared in the form of random tourists disappearing and one of the participants experiencing "shamanic sickness."[441]

In conclusion, it bears noting that at the present time Speransky and the Koliada of the Vyatichi community are developing their own system of categories of omens and signs with the aim of fixing such instances of immersion into pagan traditionality, thus presenting a view of "Native Faith" from within.[442] Yet it is the lack of systematization of manifestations of the divine and the visible and invisible presence of the gods that harbors a certain specificity which shapes this element of the new mythology. Amidst the different variations encountered, the main condition for the manifestation of a sign is the presence of a proselyte of pre-Abrahamic religiosity in a "place of power." This explains the significant percentage of pagan miracles occurring within the zone of shrines. A second criterion for obtaining a

---

441 Velimir, *"Kapishche Peruna", Derevo Zhizni. Gazeta etnicheskogo soprotivleniia 2* (Troitsk: Trovant); Ibidem, *Nravstvennaia kniga: kakim rodnovery byt' i pochemu* (Pamphlet #11; Troitsk, 2012).

442 In a correspondence with Nikolai Speransky from 26/11/2013 (author's personal archives), the volkhv remarked that seeing the will of the gods in manifestations of nature is a common phenomenon for pagans: "During rites Kazakov [the head of the Union of Slavic Communities of Slavic Native Faith] also followed the flight paths of birds and sought answers from the Gods through them and other objects. The pagans in Rodoliubie have also done this. The same has been the case in the Circle of Pagan Traditions - this is a common feature."

sign is associated with sacred space: in this case, the source of manifestation of the sacred is more "concentrated" and shifts in the direction of the man-made "shells", i.e., idols of the Slavic pagan pantheon.

***

THE PHILOSOPHY OF GENDER IN CONTEMPORARY EUROPEAN PAGANISM[443]

Elaborations on the social profile of genders and the role and place of man and woman in society occupy a central place in the worldview constructs and "pagan reactions" of the Norwegian nativist Varg Vikernes and the Russian mystical anarchist Alexey Dobrovolsky (Dobroslav) - and such, let us emphasize, concern both their "own", i.e., diasporic, "traditional" society as well as their relation to the "other", "external", "multicultural" society. The exceptionalism of the gender question in their religious systems is confirmed not only by the sheer quantity of these radicals' references to the problem of the masculine and feminine that is honed in the source massifs of these pagan leaders, but the level of significance of gender can also be judged in terms of this theme's constant interspersion in the religious opposition they construct and propose to neophytes, as well as in the whole masses of those sympathetic to their historical canvas. The socio-cultural and religious aspect of gender identity permeates literally the entirety of the historical worlds that constitute the hypothetical and evidential foundation of 20th-21st century pagan ideology. Man and woman figure in these Russian and Norwegian sketches of prehistory and are cited with respect to "tangible" historical periods. Ideal reconstructions of strong and weak genders are "caught up" in the pagan perspective of a new Golden Age.

The gender range of the worldview constructions of the Norwegian pagan Varg Vikernes encompasses several basic themes whose main content can be encountered in one form or another in many of his published works and interviews. The most acute of this Scandinavian's considerations on gender are concentrated in two angles of analyses: defining primacy in the "war of genders" and examining the religious aspect of relations between man and woman.

---
443 Article first published in *Vestnik Permskogo universiteta* [*Bulletin of Perm University*] 3:19 (2014).

An analysis of Varg Vikernes' texts shows that one of the most important spiritual luminaries for this Nordic pagan is the figure of Mother-Earth. The Norwegian syncretically associates the religious degradation of modern society with denials of the harm wreaked by the materialistic exploitation of natural resources. In particular, this pagan writes of the need for restoring mankind's respect for nature and for spirituality to be sought precisely in the surrounding environment. The Norwegian musician plans to recreate such a worldview through the rituals of religious practice. Imparting the natural world with a pantheistic element and rejecting the idea of a posthumous paradise, this ethno-radical calls upon his readers to "live here, now, and in the future on our beautiful Mother-Earth."[444] Despite this Scandinavian pagan's cultic approach to the feminine deity of Earth (Mother-Nature), Vikernes nevertheless adheres to the idea of difference between the masculine and feminine in the religious notions of his ancestors. Vikernes constructs a divine hierarchy whose highest ideal is not to be found in the feminine element: "We are earthly and divine creatures; our bodies come from Jord (Norse Jorð, "Earth"), Mother Earth, but our minds (or so-called "souls") come from Bore (Norse Búri, 'born'), the Sky God - and while the mind longs for home (Ásgarðr), the body keeps it on Earth, and will continue to do so until we have been sufficiently purified and improved."[445] As follows, in Vikernes' worldview the masculine is equivalent to the spiritual and is privileged over the feminine-earthly. To confirm his hypothesis, the Norwegian resorts to his "source steed" of Scandinavian mythology: speaking of the role and significance of the valkyries, which are by no means secondary mythical figures among Nordic myths, the founder of the Norwegian Heathen Front emphasizes that these sacred women warriors are dependent and somewhat divinely deficient, as these winged virgins are fully subordinate to Odin, the main duties of the valkyries being equipping warriors and serving at festival

---

444 Varg Vikernes, *Skandinavskaia mifologiia i mirovozzrenie* (Tambov: Poliu, 2006) p. 89.
445 Varg Vikernes, "Paganism: Part V - Sacrifices" (2005) [https://www.burzum.org/eng/library/paganismo5.shtml]; Ibidem, *Rechi Varga II*.

feasts.[446] Without a doubt, this Nordic musician also takes note of both the martial and magical "service" of the female consorts of Valhalla, but on the pages of his *Scandinavian Mythology* these "heroines' duties" are, if not altogether secondary, then at least subordinate to the "traditional" occupation of the female half of humanity.

The dominance of the masculine over the feminine is even more pronounced and acquires more open form in Vikernes' references to historical materials. This Scandinavian writer constructs his own system of gender relations in a series of articulations of a "war of genders." Since in this system the basis of masculine greatness was laid in "prehistory", of interest is a small journey, a kind of historical descent, through which we can fully imagine the role of man and woman in the world of this propagandist of alternative Scandinavian religiosity.

Presenting his point of view on the contemporary situation of the social genders, Vikernes speaks quite critically of women in the 21st century. In a 2005 interview, following a rather interesting preamble featuring an affirmation of equality between the sexes despite their differences and the equally interesting phrase "I have only positive things to say about women, but I have nothing positive to say about modern women"[447], the Norwegian lists the vices of the weaker sex today. The table of female minuses detected by this Nordic pagan include a depraved culture (contempt for cooking and an unwillingness to have children and families overall), a set of traits allowing women to become "like men" (a thirst for theoretical education, male professions, and "looking like men"). The Norwegian states in conclusion: "True women are all my equals, whom I adore and respect, but I see modern women more like disgusting, primitive and disturbed animals, or subhuman at best."[448] Further, perhaps in an attempt to "mix up" what he has said and dissociate himself from the label of a male chauvinist, the Norwegian points towards the spoiled state of modern men (Vikernes compares the stronger sex to sick dogs before

---

446 Vikernes, *Skandinavskaia mifologiia*, pp. 68-70.
447 Chris Mitchell, "Interview with Varg Vikernes" (10/5/2005) [https://www.burzum.org/eng/library/2005_interview_metalcrypt.shtml].
448 Mitchell, "Interview with Varg."

euthanasia) and all of humanity. It is to be noted in particular that he sees the root of the feminism he despises in "Judeo-Christian (anti-)culture" that has destroyed healthy gender and sex life.[449]

A series of logical questions arise: if today's women do not suit this Scandinavian pagan-thinker, then is there an ideal Nordic virgin in Vikernes' worldview? If yes, then what are the criteria for the perfect female? What does the Norwegian propose instead of the feminist, monotheistic-religious figure he rejects? In the above-cited interview, the Scandinavian deems, albeit rather tentatively, the Golden Age of "true" women to have been the era of Ancient Scandinavia. The only point of orientation allowing to chronologically outline the "correct antiquity" is once again the religious factor. For Vikernes, who *a priori* rejects Abrahamic religiosity, the longed-for time of longed-for women is the pagan and, as follows, practically timeless period of native history. The set of qualities needed for a real woman, in the opinion of this musician, includes, firstly, a selection of antonyms for the vices of the weaker half of humanity distinguished by Vikernes himself and, secondly, are based on his views referencing history - a "history with a woman's face." The descent down the ladder of the female question in the works of this Norwegian ethno-radical is pronouncedly rapid. Without plunging into temporal questions and the change of historical eras, the founder of the Norwegian Heathen Front focuses on the crimes of the bearers of the new faith of "Asiatic Christianity", with the onset of which, according to this Scandinavian thinker, millions of European women and girls would be burned alive.[450] The religious component of the female gender becomes paramount in this Norwegian writer's pagan history. Vikernes recognizes the fairer half of humanity to be skilled in magic, possessing power that was (is and will be?) concentrated in the spirit and empathy. However, having almost completely surrendered sacred power to women in the idealized pagan past, the Scandinavian puts the servants of Freya in a position dependent upon the male clergy, the priests (the "Seidrmen").[451]

---

[449] Varg Vikernes, *Rechi Varga* (Tambov: Polius, 2007), p. 32.
[450] Vikernes, *Skandinavskaia mifologiia*, pp. 88, 171.
[451] Ibid, p. 173.

Another component of the feminine ideal directly associated with the spiritual sphere is seen by this Nordic pagan in girlish innocence. It is purity that becomes the "degree", the "physical measure" allowing women to occupy a proper, dignified social position in the Golden Age of the past.[452] Thus, in outlining the desired ideal of the priestess-maiden, the Norwegian finds application in the figure of "mortal goddesses." Women are supposed to fulfill their main function of being maternal and becoming "symbols of life." Remaining true to the dictates of eugenics and hygiene, Vikernes uses the example of changing eye color to discuss the need for instituting polygamous families, exclusively in the form of polygyny.[453] The line of argumentation in defense of such family unions is based on religio-racial attitudes concerning the Aryan purity of the pagan maiden-mother. The intrafamily code, in the view of our subject, is imbued with a purely masculine tinge: cheating on a husband is punishable by death, women who lose their virginity outside of wedlock, divorcees and widows trying to remarry acquire the status of outcasts in the gender philosophy of this Norwegian as "dirty women", inferior members of society.[454] Despite the Norwegian's recognition of a sacrality, spirituality, and, finally, divinity of the female figure, the latter's designated role does not go beyond serving the male figure. Woman is only part of the whole, a fragment, even if an important one.[455]

The basis of Vikernes' views on gender ought to be sought in his interpretation of a history of confrontation between two well-known forms of primitive-communal relations: matriarchy and patriarchy. The fullest elaborations of this Scandinavian pagan's views are reflected in the chapter "The Age of the Gods" in one of his major works, *Scandinavian Mythology and Worldview*:

> Feminine nature is passive and quite consistent with conservatism, which seeks confidence in what it is, while masculine nature is to be

---
452 Vikernes, *Rechi Varga*, p. 34.
453 Ibid, p. 68.
454 Ibid, pp. 33-34.
455 Ibid.

active and to seek development and improvement; man wants to put his life and health on the line in an attempt to improve them. Therefore, cultural development and science first moved forward when society moved from matriarchy to patriarchy. The more men dominate society, the more progress is accomplished in culture and science.[456]

Without a doubt, Varg Vikernes' concept of gender is not one-hundred percent original material of his authorship. His "mythological raid" of Scandinavia and his interpretation of the figures and images of ancient myths might be related to his own creativity, but the roots of the main idea of the unconventional dominance of man should be sought in sources of a different origin. The latter include the intellectual baggage of thinkers which the scholarly community has associated with the Ariosophists, the Traditionalists, and other conservative thinkers. As Vikernes himself notes, one of the central places on the list of authors he "thinks highly of" is occupied by the writer Baron Julius Evola.[457] Perhaps it was the works of this Italian Traditionalist philosopher that played the decisive role in shaping this Norwegian as an extreme anti-feminist. Telling in this respect is Julius Evola's article with the suggestive title "Feminism and the Heroic Tradition" written in 1933. Regarding feminism as a tell-tale sign of degeneration, this Italian philosopher also remarked on the consequences of introducing social equality between the sexes, the list of which is typical of Vikernes' articulations.[458] Moreover, in a number of other articles Evola repeatedly emphasizes the antiquity and non-Aryan origin of gynecocracy (the "civilization of women"). The predominance of the feminine over the masculine encountered in such historical cultures is unequivocally regarded by this Italian thinker as a "distortion of normal relations inherent to the traditional order in its pure and absolute state."[459] Hence the pantheism derived from matriarchy, which is presented by Evola as "formless liberation, wrenched out in chaotic experiments",

---

456 Vikernes, *Skandinavskaia mifologiia*, p. 196.
457 Mitchell, "Interview with Varg."
458 Julius Evola, *"Feminizm i geroicheskaia traditsiia" in Traditsiia i Evropa* (Tambov: Ex Nord Lux, 2009), p. 170.
459 Julius Evola, *"Krasnoe znamia" in Traditsiia i Evropa* (Tambov: Ex Nord Lux, 2009), p. 133.

and hence Evola's correlation of the feminine with lunar and chthonic elements as opposed to masculine-uranic values.[460]

Albeit partially, we can also include the famous Austrian occultist Gudio von List to the list of Vikeners' well-known mentors on gender relations. The Norwegian shares the views of this mystic of the 19th-20th century European pagan revival on the privilege of the religious element in Germanic women, although with a different view on the institution of Aryan marriage. Guido von List, like Vikernes, proclaimed a so-called legal union in the form of marriage between a woman and only one man and a prohibition on extramarital affairs. List spoke of the necessity of observing racial purity and outlawing mixed marriages. However, this Austrian mystic rejected the institution of polygamy so desired by Vikernes.[461]

Finally, a third "mentor" of the Norwegian Heathen Front's founder of interest to us is to be recognized in the French writer of the late 19th century, Joseph Arthur de Gobineau. First of all, let us take note of the fact that on the pages of his major "racial work" this count expresses, in the spirit of Vikernes' masculine hegemonization, the idea of "male" and "female" (or feminized) races on earth: "With the exception of the Teutonic family, and a portion of the Sclavonic, all other groups of our part of the world are but slightly endowed with the faculty for the useful and practical; or, having already acted their part in the world's history, will not be able to recommence it."[462] Prioritizing the racial question, dividing the population of Europe into "masculine" and "feminine" or "male" and "female" races, and fixing a "chronological death" of the feminized races of the past, this author moves from the general to the particular and turns to the ideal characteristics of the Aryo-Germanic family. Gobineau, like our Norwegian (following?) him, placed this desired unit of Germanic society in a chronological timelessness, when the Aryans migrated out of Upper Asia. In Gobineau's *Essay on the*

---
460 Julius Evola, *"Zhivem li my v ginekokraticheskom obshchestve?"* in *Traditsiia i Evropa* (Tambov: Ex Nord Lux, 2009), pp. 180-181.
461 Guido von List, *Pervoosnova* (Tambov: Ex Nord Lux, 2009), pp. 146-147.
462 Count A. De Gobineau, *The Moral and Intellectual Diversity of Races* (1856) [http://www.gutenberg.org/files/37115/37115-h/37115-h.htm].

Inequality of the Human Races, the head of the Aryan family is presented in full "despotic beauty." This 19th-century thinker's conclusions on the direct dependence of a definite percentage of the Aryan folk element on female authority in society are also far from unambiguous.[463] Besides the racial-gender and "habitual gender" aspects, both Vikernes and Gobineau's thoughts are akin in their view on the role of the sexes in religion. The women of the North, in the French writer's view, were responsible for medical knowledge, witchcraft, and magical practices.[464]

Having examined Varg Vikernes' fundamental ideas on the gender question and identified the possible sources of the latter, let us turn to the social role of the sexes in Alexey Dobrovolsky's interpretation. This pantheist's series of inquiries pertaining to the sphere of the masculine and feminine overall coincide with those exhibited by the Norwegian ethno-radical. A new variant introduced by Dobroslav into the question under study is the image of the "militant maiden", which is lacking in Vikernes' constructions.

The fullest exposition of this Russian mystical anarchist's point of view on the current state of gender in Russia, and especially the role of women in the social relations of post-Soviet Russia, was presented in a letter to the present author dated 4/7/2012. Let us cite a key passage from this source:

> We live in a world where men - and, indeed, women as well, unfortunately - are guided by social concepts, prejudices, and norms set by men and oriented towards men... Without a doubt, the degraded position of woman and the limited opportunities for her self-realization hinder the spiritual renewal of society, the level of development of which is always measured by the role played by woman, for it is in her, in Lycurgus' words, that the strength of a people is hidden.[465]

In principle, "compared to Dobrovolsky", the same positions are adhered to by Vikernes and the majority of this Norwegian radical's "indirect teachers." Another matter, however, is how these elevated, initial characteristics are developed and into what.

---

463 Ibid.
464 Ibid.
465 Letter by A.A. Dobrovolsky to Roman Shizhensky (4/7/2012, author's personal archive), p. 1

The modern vices of Russian society overall and its female half in particular which are enumerated by Dobroslav are altogether close to the Scandinavian case: "Abstaining from marriage is encouraged, same-sex 'love' is welcomed, as are narcotics, racial incest, and other abominations. Our homegrown 'feminists' have taken from their Western colleagues all of the most ill and unclean things: aversion to family life, the 'right' to abortion, abandoning giving birth and raising offspring."[466]

The problem of feminism, the movement so criticized by Vikernes, however, is touched upon across the pages of this epistolary source in a fundamentally opposite way. Dobroslav not only does not oppose feminism, but puts it in the ranks of a possible alliance with neo-paganism alongside ecologists and anti-globalists. This ideologist of pagan anarchism sees in feminism the "real", unspoiled "liberation of women from the despotic patriarchal heritage of Western civilization, first and foremost in its RELIGIOUS aspect."[467] The difference with Vikernes' views is obvious here.

A survey of Dobroslav's works which directly disclose the essence of this religious side of the interrelation between the genders suggests that the "pantheons" of these Russian and Nordic pagans differ significantly in terms of hierarchy even if constructed out of the same composition. Instead of a secondary role for Mother-Earth and unlimited power for the male gods of the Northern Olympus, Dobroslav constructs a Slavic divine world in which the feminine principle is placed at the head of a host of higher powers. In the opinion of this hermit, the roots of the cult of living earth, of the great goddess of life, is not only intrinsic to primordial pan-Indo-European unity, but "all of young humanity" dates back to a time of primordial matriarchy.[468]

If in their views on the mythological function of genders our subjects are not only distant from one another, but directly opposed, then these contemporary pagans' description of the religious component of real, historical women is largely a case of worldview unison. One of the most important peculiarities

---
466 Ibid.
467 Ibid, p. 2.
468 List, *Pervoosnova*, p. 31.

"detected" by both Varg Vikernes and Alexey Dobrovolsky is feminine sacrality, the capacity to, unlike men, think in otherworldly categories. Dobrovolsky refers to specific mythical examples. He endows the personage of fables, Baba Yaga, with the gift of shamanism, the "profession" of raising children, and being a "curatrix of clan customs and leader of women's initiatory rites."[469] Using the comparative-historical method in his own way, this Russian pagan leader draws into his system of evidence examples of seeresses from ancient Germanic history.[470]

Without a doubt, yet another common gender theme is to be recognized in the accusations brought by this "Norwegian-Russian pagan tandem" against the clergy of the Christian church. The basis of these accusations is the inquisitorial persecution of the weaker half of humanity. If in Vikernes' works the condemnation of zealots of extrameres against witchcraft, equated to feminine processes, takes a total of several lines, then in Dobroslav's works analogous acts figure on a much larger scale. Employing a large quantity of foreign illustrative examples, this ideologue of the new Russian paganism draws special attention to the misogynistic practices of medieval heretic hunters, on the basis of which he puts forth a diagnosis on a certain part of the church clergy.[471] Based on the textual data, the author's position crystallizes one-hundred percent: firstly, woman (the virgin) is the main guardian and translator of "knowledge for the initiated"; secondly, in the religious persecutions of the Middle Ages the female half of humanity suffered much more than the male; thirdly, the main source of inequality inequality is monotheistic religiosity in the face of Christianity in its multiple confessions.

A final point that unites these ethno-radicals in their views on the social position of women is the function of reproduction and childbirth. Emphasizing the exceptional importance of motherhood and procreation, the Russian mystic connects and even places into direct interdependence the religious and nature-centric components.[472]

---

469 Dobroslav, *Iazychestvo: Zakat i Rassvet* (Kirov: Viatka, 2004), pp. 69-70.
470 Dobroslav, *Zov Tule* (Khlynovskii ekspress, 2006), pp. 82-83.
471 Dobroslav, *Saryn' na kichku!* (Kirov: Viatka, 2004), pp. 102-104.
472 Ibid, p. 97.

If Dobroslav's anti-Christianity is to be regarded as a worldview constant even on the question of gender, then on what platform is this constant built? The answer lies, as in the above-examined "war of the sexes", in the era of transition from matriarchy to patriarchy. Naming one "event" as the source, both Vikernes and Dobrovolsky approach its results from absolutely opposite positions. Unlike the Scandinavian, the Russian thinker associates matriarchy precisely with the origins of human culture and the lost and, perhaps, sought-after original Golden Age. Relying on his constructions on the German sociologist Erich Fromm's primordial matro-centrism, Dobroslav proclaims: "There was no 'dominance' of women. There was no power as such. There could be no talk of violence, coercion, and imposition of someone else's will when Woman was at the center of social life... The mother was more of a Deity than a chief; she was associated with Mother-Earth, and around her was structured all of family and all of social life."[473] This writer thus associates gender equality with primordial, that is matriarchal society. Accordingly, it is with the advent of patriarchy, in Dobrovolsky's opinion, that the period of the discovery of agriculture and cattle-herding began and man brought into the world "ugly offspring", i..e. the state and monotheism. In addition, proceeding from the concept of matrocentrism, Dobroslav significantly expands the sphere of female activity, thus coming into direct collision with Varg's theses on the limited functionality of the weaker sex. The Russian pagan enlightener assaults the (Varg's) main male occupation: war. On the pages of one of Alexey Dobrovolsky's late works, revolutionary and terrorist women who fought against the statist regime are presented as heroines fighting against manifestations of despotism.[474]

Without dwelling on "book institutions" and his own experience of reclusion in the forest which contributed to the formation of Dobrovolsky's matriarchal-centric views, let us highlight another author of the past whose ideas, as Dobroslav himself remarked, were dear to him on this aspect of interest to us. The person in

---

[473] Dobroslav, *Ob idolakh i idealakh* (Novaia Zemlia, 2007) pp. 15-16.
[474] Dobroslav, *"Svoim putem"* in *Ocherki Prirodovedeniia. Ubozhestvo edinobozhiia. Svoim putem. Kak khrest'iane stali krest'ianami. O glavnom*, pp. 33-35.

question is Professor Herman Felix Wirth, known to specialists as the head of the Ahnenerbe (Ancestral Heritage) society. Wirth was, in addition, the author of a number of studies (such as *The Sacred Proto-Script of Mankind* and *The Emergence of Mankind*) and the publisher and ardent defender of the Old Frisian runic book, the *Ura Linda Chronicle* (whose authenticity is the subject of great doubts).[475] Studying the latter text (translated into Russian with commentary by A.V. Kondratyev) allows us to determine the common and in some places identical conceptual constructs between Herman Wirth and Alexey Dobrovolsky. Both associated the mythical "Golden Age" of paradisal times with matriarchal rule. In his commentaries on the *Chronicle*, Professor Wirth assigned governance concentrated in the hands of the "honorary mother" and "maiden-ruler" a most important role. The main point in this system was not so much the degree of influence of Frisian chosen women on the socio-political development of their folk as much as the sacred-cult functions attributed to them: "The cult was... a social, state, and state-ordered affair. It was in the hands of women. The woman among them who was called to lead and preserve the cultic order, protect the folk tradition, and so on thus bore the highest responsibility for the administration of the state."[476] Wirth deemed such a social structure to be democracy and held such a matriarchal community to be a union of free and equals (cf. the primitive anarcho-communism of Alexey Dobrovolsky). In both of these declared systems, the passage of power from women to men, the onset of the reign of patriarchy, is conceived as regression and the end of earthly paradise. The professor, like the pagan didaskal, considered the arrival of a foreign power based on new religious principles to be one of the main attributes of the destruction of traditional archaism. Also similar between these personalities is the chronological frame of the heyday of the mother-cult. Dobrovolsky has more than once written of humanity's innovations during this primordial, female age, and Wirth directly stated: "the cult of the matres or matronae, of the 'White' and 'Wise' Dames, the 'folk mothers',

---

475 Russian edition: Khronika Ura Linda (trans. By A.V. Kondrat'ev; Moscow: Veche, 2007).
476 Ibid, p. 276.

belongs to the initial culture of the megalithic tombs of the broad North Sea circle."[477]

Let us present some summations. Firstly, an analysis of the gender question in the worldviews of Varg Vikernes and Alexey Dobrovolsky shows a significant percentage of "female material" in the considerations and interpretations of these authors. Secondly, the texts of these European pagans allow us to distinguish certain segments that ultimately form these two ethno-radicals images of the female gender. The fundamental structural components of both concepts encompass the views of these alternative religiosity leaders on the place of women in historical discourse (the history of "their own" vs. "others") and the place of the fair half of humanity in the socio-political, family, household, and religious practice of European societies. Thirdly, upon working through the content which these authors impart to this structure, it is possible to identify both the common and fundamentally differing features of these radicals' views on the feminine gender component. The common features include these pagan leaders' descriptions of the vices of the modern fairer sex with regards to the question of feminism, the quest for a feminine ideal in historical retrospective, an array of identical assertions pertaining to the dominance of the sacred, magical function of the gentle half of humanity, a particular view on the internal-family functional in which woman is equivalent to mother and continuer of the rod, and a search for an etiology of the feminine question in the religious and racial spheres (predominantly through critiques of monotheistic religiosity). Out of the mass of differences between them, the most important are these pagan leaders' approaches to the problem of the ideal social system and the directly related determination of the Golden Age.

***

---

[477] Ibid, p. 282.

III. SYMBOLS AND RITUALS

THE STAFF OF THE VOLKHV: THE QUESTION OF THE SACRED ATTRIBUTE OF TWENTY-FIRST CENTURY RUSSIAN PAGANISM[478]

In the contemporary realities of the religious space of the Russian Federation, the phenomenon of the Russian pagan worldview functions in a "symphony of rudiments" that are rather conditionally unified into narrative and substantive "blocs." It should be noted that the synergy of texts (glorifications of deities, pagan preachings) and objects (amulets and idols) has been recorded as a characteristic feature of Russian "Native Faith" since the very genesis of this variant of new religiosity. If the propaganda leaflets, self-published volkhv-ing books (volkhovniki), and monographs of nativism's ideologists continue to by and large fulfill the role of informational, educational mouthpieces, then the field of the "visual paganism" of objects is aimed in several directions beyond unconditional propagandistic work within the cultic milieu: firstly, at the constant actualization of the diaspora's claims to being a movement (an in-group); secondly, at recognizing hierarchical (caste) divisions within communities; and thirdly at confirming the historicity and authenticity of the religious component of this phenomenon. The above is accomplished through the industry of ethnic tattooing, specialized clothing brands, a widely represented market of defense products[479], and, finally, through the creation and distribution of "ritual elite accessories", i.e. cult objects. In accounting for the strategic position of the visual component in contemporary paganism, which in our opinion is central, it is the elements of the ritual, volkhv (priestly) "costume" that deserve particular attention, especially the staff.

Unlike other attributes accompanying "young-pagan" religious practice, such as the drum and the "traditional" clothing of the cult priesthood, the practical and symbolico-mythological

---

478 Article first published in *Colloquium Heptaplomeres 5* (2018).
479 R.V. Shizhensky, and E.S. Surovegina, "'Rodnovercheskii obereg': pogruzhenie v iazycheskuiu traditsiiu XXI veka", *Nauchnoe mnenie 12* (2017), pp. 10-14.

purpose of the volkhv's staff has not received proper coverage in both the scholarly community and among the community of those studied, i.e., the bearers of the Native Faith tradition. Moreover, this object and its analogues (such as the scepter and rod) are widely represented in the realities of the historical past. The staff is an invariable attribute of both religious and secular power across the traditions of the world's peoples.[480] To define the place of this object in the "theology" of contemporary Russian paganism, it is necessary to turn to the few number of extant primary sources: the texts and interview materials of the movement's Russian ideologists.

The earliest works on this subject - and the only ones published at the present time - are the chapter "Completion: On the Staff" in the work *The Ritual Interpretive Companion of Priest Rodomir* (2004) and the text "A brief word on the volkhv's staff" (2008), both by Volkhv Veleslav (I.G. Cherkasov), one of the leaders of the Veles Circle fellowship of communities. In addition, information on the staff is contained in Veleslav's travel diaries, entitled *The Sun of Heroes*, written during this volkhv's trip to the island of Rügen in 2013.

Rodomir's "Completion" is of interest by virtue of a number of (legitimized) provisions which it proposes. The priest points to the symbolic meanings of the staff, considering this object to be an image of the world tree, an invisible pillar of strength, and a symbol of the path and spiritual power of volkhvs. This text also contains a practical "taboo recommendation" for the priestly-volkhv community (the author emphasizes that both categories of cult servants have the right to use this object) on "working" with staffs: "The paths are of a direction from Bottom to Top (for this reason the staff ought not be laid flat on the ground during ritual,

---

480 E.V. Nam, "'Procthenie' simvolicheskikh znachenii 'shamanskogo' posokha v kontekste indoevropeiskikh ritual'nykh traditsii", *Izvestiia Irkutskogo gosudarstvennogo unviersiteta, seria "Politologiia. Religiovedenie"* 20 (2017), pp. 205-212; E.V. Pchelov, "Posokh, skipetr, zhezl: iz istorii regalii Moskovskogo tsarstva", *Vestnik RGGU, seria "Istoriia. Filologiia. Kul'turologiia. Vostokovedenie"* 21:201 (2012), pp. 159-173; A.Iu. Sergeeva, "Simvol i vlast' v respublike Tanzaniia: funktsiia zhezla Otsa Natsii v bor'be za prezidentskii post", *Novoe proshloe/The New Past 4* (2017), pp. 91-104; M.B. Iarovaia, "Insignii i regalii vlasti v Drevnem Rime", *Vestnik Moskovskogo gorodskogo pedagogicheskogo universiteta, seria "Iuridicheskie nauki"* 2 (2010), pp. 44-45.

but only leaned up against something, for the Axis of the World Tree is vertical, not at all horizontal!)."[481] Within the newspeak of this ideological and, more broadly, worldview phenomenon, one of the constants of contemporary paganism as a case of new religiosity[482] is thus "enriched" by Rodomir with his own references to ethnographic material, i.e., the symbols and customs in which this object figures. Veleslav's "brief word" introduces a number of additions to the emergent "ladder of sacralization" of the staff as an attribute of the theocratic group in the Russian nativist movement. Also associating the staff with the world tree, the volkhv lists the demiurges who endow this magic cane with power. The latter include the most popular deities in "Native Faith": Svarog, Perun, and Veles, who "bestow" upon this object the power of creation, strength, and wisdom, respectively.[483] Veleslav also touches upon another interesting question pertaining to the right to wield the staff. In the opinion of this ideologist, the time of obtaining the *rod* is during initiation, upon the decision of the volkhvs and by the will of the gods. We should cite in this regard a passage from R.V. Shizhensky's interview with the leader of the Svarte Aske ("Black Ash") community of pagans of both the Slavic-Russian and Scandinavian traditions, E.A. Nechkasov. Responding to our question on age restrictions for the ritual use of the staff, the head of the community replied: "I cannot refer to any sources or sacred justification for such an age, it's rather more a matter of intuition that a young man looks a little awkward with a staff. All the same, the staff is not only a 'rod' but also a 'cane', therefore it is inevitably associated with the semantics of age, wisdom, and elders."[484] Proceeding from the foregoing, let us note that the initiatic provisions pertaining to the staff are presently at the stage of developmental articulation.

Yet another passage of Veleslav's "brief word" is dedicated to the place of cult servants in the pagan communal hierarchy. In this "volkhv hyperbolization", the staff is allotted one of the

---

481 Volkhv Veleslav, *Kniga Velesovykh radenii* (Moscow: Veligor, 2008), p. 169.
482 R.V. Shizhensky, *"Osobennosti novogo iazyka ('novoiaza') russkikh iazychnikov XXI veka"*, Nauchnoe mnenie 11 (2017), pp.25-33.
483 Velslav, *Kniga Velesovykh radenii*, p. 171.
484 R.V. Shizhensky, interview with E.A. Nechkasov, 27/11/2018, from the author's personal archives.

leading roles. This object is a vessel in which one of the volkhv's two souls is concentrated. Being present at a shrine, it is through the mediating-staff that the religious leader communicates with the forces beyond: "it raises his soul up to the Gods, marveling in the Spirit up to the highest in Prav."[485]

Elsewhere, this volkhv of the Veles Circle dwells on the constituent elements of this artifact by correlating parts of the staff with the "classical" parts of the new pagan cosmogony, i.e., the worlds of Yav, Nav, and Prav. In correlation with this constructed structure, the "pommel" of the staff (the world of "Prav") either features an anthropomorphic face of a specific deity (or deities) or, according to the Veles Circle's newspeak, is to be carved in the shape of *Goy* (the pronouncedly phallic symbol of the god Rod) and is dedicated to the "All-God." In this fellowship of communities' theogony, "the unity of the native gods is in the all-god Rod."[486] The "middle" of the staff (the world of Yav) is marked by the signs of those forces which the bearer, the volkhv, "conducts" into the present world. The "bottom" (the "ash-bottom") seared in fire, personifies "Inferno", the hell of dark Nav. The type of wood is chosen by taking into account the divine patron. It is emphasized that the mystical signs and sacred formulas applied to it, consisting of the so-called *"chiry"* and *"charostavy"*, should be carefully selected and not contradict each other. Veleslav excludes the possibility of ordering such a product and proposes that the adept themself directly cut and engrave the staff.

The concluding section of Veleslav's "brief word" is devoted to practical and magical instructions, such as prohibitions and rules for "being in contact" with the volkhv's staff. The following set of actions are attributed to the sphere of taboo: keeping the staff in a dirty place, dropping the object on the floor, abusing the staff and uttering foul language around it. Prohibition is also extended to strangers touching the artifact. Veleslav also does not accept compound staffs (with replaceable "pommels"). Neglecting this list of vetos, in this author's opinion, leads to the staff losing its powers and severing the spiritual connection with its owner. In

---

485   Veleslav, *Kniga Velesovykh radenii*, p. 173.
486   Volkhv Veleslav, *Osnovy rodnoveriia. Obriadnik. Kologod.* (Saint Petersburg: Vedicheskoe nasledie, 2010), p. 384.

turn, this pagan considers the correct and necessary set of actions for gaining and accumulating the staff's power to be rubbing it with natural oils under chants and spells, hanging claws, fangs, and amulets from it, and "strengthening" the cane with talismanic knots (*nauzy*).

The most recent narrative source, Veleslav's diary kept during his trip to the island of Rügen (one of the commonly recognized sacred sites of Native Faith[487]), contains a concrete example of "acquiring" a staff. On the way to Königsstuhl ("King's Throne") cliff, Cherkasov carved a ritual staff from a beech taken from the relic forest of Jasmund national park: "The Ritual Staff with the face of the Warrior in a high, pointed helmet and long beard of the Elder. The Staff united the Princes and the Volkhvs, the Wisemen and the Warriors."[488] Let us note that variations of the union of the martial and priestly branches (whether "volkhv-warrior" or volkhv and warrior) are one of the fundamental principles of the contemporary Russian pagan worldview. The texts of the first-wave "young pagans", as well as the works of their younger "colleagues", envision the construction of a "*Civitas Solis*" whose administration would be concentrated in the hands of this duumvirate. The Golden Age of the Slavic past is also associated with the reign of those possessing both "force and spirit."[489]

An interview with Cherkasov also contains rather valuable additions pertaining to the features of "the particular staff of a particular volkhv." During the conversation, the leader of the Veles Circle was asked about this object's role in the practice of *radeniia* ("rejoicing" - an ecstatic ritual): "The leader of this rite is the person who sets the impulse. He holds the staff, the world axis, and the others attune to him. When the staff is cut, oiled, and every centimeter of it is calcined, a certain psychological attitude comes into the object. Feeling a certain weight in my hand and remembering it on the bodily level helps me to enter the state of

---

487 Dobroslav, *Zov Tule* (Khlynovsky ekspress, 2006), pp. 26-27; "*Bittsevskoe obrashchenie*", Biblioteka: *Koigi v Dome Svaroga* (7/10/2017) [http://books.pagan.ru/article/bitcevskoe-obrashhenie/].
488 Volkhv Veleslav, *Solntse Geroev (Severnyi dnevnik - 2013)* (Moscow: Institut obshchegumanitarnykh issledovanii, 2013), p. 54.
489 Volkhv Velimir, *Kniga prirodnoi very* (Moscow: Veligor, 2009), pp. 174-175; *Dobroslav, Zov Tule*, pp. 66-67.

radenie. This is a kind of self-conviction, but it really does help."[490] The aim of the following questions was to determine the level of perception of the staff as a "living" mythical personage:

> If I carve a face into the staff, then for me it becomes a living being. In the beginning it is just a stick, then you start cutting and at some point you put spirit, part of yourself, into the staff. After a certain time, you come to understand that it is a separate being. It helps you, but it is not only or not so much a continuation of you - it is "not I." The longer you use it at various rituals, the more noticeable its own "personality" takes shape. I have several staffs and I go to certain rituals with certain ones: a kind of inner tradition has been built up. When I choose which staff to take, this choice reflects my attitude, my state: 'With this friend you can go to a football match, with that one to the conservatory.' The staff, as an axis, as a symbol of the vertical, might not have a face. Then it is simply a symbol acting as a kind of resonator. But this is more of a psychological than an occult point.

To the question "Do you practice feeding your staff?", the following answer was received:

> I do not practice such, but there have been cases when there was no shrine, so I would put the staff up against a tree or stick it into the ground and present the sacrifice to the deity's image on it. I do not discount the possibility of feeding a drum or staff, but I don't do this. They are not so detached from me as to need to feed them as separate beings. Sometimes, when I am weak, it [the staff] helps me to keep up a certain level of energy. When I take it into my hands, I already know that I am doing something. I'll emphasize that it is a living being which is more of a continuation of myself than a fully autonomous, independent entity.

To highlight the main meanings of the image of the staff, which "young-pagan" circles claim has a certain system to it, we can cite the seeking of another representative of this worldview, the high-leader of the Volga Frontier Community of East-Slavic Folk Natural Faith (founded 5/3/2017), Vad Petrovich Kruchina.

---

490 R.V. Shizhensky, interview with I.G. Cherkasov (Veleslav), 24/12/2016, from the author's personal archives.

In unison with Veleslav's vision of the connection between the staff and its owner, this pagan community leader considers this volkhv attribute to be a source of power, an "object personifying one's own I."[491] His story of acquiring the material for making his staff is also sacralized. As the leader of Volga Frontier reported, in 2011 he was on a trip to the Ilet River, where he detached the top from an oak tree that had been felled by a storm. Sacred to the Indo-European tradition, the oak is a "gift of nature", the magic of the river originating in the republic of the "last pagans of Europe" - the Mari, who, without a doubt, attach magical weight to this product. As in the previous description, the respondent emphasized the creative work of the author, i.e., his own contribution as the carver to the "becoming of the staff", the widespread taboo on of strangers, of "those who are not the closest", touching the staff, etc. Unlike Veleslav, Vad devotes special attention to mythological interpretations of the "graffiti" applied to this priestly attribute.[492] In one online text by this pagan, blood figures as a magical substance associated with the staff. The semantics of rubbing blood into an object of power is also spoken to by a representative of the Nizhny Novgorod neo-pagan microcosm, the elder of the Altar of Spirit community Vukovoy (E.V. Vasilyev). In the opinion of this nativist, by "feeding it with blood" and coloring it with chiry (signs), the instrument is activated and the owner confirms his connection with the staff.[493]

To conclude this brief review, we would like to draw attention to one more feature of the contemporary Russian pagan worldview. This is the most important characteristic of the "newspeak": the re-mythologization of the sacred attribute. The owner of a staff often scripts a storyline about its acquisition, its "independent life", and an array of miracles unique to the magical staff. For example, in

---

491 V. Kruchina, *"Para slov o posokhe"*, YouTube (10/4/2017) [https://www.youtube.com/watch?v=32SG_EN6wDQ].
492 R.V. Shizhensky, interview with V.P. Kruchina, 3/12/2018, from the author's personal archives
493 R.V. Shizhensky, interview with E.V. Vasilyev, 3/12/2018, from the author's personal archives. It should be noted that anthropomorphic and zoomorphic images on a staff are most popular in the priestly-volkhv community. The top of Vukovoy's carved oak staff depicts the "faces" of Veles and Mara, while the bottom depicts one of the main deities of the community: Yashchur.

his "Northern diary" Volkhv Veleslav compares the pommel of his staff to the seaside cliffs of Arkona (the pagan religious center of the Baltic Rujani).[494] The magic of this volkhv attribute at ritual-festival events passes from the pages of specialized literature "for their own" into another genre of today's pagan literature, the *bylichki* or "folkloric tales." Perhaps it is the de-sacralization of the staff through its introduction into the comic world that "officializes" the object and allows one to speak of the staff as an "established", recognized symbol which has the right to be considered in everyday life from a game perspective. The author of the *pobrekhushki* tales, Bogumil Murin, endows the staff with the traits of a trickster arguing with a volkhv in a comical dialogue. At the same time, even in this anecdotal form the staff is "magically-significant": it speaks with its owner like an elder teaching life-wisdom to the young volkhv.[495]

Given the absence of any uniform canons in the contemporary Russian pagan social milieu, including on those positions consciously upheld by nativists, it bears paying attention to the fact that a definite percentage of these seekers of pre-Abrahamic religiosity do not share the opinion of their colleagues on the status of this "object of force." For instance, one of the founders of the neo-traditional Circle of Yashcher fellowship refers to the constructed mythology of the staff as artificial:

> In the past, the staff was an attribute of the elder-volkhv. Its purpose was for the old man to not fall while walking. Now it has been 'licked' off the image of the wiseman in order to emphasize its status, and now they've added the effects of a magical wand, à la Harry Potter, in Old Russian style. In the modern world, the majority of pagans use magical attributes thoughtlessly, to show off, and nothing more. Therefore, I cut as many of these fashionable things out from my work as possible.[496]

Analysis of these materials thus allows us to draw a number of conclusions. Firstly, the diasporic group of contemporary

---

494 Veleslav, *Solntse Geroev*, p. 93
495 B. Murin, *Pobrekhushki. Kniga pervaia. Part I* (Obninsk: Optims-Press, 2006), pp. 138-141.
496 R.V. Shizhensky, interview with A.V. Temnogor, 29/11/2018, from the author's personal archives.

Russian pagans lacks any consensus on recognizing or rejecting the staff as a sacred attribute. Secondly, the "pro-staff" side is represented by the religious leaders of the movement: volkhvs, priests, high-leaders, etc. Thirdly, the mythologem of the staff reflects an associative array: the staff is the world tree, and there is necessarily a "personal" link between the owner and the object. Fourthly, the manufacturing and use of the staff is associated with a number of "canonical prescriptions." Such include the acquisition of the material, the creative work aimed at sacralizing the product (carving, rubbing with oil or blood), and observing taboos (preserving the integrity of the object, prohibiting the use of the staff by other persons than the owner, etc.). Fifthly, the contemporary Native Faith reading of the staff fits into the general system of pagan "newspeak" and is characterized by a complex array of discourses of re-mythologization. Sixthly and finally, there is a syncretic perception and semantic unification of the contemporary volkhv staff with various traditional "versions" of this sacred object. That the staff is the vessel for the soul of the Slavic priest, the vertical of his travels through the world, and a living, "nourished" being, lies within the framework of the tradition of shamanism, and its symbolization of secular and theocratic power is an analogue of the ancient Roman insignia *(lituus)* and the Russian royal and bishopric regalia (the scepter and staff).

***

THE ARCHETYPES OF CONTEMPORARY SLAVIC PAGANISM: THE CASE OF THE FICTION FILM *GUARD OUTPOST*[497]

The paganism of the second decade of the 21st century, being at the cusp of another stage of transformation, has significantly expanded its sphere of projected ideological influence. To the traditional range of holidays, ethno-festivals, conferences, seminars, specialized periodicals, monographs, and handouts in the form of leaflets and "agitprop" communiques, has been added a whole industry of "tangible paganism" represented by a large number of "defense products" and branded clothing. Fiction literature is already beyond competition, as pagan motifs have gone far beyond the narrow specialization of the fantasy genre and now feel themselves at home in the expanses of historical tales and novels.[498] The format of the usual forms of communication between the attendants of cult (the charismatic leaders of the new religious movement[499]), the real "flock" and the "cultic milieu"[500] of prospective future pagans, has been enriched. Paid webinar series, thematic lecture DVDs, the personal sites of lone ideologues and the websites of associations, pagan news pages on social media, etc. are spreading. The "classic" book industry is also undergoing mutations. Pagan authors' works are being enriched with the inclusion of recognized source materials as well as forgotten and little-known fragments of ethnographic studies. As a result, such published syncretic products are received by

---

497 Co-authored with S.V. Zhbannikov, article first published in *Manuskript 1* (2020).
498 R.V. Shizhensky, *"Neoiazycheskii mif o kniaze Vladimire"*, Vestnik Buriatskogo gosudarstvennogo universiteta 6 (2009), pp. 250-256.
499 On the question of leadership in new religion movements, see: L.P. Gun'ko, *"Liderstvo v novykh religioznykh dvizheniiakh: ot metodologicheskikh kharakteristik k soderzhatel'nym"* in *Novye religioznye dviezheniia v Rossii: dvadtsat' let spustia. Materialy Mezhdunarodnoi nauchno-prakticheskoi konferentsii* (Moscow, 2013), pp. 78-86; R.V. Shizhensky, *"Zhrechestvo v sovremennom rossiiskom iazychstve"*, Vestnik Udmurtskogo universiteta. Seriia Istoria i filosofia 5:2 (2008), pp. 139-148.
500 "The whole sphere of non-instutionalized, non-traditional religiosity consisting of sectarian ideas and ritual practices distributed and performed among people individually outside of the context of any group" - V.A. Martinovich, *Netraditsionnaia religioznost': vozniknovenie i migratsiia* (Minsk, 2015), p. 94.

ordinary readers as reliable historical material revealing the features of distant ancestors' worldview. Moreover, at the present time the diasporic community[501] of Slavic pagans has gone beyond religious constructions and managed to develop its own gastronomy and even special language.[502]

One of the comfort-zones of contemporary paganism is, without a doubt, the field of cinematography. Pagan images and motifs appear to the viewers of mass fiction cinema both in veiled (as in *Avatar*) and fully open PR-form (*Vikings, Valhalla*). Whether deliberately or not, the directors of the new cinema often script the ideal pagan world, bringing the most important archetypes of this worldview phenomenon to the big screen.

In this respect, of considerable interest for examination are the Slavic new-pagan archetypes exhibited in the Ukrainian film *Guard Outpost* (*Storozhevaia zastava*, Kinodel Studio, Ukraine, directed by Yuri Kovalev, 2017). The script is based on the book of the same title by Vladimir Rutkovsky. The plot of *Guard Outpost* unfolds around a schoolboy, Vitya, who is transported from the 21st century to the year 1120 by a magical time portal activated during a solar eclipse. The portal transports the Ukrainian schoolboy to the era of clashes between the Rus and the Polovtsian principalities. At the center of this struggle, on the one side, is the Polovtsian Khan Andak guided by a shaman, and on the other, three heroes on the border with the horde, Ilya, Dobrynya, and Alyosha, who are led by the elder Yevsey.

---

501 Despite the fact that contemporary paganism has clearly gone beyond the level of a subculture, this term enjoys popularity among some scholars. See: L.M. Pushnaia, "*Metody issledovaniia regional'nykh subkul'tur na primer neoaizychestva*", *Vestnik Tomskogo universiteta 305* (2007), pp. 59-61. Opposed to this view of neo-paganism as a subculture is one of the most actively writing leaders of late 20th-early-21st century Russian paganism, N.N. Speransky (Velimir). See: Velimir, "*Iazychestvo - subkul'tura?*", *Slavianskii Iazycheskii Portal Spravochnik po miru slavianskogo Rodnoveriia! Lichnyi blog pisatelia Stansislava Sviridova* [http://slaviy.ru/problemnye-voprosy-rodnoveriya/yazychestvo-%E2%80%93-subkultura/].

502 R. Shizhenskiy, "The role of food in contemporary Russian Paganism" in *Walking the Old Ways in a New World: Contemporary Paganism as Lived Religion* (Katowice: Sacrum Publishing House, 2017); Ibidem, "*Osobennosti novogo iazyka ('novoiaza') russkikh iazychnikov XXI veka*", *Nauchnoe mnenie 11* (2017), pp. 25-33.

The territorial and semantic center of the film is the Rimov outpost, with which the majority of the key events of the film plot are connected. Rimov is the frontline of the Slavic defense and is portrayed as an ideal microcosm. Let us emphasize that this microcosm is Slavic, whose confrontation with the foreign ethnic other, the Polovtsians, attains to both open armed conflict with the Andak order, the imprisonment of the Khan's brother, Tugarin, in a cage, as well as mythological war: the Polovtians' path to the outpost is blocked by the swamp-dwelling Veles, and in his quest for the magic stone the shaman is aided by spirits to awaken the stone giant Golem. The border also runs through the social, everyday level: the "colorful" Rimov, with its cheerful, diverse population, is contrasted to the "black", exclusively military contingent of the Khan, and the festive feasts of the Rimovtsy are contrasted to an absence of culture among the Polovtsians. The contrast between the "light" Slavic world and the "dark" Polovtsians is intensified in the plot with a Polovtsian attack on the village of Aistovo. One of the main heroines of the motion picture, Alyonka, characterizes the inhabitants of Aistovo thusly: "The people here are good and a little strange. They aren't capable of getting angry. They do not envy. They do not fight. They are like children." The strange shapes of their houses, which look like nests, their hats, ornaments, and even Aistovo's climate are presented on screen as polar opposites to the space of the nomads. Aistovo is presented as the ideal, "peaceful" model of Rimov, the Slavic "city of the sun."

The construction of this closed ("outpost") space, which is in some respects closed not only territorially, but also ethnically, is one of the models of the young-pagan Golden Age.[503] An attempt to construct such a "Rimov-Aistovo" in the realities of Soviet times was already seen in the practical activities of the first Soviet pagan, Dobroslav (Alexey Dobrovolsky, 1938-2013). In 1990, as Dobroslav later recounted, he fulfilled his

---

503 See, for example, the ethnocentric ideas of the founder of contemporary Norwegian Odalism, Varg Vikernes in his *Rechi Varga* (Tambov, 2007), p. 82.

long-time dream and broke with civilization.[504] Such voluntary hermits are a unique case, a phenomenon with practically no analogue in the Russian version of contemporary paganism - this does not fit with, or more correctly, contradicts one of the main theses of scholars on the exclusively urban nature of this 20th-21st-century phenomenon.[505] Let us remark that Dobroslav's departure from society should not be viewed as an heroically-colored, idealized act: Dobrovolsky initially did not set off in search of the pagan El Dorado in the Kirov forests alone. In the spring of 1990, the abandoned village of Vasenevo in the Shabalinsk district sheltered a whole group and several families of contemporary nativists: "When we left Moscow, there were many people who wished to join. They bought out the whole village. But it was nice to, sitting in a warm kitchen, talk about how we will live by organic farming. In the very first summer, they couldn't stand it: the mosquitos, no hot water..."[506] Perhaps, given a favorable concurrence of circumstances, Russian society would have acquired such an ecological settlement in the days of the dying USSR, a movement that is now so popular on the contemporary territories of the post-Soviet space. However, a harsh winter spent far from the usual delights of civilizations dotted all the "i's" and left most of the urban pagans to return to their usual

---

504 "At the age of 50 I consciously and forever discarded any and all 'life-prudence' and finally broke with so-called civilization and all of its 'comforts.' I exchanged them for living amidst free Nature" - Dobroslav, *"Nabroski moego stanovleniia"*, *Poslednii rubezh 1:9* (2008), p. 3. It bears noting that the initiator of the move to Vasenevo was Dobroslav's eldest son Sergei: "This place was chosen not by me, but my son Rodostav. Him and Sasha Belov from Slavic-Goritsky fighting went far and wide. They had gone through the Yaroslav and Kostroma regions and sought out more or less non-filthy places, but all of them were already polluted and civilized. They got lost, went to an unknown idol, and understood that place is not so simple. Then they discovered the village. Rodostav returned and said: 'Father, here is where we'll move.'" - audio-recorded interview with Dobroslav in Vasenevo (26/3/2011), author's personal archive.

505 See, for example: D.Iu. Kopysov, *Sovremennye netraditsionnye religii* (Izhevsk, 2000), p. 36. V.A. Schnirelmann, *"Perun, Svarog i drugie: russkoe neoiazychestva v poiskakh sebia"* in *Neoiazychestvo na prostorakh Evrazii* (Moscow, 2001), p. 13; Y.I. Zlorovets and A.A. Mukhin, *Religioznye konfessii i sekty* (Moscow, 2015), p. 229.

506 Dobroslav, video lecture from 9/2006.

way of life.[507] In this regard, it is worth noting the special significance of unanimity that reigned in Dobroslav's family, which would be decisive in the critical years of 1990-1991. It was thanks to his sons Sergei (Rodostav) and Alexander (Vyatich) that Alexey Dobrovolsky managed to settle in the Vyatka outback and become the "forest grandfather" of Russian paganism:

> My first faithful disciples were my adult sons, who adopted the pagan names Rodostav and Vyatich and abandoned their Moscow apartment to follow me into the wilderness. My sons were dear to me not only by blood and flesh, but in spirit, for they saw and felt in me the convinced, inspired, and single-hearted person whom I really was: I WAS AND I DID NOT PASS OFF AS ONE.[508]

It is noteworthy that in a video lecture from 2006, Dobrovolsky spoke negatively of Russian ethnophores leaving cities for the countryside to create eco-settlements. There were several reasons for his position. Firstly, the massive outflow of young people to the countryside reduced healthy political opposition to a minimum, diverting the latter from struggle. Secondly, the emergence of ecological settlements reduced the pagan ideal to an absurdity, to a farcical show allowing authorities to control communities.[509]

---

507 "I had the opportunity to observe over the course of many years the experience of the famous ideologue of paganism Dobroslav's move from Moscow into the thickets of the Vyatka land. Several families moved to the Shabalinsk district and settled in the remote village of Vasenevo. Back then there were still some old-timer inhabitants there. The plan was to create a community of like-minded associates and be an example to others. The first summer they groaned, sighed, and learned to cultivate the land... And the rest was history... Dobroslav told me how the families that came with him, after making it through autumn and up to winter, began to return to Moscow. 'There's no television and they aren't capable of talking with the Spirits. They don't feel Nature. They got bored, moped, and went back." - Svetobor, "Sozdanie ekoderevni" [http://www.svar-ga.ru/archive/sozdanie_ekoderevni.htm]

508 Dobroslav, "Nabroski moego stanovleniia" in Volkhvy, pp. 3, 74. In an interview with Vyatich (Alexander) we learned that besides Vasenevo, during the first two years pagan-ecologues also lived in the village of Oborona. The number of proselytes from Moscow and Saint Petersburg was around 60. The main reasons for their departure were difficulties with food (products were sold only by ration cards and only to locals) and these "urbanites'" inability to adapt to agricultural labor. - Interview with Vyatich (Alexander Dobrovolsky) from 26/3/2011 in Shabalino, Kirov region.

509 "They will fence us off behind barbed wire. They'll show us to journalists: here is the reservation, here are the pagans." - Dobroslav, video lecture from 6/2006.

Thirdly, the creation of clan estates is impossible at the present time due to the absence of a main cementing factor: blood ties. Among neighbors and friends, in Dobrovolsky's opinion, disagreements and discord would sooner or later arise.[510]

In the early 1990s the village of Vasenevo became a kind of pagan pilgrimage center, the root of the re-mythologized world tree. As A. Stepanov would remark, people were looking for a living stream. Many did not find what they wanted in Selidor's (A.K. Belov's) Slavic-Goritsky community[511], Emelyanov's circle[512], and the meditations of pagan loners, hence "people from Moscow and Saint Petersburg somehow organized themselves and went to the summer settlements in Oborona, not far from Vasenevo where Dobroslav had settled. They set up festivals, Kupala and Perun."[513] Also telling are the words of Dobroslav's associates on the role of this village and its inhabitants in the political pagan life of the 1990s: "We all came out of Dobroslav's Vasenevo."[514]

Assuming the possibility of using the subjunctive, let us pose the question: "Should the village have kept its central headquarter's position in this developing movement, how would we see it in contemporary Russia?" I think that it would clearly be not purely urbanized. In any case, the example of the natural-village variant of the movement, albeit not finding expression in such a "Russian pagan agricultural community" as in the Dobrovolsky family[515],

510 Ibid. Yet another line of reasoning behind Dobroslav's reluctance to live alongside urban pagans boiled down to these young ecologues' progressive manners: "I am very glad that they all left. If they lived here, I myself would have fled from them. Imagine that I head out in the morning to listen to the birds and they come out to listen to the transistor radio, they can't live without it!" - audio-recorded interview with Dobroslav in Vasenevo, Shabalinsk district, Kirov region, from 26/3/2011, author's personal archive.
511 On the Slavic-Goritsky movement, see: V.B. Meranvil'd, *Slaviano-goritskoe dvizhenie kak odna is form vozrozhdeniia russkoi natsional'noi kul'tury* (Yoshkar-Ola, 2004).
512 See: *"Vsemirnyi antisionistskii i antimasonskii front 'Pamiat'"* in *Rossiia: partii, assotsiatsii, soiuzy, kluby: dokumenty i materialy* (Moscow, 1993), p. 92.
513 This is a recollection A. Stepanov shared in online correspondence from 25/11/2009, author's personal archive.
514 *"Interv'iu s pisatelem Ponomarevym"* in *Vikhor'. Natsional-sotsialisticheskoe izdanie Viatki* 2, p. 53.
515 "Dobroslav indicated by his very own example that traditional folk life is lived in the countryside and that this is a higher value than living and consuming material goods in the capital. This is his colossal plus." - online interview with Nikolai Speransky (Volkhv Velimir) from 30/12/2010, author's personal archive.

was met with approval among the emergent enlightening elite of this camp of alternative religiosity.

At the present time, the "Aistovo project" is being implemented in the form of a variety of so-called "clan estates" and "eco-settlements":

> The ecosettlement is a rather broad notion: such is not only the new settlements (it always is only de facto, but not officially) gathering people who wish to lead an ecological lifestyle in a 'pure environment.' Ecosettlements include colonies created by groups of people united by a common ideology aimed at social, informational, and economic isolation. Moving to them is generally driven by more than mere aspiration for ecological well-being. The reasons for resettling can also be romantic, philosophico-esoteric, social (escaping the consumer society and technocratic world) and even practical (striving for self-sufficiency in the event of economic crises and other cataclysms).[516]

In some cases, such a Slavic "Midgard" as the one presented by the director of *Guard Outpost* is positioned not as a local territory (i.e. village, settlement, estate), but as a really existing state entity. On this point we can cite the creed of the Sobor of Native Ukrainian Faith (the Sobor of Dazhbog Faith) registered on 28 December 2000 as a separate denomination of Ukrainian Native Faith:

> For the Holy People Dazhbog 'cut out' (*ukraiav*) the Holy Land, which people called the "Land cut-out (*ukraianoiu*) by Dazhbog" or "Ukraine" for short. Ukraine is a special country, a material world filled with the Force of Dazhbog. Her special Divine Body was formed in Ukraine and was chosen by Dazhbog. Therefore, Holy Ukraine is destined to play a special role in world history: with it begins the realization of Dazhbog's Design in the world.[517]

The leaders of this new religious current sometimes enrich the characteristics of the lost and sought-after past by deriving

---

516 A.A. Pozanenko, "*Samoizioliruiushchiesia soobshchestva. Sotsial'naia struktura poselenii rodovykh pomestii*", *Mir Rossii 1* (2016), p. 131.
517 O.S. Bezverkhii, "*Sobor Rodnoi Ukrainskoi Very*" in R.V. Shizhensky (ed.), *Indigenous Religions. 'Rus' Iazycheskaia': etnicheskaia religioznost' v Rossii i Ukraine XX-XXI vv.* (Nizhny Novgorod, 2010), p. 222.

parameters for achieving earthly paradise and even offering local models of a *"Civitas Solis."* For instance, one of the most actively writing ideologues of Slavic paganism in the late 20th and early 21st centuries, Velimir (Nikolai Speransky), holds such a place to be Russia's Northern territories with their collective system of self-government.[518] On the pages of his monograph Rodnoverie, in addition to idealizing their system in legal terms, this author draws attention to the economy and the territorial and administrative features of this exemplary form of world order. The volkhv deems the main territorial unit unifying the free Russian population be the volost with a village as its central "capital" and a mass of villages divided into courts. The volost, the product of the decision of an exclusively popular assembly free from pressure from any higher authority, covered signified land zones distributed among communities in terms of the right to work (cultivation capacity). Velimir writes:

> The volost community consisted of peasant-proprietors who owned land, mowing, forest, and partially reservoirs. It was the owners of land that had a voice at the community assembly... In the Russian tradition, the voice of an unmarried son who did not manage his own household was never equal to the voice of his father... The volost community organized the self-government of the mir. It had an inner completeness. It had the right to court, to pronounce a sentence, and the right to decide all household, economic, and social issues. The highest organ of the volost was the peasant assembly. In addition, a volost headsman (*starost*) was elected for a year.[519]

Further, Velimir emphasizes that such a system limited the movement of strangers and minimized the volost's contact with the "outside world" of government, thus creating a free person ("his own master"), working out just rules for life within the society and a kind of codex of relations between neighbors, etc.[520]

---

518 Velimir, *Darna - uchenie o zhizni v Prirode i obshchestve* (Troitsk, 2009).
519 Volkhv Velimir, *Rodnoverie* (Moscow, 2012), pp. 127-128.
520 This pagan enlightener holds that the "folk artel", in which, in his opinion, a person would have greater freedom in labor and personal life, as well as the "seasonal work" (*shabashka*) of USSR times, could be a potential, later variation for constructing such a just microcosm. - Velimir, *Volkhvy protiv globalizma* in Velimir, Veleslav, and Vlasov, *Put' Volkhva* (Donetsk, 2007), p. 851.

In definite correspondence to the Golden Age of the communal ancestral-clan system, Speransky has articulated the idea of 21st-century pagan coalitions: the "legislative" basis for this project's implementation in life remains the union of the primary elements of folk religion (paganism) and popular government. "Pagans have their own political idea which is in essence based on the traditional right of the community to complete self-governance and the achievement of agreement of opinions among all the adults and independent members of the community."[521] This thesis proclaimed by this ideologist of oppositional religiosity reinforces the conviction that the Russian pagan movement must gravitate towards a culture-forming religion through the rise of pagan self-consciousness among the popular masses in the conditions of the isolation and small population of existing communities.[522] Taking into account historical examples of the life of Russian society in conditions of popular rule as well as examples of the collapse of this system, Speransky proposes his own view on the popular-cum-pagan community under restitution. Firstly, contemporary nativist associations should solve the problem of the movement's diasporicity through mastering their own living-space and betting on increasing demographic indices. As a platform for realizing such arrangements, Velimir proposes to use suburban property and the countryside. Secondly, the planned community should fulfill a unifying function providing for unity in the discussion of problems, ritual practice, and elementary outlets human interaction. Thirdly, such "Native Faith communities" planned by Speransky are to be economically and morally self-sufficient, but they do not wield absolute independence, as they are to be included in a state bound by Russian pagan communities' contractual relations or "duty outfits" (*"nariady"*). State administration is to encompass such issues as criminal law, international relations, ecology, and the

---

[521] Volkhv Velimir, *Rodnoverie*, p. 50. Elsewhere: "The way to popular rule is returning self-consciousness of the people, returning the habit of their own social decision-making and accounting for execution... this demands mass will, readiness for accountability before oneself, and inner initiative. All of this is demanded of people in the pagan faith." - online correspondence with Nikolai Speransky from 17/1/2011, author's personal archive.

[522] Velimir, *Volkhvy protiv globalizma* in Velimir, Veleslav, and Vlasov, *Put' Volkhva*, p. 851.

coordination of the country's economic activity. Meanwhile, the life of the ordinary community member is not controlled by state organs.[523] In his constructions, Velimir does not limit himself to conceptualizing the creation of such a Slavic communal "pagan paradise", but puts forward projects for opening pagan monasteries, schools, parties and, ultimately, a pagan state.[524]

Acquaintance with the territorial units of the world of *Guard Outpost* would be incomplete without considering the system of governance of the Slavic guard outpost and the Polovtsian headquarters. Despite the apparently pronounced differences in the socio-cultural strata of the nomadic community and the population of Rimov, the apparatus of state power of these diametrical forces is identical. In both cases the society is headed by a duumvirate represented by a band of warriors (bogatyrs and khan) and religious authorities (elders and shaman). This eclectic model of military democracy plus theocracy is, according to the materials of the ideologists of contemporary Slavic paganism, the most in demand among the bearers of this worldview phenomenon. Virtually all of the most famous associations of Ukrainian neo-pagans are organized along this priority of hierarchy. The Sobor of Native Ukrainian Faith names its organizations leaders as spiritual leader of the land (who has the right to ordain priests), priest (who has the right to conduct services and initiate into the religion), and preacher (who has the right to publicly preach and lead common prayer but not to hold service and initiate). The Great Fire organization, which claims the status of the first official pagan group in Slavic countries, is led by a "prince" (an elder and cult attendant). A similar syncretism can be seen in the Association of Rodnovery of Ukraine, where the head of the community can perform the functions of priest.[525]

The data of a questionnaire survey conducted by the author in 2015 among rank-and-file followers of contemporary Russian polytheism and potential pagans gathered in such a "cultic

523 Velimir, *Nravstvennaia kniga: kakim rodnoveru byt' i pochemu*, pp. 56-57; Velimir, *Volkhvy protiv globalizma* in Velimir, Veleslav, and Vlasov, *Put' Volkhva*, p. 854; Volkhv Velimir, *Rodnoverie*, pp. 231-233.
524 See: R.V. Shizhensky, *Pochvennik ot iazychestva: mirovozzrencheskie diskursy volkhva Velimira (N.N. Speranskogo)* (Nizhny Novgorod, 2015), pp. 59-73.
525 Shizhensky (ed.), *Indigenous Religions. 'Rus' Iazycheskaia'*, pp. 183, 199, 209.

milieu" at a Kupala festival (held in the vicinity of Ignatyevskoe village in the Maloyaroslavets district of the Kaluga region, organized by the Veles Circle Fellowship of Communities) confirms the thesis of the exclusive position of the "cult of religion and power" dominant in this diasporic community. The vast majority of respondents believed the most important function of a community leader to be religious:

> The fourth question of the second bloc of the questionnaire was aimed at determining the functional duties of a pagan community leader. Out of the five answer variants of "religious", "administrative", "household-economic" (khoziastvennaia), "informational", and "other", respondents were asked to single out one of the most important functions of the leader of a Native Faith community. This question caused difficulty for nine respondents (2.1%). The latest number of pagans indicated the religious function as the determining type of activity. This option was preferred by 179 people (out of 429 respondents), or 41.7%. Second place, in the opinion of this movement's adepts, is the informational element. This position was voted for by 89 respondents (20.7%). The administrative component was highlighted as the dominant function of the community leader by 44 people or 10.3%.[526]

Correspondingly, the most popular historical figures named by polled pagans were figures of Russian statehood whose policies were, let us stress, far from democratic ideals.[527]

The organizational documents of pagan groups from the late 1990s and early 2000s also abound in examples of the affirmation of the status of religious leaders. In the *Russian Pagan Manifesto* (1997), the "pagan clergy" is allotted the role of leading the communities of Russia and Europe.[528] The Bitsevsk treaty of the Circle of Pagan Tradition (2002) regulates the creation of a unified "priestly-volkhv council" thusly:

---

526 R.V. Shizhensky and O.S. Tiutina, *"Proektsii institutsional'noi samoidentifikatsii v sovremennom slavianskom iazychestve po dannym polevykh issledovanii"*, *Mezhdunarodnyi zhurnal prikladnykh i fundamental'nykh issledovanii 1-2* (2016), pp. 280-281.
527 See Roman Shizhensky, "Contemporary Pagan Ratings of Russian Historical Figures: The Data of Field Studies" in this volume.
528 M.S. Vasil'ev, D.Zh. Georgis, N.N. Speransky, and G.I. Toporkov, *Russkii iazycheskii manifest* (Moscow, 1997), p. 6.

1. Within the framework of the movement of Slavic pagan tradition two associations (organizations) are created: the religious and the secular - with the same ultimate goal but different means of attaining such. 2. A center for public relations is being created under a priestly-volkhv Council. The Council is a coordinating structure open to authorized representatives of all pagan groups. This body's representatives do not interfere in the affairs of a particular community and do not subordinate a separate organization.[529]

Despite the above limitations on the Council's activities, a quite logical question arises: Why did the authors of the Bitsevsk agreement need to divide the already weak (both in quantitative and ideological terms) movement, isolating the religious component into a separate line? The priests and volkhvs are thereby separated from ordinary community members and are gradually turned into a closed caste.

According to the charter of the "oldest religious organization in Russia", the Union of Slavic Communities of Slavic Native Faith (SSO SRV, founded in 1997), the Veche of priests is the fundamental structural unit without which the organization cannot possibly function as a whole.[530] A separate organization of Rodnovery, the Slavia Fellowship of Natural Faith, has a similar structure. According to the fellowship's charter (2003), the veche nominates people who are ready to fulfill the duties of community priests and appoints tests for those initiated into the "volkhvdom." The fellowship's council (a regular meeting that manages Slavia's ongoing affairs) consists of volkhv, public, and business assemblies. The leader of the volkhv assembly, the *vedun*, is also the official leader of the community. The vedun's scope of activity and authorities are comprehensive, as they:

- act on behalf of Slavia without proxy;
- hold negotiations and resolve issues related to the execution of contracts and other transactions;

---

[529] "Bittsevskii Dogovor (O sozdanii ob'edinennogo Zhrechesko-Volkhovskogo Soveta Kruga Iazycheskoi Traditsii", Sodruzhestvo Prirodnoi Veri 'Slaviia' [http://slavya.ru/docs/bitc_dogov.htm].
[530] "Ustav SSO SRV" [http://www.rodnovery.ru/dokumenty/ustav-sso-srv].

- have the sole right to sign documents as "Slavia"
- represent Slavia in relations with Russian and foreign legal entities and individuals;
- issue decrees, orders, instructions, and other acts;
- delegate their authorities to the other leaders of Slavia on the basis of the charter and internal regulations adopted by the council.[531]

Other communities of the Native Faith movement either consist (or consisted) entirely of pagan clergymen (such as Shield of Simargl, Skhron ezh Sloven, and Volkhvs of Rod) or a percentage of "clerical-leaders" significantly exceeding the percentage of "lay-leaders." For instance, out of the 10 leaders of the currently active Veles Circle Fellowship of Slavic Native Faith Communities, seven are holders of "pagan rank."[532]

Beyond the system of governance presented in the film *Guard Outpost,* there is the mysterious figure of the volkhv. The image of this personage is shrouded in an aura of mystery. The volkhv is invisible (the viewer can only hear his voice) and omnipotent. This figure is sacralized when the protagonist is transported into the separate "volkhv world" and is told: "Open your innermost fears. If you say the wrong thing, you will remain in my time forever." It is the volkhv who, after testing him, tells the boy Vitya the way to return to the present. The volkhv of *Guard Outpost* is altogether close to the images of this figure created by the real ideologists of the contemporary pagan movement. This "fluid mythology"[533] manifests itself both in the literary works of these leaders, which present the volkhvs of the past and future on the pages of their programmatic documents and monographs, as well as in the figures of the 20th-21st century volkhvs themselves.

---

[531] *"Sodruzhestvo Prirodnoi Veri 'Slaviia'"* [http://slavya.ru/slavia.htm].
[532] *"Obshchiny VELESOVa KRUGa"* [http://www.velesovkrug.ru/sobyitiya/obschinyi-velesov-krug.html].
[533] "By this ['fluid mythology'] is meant the numerous tales of the mysterious and unexplainable power of leaders, the hereditary nature of their gift to help people, their gift of foresight, their ability to give wise advice and to solve unsolvable problems." - Martinovich, *Netraditsionnaia religioznost'*, p. 93.

The idea of "leaderism" can be traced in the majority of works of the Kirov thinker Dobroslav and finds full expression in his pamphlet *Volkhvs*. The principal feature of Dobrovolsky's constructed portrait of a leader is his initially and entirely dominant religious component. For Dobroslav, both the father of the family and the head of the clan are first and foremost spiritual figures and only secondly secular and political.[534] In the search for and confirmation of his hypothetical constructions, referring as is standard to the Slavic archaism of the era of "Golden Paradise", this pagan endows the primordial and main figure of Slavic theocracy, the volkhv, with the necessary set of qualities. On the pages of Dobrovolsky's texts, the image of the ancient sage is surrounded by an aura of mystery and holiness. Singling out the volkhvs from the possible hierarchy of attendants and keepers of pagan cult[535], this author leans towards Nietzschean ideals, hyperbolizing the volkhvs to the level of *Übermenschen*. The latter's sphere of activities is all-embracing. Dobroslav's volkhvs are responsible for the birth of a new, healthy generation (through the organization of wedding rites in the right places of force[536]). It is the volkhvs to whom originally belonged the prerogative of keeping and transmitting sacred legends (only with the adoption of Christianity would this function pass to fathers[537]). They are also responsible for educating and raising the Slavic ethnos.[538] Of principal importance is the fact that the volkhvs, besides their traditional everyday religious function, are endowed by Dobrovolsky with the function of socio-political institutionalizing. In the works of this hermit, the Slavic

---

534 Using as an historical example of the key cults of his own worldview platform, the worship of ancestors, Dobroslav cites the works of official historical science (e.g., S.M. Solovyov, A.S. Famintsyn) to argue that the heads of families and the elders of the *rod* assume the function of the priestly caste during ritual practice. See: Dobroslav, *Volkhvy*, pp. 49-59; A. Dobrovolsky, *Strely Yarily* (Pushchino, 1989), p. 3.
535 "Priests are simply cult officials administering sacrifices and deities. The Volkhvs are a qualitatively different notion. During the Christianization of Rus, the Volkhvs were already a relic of the communal-Veche system, hermits, sorcerers, wizards, and sages." - Letter from A.A. Dobrovolsky to R.V. Shizhensky (6/12/2007), p. 2., author's personal archive.
536 Dobroslav, *Mat'-Zemlia: chudo-chudnoe, divo-divnoe*, p. 50.
537 Dobroslav, *Iazychestvo kak volshebstvo* (Kirov: Viatka, 2004), p. 10.
538 Dobroslav, *Iazychestvo: Zakat i Rassvet* (Kirov: Viatka, 2004), p. 10.

"pagan mentors" are the spiritual leaders of the nation, the main leaders of the veche assemblies, and upon the adoption of the new faith they become the first resistance fighters, the first initiators of the popular uprisings.[539] Dobroslav also says that the volkhvs, alongside the already designated elders and fathers, represent the religious nobility whose status and position in society overlaps all the claims to leadership of secular entities.[540] No less significant is that Dobrovolsky's theocrats are militant. The volkhv is not only a shepherd, but a warrior who bears and, if necessary, defends and enforces the "Militant Good Will."[541] The purposeful aspirations of this Vyatka hermit found clearest reflection in the spiritual world of 1920s-1930s Germany which Dobrovolsky highly praised.[542] With reference to the occult Thule Society, the pagan writes:

> Eckhart and his companions strove to fulfill the dream of many mystics who had contact with politics: to create over the head of political authorities a power of a spiritual elite, knights without fear and reproach, a kind of Order of the Initiated with an advisory and decisive voice in all matters vital to the Nation... The task is to educate and put at the head of the state rulers who combine the virtuous wisdom of the Volkhv and the iron will of the Warrior. Eckhart dreamed of reviving the harmonious synthesis of semi-mythical times when secular and spiritual power were united in the hands of Leaders, of Initiated Elders.[543]

---

539 Dobroslav, *Volkhvy*, p. 13.
540 Ibid.
541 Let us note that the images drawn by Dobrovolsky are largely autobiographical. For example, the ideal volkhv in the narratives of this young-pagan is a recluse living in the forest and perceiving the secrets of nature through personal self-perfection and "penetrative world-feeling." - Dobroslav, *Volkhvy*, p. 14.
542 Despite Dobrovolsky's frequent historical excursions into the German world of the Third Reich era, many of his doctrine's provisions have parallels in the preceding period of German history: the idea of the folk has the core of political life, the elevation of the national spirit, national will, discipline, and camaraderie, prioritizing the collective community over the individual, distaste for democracy, and pronounced anti-urbanism were characteristic of conservative movements in the Weimar Republic. See: S.V. Artamoshin, *Poniatia i pozitsii konservativnoi revoliutsii: intellektual'noe techenie 'konservativnoi revoliutsii' v politicheskoi zhizni Veimarskoi respubliki* (Bryansk, 2011), pp. 18, 26-27, 52, 54, 56-57, 70, 120-122, *passim*.
543 Dobroslav, *Zov Tule*, pp. 66-67.

Maintaining a certain continuity, this elder of the Russian Liberation Movement[544] projects, if not the images of the desired caste of "warriors of the spirit", then the necessary set of qualities of theocratic leaders of the past and for the present. As noted above, the place of the volkhv was taken over by the elder of the family (the clan), and then to Dobroslav's forestage emerge the atamans and chiefs of the free robber folk. The prerogative of expressing the aspiration of peoples then passes to the leaders of the "green revolution" and, having passed through the German-Russian activists of the early 20th century, reaches modernity, finding expression in the leaders of ultra-right radical youth associations.

In the constructed projections of the ideal society of the above-mentioned "second-wave" pagan ideologue, Velimir (Nikolai Speransky), one of the main components chosen as the principle for structural organization is that of hermit-volkhvs. Velimir believes that a certain percentage of cult attendants existed outside of society, improving their sacred practices in secret settlements. It is this isolated group that was close to the gods and constituted, in Speransky's opinion, the cohort of "the main guardians of the faith." For parallels to the emerging pagan hierarchy, the former volkhv of the Koliada of the Vyatichi refers to the experience of the Old Believers Rite: "The Old Believers' sobor was a secluded religious community of elders living in purity, beyond everyday human interests. The highest representatives of the sobor live in solitude in the forest. The lower, younger ones live among people, imposing upon themselves only a kind of ascesis and moral duty."[545] Velimir places the volkhvs, the strongest of the priesthood who, in his views, possess a number of specific traits, at the top of the contemporary pagan spiritual caste. Firstly, according to the narratives of this author and his associates, intrinsic to the institution in question are features of sacralization and mythologization. The story of the appearance of these volkhv-

---

[544] Dobrovolsky himself remarked: "The Russian Liberation Movement is not an organization. It is a movement without a strict structure. A spontaneous movement of like-minded people." - audio-recording of interview with Dobroslav in Vasenevo, Shabalinsk district, Kirov region, from 26/3/2011, author's personal archive.

[545] Velimir, *Kniga prirodnoi very*, p. 170.

supermen, the "volkhv-anthropogony", is "interwoven" into the main mythological system of the Koliada of the Vyatichi, known as the "Myth of Creation." This theocosmogonic myth sees the volkhvs as disciples of Chernobog. The volkhvs possess elements of shamanic techniques (they can travel between worlds), they pray to the god Veles, and are revered by ordinary people on par with the gods.[546] Secondly, Speransky complements the religious primacy of the volkhvs in the preservation and proliferation of experience and knowledge with a national (ethnic) orientation for the high pagan clergy. The volkhvs of the chronicles and today have been independent from official state-administrative regimes (both in past Rus and contemporary Russia). Having been in opposition for more than a thousand years, according to Velimir's texts, they can possess fully tangible economic and political power and even claim the title of popular leaders with the obligatory practical experience in terms of following *lad (darna)*.[547] According to Velimir, the pagan way of life, following the rules of volkhv leaderism, assumes adherence to the principles of a structured group (the flock) and the active participation of ordinary members under the authority of the leader, who is an open example for others. At the same time, Speransky conceives of the volkhvs' political role in the future pagan system in a somewhat different spirit. Imagining the "next" Russia as an independent socialist state with a duumvirate in the form of a people's assembly and monarchy, this young-pagan leader assigns a priestly function to the monarch. In this system, the volkhvs should represent a separate humanitarian institution that is not directly connected to state authority.[548] Let us take note of how it is the spiritual chosenness of the priests and volkhvs that allows them to position themselves not only as political leaders of the nation, but as its teachers. Thus,

---

546 Mezgir, Velimir, and Peresvet, *Sut' iazycheskoi very* (Koliada Viatichei, 2008), p. 11.
547 Ibid, pp. 174-175. Highlighting the spiritual backbone of the volkhv's "power/force of the spirit" as dominating over the worldly categories of a true volkhv's service, Velimir recognizes the possibility of a rich pagan church in terms of both a luxurious temple complex and well-off life for its clergy. To the material sphere relates the kind of "pagan church tithe", or duty of the people to support (feed) its volkhvs spoken of by Speransky on more than one occasion. Ibid, pp. 175, 180.
548 Velimir, *Rodnoverie*, p. 94.

in the point of view of the Koliada of the Vyatichi leadership, the pagan religious caste is responsible for determining the measures of a human's immersion in civilization. To this should be added Velimir's personal opinion that the cultural values of pagan tradition are accumulated by "ordinary nativists" through the conceptual and practical realization of the mystical experience of the volkhv caste.[549] In the forecasted future, such a pagan elite is positioned as a universal messiah called upon to shape the spirituality of subsequent generations.[550]

The spiritual leader of the Koliada of the Vyatichi suggests that the range of "priestly-volkhv problems" can be partially resolved by creating a religious school in which today's volkhvs could pass on their experience to disciples. The first step towards opening such a school would entail the unification of the spiritual leaders of Native Faith into a volkhv union with a single curriculum. Neglecting such an association, in Speransky's opinion, would destroy all of the experience accumulated by the Russian pagan movement over the past decades: "It will turn out that if the group of today's volkhvs 'leaves the scene,' no new, trained people who would be able to inherit all the experience they've earned will come to take their place. There will simply be no one to conduct rites. This would throw today's pagan movement back 20 years and allow for the expansion of the life-space of those Ynglists who teach ritual practice to their pupils."[551] The "first swallow" of such an emerging "volkhv crisis" can be considered the polemic over the timing of the Kupala festival which unfolded across one social network. Velimir explained one of the reasons for shifting the celebration's timing to 6-7 July, which would de facto be holding a second Kupala, as an elementary shortage of religious wardens in the community: "We are forced to celebrate Kupala

---

549 Mezgir, Velimir, and Peresvet, *Sut' iazycheskoi very*, p. 14; Velimir, *Darna*, p. 49.
550 "As is evident, we are called upon to formulate the spirituality of the future civilization, whose essence is partially in returning to traditional society and balancing between traditional society and the state." - Mezgir, Velimir, Peresvet, *Sut' iazycheskoi very*, p. 31.
551 Velimir, "O perspektivakh iazycheskogo dvizheniia, shkola", *Informatsionnyi portal iazycheskoi traditsii* [http://triglav.ru/forum/index.php?showtopic=178&hl=%EF%E5%F0%F1%EF%E5%EA%F2%E8%E2%E0].

on 22 June near Moscow (in the community circle) and on 6 July near Kalyazin (with a large gathering of people) due to the fact that the activities of Koliada of the Vyatichi are held over a large area and the priesthood cannot be present in different places at once."[552]

Of further particular interest is examining the symbolism of *Guard Outpost*, most clearly presented in the depictions of "Perun's stone" and individual (worn) protection amulets. The magic stone is a central artifact of the film production, the key to the time portal and power that controls the stone monster Golem. The screenwriters depict a triskelion (triquetra), a three-rayed symbol, on the "stone of Perun." Various renditions of the swastika are among the most "recognizable" new-pagan brands of Slavic nativist communities. One of the "pioneers" of this symbol in the former USSR was the above-mentioned Dobroslav. The eight-pointed swastika, the Kolovrat, became the hallmark of the Kupala festival held by Dobrovolsky and was printed on this hermit's letters and pamphlets.[553] At present, the triskelion is the sacred symbol of the Association of Rodnovery of Ukraine neo-pagan organization and the "Yar Sun" (the eight-rayed kolovrat) is a popular symbol among "third-generation" Russian pagans.[554]

Furthermore, one of the amulets worn by the elder Yevsey is the Valknut, a symbol of Scandinavian pre-Abrahamic religiosity. In discussions on the meaning of this ethnic symbol, which does not match Slavic sacred attributes, the creators of the

---

[552] Online correspondence with Nikolai Speransky from 7/7/2013, author's personal archive. Also see the VKontakte post "KUPALA 6-7 Iiulia" [http://vk.com/event54770927].

[553] "There is also supra-communal, supra-union symbolism - like all Rodnovery, we believe one of the main symbols, signs of the world and the Gods to be the kolovrat, and we honor it in different variations. Who introduced it to contemporary paganism? Well, perhaps precedence here belongs to Dobroslav. His letters began with the words "glory to Yarilo!" with an eight-rayed swastika between these two words. He did not invent the kolovrat, it can be found in the graphics of the Poles, but he popularized it in our emergent environment." - R.V. Shizhensky, "*Interv'iu s Bogumilom (Bogumilom Ashumovichem Gasanovym)*", *Colloquium Heptaplomeres 2* (2015), p. 115.

[554] "*Svastika sviashchennyi simvol*", Ob'ednannia ridnoviriv Ukraini [http://www.oru.org.ua/index.php/bogoznavstvo/oberedi-ta-znaki/174-svastika-svyashtenniy-simvol.html]. See also: Veleslav, *Slovo o Kolovrate v Iskon Very-Vedy. Kniga Rodosveta. Kniga Sviatogora* (Moscow, 2001), pp. 127-129.

RUNARIUM information portal put forth the following versions of interpreting the Valknut:

> The meaning of this symbol is often associated with the trinity of the gods. Such can be Odin, Vili, and Vé, Odin, Honeir, and Loki, or Freya, Heimdal, and Tyr. The first trinity is obvious, as these are the gods who created the Universe. The second trinity can serve as an allegory of wisdom, physical force, and ingenuity. The third variant demonstrates the stages of a person's spiritual evolution: feelings (instincts, the subconscious world), the body (the physical world, strength and resilience) and the spirit (wisdom, consciousness). These interpretations are based on the fact that Valknut is actually three intertwined triangles. At the same time, however, the three triangles yield nine angles. For this reason, Valknut can thus be deemed the prototype of the World Tree, as in Scandinavian mythology the Universe consists of nine realities... This symbol's meaning can be based on the existential interaction of the three key worlds of Asgard (the world of the gods), Midgard (the world of people), and Helheim (the world of the dead). Valknut can also indicate the unity of the three components of the human essence: soul, spirit, and body. In general, the theme of triplicity is key to the question of the etymology of the Valknut symbol.[555]

It is noteworthy that both pagan and new-pagan symbols "feel" quite freely "at home" amidst foreign religious attributes and rites. One particularly telling scene in the film *Guard Outpost* is that of the council of the outpost's elders. The aim of this "veche" is to get to know Vitya's story of time travel. In this episode, Ilya Muromets and the other villagers wear crosses while the elder Yevsey, as already noted, brandishes both a pagan amulet and Christian (?) incense pouch. When they hear the sound of the foreign object (the megaphone), the heroes Ilya and Dobrynya make the sign of the cross. This syncretism is characteristic of new-pagan associations. Despite their emphatically positioned break with the world religions, it is enough to look at the content of the main "anti-Christian"

---

[555] "Val'knut", *Runarium* [http://runarium.ru/valknut].

(anti-monotheistic) group of pagan demotivators[556] and some elements of religious practice (such as the rites of de-baptizing and naming), which can be classified as "shape-shifting." The latter are characterized, firstly, by a partial copying and alteration of the Christian rite of baptism (with the use of water, amulets, consecrating the neophyte with the signs of pagan gods, etc.) and, secondly, by their multiplicity of stage, relative elaborateness, and in some cases spectacular character of the rite of faith (the public denunciation of the past, i.e. Christian, faith) as well as the whole complex array of ritual actions including the "charms" of the volkhv, the "connecting" of the initiate to their new pagan religion, and the adornment of the new convert with protection.

Also indicative in the context of contemporary Slavic pagan self-identification is the above-cited example of the use by a Slav, that is by the film character Yevsey, of a Scandinavian religious artifact. The Rodnovery of Russia and other Slavic states are inclined towards mixing traditions. Of principal value is often not the ethnic component of the symbol that is worn or applied (as in tattooing), but its content, such as the very belonging of an amulet to the "real" pagan past. A first-hand analysis of the tattoos of participants of the 2017 Kupala festival (organized by the Veles Circle fellowship of communities) carried out as part of the field practice of the "New Religious Movements in Contemporary Russia and Europe" research laboratory of Nizhny Novgorod State Pedagogical University showed that both the leaders of pagan communities (priests and volkhvs) and ordinary community participants combine, for instance, petroglyphic characters typical of Finno-Ugric animal style with Scandinavian runic symbols and author-specific anthropomorphic depictions of Slavic gods.

The main figures of the film's pantheon, Perun and Veles, are also central coordinates of the young-pagan system. In this

---

556 To this type of contemporary pagan demotivator should be attributed themes "hyping" the consequences of the baptism of Rus in 988, themes portraying the dogmatic ("anti-dogmatic") principles of the relation between man and god, and themes aimed at singling out prophets associated with the adoption of the new faith. See: *"Iazycheskii demotivator - 'mirovozzrencheskaia nagliadnost" sovremennoi Rossii"* in *Istoriia, iazyki i kul'tury slavianskikh narodov: ot istokov k griadushchemu: material mezhdunarodnoi nauchno-prakticheskoi konferentsii 25-26 noiabrya 2012* (Penza/Koling/Belostok: Nauchno-izdatel'skii tsentr "Sotsiosfera", 2012), pp. 72-84.

Ukrainian fantasy film, the god of power, Perun, revives the mighty Golem through his symbol, and the lord of waters, Veles, administers justice by "divining" the innocence of the protagonist, the boy from the future, Vitya, when he is plunged into the lake. Without delving into analyzing the functional features of these deities presumed by the screenwriters, let us take note of the fact that such depictions of these mythological personages are, without a doubt, among the most recognizable in the contemporary pagan community. Here we will present only a few examples. These two theonyms, Veles and Perun, figure in the names of several active associations of followers of Slavic paganism, such as Landmark of Veles, the Veles Circle, the Wheel of Veles, Children of Perun, Army of Perun, and Perun's Color. Moreover, the installation of an idol (*chur*) of Perun was one of the most colorful PR moves by one of Ukraine's central neo-pagan groups, the Association of Rodnovery of Ukraine.[557] The Russian "pagan bible", the *Book of Veles,* from the late 1970s-1980s is recognized as a "source" by contemporary Ukrainian Native Faith.[558] Furthermore, one of the classifications of the trends in Russian paganism proposed by the constructors of this pre-Abrahamic religiosity themselves includes the designations "Perunists" and "Velesists."[559]

Examining the storyline and main images of the film *Guard Outpost* thus allows us to highlight a number of archetypes which are characteristic of pagan groups and the "young-pagan" worldview as a whole. Firstly, in the overwhelming mass of its communities and associations, contemporary Slavic paganism has been and is a diasporic, ethno-oriented, semi-closed association, a kind of eclectic secret society and club of interests. The "utopia"

---

[557] "*Povernennia Peruna!*", *Svarog* 22 (2010), pp. 7-8.
[558] At the present time, one of the most visible defenders of the "*Book of Veles*" is G.Z. Maksimenko (Volkhv Slaver, the author-compiler of six editions. See: G.Z. Maksimenko, *Velesova kniga. Vedy ob uklade zhizni i istoke very slavian* (Moscow, 2018). The most "fundamental" author-specific conceptualization of this source among Ukrainian neo-pagan materials belongs to Volkhvess Zoreslava. See: G.S. Lozko, *Velesova Kniga. Volkhovnik* (Ternopol, 2010).
[559] Velimir, Veleslav, and Vlasov, *Put' Volkhva*, p. 874. This unspoken division between "divine patrons" can also be recorded in the trends and activities of central Russia's largest pagan organizations, such as the Union of Slavic Communities of Slavic Native Faith and the Veles Circle Fellowship of Slavic Native Faith Communities. The first association singles out Perun, whereas the supremoteism of the second is concentrated on Veles.

of neo-pagan reading, alongside its positioned veche structure for the social microcosm of the "society of equals", is characterized by theocratic leadership and a pronounced national component. Secondly, a significant role in the popularization of this new religious movement trend is played by the visual component. At the same time, however, "visual paganism" is altogether variable and cosmopolitan. In contrast to ethnicity or national identity being dominant in the "staffing" of a number of communities, in "visual Native Faith" the regulator and determining level of the "local hereness" (*tuteshnost'*) is the symbol itself, whether an amulet, pattern, tattoo, etc. and its belonging (as a replica or according to its author's own reading) to the old or new paganism. Thirdly, contemporary Slavic nativism is characterized by a syncretism of "all and everything": ritual practices, the source basis of "Native Faith" presented in the published narratives of contemporary volkhvs, sacred symbols, and the religious "dress-code" are filled with eclecticism. Fourthly, from the moment of its emergence up to the present time, the young-pagan pantheon has been stagnant. This historical peculiarity of the contemporary Slavic pantheon, alongside its variations of venerating "dark" and "light" gods, should be attributed to a pronounced supremotheism.

***

CHRISTIAN MYSTERY AND NEO-PAGAN RITUAL PRACTICE: THE RITES OF "DE-BAPTIZING" AND "NAMING" IN RUSSIAN NATIVE FAITH ORGANIZATIONS[560]

Two of the main and perhaps most widespread rituals practiced in contemporary Russian paganism are the rite of de-baptizing (*raskreshchivanie*)[561] and the rite of naming (*imianarechenie*). In the opinion of one representative of Slavic Native Faith, Volkhv Bogumil, "The rite of de-baptizing is carried out to remove a person from those *nav*-charms[562] imposed on him during baptism."[563] In some communities, there are restrictions on individuals wishing to undergo such cleansing. In the Slavic Heritage community of the North Caucasus, only a Slav can be de-baptized.[564] If a neophyte does not have Slavic roots on both their paternal and maternal lines, then the ceremony will not be performed. In the case of initiating a "half-breed", only the "all-powerful" priest has the right to decide. Before describing some of the particularities of this religious act in different neo-pagan associations, it is worth citing the words of one of the leaders of the Light of Svarog Slavic pagan community in Bryansk, who characterizes this rite thusly: "This rite is not canonical, its performance depends on specific people. The most important thing is to grasp the essence of the rite, it is not mandatory to follow this description in all details, it is the essence that it is important to grasp. The rest will be done by Nature herself and

---

560 Article published in *Tysiacheletie razvitiia obshchestvenno-politicheskoi i istoricheskoi mysli Rossii. Materialy Vserossiiskoi nauchnoi konferentsii 14-16 maia 2008 [A Millennium of Development of Socio-Political and Historical Thought in Russia: Materials of the Russia-wide Scientific Conference 14-16 May 2008]* (Nizhny Novgorod, 2008).
561 Other names for this rite are "ritual for purifying from baptism" and "removing faith." See Volkhv Bogumil, *"Obriad raskreshchivaniia (imianarechenie)"* [http://velesova-sloboda.org/heath/name-giving.html].
562 On the semantics on *"nav"*, see *"Yav', Prav', and Nav' as Religio-Philosophical Foundations of Slavic Neo-Paganism"* in this volume.
563 Ibid.
564 http://sva-slava.narod.ru/main/faq/obr_raskr.htm

her Spirits, and the gods of Rus will help."[565] In other words, any so-called "volkhv" can present the "process of purification" in a form of interest to him, pursuing his own moral, political, and, finally, economic interests in the course of placing the initiate into a specific "ritual" framework.

De-baptism as such is practiced in the community of the Volkhvs of Rod can be divided into two components: the rite itself of "breaking the slave collar" and the "re-connecting" of the reborn pagan with nature after the ritual act. At the heart of "de-baptizing" - an act which, without a doubt, was invented by the contemporary religious leaders of Native Faith and has no historical basis - is the "rite of shape-shifting" copied from the Christian "baptism" of their pagan ideological opponents. The main element of this act is water, into which the person is immersed for purification. Then, by analogy with the Christian practice, a *zagovor* is pronounced, such as: "I remove the baptism from myself, I break the slave collar, I am not a slave, I am a grandchild of the Russian gods!"[566] The neophyte is then supposed to pierce their finger, squeeze out a few drops of blood into the water, and continue with the words: "The blood of the Ancestor-Gods flows in my veins, the primeval shall return to the Pure Water!" Following this monologue, the person sits down in the tub of water and says the following "quatrain": "Water helped cause baptism, water can also wash it off!" The initiate then submerges headlong into the water and stays under for 20 seconds, and then emerges to say: "The baptism is gone, the grandchild of the Russian Gods has entered nature! Accept me, Mother-Nature, hear me, Great Ancient Gods!" The "ready pagan" then comes out of the water and reads appeals to the gods. The "cleansing" ends with the Rodnover's "re-connecting" to nature with the help of "magical objects" (chalk, a sickle, etc.), further blood[567], and requests put to the gods for the "adoption" of the adept.

---
565 http://www.svet-svaroga.debryansk.ru/obr-raskr.html
566 Volkhv Rodomir, *"Obriad izloma 'rabskogo osheinika'", Volkhv Roda* [http://volxv.info/izlom_rab].
567 In the opinion of Volkhv Rodimir, blood is necessary to the ritual for "charging" objects and cleansing the neophyte of Christianity on the level of energy.

Another version of this rite is practiced by the volkhvs of the Shield of Simargl community. The priest conducting the de-baptism puts the initiate on their knees[568], on a stack of hay or branches, and the person is crossed with the sign of Perun: a circle is drawn around him with a ritual knife. In correspondence with cardinal directions, the rite's needed elements are placed around the circle: a candle, a tub of water, incense, and grain in a saucer, thus symbolizing the four elements of fire, water, air, and earth. Then the volkhv washes the neophyte with the clean cold water and tears off his old shirt. The priest then purifies the person with the four elements by way of a spell of request to the gods. After cleansing, the ritual subject receives a Slavic amulet (just as a cross is received in Christianity) and the volkhv establishes protection over it. By analogy with the Christian sign, following each magical procedure (after the enacting of each element) the person is crossed with the sign of Perun.[569] After the sacrifices[570], the "reborn" person commits to a "psychological consolidation" of the experience. This procedure boils down to the destruction of Christian sacred texts: "The person should dismember the Christian scripture with an axe."[571] Following this "emancipation", the pagan is obliged to remember their "deceased previous self" (their Christian name?) three times - on the third, ninth, and fortieth following days.

We also have at our disposal the texts of another neo-pagan community, Light of Svarog. Let us dwell on only some of the peculiarities of the rite of de-baptizing practiced in this Bryansk community. The volkhvs of the community argue that a person who decides to return to the faith of their ancestors must rid themself of Christianity on three levels: the physical, the intellectual, and

---

568 The volkhvs of the Slavic Heritage community of the North Caucasus hold that the neophyte must necessarily kneel on both knees: "On two knees, not one, because he was a slave of god on this earth and wrote this cross through life." [http://sva-slava.narod.ru/main/faq/obr_raskr.htm].
569 http://pravislava.al.ru/obriad.htm
570 The person receives a bit of grain for sacrifice to the gods and a ladle of the ritual drink sur'ya to commemorate the ancestors. - Ibid.
571 However, as Volkhv Bogumil remarks in his study of this rite, these extremes were typical of Native Faith only in its beginning, whereas presently many communities do not employ such radical elements in their practice. [http://velesova-sloboda.org/heath/name-giving.html]

the energetic.⁵⁷² The physical level of purification is characterized by refusing to attend church services, observe holidays, and wear Christian symbols. In the opinion of these Rodnovery, the stage of purification entailing the greatest responsibility and difficulty is the second one: the intellectual. This stage comes when the future pagan begins to understand the utopianism and harm of the Christian creed. The third stage, getting rid of "energy dependence", directly encompasses the whole array of ritual actions described above. What is new here in comparison with the previous versions of de-baptizing is the dialogue between the volkhv and the initiate, which includes the following questions and answers:

1. Do you renounce the church? I renounce it.
2. Do you renounce the Christian trinity? I renounce it.
3. Do you renounce Jehovah? I renounce him.
4. Do you renounce Christ? I renounce him.
5. Do you renounce the holy spirit? I renounce it.
6. Do you renounce the mother of Christ? I renounce her.
7. Will you no longer don the death-bearing cross? I will not don it.
8. Will you no longer kneel before foreign gods? I will not kneel before them.
9. Are you firm in your decision? I am firm.[573]

Following this "oath" the volkhv removes the "seals" imposed at baptism[574] and "heals" the places from which hair was removed during tonsure.

Let us note that this important procedure of de-baptism does not have a clearly established standard, but is characterized by variability. It is noteworthy that the quantitative and personal composition of the pantheon of gods to which contemporary pagan communities appeal during one and the same rite can fundamentally differ. In the Volkhvs of Rod community, there

---

572 http://www.svet-svaroga.debryansk.ru/obr-raskr.html
573 Ibid.
574 Such "seals" are removed from the forehead, eyes, lips, ears, and chest, etc.

are 22 gods. Also deserving of attention is the fact that, alongside those known to scholarship, the ranks of Slavic gods come to include personages invented by contemporary Rodnovery priests, such as Morok, Blud, Yashcher, and others.[575] The Triglav community of Obninsk praises three gods during de-baptism: Svarog, Sventovid, and Perun.[576] The Shield of Simargl community honors five deities: Simargl-Svarozhich, Veles, Stribog, Mother Earth, and Living Water.

The rite of de-baptism practiced by contemporary Slavic pagan communities represents an absolutely new phenomenon. It is characterized, firstly, by partially copying and amending the Christian rite of baptism (using water in ritual practice, body amulets, consecrating the initiate with the signs of pagan gods, etc.). Secondly, it is distinct for its multistage and relatively developed structure, in some cases the rite taking on the quality of a spectacle.[577] It is marked by the renunciation of past (Christian) faith, a direct, complex array of ritual acts, the incantations and spells of volkhvs, connecting the neophyte to the new (pagan) religion, and placing protection upon the newly converted. Thirdly, the entire semantic load of the act, both on the part of the volkhv and the future adept during the passage of this "shape-shifting rite", bears a pronouncedly negative attitude towards the Christian religion (such as in one name for this rite, "breaking the slave collar", and the destruction of Christian sacred texts). Such a hostile attitude and attempts to suppress and humiliate another religion were in principle unacceptable in polytheistic societies of both the ancient world and the Middle Ages.[578]

575 http://volxv.info/site/artic/es.html
576 http://velesova-sloboda.org/heath/name-giving.html
577 Such are cases in which a rite is held in front of community members, whether at annual holidays, important meetings, etc. For example, at least three people must be present as witnesses during this rite in Slavic Heritage community. [http://sva-slava.narod.ru/main/faq/obr_raskr.htm].
578 As an example we can cite the words of one of the heroes of the Icelandic sagas, Thorir the Hound: "If I go into battle [between St. Olaf and recalcitrant locals] I will give my help to the king, for he has most need of help. And if I must believe in a God, why not in the white Christ as well as in any other?" - "Saga of Olaf Haraldson." *Internet Sacred Text Archive* [https://www.sacred-texts.com/neu/heim/08stolaf.htm]. It was typical of the Scandinavians, the ancient Slavs' closest neighbors, to adopt Christ into their pantheon of gods. See Else Roesdahl, *The Vikings* (London: Penguin, 1998). Finally, we might also mention cases of "half-baptism" which allowed Northern merchants to conduct their trading operations in Western Europe.

An equally important rite conducted by volkhvs in contemporary pagan organization is the rite of taking a name or "naming." According to the already-cited Slavic Heritage community of the North Caucasus, the rites of de-baptism and naming can be combined: "In this case, it is carried out sequentially, starting with de-baptism and smoothly transitioning into the ritual of naming. Given the combination of these rituals, the circle [drawn by the priest with a ritual knife] closes with the first and opens after the end of the second rite. In this case, three treasures, an old shirt, and a traditional Slavic shirt belt are taken into the circle with them."[579]

A different approach towards unifying these rites has been expressed by Volkhv Vladimir of the Native Faith community of Omsk: "The rite of naming is a special rite which regenerates a person by way of giving them two names: one adult, communal name and another 'secret' one."[580] The rite itself is performed with the person being completely naked in the water of a river only after they have "buried and remembered" their old life. Naming is a sacred rite that is held without other people present: only priests and the initiate themself participate.[581]

The high-leader of the Way of Prav pagan community proposes another variation for "adopting a name." The person is not taken away and isolated from the community. Instead, they stand in front of the entrance to the circle, facing the fire: "The leader of the rite says: 'We grant you your name (...)! The Gods of the Rus take you under their protection and patronage under the name (...)!. Let it be so!" The neophyte then introduces himself to the gods with a ritual bowl, asks for their patronage and strength, and offers a sacrifice: "At the exit from the circle, the community exclaims: "Glory to (name)! Glory to the Gods of the Rus!"[582]

The leading role of the priest is especially traceable in this rite. In the Obninsk community, it is the priest that chooses the date of naming[583] and the very name (given to the priest by

---
579 http://sva-slava.narod.ru/main/faq/obr_raskr.htm
580 http://pravislava.al.ru/obriad.htm
581 Ibid.
582 http://www.svet-svaroga.debryansk.ru/obr-raskr.html
583 Three days after the "commemoration" of the previous self is believed to be the ideal time for adopting a new name, while the usual variant is nine days of commemoration, and the most difficult is held to be the day after.

the gods) of the newly converted pagan. Ultimately, only priests have the right to hold and be present at the rite itself. Naming and the main role assigned to the priest in this act was the subject of an article by Krada (Irina Volkovaya), one of the members of Union of Slavic Communities of Slavic Native Faith. In Krada's opinion, the priest who announces the name of the initiate to the community assumes the role of parent: "He who grants the name fulfills the role of the father."[584] This is associated with the small number of Slavic names in Russian families and Russians' religious choice.[585] The author also remarks that the sacred role of the priest in this rite boils down to "cutting ties with the Christian egregore." This requires simultaneous presence and action in both the real world and the world beyond - which, of course, only the volkhvs have the power to accomplish. Likewise, only volkhvs can re-establish the broken spiritual ties with the ancestors: "In the rite of naming, one's soul must reach the guardian spirit...People go to a priest or volkhv for naming if they are confident that this priest has a spiritual connection with the ancestors through their native pagan faith."

When carrying out both the rite of baptism and the rite of taking a name, Slavic neo-pagan communities adhere to different substantive forms of religious activities. The leading, "pivotal" figure in both rites is that of the volkhv-priestly figure, who is endowed in a number of such cases with unlimited ideological-power functions. In addition, it is the volkhv caste of contemporary Slavic Native Faith communities that composes and "constructs" these rites, devises their attributes[586], makes amendments to them, and thus further confuses the already complex entanglement of Slavic paganism.

***

---

584 http://www.pagan.ru/name3.htm. Unlike in the Obninsk community, in the Union of Slavic Communities choosing one's name is left to the Rodnover themself.

585 Here the "religious choice" had in mind is Christianity.

586 The Volkhvs of Rod community has a whole system of amulets, including "word-amulets", "knot-amulets" (*nauzy*) (woven out of an incredible number of knots and having a narrow active intent), "sign-amulets", and *ladanki* (leather pouches embedded with symbols of Khors, Perun, etc.), patron-guardian-amulets (small images of gods), mirror-amulets (which deflect evil), mineral-amulets, plant-amulets, and magical-amulets (protective circles). Volkhv Rodomir, *"Oberegi", Volkhv Roda* [http://volxv.info/oberegi].

IV. THE PAGAN ALTERNATIVE

PER ASPERA AD ASTRA: THE BEGINNING OF THE INTERNATIONAL CONTACTS OF TWENTY-FIRST CENTURY RUSSIAN PAGANS[587]

The phenomenon of contemporary Russian paganism has drawn the attention of scholars with respect to a whole spectrum of questions on the plane of the majority of disciplines of the Humanities, from political science to cultural and religious studies.[588] However, due consideration and analysis has not been devoted to the passionary element of this new religious movement. Among the many variations of the latter (e.g. religious travels), this manifests itself in both domestic-Russian and international contacts between the leaders of pagan groups. It bears remark that studying the social mobility of Russian polytheists is first and foremost of interest in terms of the "itinerary of ideas." Quite often, borrowings and mutual influences in the ideological, intellectual, and mythological domains have imparted considerable changes to the worldviews of late 20th and early 21st century Russian pagans. In this regard, one significant research interest is the genesis of the contacts and, in particular, international cooperation between a number of Russian pagan organizations and their Lithuanian colleagues from Romuva.

The formation and development of the latter Lithuanian pagan association is tied to the name of Jonas Trinkūnas (1939-2014), an active participant in the Lithuanian ethnic movement since 1967. In October 2002, Trinkūnas was elected spiritual priest (*Krivių Krivaitis*). Trinkūnas received the Basanavičius Award for his service in preserving national culture. In addition, on

---

[587] Co-authored with E.S. Surovegina, article first published in *Gorizonty tsivilizatsii [Horizons of Civilization]* 8 (2017). Article prepared with the financial support of the Russian Humanitarian Science Foundation as part of the research project "Comprehensive Historical-Religious Study of the Phenomenon of Russian Neo-Paganism" (Project #15-31-01247).

[588] A.N. Agal'tsov, *Rossiiskoe neoiazychestvo kak religiozno-nravstvennyi fenomen* (Tula, 2010); S.M. Petkova, *Neoiazychestvo v sovremennoi evropeiskoi kul'ture (na primere rasovykh teorii)* (Rostov State University, 2009); A.B. Iartsev, *Antropologicheskie aspekty politicheskikh i sotsial'nykh uchenii v sovremennom neoiazychestve v Rossii* (Moscow: MAKS Press, 2009).

6 July 2013, Trinkūnas was the receiver of Lithuania's civil award, the Order of Grand Duke Gediminas. The international activities of Lithuanian pagans began in 1994, when European adherents of pre-Abrahamic religiosity resolved to begin work on forming an association. In Kamienic, Poland, Trinkūnas would be elected spokesman for Eastern Europe in the 1990s, a position which included informational functions aimed at reviving pagan tradition and establishing ties between the associations of different countries.

First and foremost, let us note that some representatives of the Russian scholarly community interested in "contemporary neo-paganism" have drawn attention to the fact of the development of international ties among the leaders of Russian communities. One emblematic event which served at once as the starting point for such contacts as well as, in a certain sense, their culmination, was the First World Congress of Ethnic Religions held in 1998 in Vilnius, Lithuania. Figuring among the delegates from Slavic countries and in the works of Russian specialists were Kazakov and Speransky.[589] The former, at the time, was the chairman of the Union of Slavic Communities, while the latter represented the Vyatichi society and Koliada community. The scholar S.I. Ryzhakova has put forth the assumption that the result of intensive contacts between these Lithuanian and Russian "traditionalists" over the four years between 1996 and 2000 was not supposed to be limited to mutual publications, but to include "the assimilation in Russia of Lithuanian religious concepts put forth and upheld by the members of Romuva."[590] Taking into account the importance of this event chronology in our search for the transmission of worldview elements, let us reconstruct the history of these Russian-Lithuanian pagan ties on the basis of primary sources, i.e. the direct testimonies of the interested parties.

In 1998, Nikolai Speransky (Volkhv Velimir) released a pamphlet entitled *The International Relations of the Vyatichi*

---

[589] V.A. Schnirelmann, *Russkoe rodnoverie: neoiazychestvo i natsionalizm v sovremennoi Rossii* (Moscow: BBI, 2012), pp. 237-238.

[590] S.I. Ryzhakova, "Romuva. Etnicheskaia religioznost' v Litve", *Issledovaniia po prikladnoi i neotlozhennoi etnologii 136* (Institute of Ethnology and Anthropology of the Russian Academy of Sciences, 2000), p. 4.

Society in which he described his trip to Lithuania. Later, with respect to the importance of the relevant event and the minimal print-run of this pamphlet (10 copies), an account of Vyatichi's expedition was duplicated in two of Velimir's monographic works, *Russian Paganism and Shamanism* (2006)[591], and *Book of Natural Faith* (2009). According to this account, which the community's leader expounded in the form of a diary, Russian nativists' first acquaintance with the tradition of Lithuanian Romuva took place in August 1997, when Romuva's representative in Moscow, Laimutis Vasilyanovich, brought Speransky, Kazakov, and Vasilyev to Lithuania. The culmination of this trip was the adoption on 14-15 August of the Užpaliai agreement "On Balto-Slavic Cooperation and Agreement in the field of Traditional Culture and Faith."[592]

Jonas Trinkūnas, in turn, would be the initiator of founding a "European Natural Religious Association." The activities of this organization were: (1) religio-charitable, (2) organizational-informational, (3) scientific and cultural, and (4) psycho-social and ecological ("the ecology of nature and the human soul").[593] As Speransky noted, the Balto-Slavic pagan union remained only a planned project for two reasons: "The first lies in that the Eastern Slavs are poor and do not have the resources for developing international contacts and projects. The second reason is that after some time the initiator of the European Natural Religious Association, the Lithuanian side, decided to develop not only European but international relations or, in other words, to create, instead of a European association, a movement on a much larger, international scale."[594] Thus, one of the results of the 1997 trip to Latvia by these two leaders engaged in actively developing pagan associations in central Russia was the attempt to create a Balto-Slavic and, more broadly, European religious association. Despite their lack of success, their work would find realization in 1998: on 20-24 June, Vilnius was visited by representatives of European

---

[591] Volkhv Velimir, *Russkoe iazychestvo i shamanizm* (Moscow: Institut obshchegumanitarnykh issledovanii, 2006), p. 381.
[592] Ibid.
[593] Volkhv Velimir, *Kniga prirodnoi very* (Moscow: Veligor, 2009), p. 534.
[594] Ibid, p. 382.

"ethnic religions" (pagan leaders from Norway, Belgium, Latvia, France, Denmark, Germany, Russia, Belarus, Ukraine, Greece, Poland, Sweden, Lithuania, and Czechia), as well as delegates from the US and India. The most important outcome of the congress was the establishment of the World Congress of Ethnic Religions, whose declaration contained the following provisions:

> All cultures as well as native religions and faiths should be equally valued and respected Each region and each people have their distinctive local traditions (native faith, world outlook, mythology, folklore etc.) which articulate their love of their land and history, and cultivate a regard for the sacredness of all life and the divinity of Nature... Ethnic and/or "Pagan" religions have suffered great injury and destruction in the past from religions claiming they possess the only truth. It is our sincere wish to live in peace and harmony, and to strive for cooperation with the followers of all other religions, faiths and beliefs. We believe that the dawn of a new era of individual and intellectual freedom and global exchange of views and information gives us an opportunity to start again to return to our own native spiritual roots in order to reclaim our religious heritage. We are worshippers of Nature just as most of mankind has been for the greater part of human history. True indigenous religions should give us love and respect for all that we see and feel around us, to accept all forms of worship which emphasize sincere hearts, pure thoughts and noble conduct at every moment of our life, towards all that exists... We established the "World Congress of Ethnic Religions" (WCER) to help all ethnic religions groups survive and cooperate with each other.[595]

Jonas Trinkūnas was elected chairman of the congress. At the 10th congress held in Bologna, Italy on 25-29 August 2010, participants revised the organization's name, since which the congress has been called the European Congress of Ethnic Religions. To this day, 17 congresses have been held, throughout which the Lithuanian nativist community has been organizationally dominant, facilitating seven international meetings.

---

[595] "Declaration", *European Congress of Ethnic Religions (1998)* [https://ecer-org.eu/about/declaration/]; Jonas Trinkūnas (ed.), *Of Gods and Holidays: The Baltic Heritage* (Tvermė: 1999), pp. 194-195.

In addition to the transformation of the European Natural Religious Association into the World Congress of Ethnic Religions, the 1997 trip to Užpaliai was significant in terms of two other developments. Firstly, the leader of the Union of Slavic Communities, Kazakov, who had played an actively role in the establishment of the European Natural Religious Association, in particular putting forth the organization's slogan, "Unity in Diversity", conducted a pagan rite for those gathered and was initiated among the Lithuanian priests:

> August 1997, Užpaliai. Romuva's summer camp. On Jonas' request, all delegates demonstrated some kind of rites and who is strong in what. For instance, Todor Kashkurevich played the flute. Edda from Austria conducted some kind of magical rites (I didn't see them). I invited the Lithuanians and everyone interested to a tone (*zachin*) in our custom and took Maxim Vasilyev as my assistant. Together we held the rite of praising for Spozhniki. Beforehand I explained to the Lithuanians what they needed to do. They all knew Russian excellently. Even the youth, which was surprising (they watched movies in Russian). Therefore, there were no difficulties in understanding each other. The Lithuanians stood at the semi-circle and started the rite. After it there were games. Everyone liked it. Then Jonas turned and spoke to his associates in Lithuanian, and all of them nodded their heads in agreement. He then gave me a ring and said: "You are a real priest. This is the sign of the Romuvis, 20 in total, and now you will have the 21st. You can conduct rites among Lithuanians" (later in Kaluga I would grant names to the children of Laimutis Vasilyanovich). In addition, they gifted me a silver axe of Perkunas, a copy of the axe from Kernavė.[596]

The verbal part of the rite of Spozhniki consisted of such "praises" as "Praise of the great Triglav" and "Bounty (*shchedry*) of Veles", which are chapters from the famous 20th century forgery, the *Book of Veles*. At the present time in Russia, one of the most active popularizers of the *Book of Veles* is a member of the Academy of DNA-Genealogy, Georgy Maksimenko (Slaver). In 2017, Maksimenko prepared a fifth translation edition of the *Book of Veles* that was advertised and published en masse in the 1990s

---

596 Online interview with G.S. Lozko from 5/10/2010, author's personal archive.

by A.I. Asov (Barashkov). According to the version of the religious leader of the Veles Circle fellowship of communities, Bogumil (B.A. Gasanov), the history of this ritual "tone" was the following "The tone took shape in 1994... We communities, upon meeting, conducted the first rites with them [Kazakov's community] and set up the first shrine, they looked upon and memorized it."[597] Thus, the example of Kazakov's initiation and the passionarity of this leader of the Union of Slavic Communities manifest in such active work on international pagan organizing, as well as the use of developed ritual elements and sacred texts, suggests that already by 1997, when Russian "young paganism" entered the European polytheist stage, the Russian pagan community possessed its own group of "religious virtuosos" (à la Weber). It bears emphasizing again that the "virtuosity" of the new priestly-volkhv group presented at Užpaliai encompassed both religious acts and verbal content for ritual practice.

Secondly, despite the complex array of factors preventing the formation of a Russian-Lithuanian pagan union, after 1997 the definition *darna* entered the terminological and worldview collection of one of the congress delegates, Nikolai Speransky (Volkhv Velimir). Having examined the history of this term in other works[598], here we will restrict ourselves only to revealing the semantics of this notion of *darna*. According to Jonas Trinkūnas, who created this definition in the 1980s, "*Darna* has been understood as 'harmony', but in the Romuva tradition it has acquired a religious meaning."[599] *Darna*, without a doubt, is a national-oriented, religio-ethical product with a fixed point of prime in the era of the rule of Grand Duke Gediminas, and an array of typical artifacts. The latter include the pantheistic worldview, the presence of two systematizing poles of perceiving and reflecting surrounding reality (the socio-

---

597 Online correspondence with B.A. Gasanov from 29/1/2017, author's personal archive.

598 R.V. Shizhensky, "*Darna kak religioznaia kategoriia sovremennykh litvoskikh iazychnikov*", *Vestnik buriatskogo gosudarstvennogo universiteta* 6 (Ulan-Ude: Buryat State University, 2013) pp. 171-174; Ibidem, *Pochvennik ot iazychestva: mirovozzrencheskie diskursy volkhva Velimira (N.N. Speranskogo)* (Nizhny Novgorod: Povolzh'e, 2015), pp. 75-92.

599 Online correspondence with Jonas Trinkūnas from 7/11/2012, author's personal archive.

onomic and bionomic), and the recognition of balance as the most important worldview foundation. Materials from two personal records by the head of the Koliada of the Vyatichi allow for determining the precise date of this Russian pagan's acquaintance with such religious harmony. Speransky first heard of darna on 12 August, during a lecture by the ethnologist, bioenergist, and Romuva member Vaclovas Mikajlenis.[600] However, we propose that Nikolai Speransky's more detailed acquaintance with Lithuanian darna came as a result of contact with its creator, Jonas Trinkūnas. This representative of Russian "tradition" not only met Trinkūnas in 1997 and during the World Congress of Ethnic Religions in 1998, but also had more "lively" contact with Jonas Trinkūnas during these years:

> Then, in the summer of 1997, on one sunny day we drove around the center of Vilnius and talked. Jonas was driving the car and meditatively, with an intonation of phrases, voiced a proposition which I then wrote down at his house as soon as I got my hands on a pencil and paper: "When we sing our ancient songs, we lose our individual element. Within us opens that common, ancestral, tribal element that is within our soul. Then it becomes clear that the most important thing in us is not the individual, but the common, ancestral, tribal element. During such singing there is a unification with the ancestors and all of our rod, similar to that which comes after death. Hence why it is so important to preserve the ancient form of songs, without losing the intonation, the emphasis on sounds in time, and the words, whose meanings seem to be lost to our modern consciousness. Observing this makes the connection with the ancestors more durable and constant." I believed this phrase to be key to understanding the paganism of Romuva. The Lithuanians are much more conservative than we are.[601]

Some time later, Speransky maintained a correspondence with Trinkūnas.[602] Despite the impossibility of Speransky paying

---
600 Velimir, *Russkoe iazychestvo i shamanizm*, pp. 360, 363-364.
601 Online correspondence with Nikolai Speransky from 30/1/2013, author's personal archive.
602 Online correspondence with Jonas Trinkūnas from 7/11/2012, author's personal archive.

regular visits to his like-minded Lithuanian associates, the link with the Baltic pagans was maintained both by members of Koliada of the Vyatichi and representatives of the union communities constituting the Circle of Pagan Tradition. During the sixth Congress of Ethnic Traditions, a deputy from the Slaviia community, Pravoslav, gave Trinkūnas a copy of Velimir's book *Darna, or the Doctrine of Life in Nature*.[603] The further "life path" of this "harmony" consisted in the de facto Russification of "darna" and its elevation to the rank of the most important element of Volkhv Velimir's projection of pagan morality. It is noteworthy that *darna* would not be highlighted as a worldview principle in the narratives of the other representatives of Russian paganism present on these "Lithuanian journeys." The reasons for the Native Faith masses' "decline" (if indeed there was one?) to employ this definition could be pondered infinitely. For us, the most important point is the definite, unpredicted, unconscious "monopolization" of darna by Velimir. Returning to S.I. Ryzhakova's presumption of a possible Lithuanian conceptual influence on the worldview choice of Russia's pagans, we can admit a resultant "halfness." On the one hand, Speransky, as the author and propagandist of Russian darna in the form of "*lad*" (the synonymity of these terms has been confirmed by the leader of Romuva himself), over the span of fourteen years managed to expound his views of socio-natural harmony in more than seven publications. Some of these works were collective, from which it follows that a definite percentage of contemporary "religious autochthonists" share the pagan philosophy developed and put forth by Velimir. The presence of "darna" in collective documents speaks most clearly in favor of this thesis. For instance, in autumn 1998, five community members of Koliada of the Vyatichi reported the existence of their group to the Moscow Committee on Religious Questions and sent this state organization their formula of creed. Out of this program's eight points, three mentioned darna, which was held by these pagans to be ascesis and one of the main elements of their

---

603 Pravoslav, "*Shestoi Mirovoi Kongress Etnicheskikh Religii*", *Derevo Zhizni. Gazeta etnichesvkogo soprotivleniia* (Troitsk: Trovant); M.S. Vasilev, "Our experience of religious building" in *The Oaks: The Official Publication of the World Congress of Ethnic Religions 4* (Vilnius, Summer 2001), p. 4

religious teaching.⁶⁰⁴ Later, Speransky's idea of darna would figure in the *Manifesto of Pagan Tradition*, the foundational document of the Circle of Pagan Tradition, which speaks to the recognition of this lad beyond community boundaries and the entry of this religious harmony onto the level of the international movement.⁶⁰⁵ In the 52nd issue of the Koliada of the Vyatichi's community newspaper from 2012, *darna* was "played with new colors", becoming a necessary attribute of the self-perfection of the contemporary cult attendant, the priest, as well as an aim of the followers of "Bodra", one of the elements of the Slavic system of healing.⁶⁰⁶ On the other hand, darna has not become a mass, commonly recognized project with the status of mainstream pagan philosophy over the course of the 14 years since. Perhaps Velimir's reflections on the Russian pagan movement of the 1990s are quite sufficient for explaining the quietness and "calm reaction" of Russian nativists towards this *lad*:

> I should say that in the '90s spiritual ideas as such did not particularly concern Russian pagans. What was valued was gathering more and more people and formally unifying them into a single religious organization. Pagan spirituality as such was then not yet conceptualized as something which people needed and in demand for the pagan religious institution. The understanding that beyond ritual activities there is also psychology and deep experiences which should find embodiment in the images of faith, and that to this end the language of faith should be developed - many pagans clearly do not understand this to this day. Back in the '90s, no one at all understood or formulated the spiritual needs of pagans on a conscious level in any way. Religious spirituality was substituted with the joy of being in touch with one another, sewing shirts, and creating shrines or studying ethnography.⁶⁰⁷

---

604   N.N. Speransky (Velimir), *"Istoria i vera 'Koliady Viatichei'", Informatsionnyi Portal Iazycheskoi Traditsii* [http://www.triglav.ru/forum/index.%20php?showtopic=236]
605   D.A. Gravilov, N.P. Brutal'skii, D.D. Avdonina, N.N. Speransky, *Manifest iazycheskoi Traditsii* (Moscow: Ladoga-100, 2007), p. 10.
606   *Derevo Zhizni. Gazeta ethnicheskogo vozrozhdeniia 52* (2012).
607   Online correspondence with Nikolai Speransky from 30/12/2012, author's personal archive.

At the same time, we cannot exclude from the evidence of *darna*'s weak popularity one of the main issues of late 20th and early 21st-century Native Faith, namely, Russian pagan "leaderism" and the array of weakness intrinsic to this phenomenon, such as in the form of the creation of unrepeatable, "true", and, most importantly, ethnically-original doctrines with sets of author-specific literature (which acquire the status of sacred texts within communities), author-specific symbolism, author-specific formulations of preferred places of force, etc. The "tug-of-rope" among the movement's leaders has naturally made itself felt in the external shaping of communities, turning them into diasporic interest-circles unifying "our own among others and others among our own." The Russian pagan religiosity of the chronological period under consideration fully fits into the definition of a "polis religion" proposed by Rudolf Itz. The latter scholar assesses this phenomenon of early class society thusly: "People segregate themselves off in their beliefs, like bees in honeycomb cells, fencing themselves off from one another by a wall of non-acceptance of foreign gods and spirits, other rites and customs, and foreign language and culture."[608] Taking into account the weak interest of the pagans of the 1990s in any sacred dimensions for the doctrine they propagated and the consequential dominance, up to the present time, of the ideas of leaderism and chosenness, we can explain the success and failures of *darna* in the contemporary nativist space of the Russian Federation.

As noted above, on 20-24 June 1998 the first congress of the World Congress of Ethnic Religions was held in Vilnius.[609] Besides the very fact of this global community of ethnic religions' documentary formation, the organization of this event is of interest for its fixing of a new term that has come to characterize contemporary Russian paganism. In his presentation "The Slavic Worldview in Russia in the 1990s", alongside the idea of "Slavdom" or "Slavism" Kazakov put forth the phrase "Native

---

[608] Rudolf Itz, *Shepot Zemli i molchanie Neba. Etnograficheskie etiudy o traditsionnykh narodnykh verovaniiakh* (Moscow: Politizdat, 1990), p. 203.

[609] Jonas Trinkūnas, "Vsemirnyi kongress ethnicheskikh religii v Vil'niuse", *Nasledie predkov* 6, p. 6; I. Kravchuk, "Svitovii kongres etnichnikh religii", *Svarog* 8 (Kiev, 1998), pp. 7-8.

Faith" (*rodnaia vera*). At the present time, Russian adherents of pre-Abrahamic religiosity practically unanimously hold *rodnaia vera* (=*rodnoverie*) to be "their" definition, contrasting this notion to the rejected terms "neo-paganism", "paganism", etc. For example: "Do not confuse Paganism and Russian Folk Faith. The Russian Person who appeals to the God of the Sun, to the Egyptian Aten, is a Pagan. The Russian Person who appeals to Yarilo, the Russian God of the Sun, is a follower of Russian Folk Faith."[610] At the same time, the term *rodnoverie* and the derivative self-designation of a portion of contemporary pagans, *rodnovery*, have an altogether ambiguous history of origin. According to the point of view of the leader of the Association of Ukrainian Native Faith, G.S. Lozko (Volkhvess Zoreslava), *"rodnoverie"* is only an abstraction, a scientific form of the term *rodnaia vera*. The notion of *"ridna vira"* was first used by the founder of modern Ukrainian paganism, V. Shayan, in his religious seeking at the beginning of the previous century. At virtually the same time, through the efforts of Jan Stachniuk "rodzima wiara" entered the Polish "pagan lexicon."[611] It bears noting that on the pages of Internet forums one can encounter the theory that this term is of Polish origin and its emergence is associated with the 19th century.[612] In addition, one of the participants in such discussions believes that the Russian variant of this notion, *rodnoverie*, appeared in Russia through Ukrainian pagans. The direction is thus from the Polish *Rodzima Wiara* to the Ukrainian *Ridna Vira* to the Russian *Rodnoverie*. A different version of the origin of this term is presented by the volkhv of the Ryazan-based Troesvet pagan community, Bogumil (B.A. Gasanov), who believes that Rodnoverie began in 1997 with the establishment of the Union of Slavic Communities. Thanks to Bogumila's active position, this name has been appended with another part: "Slavic", hence "Slavic Native Faith" (*Slavianskaia Rodnaia Vera*). The spiritual head of Troesvet has remarked that this step was taken to specify the ethnic and religious component of the future union. Gasanov, however, admits that when he

---

610 Petkova, *Neoiazychestvo v sovremennoi evropeiskoi kul'ture*, p. 29.
611 Online interview with G.S. Lozko from 5/10/2010, author's personal archive.
612 "Slavianskoe Rodnoverie", *Tonkii Mir* [http://tonkiimir.ru/topic1853-60.html] (2010).

created this term he was oriented towards the Polish tradition. The transformation of *rodnaia vera* into the definitional rodnoverie, in Bogumil's opinion, took place at the turn of the millennium. The term was introduced into the contemporary Russian pagan milieu by the volkhv of the Rodoliubie community, Veleslav (I.G. Cherkasov).[613] Presently, the term *rodnoverie* is also actively spreading in the scholarly world.[614]

One final development deserving recognition, whose causation is to be sought in the founding and subsequent functioning of the World Congress of Ethnic Religious, was the opening of yet another ethno-oriented pagan organization, the Ancestral Slavic Veche. The first assembly of the Ancestral Slavic Veche's members took place in Kiev in 2003 and its most recent, eighth veche was held in Saint Petersburg in 2011. As one of the leaders of the Veche, Buyan (P.V. Tulaev), has remarked: "The Ancestral Slavic Community arose as an alternative and supplement to the World Congress of Ethnic Religions, at whose core lies the juridical principle of the equality of peoples. We proceed from ancestral clan logic."[615]

Thus, Russian-Lithuanian contacts and the international pagan projects of the 1990s have had a number of "visible" effects for, in the very least, the Russian side. The results of this cooperation which can be observed in the present version of Russian polytheism also affected both the organizational and sacred sides of this worldview phenomenon. The most important of these include: firstly, the entry of Russian "young pagans"

---

613 Online correspondence with B.A. Gasanov from 29/1/2017, author's personal archive.
614 A.V. Gaidukov, *"Slavianskoe novoe iazychestvo v Rossii: issledovaniia"* in E.S. Elbakian, S.I. Ivanenko, I.Ia. Kanterov, and M.N. Sitnikov (eds.), *Novye religii v Rossii: dvatsat' let spustia. Materialy Mezhdunarodnoi nauchno-prakticheskoi konferentsii* [Moscow: Dom Zhurnalista, 14 December 2012] (Moscow: Drevo zhizni, 2013); R.V. Shizhensky, *"Interv'iu s chlenom obshchestva religiovedov Finliandii Kaarinoi Aitamurto"*, Novostnaia lenta. Issledovatel'skaia laboratoriia 'NRD v sovremennoi Rossii i stranakh Evropy [http://nrdlab.ru/posts/1006557]; I.A. Bessonov, *"Kalendarnye prazdniki sovremennykh ekoposelenii (na materiale subkul'tury 'anastasievtsev')"* in *Kompleksnye issledovaniia traditsionnoi kul'tury v postsovetskii period 4* (Moscow: State Republican Center for Russian Folklore, 2011), p. 405.
615 *"Real'nye dostizheniia i problemy razvitiia rodnoi very v slavianskikh stranakh"*, *Slava! Vestnik Rodovogo Slavianskogo Vecha* (Moscow: Atenei), p. 3.

onto the European "religious scene" and their leading position in the development of the provisions of the European Natural Religious Association; secondly, the European pagan recognition of the ritual practice of the then emergent Russian priestly-volkhv "caste"; thirdly, proceeding from the second point, at the time of the presentation of this ritual stock in Lithuania, the leaders of contemporary nativism were already actively developing the theoretical and practical foundations of their constructed religiosity; fourthly, acquaintance with Lithuanian pagan tradition and the reconceptualization of the latter through the peculiarities of an author-specific worldview allowed for the development of one of the first models of Russian pagan morality in Russia; and fifthly, it was at the Lithuanian congress that the term "Native Faith" (*rodnaia vera*, subsequently *rodnoverie*) was promulgated, since which it has become the recognized definition of the Russian pagan community in Russia.

***

THE SLAVIC RELIGIOUS ALTERNATIVE: THE SLOVENIAN VARIANT[616]

One of the worldview artifacts which European society has inherited from the 20th century is the phenomenon of the modern pagan revival. At the present time, "indigenous religious" movements are represented in the "Old World" by a whole number of currents in one way or another concerned with all the nodal spheres of human community life - from world ecology to the political structure of specific states. This striving for a shift in worldview priorities based on the reconstruction of traditional beliefs, coupled with the proselytes of paganism's own constructs as well as parallel or even alternative religious and socio-political systems, has generated a certain resonance in European society. One vivid example of the "new life of the old gods" is the inclusion of the Asatru and Druidist movements into the orbit of "official religiosity."[617] According to Internet resources used by both opponents and representatives of contemporary paganism, the 20th-21st-century Slavic version of nativism occupies one of the leading positions in this pan-European movement. Russian historiography on this subject numbers several hundred publications devoted to analyzing the peculiarities of the formation and the development of this alternative religiosity in the East-Slavic bloc of Russia, Ukraine, and Belarus. Besides the natural, traditional research aims, scholarly and publicistic interest has been conditioned by the longevity and varying diversity of Slavic paganism which, since its rebirth (conventionally dated to the early 20th century), has gone far beyond the bounds of "pure" religiosity. However, the other territorial pole of Slavic "*ethnica*" has not received proper coverage in specialist literature, though it undoubtedly deserves the closest attention by virtue of its uniqueness as well as its worldview parallelism with the pagan movements of fraternal peoples and European folk-religiosity in general.

---

616   Article first published in the conference volume *Religiia - Nauka - Obshchestvo: problemy i perspektivy vzaimodeistviia* [Religion - Science - Society: Problems and Prospects of Interaction] (Penza: Sotsiosfera Scientific-Publishing Center, 2011).
617   See, for instance, the Scandinavian Travel Agency's entry "Iceland-Religion" [http://scantravel.ru/countries/iceland/about/1803.html].

Alongside the rather well-known associations of Moscow and Kiev's "metropolitan pagans", the urban variant of this autochthonous worldview is also represented in its Balkan variant by the Svetovid community of Ljubljana, the capital of the Republic of Slovenia. Information on the development of this 21st-century "Alpine paganism" has been obtained in the course of online correspondences with the leader of this community, the historian and cultural scholar Matjaž Vratislav Anžur.[618] According to this Slovenian pagan leader, at the present time the organization counts 100 people of differing ages and social statuses.[619] This figure is rather impressive given that the average membership of such communities of pre-Abrahamic religiosity rarely exceeds 10-15 proselytes. Comparing the number of pagans of Svetovid with the total population of Slovenia (2,053,355 people), we have an altogether considerable percentage of nativists for such a small European country. Despite its young age (Svetovid appeared in 2005), the community plays an active part in both the domestic-Slovenian and international pagan movement. In particular, Svetovid is a member of the Slovenian movement of "Old Believers", *Staroverci*, the Ancestral Slavic Veche association of Slavic pagans, and other associations.[620] The community has its

---

[618] Online interview with Matjaž Vratislav Anžur from 22/3/2011, author's personal archive.

[619] Without a doubt, the tendency towards preserving and transmitting the contemporary tradition from generation to generation should be seen as novel in the new pagan construct. If at the dawn of its emergence in Russia in the late 1970s the Russian alternatively religiosity was characterized by a colorful individualism, and in the 1980s-'90s by the creation of communities and unions of pagans "in terms of interest", then in contemporary conditions a portion of Russian as well as foreign nativist associations have opted for building communities on "family" and "clan" grounds. One vivid example of this type of organization is the Ryazan community Troesvet, whose core is composed of seven families.

[620] The Ancestral Slavic Veche (*Rodovoe Slavianskoe Veche*) is an association of pagans from Slavic countries. The first assembly of the ASV's members was held in Kiev in 2003 and the recent, 8th Veche was held in Saint Petersburg in 2011. The sixth congress took place in Slovenia. The Svetovid community acted as the organizer of this event. One of the leaders of the Ancestral Slavic Veche, Buyan (P.V. Tulaev), has remarked: "The Ancestral Slavic Community arose as an alternative and supplement to the World Congress of Ethnic Religions, at whose core lies the juridical principle of the equality of peoples. We proceed from an ancestral clan logic." - Buyan, *"Real'nye dostizheniia i problemy razvitiia rodnoi very v slavianskikh stranakh"* in Slava! *Vestnik Rodovogo Slavianskogo Vecha* (Moscow: Ateney), p. 3.

own website and the leader of the organization has published a number of print works.[621]

Among the striking features of this movement, we should first and foremost refer to the very fact of Svetovid's establishment, which arose partly due to the external factor of pagan influence from abroad. The catalyst accelerating the emergence of "contemporary paganism *à la Sloveniene*" was the Association of Rodnovery of Ukraine.[622] Both the source basis and etymological legend, including the self-designation of these adherents of indigenous religiosity, fall into the sphere of borrowings.[623] In response to the question of whether the community has (or does not have) "sacred texts", Anžur singled out the Rig-Veda and *Book of Veles*[624] as

---

[621] See Triglav, *"Religozni pomen pri Slovanih"* in Matjaž Anžur (dd.), *Zbornik prispevkov šeste mednarodne conference "Slovanska dediščina" na gradu Struga od 8. do 9. avgusta 2009* (Ljubljana: Jutro, 2010); Matjaž Anžur, *Vojaška zgodovina bodočih slovanov* (Ljubljana: Jutro, 2007). The Internet page of the Staroverci is http://www.ajdi.org/.

[622] In correspondence, Svetovid's leader confirmed that it was the Ukrainian variant of "indigenous religion" that has had a high degree of influence on 21st century Slovenian pagans.

[623] The term rodnoverie and the derivative self-designation of a portion of contemporary pagans, rodnovery, have an altogether ambiguous history of origin. According to the point of view of the leader of the Association of Ukrainian Native Faith, G.S. Lozko (Volkhvess Zoreslava), *"rodnoverie"* is only an abstraction, a scientific form of the term *rodnaia vera*. The notion of *"ridna vira"* was first used by the founder of modern Ukrainian paganism, V. Shayan, in his religious seeking at the beginning of the previous century. At virtually the same time, through the efforts of Jan Stachniuk, *"rodzima wiara"* entered the Polish "pagan lexicon" (- online interview with G.S. Lozko, 5/10/2010, author's personal archive). A different version of the origin of this term is presented by the volkhv of the Ryazan-based Troesvet pagan community, Bogumil (B.A. Gasanov), who believes that Rodnoverie began in 1997 with the establishment of the Union of Slavic Communities. Thanks to Bogumila's active position, this name has been appended with another part: "Slavic", hence "Slavic Native Faith" (*Slavianskaia Rodnaia Vera*). The spiritual head of Troesvet has remarked that this step was taken to specify the ethnic and religious component of the future union. B.A. Gasanov, however, admits that when he created this term he was oriented towards the Polish tradition. The transformation of *rodnaia vera* into the definitional *rodnoverie*, in Bogumil's opinion, took place at the turn of the millennium. The term was introduced into the contemporary Russian pagan milieu by the volkhv of the Rodoliubie community, Veleslav (I.G. Cherkasov) (-audio interview with Bogumil in Ryazan, 13/8/2011, author's personal archive). See "The Slavic Religious Alternative: The Slovenian Variant" in this volume. A definite victory of these adherents of pre-Abrahamic religiosity is the use (and recognition) of this definition by the scholarly community. See, for example, I.A. Bessonov, *Kalendarnye prazdniki sovremennykh ekoposelenii (na materiale subkul'tury 'anastasievtsev')"* in *Kompleksnye issledovaniia traditsionnoi kul'tury v postsovetskii period 14* (Moscow: State Republican Center of Russian Folklore, 2011), p. 405.

[624] *"The Rig Veda* and the *Book of Veles* are our BIBLE" - online interview with Matjaž Vratislav Anžur from 25/5/2011, author's personal archive.

works which fall into the category of foundational narratives. If the historicity of the first source, the "book of hymns", is quite obvious, then the *"Book of Veles"* has no such status, as it is, according to the conclusions of a range of Humanities scholarship, a forgery.[625] Ideas of "Aryandom" and Vedic tradition became altogether widespread in the Slavic pagan milieu in the mid-20th century. The "sensational" finds of "the most ancient Slavic narratives" also belong to the same period. However, if Russian alternative religiosity has mostly parted ways with or reduced its borrowing "from the outside", has since the end of the last century focused its efforts instead on searching for domestic pre-Abrahamic roots, and has defined its attitude towards pseudo-sources, then the Rodnovery of Ukraine have continued the quest for their proto-roots in the European and, more broadly, "pan-Aryan" world. The *Book of Veles* is widely advertised, regularly reissued in "new" versions, and is actively used in ritual practice.[626]

The worldview model of the "Old Believers" of Svetovid has been constructed in accordance with this choice of sources. In particular, at the core of the social structure of Anžur's community lies the Vedic principle of the four castes, "translated" into Slovenian as the *barači, kasazi, vaščani,* and *šodre* (the volkhvs / brahmans, knights / Kshatriyas, masters / vaishya, and laborers / shudras). The terminology and basic elements of the above-considered works are actively used in Slovenian "Native Faith philosophy." Considering the integration of man into the natural order, taking care of one's health, and active creativity to be the most important poles of pagan life, the leader of Svetovid focuses on the cyclical

---

[625] See, for example, *Chto dumaiut uchenye o 'Velesovoi knige'* (Saint Petersburg: Nauka, 2004). In addition, the fact should be noted that the first publisher of the *Book of Veles* in the USSR, V.I. Skurlatov (published in 1976 in the weekly *Nedelia*), considered the tablets to be forgeries since the moment he discovered them. In his words: "This source of dubious origin should be considered as an impulse for studying our distant past" - recorded interview with V.I. Skurlatov (Moscow, 25/1/2009, author's personal archive).

[626] One of the most zealous defenders and popularizers of the *Book of Veles* in contemporary East-Slavic paganism is the head of the Association of Rodnovery of Ukraine, the Volkhvess Zoreslava (G.S. Lozko). See: G.S. Lozko, *Velesova Kniga - Volkhovnik* (Ternopol: Mandrivets, 2010). Among the Russian Rodnovery milieu, a similar position is held by the spiritual leader of the Ancestral Union of Slavs (*Rodovyi Soiuz Slavian*), Volkhv Slaver (G.Z. Maksimenko). See: G.Z. Maksimenko, *Velesova Kniga. Vedy ob uklade zhizni i istoke very slavian* (Moscow: Akademiia upravleniia, 2008).

spirality of being. In his opinion, by the end of one's life (which is only one of multiple periods, in Anžur's interpretation), a pagan should be physically and spiritually healthy. Emotional mood is held to be a factor capable of exerting a beneficial influence on the well-being of both the individual and society as a whole. In the opinion of this pagan ideologist, negative emotions have not been intrinsic to the Slavic ethnos since its origination. By taking the path of a negative mood, a person undermines the sense of harmony in society and the right to mental and physical health. Emphasizing the social component, Matjaž Anžur proposes to reintegrate traditional Slavic values into the modern world, such as through hospitality, respect and a dignified approach to the surrounding environment, etc. Physical violence is not acceptable, except in cases of self-defense. Also relating to the pan-Slavic "pagan key" is the Slovenian "Rodnovery" approach to the modern ills of society. Alcohol, narcotics, gluttony, sex, television, the Internet, and gambling are seen as the "horsemen of the apocalypse", the main problematic fields of the modern world. However, while holding the effects of these minuses on the individual's soul and state to be ruinous, the "Old Believers" nonetheless leave a person with the right to choose, believing that to one extent or another everyone must undergo such an experiential test.

Recognizing a "diversity of worlds" and the existence of "this" world and "that" world, this pagan ideologist uses a conceptual apparatus to designate these categories whose roots go back to the above-named Book of Veles. For instance, Anžur calls the present world *"Yav"* and the world beyond *"Nav."* The alleged founding author of these constructs, which to this day remain core notions of reconstructed Slavic paganism, was Miroliubov. Even in the works of this person who gave the world the *Book of Veles*, however, the origin of these terms and their real existence is a matter of doubt.[627]

In these Slovenian "new pagans'" conception of the universe and the place of man in the surrounding world, it bears taking note of the presence of provisions that are common and largely identical to those peculiar to the whole reconstructed and

---

627 See Roman Shizhensky, *"Yav', Prav',* and *Nav'* as Religio-Philosophical Foundations of Slavic Neo-Paganism" in this volume.

constructed East-Slavic pagan movement. The most important elements of this worldview-arrangement include the deification of nature in all of its diversity and the dominance of a synergetic approach in accordance with which, firstly, the human individual is recognized as a parcel-unit of the universe, and, secondly, the whole world harbors energies bound together in a single energy field.[628] Proceeding from this, the theological explorations of Svetovid are built on recognizing the gods to be elements, components of one single deity - the universe. In their deification of the planet's natural phenomena, such as water, earth, wind, fire, thunder, lightning, etc., as well as the cosmonyms, the sun and moon, these Slovenian "Rodnovery" cite texts from the Vedas as well as the experience of their distant ancestors.[629] In accordance with their foundational thesis on the divinity of nature, the Slovenian pagans approach the planet's living organisms (particularly mammals) from a standpoint of equal partnership. These nativists oppose characterizing the animal world as an economic resource alone, and they are concerned about the decline in the number of species and humanity's encroachment upon the natural habitats. They also consider the use of animals as medical test-samples to be unacceptable.

Of considerable interest are Matjaž Anžur's conceptions of the social world and the array of problems associated with society. This pagan proposes to take the above-cited Vedic principle, taking into account changes in the natural, social, and technological

---

628 For greater clarity, Anžur's postulation of a kind of single world energy field might be compared to the "Eywa" life force connecting the characters of the fictional planet Pandora as created by director James Cameron's for his movie "Avatar." In the opinion of a number of pagan leaders, the release of "Avatar" in 2010 ought to be seen as one of the important landmarks of the spread of pagan views in the 21st century. See: D.A. Gavrilov (Volkhv Yggeld), *Materialy interv'iu in Indigenous Religions: 'Rus' Iazycheskaia': Etnicheskaia religioznost' v Rossii i Ukraine XX-XXI vv.* (Nizhny Novgorod: Nizhny Novgorod State Pedagogical University, 2010), p. 109.

629 To designate this single unifying force or energy, Slovenian pagans use the special term *Vsežar*. This term is associated with another notion, Vsezapis, or a place of force within the *Vsežar*. The Vsezapis unites the past, future, and present. The parallelism of Slavic pagan religion figures in the names of some holidays celebrated by the proselytes of Svetovid. The main "holy days" of the community are Bozich-Svarozhich (21 December), Yarnik-Yarilo (21 March), Kresnik-Kupala (23 June), and Mara-Morana (23 September) - in other words, the traditional days of the equinox and summer and winter solstices.

spheres, as the basis of social structure. The pagan leader rejects existing models of state structure. Deliberating on his view of the Western type of political structure, democracy, Anžur wrote in an interview reply: "We are skeptical of democracy, because with the power of parties arises corruption and 'cronyism.'" In turn, the head of Svetovid proposes to replace existing political realities with his own "pagan project" entailing minimum and maximum programs. In the long-term perspective, this community of Slovenian pagans aims for the establishment of an updated model of the Vedic social and political system. The main goal for the near future is reforming the existing political system along ethical lines.[630] Although the nuances of their program did not make it into the clarifying discussion, attention is to be drawn to these "Old Believers'" very orientation towards changing (or breaking?) the extant order. On the one hand, their course for political and social renewal and their unwillingness to live in the present reality certainly absolve these Slovenian nativists (and, overall, the whole Indo-European variation of adherents of autochthonous religiosity) of the slightest features of the mainstream. On the other hand, such allows us to speak of a predominance in this current of a diasporic element allowing the "Old Believers" to build their own small, separate state within their community. In addition, their voluntary isolation and the presence of a program and potential steps also absolve Svetovid of the scholarly "label" of escapism. Matjaž Anžur's followers do not run away into a fantasy world, but strive to build one in reality. Touching upon the economic

---

[630] The question of morality and ethical ideals is one of the foundational components shaping the philosophical basis of Slavic paganism. In his attempt to "reanimate" and return the moral element to social institutions, Anžur shares the position of one of the oldest adherents of the Russian variant of the movement, Dobroslav (Alexey Dobrovolsky), for whom "nature-loving ethics" and "moral law" are the very foundation of the pagan worldview. See: Dobroslav, *Promysel Prirody i nerazumnyi homo sapiens* (Kharkov: Sfera), p. 34. A fundamentally different approach to categories of "morality" is held by Volkhv Veleslav of the Rodoliubie community. Counter to Dobroslav's point of view on the exclusive, exceptional importance of moral laws in the pagan worldview, Veleslav writes: "Paganism as such is neither moral nor amoral. It is beyond-moral. Morality can be used as an instrument in creating any social system in our Iron Age, but it can never be an end in itself for a Pagan. And, of course, it is not morality that conditions the True Spirituality of man" - Volkhv Veleslav, *"Dvenadtsat' voprosov o Iazychestve"* in Veleslav, *Osnovy Rodnoveriia. Obriadnik. Kologod* (Saint Petersburg: Vedicheskoe nasledie, 2010), p. 314.

sphere, the leader of Svetovid emphasized that the ideal for pagans in this sphere is the old European model of a social market economy built on the principle of common industriousness.[631] The economy, in Anžur's opinion, should be geared towards ensuring the material well-being of all of society, and not only the elite of global capital. As a negative example, this organizer of the Sixth Veche of Rodnovery referred to the contemporary process of neoliberal globalization. In accordance with their proposed reforms, these Slovenian "naturopaths" also construct a certain approach to science. While recognizing modern science to be mistaken in many ways and built, as Anžur remarked, on the principles of the materialism of the scientific-technological and industrial revolution, this pagan simultaneously notes a positive side of scientific progress.[632] Accounting for both "good" and "bad" in the modern, post-industrial world, the ideologist of Slovenian paganism proposes using the experience of both the materialist and traditional, pagan, spiritually-oriented models in the future.

Also deserving of attention and examination are the views of this representative of alternative Slovenian religiosity on the problem of population. The head of Svetovid believes that the contemporary planet is overpopulated. Anžur blames the excess of human resources on the Abrahamic religions for what is, in his opinion, their calling upon their followers to maximize birth rates. The seven-billion-strong population of *Homo sapiens* rules out the possibility of the Earth's regeneration and causes irreversible harm to other inhabitants of the planet. Moving from global problems to the particular topic of Slovenia, Matjaž Anžur touched upon the question of the ethnic self-identification of the republic's pagans. He wrote: "Slovenes are presently part of the so-called Slavic super-ethnos linked by common linguistic and cultural history. It is thanks to these common roots that the Slavs will

---

631 The Slovenian pagan leader cited as one example of "traditional economics" the idealization of agriculture upheld by pagans in which development is to be constructed with the use of the latest ecological applications. Moreover, according to the plans of these "Old Believers", agriculture should be seen as comprising small and mid-range holdings which produce directly for consumers without intermediaries. Any stimulants for crop growth, additives, steroids, and genetically modified products are rejected.

632 Anžur considers medicine, the military industry, and ecology to be the most problematic zones of modern science.

enter a future based on solidarity, cooperation, and mutual aid."[633] The list of "distant relatives", according to this Slovenian pagan's theory, includes the population of the European climatic zone. Such perspectives, aimed at finding "one's own" among the Earth's polyethnic population, are completely typical of both the Slavic variation of the reborn traditional worldview and their European colleagues.[634] Characteristic of Matjaž Anžur's deliberations on population and the ethnic roots of peoples are the same ideas peculiar to the radical pagan wing. Upon designating the problem of European overpopulation, this "Old Believer" proposed his own way out of this situation: reducing the population to the formula of "one person, one hectare" (for which, as this historian remarked, Slovenia is ideal in terms of demography and land ownership). Anžur does not prescribe the method for such reduction, but simply states: "I strongly support all measures for preserving the moderate biological and demographic growth of the Slovenian people." Continuing this thought, the leader of Svetovid expressed his dissatisfaction with migration policy and the relocation of groups from certain countries to others. "Bridging" migration to the racial question, this "Rodnover" expressed the general opinion of this movement's proselytes by taking the position of "racial hygiene" and opposing the mixing and amalgamation of ethnoi, whose diversity is what embodies the beauty and diversity of the planet. This position brings this Slovenian pagan ideologist close to the ideas of other Indo-European enlighteners of the "indigenous religions" camp, in particular one of the oldest Russian didaskals of the Russian oppositional worldview, the hermit Dobroslav (Alexey Dobrovolsky), the Norwegian pagan Varg Vikernes, the Finnish writer Kaarlo Pentti Linkola, and others. Like our respondent, these other leaders of the pagan movement are in favor of controlling population growth, preserving ethnic purity,

---

633 Recognizing the population of Slovenia to be part of a whole "Slavic organism", this pagan leader at the same time rejects the ideas of Pan-Slavism, believing the latter's political models to be relics of the past which do not correspond to the "historical truth of the ethnogenesis of the Slavs."

634 For example, we can cite the statement of one of the ideologues of Norwegian 20th-21st century paganism, Varg Vikernes: "My Norwegian nationalism grew into pan-Germanic nationalism (Pan-Germanism) and even into pan-European nationalism (in a racial sense)." - Varg Vikernes, *Rechi Varga* (Tambov, 2007), p. 14.

increasing the share of traditional, national-oriented occupations and crafts in the economy, and stand against urbanization, industrialization, etc. Moreover, the ideas of this representative of the Svetovid community can be characterized from the standpoint of radical traditionalism. Believing that the contemporary "pagan dawn" arose thanks to the fall of socialism and communism, Anžur and the organization headed by him have taken the "post-atheist" path, one of the characteristic traits of which is the revival of religious archaism with elements of diasporic escapism.

The Slovenian variant of contemporary Slavic paganism is typified by a number of peculiarities. Firstly, there is its synergism, which borders with its direct borrowing of sources from Ukrainian Native Faith. Secondly, present in the ideological basis of Svetovid are features of "movement syncretism", which is to say such "programs" as those which have been intrinsic to the different currents of reborn nativism on matters ranging from the ecological to the "ultra" pagan political orientation. Thirdly, Matjaž Anžur's young community represents a colorful case of the aspirations of 21st-century Old World ethnophores. The common problematic zones uniting the "young pagans" of Europe (together with Russia) presently encompass a whole spectrum of traditional systems - political, economic, ecological, religious, and social. Consequently, the paganism of the new millennium goes far beyond the scope of religiosity and proclaims itself to be a fully-fledged worldview complex attempting not simply to enter the existing world order, but to change it, albeit within the scope of individual communities.

***

THE TERM *RODINA* (HOMELAND) IN THE CONCEPTUAL STOCK OF THE CONTEMPORARY PAGAN DIASPORA: THE DATA OF FIELD STUDIES[635]

On 17-23 June 2014, the team of the scientific research laboratory "New Religious Movements in Contemporary Russia and Europe" at Kozma Minin Nizhny Novgorod State Pedagogical University conducted a questionnaire survey among representatives of Russian pagan communities gathered at a Kupala festival. The laboratory's team had already surveyed ordinary members of these union communities in 2013.[636] This event is unique in terms of its projection. For the second year in a row, the organizer of this festival was a pagan confederation, i.e. an association of two unions of contemporary bearers of this alternative worldview, consisting of the Veles Circle fellowship of communities (founded in 1999) and the Union of Slavic Communities of Slavic Native Faith (founded in 1997).[637] This joint Kupala was held at Krasny Lug near Maloyaroslavets in the Ignatyevskoe village of the Kaluga region. According to the organizers' data, this festival event was participated in by 1200 people in 2014 (the first such Kupala in 1998 counted 20 community members, while the 2013 festival gathered between 1500 and 1800 people). Besides direct participation in the Kupala mystery, the ritual component of the festival included pagan weddings, rites of purification and naming, etc.

---

635 Article first published online at *Pantheon.Today* [https://pantheon.today/paganka/termin-rodina-v-ponyatijnom-bagazhe-sovremennoj-yazycheskoj-diaspory/].
636 See Roman Shizhensky, "Aspects of the Codification of Contemporary Slavic Paganism: The Data of Field Studies" in this volume.
637 One experience of successful pagan cooperation has already taken place in the Russian Federation: the assembly of pagan organizations over the desecration of the shrine complex in Tsaritsyno Park. The meeting took place on 27 July 2008 with approximately 40 Rodnovery, including representatives of the Circle of Pagan Tradition, the Veles Circle, the Union of Slavic Communities of Slavic Native Faith, and the religious group Slaviia. Lone-pagans were also present, and a representative of the Skhron Ezh Sloven community spoke to the gathering via telephone. See: Yggeld, *"Soveshchanie na 'Baran'em Lbu'", Derevo Zhizni: Gazeta etnicheskogo vozrozhdeniia 23* (Troitsk: 2008). However, the authority of those gathered was of a consultative character and not focused on the question of rite, i.e., the most important component of this religious system.

267

During the 2014 survey, the research team encountered the specific peculiarities of working in the "large-scale pagan field." To these should be attributed, firstly, a significant percentage of refusals to fill out the questionnaires due to potential respondents' engagements (preparing camp, participating in organizational events, etc.) as well distrust of the interviewers, and, secondly, as noted by the Kupala organizers themselves, the presence at the festival of a huge number of "mummers" (people who come for regular outdoor recreation, dressing up in costume, and religious components with the prefix "ethno-"). In order to estimate the percentage of such "untrusting" participants and to verify the previously expressed argument that the contemporary pagan community is predominantly diasporic[638], the 2014 survey included two "proposals" for respondents: writing in their email address on the questionnaire form and an acceptable format for contact, if possible, for future correspondence. Analysis of the results of this "covert survey" revealed a significant percentage of anonymous individuals who are categorically reluctant to provide additional information about themselves. Answers were lacking from 153 (65.4%) respondents. Twenty-nine people (12.4%) preferred to indicate only their email address. Fifty respondents gave only their first names on the questionnaire forms. Noteworthy is the fact that in subsequent correspondences most respondents preferred to use their everyday, civilian first name without indicating their pagan names. Thirty-six "traditional" names (15.4%) were given in comparison to 14 pagan names (6%). This paradox cannot be explained solely on the basis of the survey material. The reason for this lack of anthroponymic uniformity among those present at the festival might lie in the very organizational point and semantic "lodging" of the Maloyaroslavets Kupala, which turned from a religion-sacred act into a festival: "At the present moment we can say: 'The present Kupala has a festival background.' We also announce it as a festival-reconstruction of the ancient Slavic holiday."[639] Hence the presence at this "holy day" of different groups and individuals

---

[638] See Roman Shizhensky, "The Russian Pagan Diaspora: Definitions of Neo-Paganism in Contemporary Russia" in this volume.
[639] Audio-recorded interview with B.A. Gasanov (Volkhv Bogumil) in Ryazan from 17/8/2014, author's personal archive.

who at times distance themselves from the "pagan basis." Moreover, the reasons for this might be hidden in the banal unwillingness of respondents to give a research group, i.e., an outside group, their secret name used in their circles, or in the elementary absence of a communal name in connection with neophyte status on the part of someone present at the festival. In the latter case, the acquisition of a new name is a matter of time, of passing through the rite of "naming." Despite the complete or partial concealment of additional data by a significant mass of respondents, still 47 people (20.1%) reported both their online addresses and names. In addition, three respondents gave their phone numbers, and two left comments. Naturally, against the general backdrop of such "refuseniks", such phenomena of trust are more than minimal.

The questionnaire consisted of 19 multilevel questions, including both "control questions" and "open-ended questions" which required respondents to give their most self-styled answers as possible. This main focus of this article is analyzing the questions of the first bloc, which contained information about respondents (their gender, age, level of education, occupation, and place of residence) as well as the open question "What is the Homeland (Rodina) in your understanding?" This survey was participated in by 234 people. Of them, there were 138 males (59%) and 93 women (39.7%), and three respondents (1.3%) did not answer this question.

The second question concerning the age of the interviewees was found to be difficult for four respondents (1.7%). The most common age group of those at the Kupala festival was young: from ages 14 to 30. Under this classification fell 126 people or 53.4% of respondents. Let us note that within this group there was a tendency towards greater age among pagan proselytes. For instance, the total composition of youth aged 14-21 consisted of 18 people, whereas there were 108 people between the ages of 22 and 30. The most common age was 28, counting 23 people. Second place was taken by the age category of 31-50 years old, with 93 people (40%). Observable within this group, unlike in the previous, is a clear gravitation towards the upper age boundary. The total number of respondents aged 31-39 was 65. The most "popular" age group was 31 years old (11 people). The smallest age category, according to the questionnaire data, was those older than 51, of which there were 10 people (4.3%). Thus, the lowest age boundary of respondents was 10 years old (one person) and the highest was 66 (one person), the average age of the "ordinary pagan" present at the Kupala festival thus being 31. In the opinion of the scholar of religion A. Gaydukov, the statistically average age group of pagans is 17-35.[640]

Quite telling are the results obtained in response to the question concerning the level of education among followers of contemporary pre-Abrahamic religiosity. Besides an absence of data from 9 people (3.8%), the overwhelming majority of respondents had higher education: 162 people or 69.2% of the total number of respondents. Moreover, in the column "education level" two representatives of the diaspora selected the answer "academic degree." Second place was taken by secondary vocational education. This option was chosen by 39 people (16.7%). At the bottom of the list were holders of secondary general education - 17 people (7.3%) - and basic general education - 5 people (2.1%).

The question on occupation type (profession) caused difficulty for five people (2.1%). The rest of the respondents answered as follows: (1) enterprise director (13 people, 5.6%), (2) middle manager (37 people, 15.8%), (3) businessman, entrepreneur, independent business owner (27 people, 11.5%), specialist (71 people, 30.3%), office worker (11 people, 4.7%), worker (15 people, 6.4%), student (14 people, 6%), pensioner (3 people, 1.3%), unemployed (4 people, 1.7%), and homekeeper (6 people, 2.6%). The category "other" was chosen by 28 respondents or 12% of those surveyed. The professions which were not included in the proposed list but which were written in by pagans on the questionnaire were: teacher (3 people), artisan (3 people), film industry worker (2 people), artist (2 people) head of musical group, author, organizer of Russian holidays and festivals,

---

640 A. Gaidukov, "*Molodezhnaia Subkul'tura slavianskogo neoiazychestva v Pterburge*" in V. Kostiushev (ed.), *Molodezhnye dvizheniia i subkul'tury Sankt-Peterburga: Sotsiologiia i anthropologicheskii analiz* (Saint Petersburg: Institute of Sociology of the Russian Academy of Sciences, Filial, Norma, 1999) [http://subculture.narod.ru/texts/book2/gaidukov.htm].

farmer, builder, military, courier, blacksmith, politician, site administrator, and "helper", etc.[641]

The final question of the first bloc was aimed at determining residents' place of residence. Seven people (3%) declined to answer. Ten people (4.3%) lived in an urban settlement, 17 (7.3%) in a rural settlement, 27 (11.5%) in a district center (a city of district subordination), and 42 respondents (17.9%) in a regional center (city of regional subordination). The largest concentration of the "Kupala pagans" was in cities of federal significance. This item was chosen by 131 respondents (56%).

Thus, based on the data of the responses to the questions of the bloc "Information about yourself", the statistically average participant of the Kupala festival was a male of 31 years of age with complete higher education working as a specialist and living in a city of federal significance.

It bears emphasizing that those materials of Russian scholars of the phenomenon of contemporary paganism which have touched upon the problematic field pertaining to the survey's first bloc of questions both confirm and contradict this data acquired in the field. For instance, these pagans' responses to the question aimed at determining their place of residence confirmed the scholarly community's notion of the urban nature of contemporary Russian polytheism and its adherents: "Modern paganism originated precisely in the urban environment and remains largely a religion of city folk, being a special kind of nostalgia for a previously lost, imaginary, harmonious fusion with nature."[642]

---

[641] Despite the lack of specialist studies aiming to define the trajectory of this resultant formation, I.A. Ginder cites the opinion of Volkhv Ogneyar (K.V. Beggin) that "the majority of neo-pagans are people with higher education in the humanities." See: I.A. Ginder, *"Obzor problemy slavianskogo neoiazychestva v sovremennoi Rossii"* in V.V. Suveizda (comp.), *Molodezh' i nauka - tret'e tysiacheletie. Sbornik materialov vserossiiskoi nauchnoi konferentsii studentov, aspirantov, i molodykh uchenykh 16 dekabira 2004 g.* (Krasnoyarsk: GUTSMiZ, KRO NS Integratsiia, 2004), p. 99. In the case of the Kupala survey, half of this is confirmed, as the majority of contemporary pagans have higher education.

[642] A.A. Nakorchevskii, *"Metodologicheskie osnovy i podkhody k izucheniiu ukrainskogo rodnoveriia (ridnovirstvo)", Religiovedenie 2* (2008), p. 73; A.V. Gaidukov, *"Slavianskoe novoe iazychestvo v Rossii: issledovaniia"* in E.S. Elbakian, S.I. Ivanenko, I.Ia. Kanterov, and M.N. Sitnikov (eds.), *Novye religii v Rossii: dvatsat' let spustia. Materialy Mezhdunarodnoi nauchno-prakticheskoi konferentsii* [Moscow: Dom Zhurnalista, 14 December 2012] (Moscow: Drevo zhizni, 2013), pp. 172-173; A. Kompaneets, *"Iazycheskie bogi vykhodiat iz podpol'ia", Ateisticheskii sait (26/11/2001)* [http://www.ateism.ru/articles/russo2.htm]; A. Shchipkov, *Vo chto verit Rossiia. Religioznye protsessy v postperestroechnoi Rossii* (Saint Petersburg: Russian Christian Humanitarian Institute, 1998).

At the same time, however, the education level, social status, and, finally, intellectual baggage of contemporary pagans has not been assessed by the scholarly community without ambiguity. For instance, a number of specialists consider the intelligentsia to be the author of contemporary Russian pagan projects.[643] This assumption of a leading role for the intelligentsia, albeit indirectly, is confirmed by the data from the Kupala questionnaires' points disclosing respondents' education and profession. Opponents, on the other hand, see the basis of today's nativism in marginal milieux.[644] A "golden mean" is found in the historiography of this question, as the Moscow scholar O.I. Kavykin writes: "The sociocultural environment of neo-paganism is the marginal urban intelligentsia."[645]

The open-ended question "What is the Homeland (Rodina) in your understanding?" proved difficult to answer for 26 people. The other varying responses (208) were combined into the following semantic groups in terms of the most frequently used words and phrases:

1. "land, native land, my land" - 77 people
2. "place (locality)" - 47 people
3. "Ancestors" - 46 people
4. "*Rod*, family, children" - 35 people
5. "People [folk/nation]" - 20 people
6. "Cultural-historical values, traditions" - 18 people
7. "Cosmopolitanism (the entire globe, a place towards which the soul strives, an abstract concept not associated

---

643 L.S. Klein, *Voskreshenie Peruna. K rekonstruktsii vostochnoslavianskogo iazychstva* (Saint Petersburg: Evraziia, 2004), p. 123; V. Cherva, "Neoiazychestvo i molodezhnaia kul'tura: v poiskakh novykh religioznykh i kul'turnykh orientirov", *Mezhdunarodnye chteniia po teorii, historii i filosofii kul'tury 18* (Saint Petersburg: Eidos, 2004), p. 440; A.V. Gridin, "Mify o Zolotom Veke i nepreryvnoi Traditsii kak sotsiokul'turnoe osnovanie neoiazychestva", *Samizdat* (2006) [http://samlib.ru/g/gridin_aleksej_wladimirowich/pagan.shtml].

644 I. Afagonov, "Neoiazycheskie i antikhristianskie tendentsii v soveremennoi obshchestvenno-politicheskoi zhizni", *Tul'skii informatsionno-konsul'tativnyi tsentr po voprosam sektanstva* [http://www.sektainfo.ru/allsekts/neoyaz2.htm]; M. Sitnikov, "Idoly v dolinách Moskva-reki" [http://www.rusglobus.net/Sitnikov/idols.htm].

645 O.I. Kavykin, *Konstruirovanie etnicheskoi identichnosti v srede russkikh neoiazychnikov* (Dissertation for Candidate of Historical Sciences, Moscow, 2006), p. 7.

with a specific place, the whole world, etc.)" - 16 people
8. "Nationalism (blood, soil, Slavs, nation, lands of the Slavs)" - 15 people
9. "Home" - 14 people
10. "Religious faith, spiritual views" - 10 people
11. "Country" - 10 people
12. "Rus" - 9 people
13. "Russia" - 9 people
14. "Nature" - 3 people

Among the individual responses indicated, let us record the following: "The Grand Duchy of Lithuania", "the content of the Russian anthem", "historical Russia before 1917", "faith in people and the state in which you live", "all of pagan Rus", "a plot of land around your home which you can walk in a day", "nature, homeland, and folk", etc.

This distribution of "pagan voices" on display allows us to draw the following conclusions on the sum of "concept-codes" which respondents associated with the term "Homeland" (*Rodina*). The content of the first two most widespread responses (124 people) testifies to the predominance of a kind of "*Pochvennik*" sentiment in this milieu. One-hundred and thirteen people in total elected in favor of the next three thematic groups reflecting family and, more broadly, folk orientations vested by Kupala participants into this term. This pagan orientation can be characterized with the phrase employed by the Belarusian scholar I.B. Mikheeva: "cult of roots."[646]

It is worth noting that such answer variants as "country", "Russia", and "Rus", which would emphasize a patriotic mentality among the followers of the contemporary pre-Abrahamic worldview, are not very popular in this community. This at first glance illogical choice becomes quite explainable upon taking into account the specifics of the formation and current state of the Slavic pagan movement in the Russian Federation. As has been emphasized

---

[646] I.B. Mikheeva, *"Fenomen neoiazychestva: problema kontseptualizatsii (obzor osnovnich issledovatel'skikh paradigm)"* (2003) [http://scipeople.ru/publication/66848/].

previously, at the core of this minimization of "state patriotism" lies the principle of "diasporicity", a distinctive community of "one's own" among "young-pagan" associations which find themselves in a socio-cultural environment which they have constructed. Moreover, the internal insularity and self-isolation of the pagan masses is intensified by an ideological, organizational component in the form of the propagandist work of its leaders and their creation of a new mythology.[647] The result of the "work" and interaction of these components, as can be seen from the survey figures, is manifest in the pagan collective's general reluctance towards defining "Homeland" in the forms of "Russia", "country", etc. Meanwhile, the respondents of this Kupala festival quite clearly associate the notion of "Homeland" with "native land", "place", and blood and kin ties.

It is especially worth noting the more than insignificant percentage of responses pertaining to both such radical, antagonistic notions as "cosmopolitanism" and "nationalism." If the former antonym for all intents and purposes does not figure in studies devoted to Russian paganism of the past two centuries, then the second, in its extreme forms, is presented as dominant and as, more often than not, the only variation of the manifestation of the contemporary pagan worldview.[648] Without

---

647 As an example we can cite the worldview concepts of two late-20th-early 21st century Russian ideologists of the alternative religiosity under examination: the eco-anarchism of Dobroslav (Alexey Dobrovolsky) and the pagan (nativist) statism of Velimir (Nikolai Speransky). By "new mythology" is meant pagans' creation of their own mythological products and their ensuing partial or full immersion. See R.V. Shizhensky, *Filosofiia dobroi sily: zhizn' i tvorchestvo Dobroslava (A.A. Dobrovol'skogo)* (Moscow: Orbita-m, 2013); Ibidem, *Pochvennik ot iazychestva: mirovozzrencheskie diskursy volkhva Velimira (N.N. Speranskogo)* (Nizhny Novgorod: Povolzh'e, 2014). See also Gridin, *"Mify o Zolotom Veke i nepreryvnoi Traditsii kak sotsiokul'turnoe osnovanie neoiazychestva."*

648 The works of V.A. Schnirelmann should be recognized as one such line of promoting the idea that Russian pagan associations harbor an extreme nationalism. See, for example, V. Schnirelmann, *Russkoe rodnoverie: neoiazychestvo i natsionalizm v sovremennoi Rossii* (Moscow: BBI, 2012). On the topic of pagan extremism and radicalism see also I. Afagonov, *"Neoiazycheskie i antikhristianskie tendentsii";* M.T. Yakupov, *"Vozvrashchenie iazychestva i transformatsii religii", Religiovedenie* 3 (2009), p. 177; A. Suvorov, *"Neoiazychestvo", Nash sovremennik* 7 (2002) [http://nash-sovremennik.ru/p.php?y=2002&n=7&id=5]. An alternative point of view on determining the degree of radicalization of Russian pagan groups has been expressed by Gaidukov. Citing as an example the "religious characteristics" of the organizers of terrorist attacks in 2008-2010, this scholar of religion writes: "The bombers called themselves 'Rodnovery', which ultimately implicated all Slavic pagans (!) not only with skinheads, but with extremists in the eyes of the ignorant public and officials, and thus several people could discredit the good endeavors of many good, respectable citizens." - A.V. Gaidukov, *Slavianskoe novoe iazychestvo v Rossii,* p. 177.

a doubt, the results of this survey, though massive (taking into account the specifics of this group), cannot act as an "axiom of fallibility" for the scholarly community seeking out radical pagan nationalists. However, the altogether modest quantity of Kupala participants who elected to define "Homeland" as "blood and soil" illustrates the heterogeneity of the pagan camp when it comes to the question of nationalism.

***

CONTEMPORARY PAGAN RATINGS OF RUSSIAN HISTORICAL FIGURES: THE DATA OF FIELD STUDIES[649]

For the third year in a row, representatives of the "New Religious Movements in Contemporary Russia and Europe" research laboratory at Kozma Minin State Pedagogical University of Nizhny Novgorod have conducted a questionnaire survey among the Russian pagan communities and unions gathered at the Kupala festival held in the village of Ignatyevskoe in the Maloyaroslavets district of the Kaluga region. According to the data of the festival's organizers, the Veles Circle fellowship of communities, around 1400 people participated in the event on 19-21 June 2015.

The 2015 questionnaire form consisted of five blocs of questions containing both open-ended and closed questions. This article examines the particularities of the data of bloc #1 which was aimed at disclosing the "social portrait" of ordinary pagan proselytes and the movement's sympathizers, as well as the open question of bloc #5 (question 5.3), dedicated to determining a first-rate historical figure of Russia in the opinion of the Kupala participants. The 2015 survey was participated in by 429 respondents. Thirty-eight people - 24 men and 14 women - declined to fill out the questionnaire.

The first bloc of the 2015 survey consisted of eight questions whose aim was to exhibit respondents' personal data. We can conditionally designate this bloc as "factological." The first question asked respondents to indicate their gender: one respondent (2% of those surveyed) declined to answer. The obtained data showed that the male component is quantitatively predominant over the female. Out of 429 people surveyed, 257 or 60% were men and 40% or 171 respondents

---

[649] Article first published in *Colloquium Heptaplomeres 2* (2015), prepared with the financial support of the Russian Humanitarian Science Foundation as part of the research project "Comprehensive Historical-Religious Study of the Phenomenon of Russian Neo-Paganism" (Project #15-31-01247).

were women.[650] This proportion finds confirmation in Russian historiography, in which contemporary Russian paganism has traditionally been seen as a "male movement."[651]

The second survey question was intended to reveal the age groupings typical of the Russian polytheist milieu. Over the course of surveying, it turned out that two people younger than 14 (.2% of respondents) were present at the Kupala festival. Another 3% of these young pagans were not of full adult age (13 people). The age group of 15-29 composed 42.9% of those surveyed (184 people), which is much higher than the statistically average picture for throughout the country.[652] The age group of 30-49 was represented in the pagan wing by 197 participants, making up 45.9% of the total number of respondents.[653] Around 5% (25 respondents) of those gathered at the pagan festival were people beyond the threshold of 50 years of age. This index is almost five times lower than the Russia-wide figure, in which the age group of over 50 is 34.5% (49,622,000 people). The lower age boundary of the pagans and sympathizers who participated in the survey was 11 years of age, and the upper age limit was 67. The average age was 28.7 years.[654]

---

650   This gender correlation is not typical of the whole Russian Federation, where in 2014 the female share of the population exceeded the male population by 8%: 54% female (77.1 million) compared to 46% male (66.6 million), according to the Federal Service of State Statistics. However, this "gender" proportion of 60-40 has been maintained since 2014, when 138 women (59% of 234) and 93 men (39.7% of 234) were surveyed. See: R.V. Shizhensky and M.Iu. Shliakhov, *"Pis'mennye istochniki sovremennykh rossiiskikh iazychnikov po dannym polevykh issledovanii"*, Istoricheskie, filosofskie, politicheskie, i iuridicheskie nauki, kul'turologiia i isukusstvovedenie. Voprosy teorii i praktiki 8:58 (Tambov: Gramota, 2015), p. 211.

651   I.A. Ginder, *"Obzor problemy slavianskogo neoiazychestva v sovremennoi Rossii"* in V.V. Suveizda (comp.), *Molodezh' i nauka - tret'e tysiacheletie. Sbornik materialov vserossiiskoi nauchnoi konferentsii studentov, aspirantov, i molodykh uchenykh 16 dekabira 2004 g.* (Krasnoyarsk: GUTSMiZ, KRO NS Integratsiia, 2004), pp. 98-99.

652   According to the Russian statistical service's data for 2014, the number of citizens of this age category makes up 20.5% of the population.

653   This percentage is greater than countrywide indices, which in 2014 approximated 29%.

654   This data only partially coincides with the age characteristics of pagans which have been established by the scholarly community. A. Gaidukov, for instance, notes that the most widespread "Native Faith" age is 17-35. See: A.V. Gaidukov, *"Slavianskoe novoe iazychestvo v Rossii: opyt religiovedcheskogo issledovaniia"*, Tsentr religiovedcheskikh issledovanii 'Religiopolis' (22/1/2013) [http://religiopolis.org/religiovedenie/5730-rodnoverie.html]. S.V. Ryazanova and A.I. Tsolova speak of a greater share of youth up to the age of 35 in the neo-pagan movement. See: S.V. Ryazanova and A.I. Tsolova, *"Sovremennoe 'neoiazychestvo': klassifikatsiia, spetsifika i lokal'nye varianty"*, Vestnik Moskovskogo universiteta - Seria 7: filosofiia 1 (Moscow, 2015). Let us note that the age of respondents in 2015 was almost two times younger than the analogous group present at the Kupala festival in 2014. See: Shizhensky and Shliakhov, *"Pis'mennye istochniki."*

The "rejuvenation" of the pagan movement represented at Kupala came at the cost of the overall share of youth (from 14-30 years of age), which fell from 53.4% in 2014 to 47.3% (203 respondents) in 2015, but did see a redistribution of age groups within the "youth" category. The number of young pagans of ages 14-21 increased by 1.4% (from 7.7% in 2014 to 9.1% in 2015). The share of pagans whose age falls in the range of 22-30, on the contrary, decreased by 7.95%: from 46.15% of pagans in this age category in 2014 to 38.2% at Kupala in 2015. The 21-50 age range made up 42.9% (184 people) as opposed to 40% in 2014.[655] The most common pagan age, indicated by 30 respondents making up 7% of the total of the surveyed, is 31. It should be noted that the most common age at Kupala in 2014 was 28 (nearly 10% of respondents).

The third survey question was aimed at determining the level of education among representatives of the new pagan religiosity. The column "higher education" was the most mass represented, filled in by 63.9% or 274 respondents. In second place was specialized secondary education with 98 pagans (22.8%). Twenty-seven respondents (6.3%) possessed general secondary education. Eleven of those surveyed (2.6%) had a general education. It is noteworthy that eight adepts (1.9%) had an academic degree. This question caused difficulty for 11 respondents (2.6%).[656] Thus, despite a certain chronological interval (indices stretching over five years), the level of education among contemporary pagans at Kupala in 2015 is almost three times higher than the Russia-wide figures.

The fourth question of the questionnaire asked respondents to choose their type of professional affiliation according to the classification of E.A. Klimov.[657] The majority of respondents (143 people, 33.3%) indicated "person - person." Next in terms of polarity was the variant "person - nature", which was chosen

---

655 Shizhensky and Shliakhov, *"Pis'mennye istochniki"*, p. 211.
656 It bears noting that according to the Russia-wide census data of 2010, only 27.5% of Russians had higher education, 21.5% had completed average education, and 6.7% had average specialized education. Only 0.7% of those surveyed had post-college education. - *"Vserossiiskaia perepis' naseleniia 2010"*, *Demoskop weekly* (2011) [http://www.demoscope.ru/weekly/2011/0491/perep01.php].
657 E.A. Klimov, *Psikhologiia professional'nogo samoopredeleniia* (Rostov-on-Don: Feniks, 1996).

by 23.1% of those surveyed (99 respondents). In third place in this typologization was the module "person - technology", which was indicated by 21.4% of pagans (92 respondents). Seventy-six adepts (17.7%) associated themselves with the "person - artistic image" typology. The last position on the list with 3.3% was the module "person - sign system", chosen by 14 respondents. Only five respondents, which amounted to 1.2% of the total, had difficulty answering this question. Based on the above, it can be said that among the Russian pagan milieu the predominant type of engagement is the extraverted, anthropo-oriented professional module "person - person." The individual is the direct object of labor.[658] The "person - nature" type is also common among the representatives of pre-Abrahamic religiosity, which in many respects explains the certain nature-centricity of the movement. The minimal percentage of the "person - sign system" module was conditioned, in our opinion, by a certain type of perception of reality among the representatives of this new religiosity whose world-perceptive potential is rather directed along an empirical-constructive rather than rational-transformative vector.

The fifth question of the survey asked those present at the Kupala festival to indicate their occupation. This question was difficult for three respondents (0.7% of respondents). The professional engagement of the rest of those surveyed was distributed as follows. Twenty-nine pagans (6.8%) called themselves top-level managers (directors, etc.). Fifty-nine respondents (13.8%) were mid-level managers, and slightly fewer of this movement's adherents were from the business world: 56 people or 13.1%. The most numerous professional group was office workers, making up 17.9% or 77 respondents. Also sufficiently widely represented was the contingent of workers, numbering 67 people or 15.6%. Twenty-eight people (6.5%) were students, five were pensioners (1.2%), and 12 were unemployed (2.8%). Twenty-six respondents (6.1%) indicated their main form of occupation as homekeeping.

---

[658] It is noteworthy that researchers of this movement are inclined to attach priority to the professional orientation of Russian nativists or "techies" or attribute the contribution of those trained in the humanitarian sphere to only the initial stage of the diaspora's emergence. - Ginder, *"Obzor problemy"*, p. 99.

Other professional occupations were chosen by 67 people (15.6%). The latter category included the following answers: teacher (11 people, 2.56%), artisan (7 people, 1.6%), adolescent student (5 people), programmer and musician (four answers each), researcher and artist (three responses each), military, engineer, freelancer, psychologist, photographer, and florist (two responses each). Among answers with only one response figured: media worker (questionnaire #7), volkhv (questionnaire #169), healer (questionnaire #170), warrior (questionnaire #173), doctor (questionnaire #122), beekeeper (questionnaire #341), museum worker (questionnaire #75), tattoo artist (questionnaire #284), biotechnologist (questionnaire #275), call worker (questionnaire #383), artist (questionnaire #371), and film director (questionnaire #299).

The aim of the sixth question was to determine respondents' place of residence. Among the representatives of alternative religiosity surveyed, 250 (58.3%) live in cities of federal significance and 85 (19.8%) are residents of regional centers. Sixty-one respondents (14.2%) live in a district center. Eighteen of the pagans indicated their place of residence as an urban settlement (4.2%), and thirteen indicated rural residence (3%). Only two respondents, or 0.5%, declined to answer this question. Thus, we can observe a significant prevalence of share of the urban population at this pagan festival: 96.5% of the pagans surveyed are urban residents. The data obtained from these answers is fully consistent with the character of the contemporary Russian pagan movement, the emergence and spread of which has been discerned by Russian scholars of religion in the activities of exclusively its urban representatives.[659]

---

[659] D.Iu. Kopysov, *Sovremennye netraditsionnye religii* (Izhevsk, 2000), p. 36; Schnirelmann, *"Perun, Svarog i drugie: russkoe neoiazychestvo v poiskakh sebia"* in *Neoiazychestvo na prostorakh Evrazii* (Moscow: St. Apostle Andrey Biblical-Theological Institute: 2001), p. 13; V. Cherva, *"Neoiazychestvo i molodezhnaia kul'tura: v poiskakh novykh religioznykh i kul'turnykh orientirov"* in *Differentsiatsia i integratsiia mirovozzrenii: filosofskii i religioznyi opyt: Mezhdunarodnye chteniia po teorii, istorii i filosofii kul'tury 18* (Saint Petersburg: Eidos, 2004), pp. 434-442; Ia.I. Zdrovoets i A.A. Mukhin, *Religioznye konfessii i sekty* (Moscow, 2005), p. 229. It is interesting to note that according to the data of the Russian statistical service the share of the urban population in Russia in mid-2014 was 74% compared to 26% rural. Thus, it can be said that the urban component of the new pagan religiosity is much higher than the countrywide average.

For question #7 respondents were asked to describe their religious views with one word. This question posed difficulty to 11.2% of pagans (48 respondents did not answer). The most popular variation of self-designation among these diaspora representatives was Rodnoverie ("Native Faith"), which was elected by 111 respondents or 25.9%. In second place in popularity was the name *iazychnik* ("pagan") - 110 respondents (25.6%) answered thusly.[660] Thirty-two out of 429 respondents (7.5%) identified their worldview as atheistic. One hundred twenty-eight respondents (29.8%) proposed other answer variations, among which, in our opinion, the following are especially interesting: *"pravoslavnyi"* (potentially "Orthodox"[661] - 16 people, 3.7%), agnostic (11 people, 2.56%), Christian (8 people, 1.86%), traditionalist (5 people, 1.16%), Vedism, shamanism and cosmism (three answers each). "Natural faith", "realist", "pantheist", "Buddhist", "animist", "cosmopolitan", "Slav", and "I believe in god" had two responses. The number of singular responses included: anarchist (questionnaire #427), Russian warlock (questionnaire #208), Pastafarian (questionnaire #205)[662], materialist (questionnaire #17), Odinist (questionnaire #266), Wotanist (questionnaire #284), New Age follower (questionnaire #97), Shivaist (questionnaire #82), gnostic (questionnaire #78), chaognostic (questionnaire #262), and wizard (questionnaire #282).

The question of the terminology of the contemporary variation of Russian paganism is currently very far from being resolved, both among its representatives and the scholarly circles

---

[660] Two people considered themselves Rodnovery-pagans (questionnaires #39 and 398). It bears noting that compared to the same question on the 2014 questionnaire, the share of those who associate themselves precisely with *"Rodnoverie"* fell from 30% to 25.9%, while the number of self-proclaimed pagans also decreased from 34% to 25.6%. Meanwhile, the number of respondents who characterized their worldview orientation by choosing "atheism" rose by 1.5%. The number of neo-pagans who preferred other answers to this question also rose from 18.8% of those surveyed in 2014 to nearly 29.8% at the 2015 Kupala.

[661] The difficulty of determining the percentage of Orthodox Christians participating in this festival lies in the substitution of notions and "play on words" widespread among followers of this alternative religiosity, whereby *"pravoslavnyi"* (usually "Orthodox [Christian]") can mean "glorifying Prav'".

[662] Pastafarianism, i.e. the "Church of the Flying Spaghetti Monster."

studying this worldview.[663] However, the definition *rodnoverie* ("Native Faith") recently defended by part of the pagan diaspora has entered into scholarly circulation and posed competition to the term "neo-paganism" that is rejected by a portion of the pagan community.[664] The notion of *rodnoverie* and the self-designation derived from it, rodnovery, has an altogether ambiguous history of origin. According to the point of view of the leader of the Association of Ukrainian Native Faith, G.S. Lozko (Volkhvess Zoreslava), *"rodnoverie"* is only an abstraction, a scientific form of the term *rodnaia vera*. The notion of *"ridna vira"* was first used by the founder of modern Ukrainian paganism, V. Shayan, in his religious seeking at the beginning of the previous century. At virtually the same time, through the efforts of Jan Stachniuk *"rodzima wiara"* entered the Polish "pagan lexicon."[665] It bears noting that on the pages of Internet forums one can encounter the theory that this term is of Polish origin and its emergence is associated with the 19th century. In addition, one of the participants in such discussions believes that the Russian variant of this notion, *rodnoverie,* appeared in Russia through Ukrainian pagans. The direction is thus from the Polish *Rodzima Wiara* to the Ukrainian *Ridna Vira* to the Russian *Rodnoverie*.[666] A different version of the origin of this term is presented by the volkhv of the Ryazan-based Troesvet pagan community, Bogumil (B.A. Gasanov), who believes that Rodnoverie began in 1997 with the establishment of the Union of Slavic Communities. Thanks to Bogumila's active position, this name has been appended with

---

663 A.A. Beskov, *"Paradoksy russkogo neoiazychestva"*, Colloquium Hepatplomeres 1 (2014), pp. 12-14; E.V. Smul'sky, *"K razvitiu voprosa o poniatii 'neoiazychestvo'"*, Colloquium Heptaplomeres 1 (2014); I.B. Mikheeva, *"Neoiazychestvo kak religiozno-kul'turnyi fenomen sovremennosti: problema definitsii"*, Filosofskie i sotsial'nye nauki. Nauchnyi zhurnal 2 (Minsk: Izdatel'skii tsentr BGU, 2010); See Roman Shizhensky, "On the Question of the Terminology of Slavic Variations of 'Indigenous Religions': The Case of the Term 'Neo-Paganism'" in this volume.

664 *Krug Iazycheskoi Traditsii, "Tsaritsynoskoe obrashchenie"* [http://slavya.ru/delo/krug/05/neo.htm]; *"Russkii dukh i kak ego shel'muiut", Derevo Zhizni* (Troitsk, 2007), p. 3; S.V. Zobnina, D.Zh. Georgis, D.A. Gavrilov, V.Iu. Vinnik, *"Analiz sovremennogo mifotvorchestva v noveishikh issledovaniiakh po iazychestvu (kritika stat'i V.A. Schnirelmana "Ot 'Sovetskogo naroda' k 'organicheskoi obshchnosti': obraz mira russikh i ukrainskikh neoiazychnikov'"*.

665 Online correspondence with G.S. Lozko (pl. Kiev) from 13/5/2013.

666 *"Slavianskoe Rodnoverie", Tonkii Mir* [http://tonkiimir.ru/topic1853-60.html] (2010).

another part: "Slavic", hence "Slavic Native Faith" (*Slavianskaia Rodnaia Vera*). The spiritual head of Troesvet has remarked that this step was taken to specify the ethnic and religious component of the future union. B.A. Gasanov, however, admits that when he created this term he was oriented towards the Polish tradition. The transformation of *rodnaia very* into the definitional rodnoverie, in Bogumil's opinion, took place at the turn of the millennium. The term was introduced into the contemporary Russian pagan milieu by the volkhv of the Rodoliubie community, Veleslav (I.G. Cherkasov).[667]

Thus, in considering the question of the terminology of this 20th-21st century worldview phenomenon, it bears paying attention to how the term rodnoverie, used as a self-designation and often acting as a marker of contradiction with regards to other definitions (particularly "neo-paganism"), has undergone a certain semantic transformation, taking on the trait of an "exo-ethnonym" for the new religiosity. The decline in the share of respondents using this definition to name themselves might testify to its "displacement" from narrowly pagan circles onto the scholarly level.[668]

One possible explanation for the considerable percentage of respondents who chose "atheism" as their answer might be the violation of cause-and-effect relationships ("non sequitur"). In other words, a non-theistic position might be treated or interpreted "atheistically." One of the forms of pantheism is the dissolution of the divine in the naturalistic, which is quite close in its denial of a personified deity of a higher order to idealistic atheism. Moreover, this assumption in many ways explains the sharp increase (by 11%) of the number of proselytes of the movement who prefer

---

[667] Audio-recorded interview with B.A. Gasanov (Bogumil, pl. Ryazan) from 13/8/2011.
[668] The "legitimacy" of the definition "*Rodnoverie*" is recognized in a number of scholarly works, such as K. Aitamurto, *Paganism, Traditionalism, Nationalism: Narratives of Russian Rodnoverie* (dissertation, Department of World Cultures, University of Helsinki, 2011); V.N. Sheremet'eva, "*Nekotorye problemy stanovleniia rodnoveriia v sovremennoi issledovatel'skoi literature. Problema termina*", Vestnik Omskogo universiteta 1:71 (2014); Gaidukov, "*Slavianskoe novoe iazychestvo*"; O.I. Kavykin *Rodnovery: Samoidentifikatsiia neoiazychnikov v sovremennoi Rossii* (Moscow, 2007); E.S. Elbakian, *Religii Rossii. Slovar'-spravochnik* (Moscow: Entsiklopediia, 2012). It also bears noting that in the latter two publications the definitions "*Rodnoverie*" and "neo-paganism" (*neoiazychestvo*) are employed as synonyms.

other variations for characterizing their worldview. This might also explain why this question was the most "difficult" among the first bloc of the survey - 48 respondents did not answer it (11.2% of those surveyed, as opposed to 5% of last year's sample).

The final question of the first bloc aimed to determine the community status of those present at the Kupala festival. This question posed difficulty to 47 of those surveyed (11% of the total). The vast majority of pagans present - 321 people (74.5%) - were not members of any community structure. Accordingly, only 61 respondents (14.2%) belonged to one or another pagan organization. Fifty-two respondents indicated the name of their community structure, while nine people preferred to not disclose this information. In turning to analyze the structures represented, two forms of the organization of pagan fellowships should be highlighted: the community and the union. According to the materials of the questionnaires, three unions were present at the 2015 Kupala festival: the Veles Circle fellowship of communities, the Union of Slavic Communities of Slavic Native Faith, and the Circle of Pagan Tradition. The first organization was indicated by 18 respondents (4.2%) on their questionnaires. Both the full name of the Veles Circle fellowship and the abbreviation "VK" were marked. With the second union, the research group had problems counting membership with abbreviations of this organization's name. The commonly accepted abbreviation "SSO SRV" did not figure on the questionnaire forms, whereas the following combinations were encountered: "SSO" (two respondents), "OOOSRV" (also two), and "SSO RV" (one). If we attribute all of these listed names to the union in question, then the total number of members of the Union of Slavic Communities of Slavic Native Faith who took part in the survey would be five (1.16%). It should be noted that the questionnaires were also found to contain the names of the specific communities which these unions comprise. The recorded communities belonging to the Veles Circle were: Rodolad (city: Astrakhan), Troesvet (Ryazan), Svarozhichi (Yaiva, Perm territory), with three responses, as well as Rodoliubie (Moscow) and Khorovod (Kostroma).

As follows, the total number of community members of this fellowship, according to the survey data, was 25 people (5.8%). Names of groups belonging to the Union of Slavic Communities of Slavic Native Faith were absent in the collected material. The Circle of Pagan Tradition was represented at the Kupala near Maloyaroslavets by the Velesye (Moscow, six people) and Vyatichi (Dolgoprudny, one person) communities, or seven respondents (1.6%) total. In addition, among the single-attested answers were encountered the following: the Prince's Banner military-historical club (Kolomna)[669], the White Stone historical-ethnographic club (Moscow), the Yarga community (Nizhny Novgorod), Svarga (Moscow), Rodnover (?), Yara Svarga (?), Vezha (?), Makosha (?), and the House of Ash association (Moscow). Among the "unconventional" answers were: "a certain esoteric group" (questionnaire #218), the Society of UFO Worship (questionnaire #291), and Chingachuk (questionnaire #397).

Without a doubt, one feature of the composition of this festival's participants from the community-union environment was the altogether modest share of the latter in the general context of those present at Kupala.[670] Both scholars of this phenomenon and the followers of 20th-21st century paganism themselves have yet to understand the reasons for this observed individualization.[671] However, proceeding from the above we can speak of a certain erosion of religious-worldview orientations within contemporary pagan religiosity. The observed terminological bricolage characterizing respondents' religious views is, in our opinion, directly related to the weak institutionalization of Slavic paganism, which once again

---

[669] The question mark here and further marks organizations about which the author had no reliable information at the time of this article's writing.
[670] Very telling is the negligible percentage of present community members from one of the organizing groups of the Kupala festival, the Veles Circle.
[671] For example, one of the ideologists of contemporary Russian paganism, Nikolai Speransky (Volkhv Velimir) believes that the lack of desire of potential community members to unite in organizational forms lies in a fear of priestly-volkhv diktat that would infringe upon spiritual freedom, as well as inter-communal fundraising which would affect a pagan's material wellbeing. - Velimir, *"Iazycheskaia Tserkov': Kto Za i kto Protiv?", Forum Samoteka* [http://forum.samoteka.su/viewtopic.php?p=5751].

testifies to the diversity and heterogeneity of this phenomenon both in form (lack of developed community structure) and content (the majority of adepts lack both dogmatic and ritual creed components).

In accordance with the program of applied sociological study of the discourses of the Russian pagan diaspora of the Russian Federation, the questionnaire survey-study included an open question aimed at determining the historical personalities which have played the greatest role in Russian history. According to hypothesis #2 put forth at the time of the field survey, the majority of respondents should have agreed with the following constant: "The greatest role in the history of Russia was played by Prince Svyatoslav Igorevich."

The question "What historical figures, in your opinion, have played the greatest role in the history of Russia?" received 947 responses. This question caused difficulty for 68 respondents (15.9% out of 429). Moreover, 16 people (3.7%) gave very vague answers, among which figured the following: "all of them (or many of them)" expressed by five people (1.2% out of 947), "it is hard to say, because the history of Rus has been distorted" (one respondent), "officers of the Russian Empire" (one person), and "the whole people" (one person). One of the respondents also answered this question negatively.

The data obtained from responses, in line with the particularity of the question, was broken down into the following subgroups: "rulers (princes, tsars, emperors, etc.)", "military leaders", "representatives of science", "political figures", "mythological personages", and "spiritual figures."

The subgroup "rulers" counted the greatest mass of responses. Princes, tsars, etc. were mentioned 738 times (78% out of 947 total responses). In this first subgroup, according to the obtained questionnaire data, the most popular are the princes of Kievan Rus. Names of the latter were recorded 198 times (27% out of 738 or 21% out of 947 total). The leader of this group was Prince Svyatoslav Igorevich (marked 119 times, 60% out of 198 or 46% out of 429). Altogether unexpectedly (in light of the field of respondents), Vladimir Svyatoslavich, the baptizer of Rus, came in second place.⁶⁷² This Kievan ruler was indicated 51 times (26% out of 198, or 12% out of 429). The third place of this subgroup was shared by Princess Olga and Yaroslav Vladimirovich (the Wise), who gathered 10 "votes" each. The "Kievan bloc" was closed by Princes Igor and Vladimir Vsevolodovich (Monomakh) with four mentions each on the questionnaires.

In the second subgroup of "tsars and emperors" (194 mentions, or 20.5% out of 947), the most popular ruler was Petr Alekseevich (Peter I or Peter the Great), elected by 122 people (63% of 194 mentions or 28.4% out of 429). The Kupala participants put Empress Ekaterina Alekseevna (Catherine II or Catherine the Great) in second place (35 votes, 18% out of 194 or 8.1% out of 429). Then followed Nikolai Aleksandrovich (Nicholas II) with 13 mentions (6.7% of 194, 3% of 429), Aleksandr Nikolaevich (Alexander II), chosen by 11 people (5.7% of 194 or 2.6% of 429), Aleksandr Pavlovich (Alexander I) with six mentions (3.1% out of 194, 1.4% of 429), etc.

The third most numerous subgroup included names from the leadership of the USSR (161 mentions, or 17% out of 947). The leader of this list was I.V. Dzhugashvili (Stalin).⁶⁷³ The latter leader was recorded 100 times (62% out of 161, 23.3% out of 429). Second and third places, respectively, were taken by V.I. Ulyanov (Lenin) (49 mentions, or 30.4% of 161, 11.4% of 429), and M.S. Gorbachev (11 mentions, 6.8% of 161, 2.5% of 429). One "vote" was cast for Leonid Brezhnev.

Among the rulers of Muscovite Rus (97 responses, 10.2% of 947), the greatest number of mentions fell to Ivan Vasilyevich (the Terrible) with 81 mentions (83% of 97 responses, 18.9% of

---

672 According to the narratives of the majority of leaders of this camp of alternative religiosity, Vladimir Svyatoslavovich is one of the main anti-heroes of contemporary paganism, first and foremost for his second religious reform, the baptism of Rus, as well as his - according to a theory held by a number of 20th-21st century pagan proselytes - Semitic origin. Vladimir Svyatoslavovich is thus taken as an antipode to his father. See: R.V. Shizhensky, *"Istoricheskii portret Vladimira Sviatogo: mify i fakty", Politicheskaia zhizn' Zapadnoi Evropy: antichnost, srednie veka, novou i noveshee vrema: mezhvuzovskii sbornik nauchnykh statei 6* (Arzamas: AGPI, 2010).
673 On the positive attitude of various pagan groups, such as the Union of the Venedy, to this figure as "leader of peoples", see E.L. Moroz, *"Iazychniki v Sankt-Peterburge" in Neoiazychestvo na prostorakh Evrazii* (Moscow: St. Apostle Andrey Biblical-Theological Institute: 2001) pp. 42-43, 48.

429). Then followed Dmitry Ivanovich (Donskoy), chosen by 9 people (9.3% of 97 responses, 2.1% of 429), Ivan (Kalita) with four responses, and Ivan III with three responses.

The country's leadership in most recent times was selected by 44 pagans (4.6% of 947). The name of the current president, Vladimir Vladimirovich Putin, figured 38 times on the questionnaires (86.3% of 44, 8.8% of 429), and the first president of Russia, Boris Yeltsin, six times (13.6% of 44, 1.4% of 429).

The smallest number of mentions on the questionnaires was noted for the founders of the ancient Russian state, counting 23 mentions in total (5.4% of 429): Oleg with 18, Rurik with five, the princes of the era of feudal fragmentation with 21 (4.9% of 429), Alexander Yaroslavich (Nevsky) with 19, and Andrey Yuryevich (Bogoliubsky) and Vsevolod Yuryevich (the Great Nest) each with one.

Thus, according to the obtained data, in the category of "rulers" the greatest popularity among neophytes of contemporary paganism, the proselytes of this worldview, and the masses of its sympathizers who gathered at the Kupala festival near Maloyaroslavets, was enjoyed by the following figures: Petr Alekseevich (Peter I) with 122 mentions, Svyatoslav Igorevich with 119 mentions, I.V. Dzhugashvili (Stalin) with 100, and Ivan Vasilyevich (the Terrible), who was marked 81 times.

The second category of answers to the open question under consideration included the names of military leaders, that is, people who to one extent or another were "famous by arms." Representatives of military affairs were chosen 53 times (5.6% of 947 total respondents), which is significantly inferior to the number of those who "voted" for state rulers. Of the answers provided, the name of Generalissimo A.V. Suvorov figured the most often - 16 times (30.1% of 53, or 3.7% of 429) total responses). Marshal of the Soviet Union G.K. Zhukov was marked on seven surveys (13.2% of 53, 1.6% of 429 total answers). The festival participants gave third place to the organizers of the second people's militia, Kuzma (Kozma) Minin and Dmitry Pozharsky (6 mentions each, or 11.3% of 53, 1.4% of 429). Next followed Stepan Timofeevich Razin (3 mentions), Nestor Ivanovich Makhno,

Ermak Timofeevich, and Fedor Fedorovich Ushakov (2 mentions each) and, with one mention each, Tamerlane, Evelyn Ivanovich Pugachev, Mikhail Illarionovich Kutuzov, Aleksei Petrovich Ermolov, Pavel Stepanovich Nakhimov, Anton Ivanovich Denikin, Alexander Vasliyevich Kolchak, Petr Nikolaevich Krasno, and Nikolai Gerasimovich Kuznestov.

Literary and scientific figures were marked 36 times (3.8% of 947 total responses to the question). The top three leaders were Mikhail Lomonosov (11 times, or 30.5% of 36 and 2.5% of 429 total responses), Alexander Pushkin (marked nine times, or 25% of 36, 2.1% of 429), and Leo Tolstoy (three times, or 8.3% of 36, 2.5% of 429). The range of other figures who reaped one vote were Vladimir Nabokov, Mikhail Bulgakov, Boris Pasternak, Ivan Pavlov, etc.

Even fewer respondents opted for representatives of the political sphere. In total, 32 responses (3.4% of 947 total responses) to the question "Which historical figures, in your opinion, have played the greatest role in the history of Russia?", contained such data on political leaders. It bears emphasis that only two politicians made up the core of this group of responses. The name Petr Arkadyevich Stolypin figured 14 times on questionnaires (43.8% of 32, 3.3% of 429) and that of Adolf Hitler eight times (25% of 32, 1.9% of 429). Regarding the latter answer, of noteworthiness is the fact that the interviewees who attempted to explain such an odious answer emphasized that they meant their desire to live under "our own Russian Hitler." Among the other political figures who received one vote figured: Alexander Danilovich Menshikov, Alexey Petrovich Bestuzhiev-Ryumin, Sergei Yulyevich Witte, Lavrenty Pavlovich Beria, etc.

The group of mythological personages chosen by a total of 12 respondents (1.27% of 947) was mainly represented by the semi-legendary Ryazan hero Evpaty Kolovrat (seven respondents, or 58% of 12 people, 2.8% of 429). In addition, Ilya Muromets, Bus Beloyar, Taras Bulba, Veles, and Hvitserk were each chosen once. This concluding list by and of itself confirms that those present at the Kupala near Maloyaroslavets included not only representatives of the Russian pagan diaspora, but also a definite percentage of "dissidents." This circumstance confirms the organizers' thesis that this originally religious event has gradually turned into a festival.

Among the "spiritual figures" group, five personalities surfaced, among which the leader in number of mentions was Sergius of Radonezh with five answers out of eight (1.9% out of 429). Next in line were Seraphim of Sarov, Nikon, and the Dalai Lama, who each received one vote.[674]

To return to the hypothesis on this open-ended question, we find that the historical figure said to have played the greatest role in the history of Russia was not Kievan Prince Svyatoslav Igorevich, as presumed by the survey's compilers, but Russian Emperor Peter I.[675]

It bears noting that, upon comparing the responses received to this open-ended question in the 2015 Kupala survey with the existing scholarly research load, which has accumulated predominantly in the conditions of desk studies, we can record the presence of both identical and opposite concepts. To a certain degree, the assumptions of the scholarly community correlate with the survey data. At the same time, however, there are also theses which diametrically contradict the received survey responses. For instance, the archaeologist L.S. Klein came to the conclusion in his considerations of the worldview paradigms of contemporary

---

674 That Orthodox saints figured in the responses has parallels in the works of the pagan authors A.V. Guselnikov and S.N. Udalov. As Schnirelmann notes: "These authors refer with respect to Russian Christian saints, hermits, Sergius of Radonezh and Seraphim of Sarov, but not calling them Christians, instead portraying them as inhabitant of remote thickets, close to the truth of nature and, of course, involved in the 'Russian Vedic heritage.'" - Schnirelmann, *Russkoe Rodnoverie*, p. 179. The figures Sergius of Radonezh and Seraphim of Sarov acquire sacred traits in what is N.O. Chanysheva's opinion a similar organization, the Bazhevsky Academy of Secret Knowledge. - N.O. Chanysheva, *"Russkoe neoiazychestvo (na primere drevnerusskoi pravoslavnoi ingliisticheskoi tserkvi i dvizheniia 'Troyanova Tropa' v g. Omske)"* (1999) [http://www.ic.omskreg.ru/~religion/kult/neoyaz/trop_main.htm].

675 Despite Svyatoslav's popularity in the contemporary pagan milieu, at the present some organization leaders attribute this historical figure to the camp of enemies of our country. The problems associated with this prince's rule were expounded in the "Word on False Greatness" published online in 2014 and compiled by official representatives of the Union of Slavic Communities of Slavic Native Faith and the Circle of Pagan Tradition. In 2015, this "evidence base" of the fallacy of the Russian cult of Svyatoslav made its way to the pages of the journal Rodnoverie. See: D. Gavrilov and V. Kazakov, *"O kniaze Sviatoslave. Razvenchanie sovremennogo mifotvorchestva"*, Rodnoverie 10:1 (2015), pp. 62-67.

Russian pagans that some have striven to create their own "national idol and firm hand, not European and not Petrine." As noted above, in the very least the pagans at Kupala actually see such a "strong hand" in Peter the Great. This "schema of partial coincidence" also includes other conclusions of the scholarly community on the most significant Russian historical figures. Russian scholars have deemed the Kievan Prince Svyatoslav Igorevich to be an especially reserved personality for the worldview phenomenon under examination.[676] Peter Alekseevich, however, who turned out to be the leader of the Kupala survey, has not been singled out as a young-pagan "historical banner" by the interested scholarly collective.[677]

Without a doubt, it is too early to draw final conclusions to explain the priorities of this pagan historical "election." However, attention begs itself to one possible reason for respondents' "concentration" on strong rulers who have radically changed the domestic and external political field. In our opinion, this choice is conditioned by the very specifics of both the rank-in-file and leadership of the contemporary Slavic pagan diaspora in the Russian Federation. This diaspora aims for cardinal changes and transformations of the existing Russian and, more broadly, European world order. The most apt term for characterizing the state of theoretical and practical seeking of these Russian young pagans is "excessivity." At the present time, this notion is being articulated and operationalized for application to new religious movements by the scholar of religion L.I. Grigoryeva, and we are confident that it is precisely the pagan milieu, with the passionarity of its members, that will become the ideal field of research for checking the representative relevance of such state-of-the-art indicators.

***

---

[676] Schnirelmann, *Russkoe rodnoverie: neoiazychestvo i natsionalizm*, pp. 175, 177, 216. A similar position is held by Ukrainian researchers. See: G.S. Lozko, *Aktualizatsiia ukrainskoi etnoreligii v evropeiskomu konteksti* (Dissertation for Doctorate of Philosophical Sciences; Kiev, 2007), pp. 13-14.

[677] For example, in his monograph Kavykin restricts himself to merely citing pagans themselves on rulers of the Russian state, such as Petr I and Ivan the Terrible. - Kavykin, *Rodnovery: Samoidentifikatsiia neoiazychnikov*, p. 129.

PAGAN TOLERANCE: THE EXPERIENCE OF QUESTIONNAIRE SURVEYING[678]

In the summer of 2016, the collaborators of the scientific research laboratory "New Religious Movements in Contemporary Russia and Europe" of Kozma Minin Nizhny Novgorod State Pedagogical University conducted a questionnaire survey among rank-and-file representatives of Russian pagan communities and unions gathered at the Kupala festival in the village of Lukino in the Ruzsky district of the Moscow region. The event was organized by two unions of communities: the Veles Circle and the Circle of Yar (Kolo Yara). It should be noted that if the Veles Circle has established itself in the role of organizing the most massive "Native Faith" festivals in Russia, then the Circle of Yar here figured as an "organizational platform" for the first time (information on this organization is virtually absent, even on this community's page on the social network VKontakte[679]). According to the data of the festival's organizers, around 800 people participated in this event on 24-26 June 2016.

The 2016 questionnaire consisted of four blocs of questions encompassing both open-ended and closed questions. This article will examine the particularities of the open-ended question #14, which was part of the second bloc of the survey, and the 63rd question of bloc #4 on the survey, which aimed to determine the level of tolerance among representatives of the contemporary pagan movement.

In the open-ended question, respondents were asked to characterize their religious/spiritual views. This question caused difficulties for 46 out of the 163 respondents who participated in the survey (28.2%). The most popular variation of self-identification among those gathered at the Kupala festival was *rodnoverie*, "Native Faith" (or "I am a *rodnover*"), which 13 respondents (7.9%) chose. It bears noting that this version of religious self-designation ranked first in the 2015 survey.[680] Second place in popularity was taken by the

---

678 Article first published in *Colloquium Heptaplomeres 3* (2016).
679 [https://vk.com/kolo_yara].
680 See Roman Shizhensky, "Contemporary Pagan Ratings of Russian Historical Figures: The Data of Field Studies" in this volume.

variant "paganism" (or "I am a pagan" or "Slavic paganism"), this answer being provided by 11 of the Kupala festival's participants (6.7% of respondents). Seven people (4.2%) characterized their religious views as "Vedic." The same number of interviewed respondents identified their worldview as pravoslavie (potentially "Orthodox Christianity"[681]). Four participants (2.4%) of the festival called themselves atheists, while "agnosticism" and "Buddhism" garnered two responses (1.2%). Sixty-six interviewees (40.4%) indicated other variations. Among the latter, the most interesting were: *rodnaia vera* (a variation of "Native Faith"), "I believe in good", and "broad" (two responses). Among answers with only one attestation, we can single out: "starorus" ("Old Rus" - questionnaire #19), "a pagan languishing away from Christianity" (questionnaire #21), "a descendant of the gods" (questionnaire #29), "I believe in the power of nature" (questionnaire #43), "three-fifths pagan" (questionnaire #50), "the faith of our ancestors" (questionnaire #80), "no religion, but I believe in god" (questionnaire #99), "I am interested in Slavdom" (questionnaire #100), "I am a worshipper of mother-nature" (questionnaire #108), "atheism with an interest in tradition" (questionnaire #112), "animism" (questionnaire #137), "everything is living, everything is god" (questionnaire #142) [See Figure 1].

Figure 1

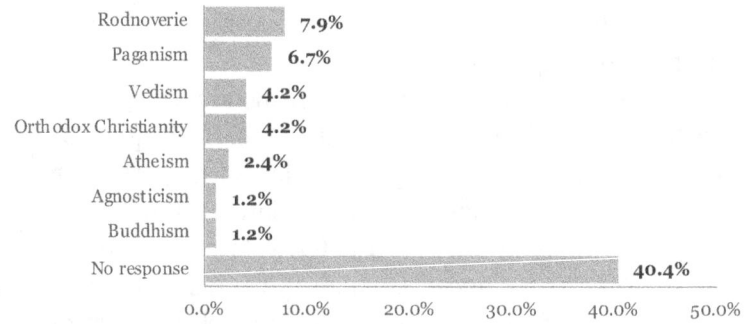

---

681 The difficulty of determining the percentage of Orthodox Christians in attendance at the festival lies in that among followers of this alternative religiosity there is a widespread substitution of notions or play on words with *pravoslavie*. The definition of *pravoslavie* can, in this particular setting, mean "glorifying *Prav*'", i.e., worshiping the higher divine realm, as well as other variations.

For question #63 in questionnaire bloc #4, respondents were asked to rank typical followers of religious/spiritual doctrines with regards to the degree of acceptability of their religious choices. Survey participants were presented the following seven associative answer variations: (1) "acceptable as a close relative (for example, a partner through marriage)"; (2) "acceptable as a close friend"; (3) "acceptable as a neighbor"; (4) "acceptable as a work colleague"; (5) "acceptable as a citizen of my country"; (6) "acceptable as a guest (tourist) in my country"; and (7) "I would not like to see them in my country." The following variants of religious/spiritual doctrines were presented: "paganism", *"rodnoverie"* ("Native Faith"), "Ynglism"[682], "Orthodox Christianity", "Catholicism", "Islam", "Judaism", "Buddhism", "Atheism", and "Jehovah's Witnesses."

Figure 2

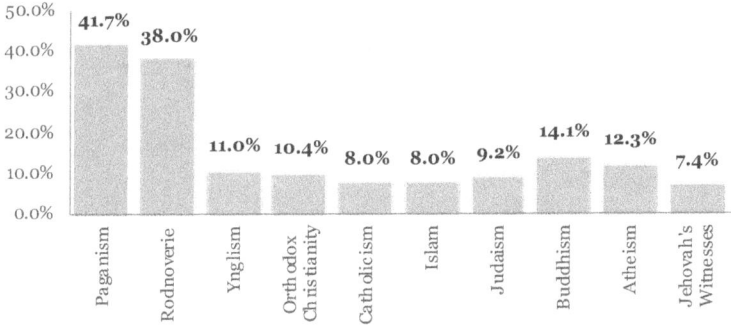

As for the first variant, where respondents were asked to indicate the extent of possibility and desirability of accepting a typical representative of a religious worldview "as a close relative (for example, a partner through marriage)", the quantitatively leading answer was "paganism", which gathered 41.7% or 68 of the total number of respondents. In second place were followers

---

682 Ynglism, or the Ancient Russian Ynglist Church of the Orthodox Old Believer Ynglings, is a new religious movement that is regarded by a number of Native Faith associations as pseudo-pagan. The Circle of Pagan Tradition and the Union of Slavic Communities of Slavic Native Faith deemed Ynglism to be "pseudo-paganism" in an official joint statement in 2009, entitled "On the Substitution of Notions in the Language and History of the Slavs and Pseudo-Paganism" [http://www.rodnovery.ru/dokumenty/o-podmenakh-ponyatij].

of rodnoverie ("Native Faith") with 62 answers or 38%. Twenty-three people (14.1%) were ready to accept a Buddhist as a close relative. "Atheism" was chosen by 20 people (12.3%), Ynglism by 18 (11%), and Orthodoxy by 17 (10.4%). Fifteen people (9.2%) selected Judaism. Catholicism and Islam were answered 13 times each (8%) [See Figure 2].

The second question from the series of variable questions aimed to identify the level of acceptability of different-minded people under the category of "close friend." In first place in number of responses were the pagan and Native Faith camps with 29 (17.8%) respondents. Eighteen or 11% of those surveyed were ready to accept a Buddhist as a close friend. Seventeen respondents (10.4%) expressed support for friendship with adepts of Orthodox Christianity. Such religio-spiritual tendencies as Ynglism, Catholicism, and Atheism were chosen nine times (6.1%). Islam was chosen by eight respondents (4.9%), and Judaism by six (3.7%). The smallest number of respondents wished to see a representative of Jehovah's Witnesses as a close friend [See Figure 3].

Figure 3

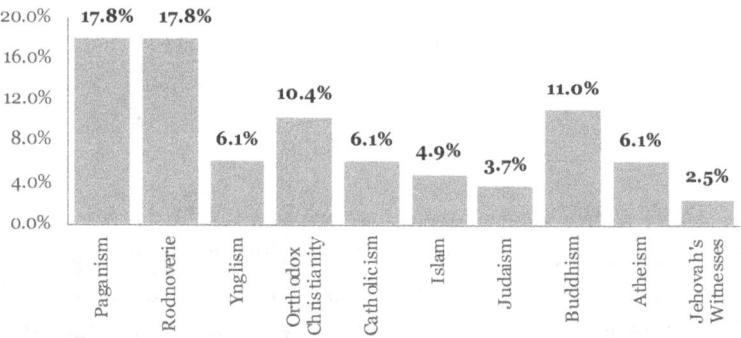

Twenty-six people (16%) preferred to see an atheist as a neighbor. Buddhists took second place with 17 respondents (10.4%). Fourteen respondents (8.6%) were ready to accept followers of Orthodox Christianity and Catholicism as neighbors. Twelve of the participants at the Kupala festival (7.4% of those surveyed) considered it possible to live next to representatives of the "Ancient Russian Ynglist Church of Orthodox Old Believer

Ynglings." Eleven respondents (6.7%) would agree to be neighbors with adherents of Judaism, and nine (5.5%) with followers of Islam. "Paganism" in the given variant was chosen by seven respondents (4.3%), while rodnoverie received six (3.7%). Only four people (2.5%) considered it possible to accept a Jehovah's Witness as a neighbor. [See Figure 4].

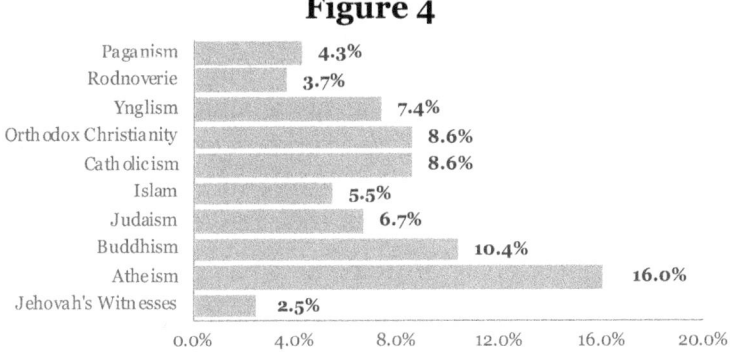

Figure 4

Nineteen respondents (11.7%) could see an atheist as a colleague. In second place came followers of Buddhism with 12 people (7.4%). Nine people (5.5%) voiced their preference for an Orthodox Christian. Eight of those surveyed (4.9%) were ready to become "work colleagues" with a Jehovah's Witness, and seven (4.3%) with a follower of Judaism. Catholicism and Islam received six responses (3.7%). Four respondents (2.5%) could see representatives of paganism and Native Faith as their colleagues. Only one person in this category chose Ynglism. [See Figure 5].

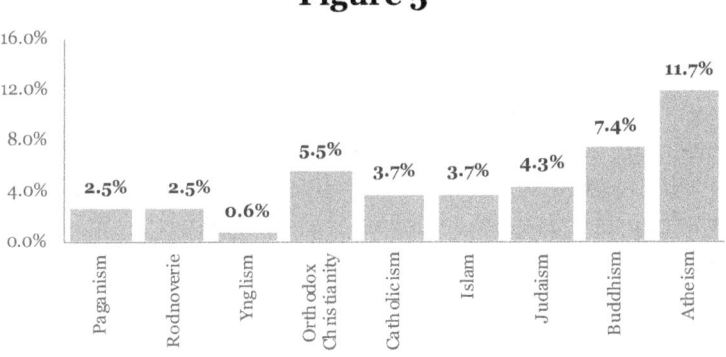

Figure 5

With regards to the proposed "religious ranking", Kupala festival participants least of all (6.7%, 11 responses) wished to see representatives of paganism and Jehovah's Witnesses as citizens of their country. Thirteen people (8%) chose Native Faith. For 10.4% or 17 of those surveyed, a representative of Judaism could be a citizen of their country. Followers of Islam were accepted by 19 people. Meanwhile, such religious currents as Ynglism and Buddhism garnered 12 responses (12.3%). Twenty-two people (13.5%) considered representatives of Catholicism as fellow citizens. In second place of popularity was atheism with 24 people (14.7%). In first place among the variants under consideration were people who profess Orthodox Christianity: 36 people (22.1%) spoke in favor of Orthodox citizens. [See Figure 6].

Figure 6

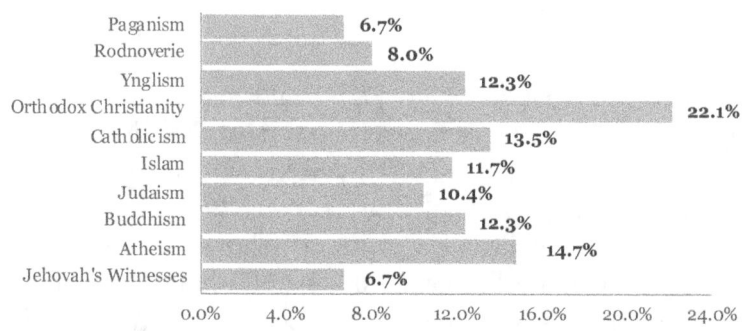

As a guest (tourist) in their country, 31 respondents (19%) could see an adherent of the Christian current of Catholicism. In second place was Judaism with 16% of responses (26 people). Twenty-four people (14.7%) were ready to see representatives of Islam as guests in their country, and 23 respondents (14.1%) were content with representatives of the religio-philosophical doctrine of Buddhism. Followers of the Jehovah's Witnesses religious organization were acceptable as guests in their country by 20 people (12.3%). Nineteen respondents (11.7%) spoke in favor of the Ynglism current. Orthodox Christianity was selected by 15 people (9.2%). Ten respondents (6.1%) selected atheists as guests. Native Faith tourists were indicated by four of the festival's participants (2.5%), while only two people singled out pagans as potential guests. [See Figure 7].

Figure 7

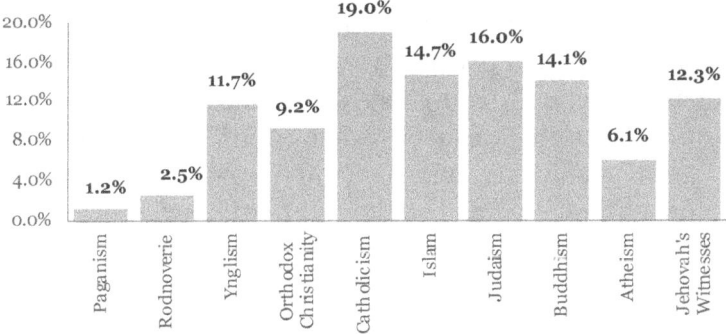

The final, seventh variation of question #63 read "I would not like to see them in my country." Sixty respondents (36.8%) did not wish to see followers of the group Jehovah's Witnesses in their country. In second place of "undesirability" were Muslims: 40 people (24.5% of respondents) indicated members of this confession on their questionnaires. Thirty-six people (22.1%) considered the presence of representatives of Judaism in their country unacceptable, and 32 survey participants (19.6%) spoke against Ynglism. Twenty-two people (13.5%) would refuse to accept a Catholic. Eighty percent of those surveyed (13 respondents) indicated Orthodox Christians, and 6.7% (11 people) atheists. Only three people considered the presence of a Native Faith believer unacceptable, and only two said the same of adherents of the pagan worldview. [See Figure 8].

Figure 8

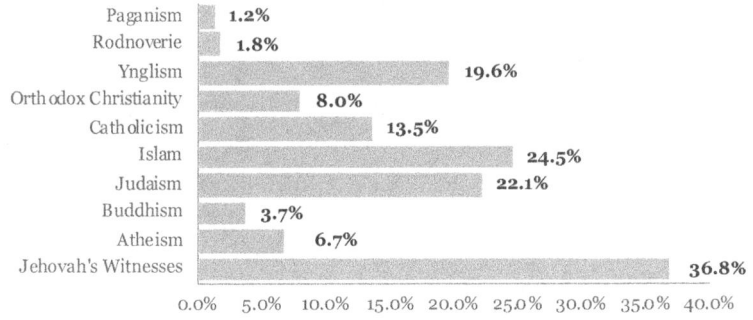

Let us note that out of the ten distinguished, typical religious/spiritual doctrines, the question of tolerance in the bloc on paganism was difficult for 40 people (24.5%). The blocs of Native Faith and Orthodox Christianity were left without answer by 42 respondents (25.8%). The greatest difficulty was caused by the bloc on Ynglism, to which 51 people (31.3%) did not provide a response. Forty-five respondents (27.6%) did not respond to the blocs on Catholicism and Judaism. Forty-four people (27.6% of those surveyed) also did not respond to the blocs on Islam, Buddhism, and Jehovah's Witnesses. The bloc on atheism was left without response by 43 respondents (26.4%).

To dwell on the results of the first question devoted to determining the religious views of respondents, let us take note of the significant decrease in the share of adepts of paganism and Native Faith (221 people or 51.5%) compared to the growth of responses under the categories "I find it difficult to answer" (46 respondents or 11.2%) and "other" (128 participants or 29.8%). In our opinion, this observed self-identification dissonance among participants at a pagan summer solstice festival can be explained by several factors. First of all, as has been noted in previous articles, in recent years the Kupala organized by the Veles Circle has been of a festival character. This specificity radically affects, among other things, the percentage of "pure" pagans present at the festival, which comes to include groups of interested, undecided people, neophytes, representatives of other religious and worldview currents (from neutral atheists to hostile Christians) as well as "mummers" or "guisers", who are becoming one of the most significant strata receptive to and developing "pagan fashion" through the adoption of external attributes (clothing, literature, cult objects, dishes, etc.). Secondly, a point which we have also emphasized in the past is the very process of the development of today's variation of the movement, namely, both new participants in the pagan world as well as its leaders' seeking for a new ideology and new practice instead of the (possibly) retiring pagan variations from the late 20th century. Thirdly, one peculiarity of the Kupala festival in 2016 organized by the "Velesites" was its new location and new union of communities and, as a result, the appearance of new participants with new worldview stocks.

Accordingly, in their analysis of the data of bloc #4 (question #63 on the survey), which was aimed at determining the tolerance on the part of adherents of the contemporary pagan worldview, the authors singled out three leaders for each of the criteria considered in the question. Thus, in first place in degree of acceptance from among the seven criteria were representatives of the religio-philosophical doctrine of Buddhism. This answer ended up in the top three of the five indicated criteria. The question of such an "exotic" choice on the part of pagans demands a separate study. Here we only dare to propose that Buddhism as a religio-philosophical doctrine is quite close to the constructors of today's paganism on a number of provisions (for instance, the absence of such features as an omnipotent creator-god figure, the problem of the world's creation, atonement for sins, etc.).

Followers of Orthodox Christianity were mentioned in four of the seven criteria of the question, which corresponds to second place. In three of the criteria, the leading place was taken by adherents of paganism, Native Faith, and atheism. Such religious/spiritual currents as Catholicism, Judaism, Islam, and Ynglism were chosen once, which indicates a lesser degree of acceptance of these movements by the participants of the 2016 Kupala festival. At the same time, note should be made of the fact that in the first, most intimate variant of interaction involving such things as marriage, pagans and Rodnovery shared preference. The same proportion remained in the second category of "level of trust": "close friend." The most important reason behind accepting Rodnovery and pagans into one's circle of family and friends should be seen in what we have more than once noted to be the shared character and, more broadly, lifestyle, peculiar to the majority of both community associations and lone pagans. This is a striving for a certain isolation and closing oneself off from other persuasions, and for the creation of a unique pagan brotherhood. Connections are preserved and successfully developed within this microcosm. This thereby allows, for example, for the "caste" of cult priests and ordinary pagans of one or another association to attend festival events organized by other communities, to conduct "pagan debates" on social networks, and to organize joint structural projects, etc.[683]

***

---

[683] One of the most recent collective projects of Russian pagans was the creation of the Veche Center and the Fellowship of Pagan Associations. See: *"Slovo 2016 - Slovo o vechevom tsentre i sodruzhestve iazycheskikh ob'edinenii"*, Union of Slavic Communities of Slavic Native Faith (28/9/2016) [http://www.rodnovery.ru/novosti/838-slovo-o-vechevom-tsentre-i-sodruzhestve-yazycheskikh-ob-edinenij].

SELECTED BIBLIOGRAPHY

Afanas'ev, A.N. *Poeticheskie vozzreniia slavian na prirodu t. 3.* Moscow: Sovremennyi pisatel', 1995.

Agal'tsov, A.N. *Rossiiskoe neoiazychestvo kak religiozno-nravstvennyi fenomen.* Dissertation for Candidate of Philosophical Sciences; Lev Tolstoy Tula State Pedagogical University, 2010.

Aitamurto, Kaarina. *"The liaison of nationalism, conservatism and leftist ideology within Rodnoverie - approaching the paradox."* Paper presented at the annual conference of the American Academy of Religion, 2010.

_____*Paganism, Traditionalism, Nationalism: Narratives of Russian Rodnoverie.* London: Routledge, 2016.

Anderson, Benedict. *Imagined Communities: Reflections on the Origin and Spread of Nationalism.* London: Verso, 2006.

Anichkov, E.V. *Iazychestvo i drevniaia Rus'.* Moscow: Indrik, 2003.

Artamoshin, S.V. *Poniatia i pozitsii konservativnoi revoliutsii: intellektual'noe techenie 'konservativnoi revoliutsii' v politicheskoi zhizni Veimarskoi respubliki.* Bryansk: Ivan Petrovsky Bryansk State University, 2011.

Aseev, O.V. *Iazychestvo v sovremennoi Rossii: sotsial'nyi i etnopoliticheskii aspekty.* Dissertation for Candidate of Philosophical Sciences; Moscow: Moscow State University, 1999.

Avdeev, V.B. *Preodolenie khristianstva (opyt adogmaticheskoi propovedi).* Moscow: Russkaia Pravda, 2006.

Belov, A. *Iazychestvo kak fenomen sovremennoi rossiiskoi religioznosti. Chast' 2* [http://www.portal-credo.ru/site/?act=fresh&id=458].

_____*"Iazychestvo kak fenomen sovremennoi rossiiskoi religioznosti, Chast' 3". LiveJournal,* 27/92007. [https://mahiravana.livejournal.com/9006.html].

_____ "Uzok ikh Krug", *Nezavisimaia gazeta* (21/12/2011) [http://www.ng.ru/ problems/2011-12-21/5_krug.html].

_____ *Veles - Bog Rusov. Neizvestnaia istoriia russkogo naroda*. Moscow: Amrita-Rus', 2007.

Benoist, Alain de. *On Being a Pagan*. Translated by Jon Graham. North Augusta: Arcana Europa, 2018.

Berdnik, G.O. *Znaki karpatskoi magii: taemnitsa starego mol'fara*. Kiev: Gamazin, 2008.

Beskov, A.A. "*Paradoksy russkogo neoiazychestva*". Colloquium Hepatplomeres 1, 2014.

Bessonov, A. "Kalendarnye prazdniki sovremennykh ekoposelenii (na materiale subkul'tury 'anastasievtsev')". In: *Kompleksnye issledovaniia traditsionnoi kul'tury v postsovetskii period 14* (Moscow: State Republican Center of Russian Folklore, 2011).

Bezverkhii, O.S. "Sobor Rodnoi Ukrainskoi Very". In: R.V. Shizhensky (ed.), *Indigenous Religions. 'Rus' Iazycheskaia': etnicheskaia religioznost' v Rossii i Ukraine XX-XXI vv*. (Nizhny Novgorod, 2010).

Blackwell, Christopher. "Russian Paganism: Interview with Yggeld." *Alternative Religions Education Network*. [http://aren.org/newsletter/2009-mabon/action.php?num=4].

Bogumir. *Rodnaia Vera. Istochnik schast'ia*. Khmelnitsky: Dukhovnoe izdanie Rodovogo Ognishcha Rodnoi Pravoslavnoi Very, 2007.

Bundina, A., P. Kozlov, and A. Mukhin. *Religioznye organizatsii Rossii*. Moscow: Tsentr polit. Informatsii, 2001.

Chanysheva, N.O. "*Russkoe neoiazychestvo (na primere drevnerusskoi pravoslavnoi ingliisticheskoi tserkvi i dvizheniia 'Troyanova Tropa' v g. Omske)*". 1999. [http://www.ic.omskreg.ru/~religion/kult/neoyaz/trop_main.htm].

Chernitsky, A. *Bolshoi mifologicheskii slovar'*. Moscow: GElios, 2008.

Cherniy, A.M. *Religieznavstvo. Posibnik*. Kiev: Akademvidav, 2003.

Cherva, V. *"Neoiazychestvo i molodezhnaia kul'tura: v poiskakh novykh religioznykh i kul'turnykh orientirov"*. *Mezhdunarodnye chteniia po teorii, historii i filosofii kul'tury 18*. Saint Petersburg: Eidos, 2004.

Chudinov, V. *"Kul'turno-mifologicheskoe nasledie slavian i neoiazychestva"*. Institute of Ancient Slavic Literature and Ancient Eurasian Civilization [https://www.runitsa.ru/index.php#36191].

Cunningham, Scott. *Wicca: A Guide for the Solitary Practitioner*. St. Paul: Llewellyn Publications, 2003.

DiZerega, Gus. *Christians and Pagans: The Personal Spiritual Experience*. St. Paul: Llewellyn Publications, 2001.

Dobroslav. *Bezbozhnye chudesa zhivoi prirody*. Kharkov: Sfera.

_____ *Iazychestvo kak volshebstvo*. Kirov: Viatka, 2004.

_____ *Iazychestvo: Zakat i Rassvet*. Kirov: Viatka, 2004.

_____ *Mat'-Zemlia, Chudo-Chudnoe, Divo-Divnoe (vvedenie v geobiologiiu)*.

_____ *"Nabroski moego stanovleniia"*. *Poslednii rubezh 1:9*, 2008.

_____ *Ob idolakh i idealakh*. Novaia Zemlia, 2007.

_____ *Ocherki Prirodovedeniia. Ubozhestvo edinobozhiia. Svoim putem. Kak khrest'iane stali krest'ianami. O glavnom.* 2012.

_____ *Prirodoliubivaia religiia budushchego*. Kirov: Viatka, 2004.

_____ *"Prirodnye korni Russkogo Natsional'nogo Sotsializma"*. *Russkaia Pravda 1:3*, 1996.

_____ *Prizrak Kudeiara (Nizhny Novgorod)*.

_____ *Promysel prirody i nerazumnyi homo sapiens*. Kharkov: Sfera.

_____ *Saryn' na kichku!*. Kirov: Viatka, 2004.

_____*Svetoslavie (ocherki iazycheskogo mirochuvstvovaniia)*. Kirov: Viatka, 2004.

_____ *Tsyplenki tozhe khochu zhit'!*

_____ *Volkhvy*.

_____ *Zov Tule*. Khlynovsky ekspress, 2006.

Dobrovolsky, A.A. *Strely Yarily*. Pushchino: 1989.

Doroshenko, M. "Slavianskoe neoiazychestvo". In: *XI Rozhdestvenskie obrazovatel'nye chteniia*. Informatsionno-konsul'tatsionnyi tsentr sv. Irineia Lionskogo [http://www.iriney.ru/sects/heathen/news009.htm].

Dvorkin, A.L. *Neoiazychestvo v Rossii: nativistskie sekty*. In: *Sektovedenie. Totalitarnye sekty. Opyt sistematicheskogo issledovaniia (3rd edition)*. Nizhny Novgorod: Izdatel'stvo bratstva vo ima sv. kniazia Aleksandra Nevskogo, 2002.

Famintsyn, A.S. *Bozhestva drevnikh slavian*. Saint Petersburg: Aleteia, 1995.

Elbakian, E.S. *Religii Rossii. Slovar'-spravochnik*. Moscow: Entsiklopediia, 2012.

_____"Slavianskoe novoe iazychestvo v Rossii: opyt religiovedcheskogo issledovaniia". In Elbakian, E.S., S.I. Ivanenko, I.Ia. Kanterov, and M.N. Sitnikov (eds.), *Novye religii v Rossii: dvatsat' let spustia. Materialy Mezhdunarodnoi nauchno-prakticheskoi konferentsii* [Moscow: Dom Zhurnalista, 14 December 2012] (Moscow: Drevo zhizni, 2013).

Elbakian, E.S., S.I. Ivanenko, I.Ia. Kanterov, and M.N. Sitnikov (eds.). *Novye religii v Rossii: dvatsat' let spustia. Materialy Mezhdunarodnoi nauchno-prakticheskoi konferentsii* [Moscow: Dom Zhurnalista, 14 December 2012]. Moscow: Drevo zhizni, 2013.

Emel'ianov, V.N. *Desionizatsiia*. Moscow: Russkaia Pravda, 2002/2005.

Fasmer, M. *Etimologicheskii slovar' russkogo iazyka t. III*. Moscow: Progress, 1987.

Gaidukov, A.V. *"Ideologiia i praktika sovremennogo slavianskogo neoiazychestva"*. Dissertation for Candidate of Philosophical Sciences; Saint Petersburg: Herzen Russian State Pedagogical University, 2000.

_____ *"Molodezhnaia Subkul'tura slavianskogo neoiazychestva v Peterburge"*. In: Kostiushev, V. (ed.), *Molodezhnye dvizheniia i subkul'tury Sankt-Peterburga: Sotsiologiia i anthropologicheskii analiz*. Saint Petersburg: Institute of Sociology of the Russian Academy of Sciences, Filial, Norma, 1999.

_____ *"Neoiazychestvo. Programma kursa po vyboru"*. In: *Gertsenovskie chteniia 2004: Aktual'nye problemy sotsial'nykh nauk*. Saint Petersburg: Faculty of Sociological Sciences of Herzen State Pedagogical University of Russia, 2004.

_____ *"Politicheskie aspect vozniknoveniia neoiazychestva v Rossii"*. In: *Gertsenovskie chteniia 1997: Aktual'nye problemy sotsial'nykh nauk*. Saint Petersburg: Faculty of Sociological Sciences of Herzen State Pedagogical University of Russia, 2004.

_____ *"Slavianskoe novoe iazychestvo v Rossii: opyt religiovedcheskogo issledovaniia"*. Tsentr religiovedcheskikh issledovanii 'Religiopolis', 22/1/2013. [http://religiopolis.org/religiovedenie/5730-rodnoverie.html].

Gal'kovsky, N.M. *Bor'ba khristianstva s ostatkami iazychestva v Drevnei Rusi*. Moscow/Kharkov, 1913/1916.

Gavrilov, D.A., N.P. Brutal'sky, D.D. Avdonina, and N.N. Speransky. *Manifest iazycheskoi Traditsii*. Moscow: Ladoga-100, 2007.

Gavrilov, D.A. and S.E. Ermakov (eds.). *Russkoe iazycheskoe mirovozzrenie: prostranstvo smyslov. Opyt slovariia s poiasneniiami*. Moscow: Ladoga-100, 2008.

Gavrilov, D. and V. Kazakov. "O kniaze Sviatoslave. Razvenchanie sovremennogo mifotvorchestva". Rodnoverie 10:1, 2015: 62-67.

Ginder, I.A. "Obzor problemy slavianskogo neoiazychestva v sovremennoi Rossii". In: Suveizda, V.V. (comp.), *Molodezh' i nauka - tret'e tysiacheletie. Sbornik materialov vserossiiskoi nauchnoi konferentsii studentov, aspirantov, i molodykh uchenykh 16 dekabira 2004 g*. Krasnoyarsk: GUTSMiZ, KRO NS Integratsiia, 2004.

Gomeniuk, G. and S. Tereshchenko. "Russkoe i ukrainskoe neoiazychestvo". *Center for Apologetic Studies*. 2003. [http://ansobor.ru/articles.php?id=136].

Gnatiuk, Y.V. *Dovelesova kniga. Drevneishie skazaniia Rusi*. Moscow: Amrita-Rus', 2007.

Gridin, A.V. "Mify o Zolotom Veke i nepreryvnoi Traditsii kak sotsiokul'turnoe osnovanie neoiazychestva". *Samizdat*, 2006. [http://samlib.ru/g/gridin_aleksej_wladimirowich/pagan.shtml].

Grushko, E.A. and Y.M. Medvedev. *Slovar' slavianskoi mifologii*. Nizhny Novgorod: Russkii kupets & Bratia Slaviane, 1996.

Gun'ko, L.P. "Liderstvo v novykh religioznykh dvizheniiakh: ot metodologicheskikh kharakteristik k soderzhatel'nym". In: *Novye religioznye dviezheniia v Rossii: dvadtsat' let spustia. Materialy Mezhdunarodnoi nauchno-prakticheskoi konferentsii*. Moscow, 2013.

Gurko, A.V. *Neoiazychestvo v Belarusi: predposylki i usloviia vozniknoveniia, organizatsionnye formy, perspektivy*. In: *Neoiazychestvo na prostorakh Evrazii. Prilozhenie k zhurnalu "Stranitsy"*. Moscow: St. Apostle Andrey Biblical-Theological Institute: 2001.

Iakovenko, B. *Iazychestvo slavian Kievskoi Rusi*. Kiev: Poligraf.

Iarovaia, M.B. *"Insignii i regalii vlasti v Drevnem Rime"*. Vestnik Moskovskogo gorodskogo pedagogicheskogo universiteta, seria *"Iuridicheskie nauki"* 2, 2010.

Iartsev, A.B. *Antropologicheskie aspekty politicheskikh i sotisial'nykh uchenii v sovremennom neoiazychestve v Rossii* (Moscow: Maks Press, 2009/BBI, 2012/

Istarkhov, V.A. *Udar russkikh bogov*. Saint Petersburg: Redaktor, 2001.

Itz, Rudolf. *Shepot Zemli i molchanie Neba. Etnograficheskie etiudy o traditsionnykh narodnykh verovaniiakh*. Moscow: Politizdat, 1990.

Judith, Anodea. *The Truth about Neo-Paganism*. St. Paul: Llewellyn Publications, 1994.

Kavykin, O.I. *Konstruirovanie etnicheskoi identichnosti v srede russkikh neoiazychnikov*. Dissertation for Candidate of Historical Sciences; Moscow: Institute of Africa of the Russian Academy of Sciences, 2006.

_____*"Rodnovery": Samoidentifikatsiia neoiazychnikov v sovremennoi Rossii*. Moscow: Institute of Africa of the Russian Academy of Sciences, 2007.

Kazakov, V.S. *Imenoslov*. Moscow: Russkaia Pravda, 2005/2011.

_____*Mir Slavianskikh Bogov*. Moscow/Kaluga: 2006.

_____*"Slavianskie obriady i obychai na Kaluzhskoi zemle"*. Soiuz Slavianskikh Obshchin Slavianskoi Rodnoi Very. 1998. [http://www.rodnovery.ru/stati/91-slavyanskie-obryady-i-obychai-na-kaluzhskoj-zemle].

Klein, L.S. *Voskreshenie Peruna. K rekonstruktsii vostochno-slavianskogo iazychestva*. Saint Petersburg: Evraziia, 2004.

Klimov, E.A. *Psikhologiia professional'nogo samoopredeleniia*. Rostov-on-Don: Feniks, 1996.

Kolkunova, K.A. *"Novye religii v postsovetskom sotsiume"*. In: Elbakian, E.S., S.I. Ivanenko, I.Ia. Kanterov, and M.N. Sitnikov (eds.), *Novye religii v Rossii: dvatsat' let spustia. Materialy Mezhdunarodnoi nauchno-prakticheskoi konferentsii [Moscow: Dom Zhurnalista, 14 December 2012]*. Moscow: Drevo zhizni, 2013.

Kompaneets, A. *"Iazycheskie bogi vykhodiat iz podpol'ia"*. *Ateisticheskii sait*. 26/11/2001. [http://www.ateism.ru/articles/russ02.htm].

Kopysov, D.Y. *Sovremennye netraditsionnye religii*. Izhevsk, 2000.

Kozlov, V.P. *"Khlestakov otechestvennoi 'arkheologii', ili tri zhiznii A.I. Sudakadzeva"*. In: *Chto dumaiut uchenye o 'Velesovoi knige'*. Saint Petersburg: Nauka, 2004.

Kravchuk, I. *"Svitovii kongres etnichnikh religii"*. *Svarog 8*. Kiev: 1998.

Krinichnaia, N.A. *Russkaia narodnaia mifologicheskaia proza: Istoki i polisemantizm obrazov t. I*. Saint Petersburg: Nauka, 2001.

Lifant'ev, S.S. *Azbuka nachinaiushchego iazychnika*. 2003.

Lozko, G.S. *Aktualizatsiia ukrainskoi etnoreligii v evropeiskomu konteksti*. Dissertation for Doctorate of Philosophical Sciences; Kiev, 2007.

_____ *Kolo Svarozhe*. Kiev: Ukrainskii pis'mennik, 2005.

_____ *Probudzhena Eneia*. Kharkov: 2006.

_____ *Velesova Kniga - Volkhovnik*. Ternopol: Mandrivets, 2010.

Liubomir. *"Sovmestnoe zaiavlenie WCER i KYT k sammitu religioznykh liderov"*. *Valhalla*. [http://valhalla.ulver.com/f63/t5731.html].

Mansikka, Viljo Johannes. *Religiia vostochnyskh slavian*. Moscow: Gorky Institute of World Literature of the Russian Academy of Sciences, 2005.

Martinovich, V.A. *Netraditsionnaia religioznost': vozniknovenie i migratsiia*. Minsk, 2015.

Martynov, A.I. *Arkheologiia*. Moscow: Vysshaia shkola, 1996.

Matiushin, G.N. *Arkheologicheskii slovar'*. Moscow: Prosveshchenie, 1996.

Meranvild, V.B. *Slaviano-goritskoe dvizhenia kak Edna iz form proiavleniia russkoi natsional'noi kul'tury*. Dissertation for Candidate of Philosophical Sciences; Yoshkar-Ola: Mari State University, 2002.

Mezgir. *"Otkrytoe pis'mo. Otvet 'neopravoslavnym'm 'neoiudeiam', a takzhe 'neozhurnalistam' i 'neoistorikam'"*. In: *V zashchitu drevnei Very (Vedy) russko-slavianskoi*. Moscow, 2002.

Mezgir, Velimir, and Peresvet. *Sut' iazycheskoi very*. Koliada Viatichei, 2008.

Mikheeva, I.B. *"Fenomen neoiazychestva: problema kontseptualizatsii (obzor osnovnich issledovatel'skikh paradigm)"*. 2003. [http://scipeople.ru/publication/66848/].

_____ *"Neoiazychestvo kak religiozno-kul'turnyi fenomen sovremennosti: problema definitsii"*. *Filosofskie i sotsial'nye nauki. Nauchnyi zhurnal 2*. Minsk: Publishing Center of Belarusian State University, 2010.

Militarev, A. *"O soderazhanii termina 'diaspora' i k vyrabotke ego opredeleniia"*. *Russkii arkhipelag: Setevoi proekt "Russkogo Mira"*. 1999/2009.

Miroliubov, Yuri. *Slaviano-russkii fol'klor*. Munich, 1984.

Mitchell, Chris. "Interview with Varg Vikernes". 10/5/2005. [https://www.burzum.org/eng/library/2005_interview_metalcrypt.shtml].

Moroz, E.L. *"Iazychniki v Sankt-Peterburge"*. In: *Neoiazychestvo na prostorakh Evrazii*. Moscow: St. Apostle Andrey Biblical-Theological Institute: 2001.

Nagovitsyn, A.E. N and D.A. Gavrilov. *"O sovremennykh tendentsiiakh vozrozhdenia traditsionnykh politeisticheskikh verovaniy"*. In: *Schola-2004, Sbornik nauchnykh statei filosofskogo fakul'teta MGU*. Moscow: Moscow State University, 2004.

Nakorchevskii, A.A. *"Metodologicheskie osnovy i podkhody k izucheniiu ukrainskogo rodnoveriia (ridnovirstvo)"*, Religiovedenie 2, 2008.

Nam, E.V. *"'Procthenie' simvolicheskikh znachenii 'shamanskogo' posokha v kontekste indoevropeiskikh ritual'nykh traditsii"*. *Izvestiia Irkutskogo gosudarstvennogo unviersiteta, seria "Politologiia. Religiovedenie"* 20, 2017.

Nazarov, R. *"Etnicheskie diaspory kak faktor razvitiia ethnopoliticheskikh i mezhgosudarstvennykh otnoshenii v Tsentral'noi Azii"*. *Informatsionno-Analiticheskii Tsentr*. 28/9/2008. [https://ia-centr.ru/experts/2638/].

Niederle, Lubor. *Slavianskie drevnosti*. Moscow: Aleteia, 2000.

Nikitina, A.V. *Russkaia demonologiia*. Saint Petersburg: Saint Petersburg University, 2006.

Ozhiganova, A.A. *"Konstruirovanie traditsii v neoiazycheskoi obshchine 'Pravo-Vedi'"*. *Colloquium Heptaplomeres* 2, 2015.

Ozhiganova, A.A. and Iu.V. Filippov. *Novaia religioznost' v sovermennoi Rossii: uchenia, formy i praktiki*. Moscow: Institute of Ethnology and Anthropology of the Russian Academy of Sciences, 2006.

Pchelov, E.V. *"Posokh, skipetr, zhezl: iz istorii regalii Moskovskogo tsarstva"*. *Vestnik RGGU, seria "Istoriia. Filologiia. Kul'turologiia. Vostokovedenie"* 21:201, 2012: 159-173.

Pennick, Nigel and Prudence Jones. *A History of Pagan Europe*. London: Routledge, 1995.

Petkova, S.M. *Neoiazychestvo v sovremennoi evropeiskoi kul'ture (na primere rasovykh teorii)*. Rostov State University, 2009.

Polishchuk, M.I. *Kalendar viznachnikh ukrainskikh narodnikh sviat*. Lutsk: Tverdinia, 2006.

Poloskova, T.V. *"Diaspory i vneshniaia politika"*. *Mezhdunarodnaia zhizn' 11*, 1999.

Popov, N.S. and A.I. Tanygin. *"Sovremennye predstavlieniia mariitsev o Boge"*. In: *Iumyniüla (Osnovy traditsionnoi mariiskoi religii)*. Yoshkar-Ola: GUP Mariiskii poligr.-izdat. komb., 2003: pp. 132-140.

Pozanenko, A.A. *"Samoizioliruiushchiesia soobshchestva. Sotsial'naia struktura poselenii rodovykh pomestii"*. *Mir Rossii 1*, 2016.

Pribylovskii, V. *"Ideinye tsentry politicheskikh neoiazychnikov"*. *RELIGARE: Pravoslavnyi pravozashchitnyi tsentr 'Territoriia tserkvi'*. 2004. [http://www.religare.ru/2_9726.html].

Prokof'ev, A.V. *"Sovremennoe slavianskoe neoiazychestvo (obzor)"*. In: *Entsiklopedia sovremennoi religioznoi zhizni v Rossii*. 2012. [http://www.avatargroup.ru/booksreader.aspx?dbid=259].

Protasenia, P.F. *Problemy obshcheniia i myshleniia pervobytnykh liudei*. Minsk: Izdatel'stvo ministerstva vysshego, srednego spetsial'nogo i professional'nogo obrazovaniia BSSR, 1961.

Pushnaia, L.M. *"Metody issledovaniia regional'nykh subkul'tur na primer neoaizychestva"*. *Vestnik Tomskogo universiteta 305*, 2007.

Rezunkov, A.G. (ed.). *Kolovorot 2008. Slavianskii solnechnolunnyi kalendar'-mesiatseslov*. Saint Petersburg: Tsentr strategicheskikh issledovanii, 2007.

Rodoslav. *Izvilistye puti Traditsii*. Moscow: 2006.

Roesdahl, Else. *The Vikings*. London: Penguin, 1998.

Ryazanova, S.V. and A.I. Tsolova. *"Sovremennoe 'neoiazychestvo': klassifikatsiia, spetsifika i lokal'nye varianty"*. *Vestnik Moskovskogo universiteta - Seria 7: filosofiia 1*, 2015.

Rybakov, B.A. *Iazychestvo drevnikh slavian*. Moscow: Nauka, 1981.

Ryzhakova, S.I. *"Romuva. Etnicheskaia religioznost' v Litve". Issledovaniia po prikladnoi i neotlozhennoi etnologii 136.* Institute of Ethnology and Anthropology of the Russian Academy of Sciences, 2000.

Samoilova, G.S. *"Antroponimy kak sposob samovyrazheniia v novykh iazycheskikh techeniiakh"*. In: *Iazychestvo v sovremmennoi Rossii: opyt mezhdistsiplinarnogo issledovaniia*. Nizhny Novgorod: Kozma Minin Nizhny Novgorod State Pedagogical University, 2016.

Schnirelmann, V.A. *Ariiskii mif v sovremennom mire - tom I*. Moscow: Novoe literaturnoe obozrenie, 2015.

_____ *"Perun, Svarog i drugie: russkoe neoiazychestvo v poiskakh sebia"*. In: *Neoiazychestvo na prostorakh Evrazii*. Moscow, 2001.

_____ *Russkoe rodnoverie: neoiazychestvo i natsionalizm v sovremennoi Rossii*. Moscow: BBI, 2012.

_____ *"Russkoe neoiazychestvo: kvazireligiia natsionalizma i ksenofobii"*. *Religio*. [http://www.religio/ru/relisoc/27_print.html].

_____ *"Neoiazychestvo i natsionalizm (vostochnoevropeiskii areal)"*. *Issledovaniia po prikladnoi i neotlozhnoi etnologii 114*. [http://www.iea.ras.ru/lib/neotl/07/2002062247.htm].

Shelbanova T.V. and Iu.G. Bolotova. *"Iazycheskoe nasledie v sovermennoi dukhuvnoi kul'ture"*. In: *Sbornik nauchnykh rabot studentov vysshikh uchebnykh zavedeniy Respubliki, NIRS 2004 Belarus*. Minsk: 2005.

Semenov, Iu. *"Etnos, natsiia, diaspora"*. *Etnograficheskoe obozrene 2*, 2000.

Shcheglov, A.M. *Iazycheskaia zaria*. Moscow: 2001.

_____ *Vozvrashchenie bogov*. Moscow: 1999.

Shchipkov, A. *Vo chto verit Rossiia. Religioznye protsessy v postperestroechnoi Rossii*. Saint Petersburg: Russian Christian Humanitarian Institute, 1998.

Shepping, D.O. *Mify slavianskogo iazychestva*. Moscow: TERRA, 1997.

Sheremet'eva, V.N. "Nekotorye problemy stanovleniia rodnoveriia v sovremennoi issledovatel'skoi literature. Problema termina". *Vestnik Omskogo universiteta* 1:71, 2014.

Shiropaev, A. "Neoiazychestvo i 'rodnoverie'". *LiveJournal*, 18/6/2007. [https://shiropaev.livejournal.com/8643.html].

Shizhenskiy, R. "The role of food in contemporary Russian Paganism". In: *Walking the Old Ways in a New World: Contemporary Paganism as Lived Religion*. Katowice: Sacrum Publishing House, 2017.

Shizhensky, R.V. "Darna kak religioznaia kategoriia sovremennykh litvoskikh iazychnikov". *Vestnik buriatskogo gosudarstvennogo universiteta* 6. Ulan-Ude: Buryat State University, 2013.

_____*Filosofiia dobroi sily: zhizn' i tvorchestvo Dobroslava (A.A. Dobrovol'skogo)*. Moscow: Orbita-m, 2013.

_____*Pochvennik ot iazychestva: mirovozzrencheskie diskursy volkhva Velimira (N.N. Speranskogo)*. Nizhny Novgorod: Tipografiia Povolzh'e, 2015.

_____ (ed.). *Indigenous Religions. 'Rus' Iazycheskaia: etnicheskaia religioznost' v Rossii i Ukraine XX-XXI vv*. Nizhny Novgorod, 2010.

_____ *"Ia iazychnik! - k voprosu o samoopredelenii prozelitov slaviankogo pagan-dvizhenia (na primere iaroslavskoi obshchiny 'Velesovo Urochishche'"*. In: *Mirovozzrenie naseleniia Iuzhnoi Sibiri i Tsentral'noi Azii v istoricheskoi retrospektive 7*. Barnaul: Altai State University, 2014.

_____"Iazycheskii demotivator - 'mirovozzrencheskaia nagliadnost'" sovremennoi Rossii". In: Istoriia, iazyki i kul'tury slavianskikh narodov: ot istokov k griadushchemu: material mezhdunarodnoi nauchno-prakticheskoi konferentsii 25-26 noiabrya 2012. Penza/Koling/Belostok: Nauchno-izdatel'skii tsentr "Sotsiosfera", 2012.

_____"Interv'iu s Bogumilom (B.A. Gasanovym)". Colloquium Heptaplomeres 2, 2015: 102-116.

_____"Interv'iu s chlenom obshchestva religiovedov Finliandii Kaarinoi Aitamurto", Novostnaia lenta. Issledovatel'skaia laboratoriia 'NRD v sovremennoi Rossii i stranakh Evropy [http://nrdlab.ru/posts/1006557].

_____"Interv'iu s Veleslavom". Colloquium Heptaplomeres 1, 2014: 177-184.

_____"Interv'iu s Velimirom". Colloquium Heptaplomeres 1, 2014: 171-176.

_____"Istoricheskii portret Vladimira Sviatogo: mify i fakty". In: Politicheskaia'zhizn' Zapadnoi Evropy: antichnost, srednie veka, novou i noveshee vrema: mezhvuzovskii sbornik nauchnykh statei 6. Arzamas: AGPI, 2010.

_____"Materialy interv'iu s S.A. Dorofeevym". In: Indigenous Religions. Nizhny Novgorord: Kozma Minin Nizhny Novgorod State Pedagogical University, 2010.

_____"Neoiazycheskii mif o kniaze Vladimire". Vestnik Buriatskogo gosudarstvennogo universiteta 6, 2009.

_____"Osobennosti novogo iazyka ('novoiaza') russkikh iazychnikov XXI veka". Nauchnoe mnenie 11, 2017.

_____"Zhrechestvo v sovremennom russkom iazychestve". Vestnik udmurtskogo universiteta. Seriia istoriia i filologiia 5:2, 2008.

Shizhensky, R.V. and M.Y. Shliakhov. *"Pis'mennye istochniki sovremennykh rossiiskikh iazychnikov po dannym polevykh issledovanii"*. *Istoricheskie, filosofskie, politicheskie i iuridiceheskie nauki, kul'turologiia i iskustvovedenie. Voprosy teorii i praktiki* 8:3(58), 2015.

Shizhensky, R.V. and E.S. Surovegina. *"'Pochemu ia stal iazychnikom': opyt oprosa liderov diaspory"*. *Istoricheskie, filosofskie, politicheskie i iuridiceheskie nauki, kul'turologiia i iskustvovedenie. Voprosy teorii i praktiki* 6:68, 2016.

_____ *"'Rodnovercheskii obereg': pogruzhenie v iazycheskuiu traditsiiu XXI veka"*. *Nauchnoe mnenie* 12, 2017.

Shizhensky, R.V. and O.S. Tiutina. *"Proektsii institutsional'noi samoidentifikatsii v sovremennom slavianskom iazychestve po dannym polevykh issledovanii"*. *Mezhdunarodnyi zhurnal prikladnykh i fundamental'nykh issledovanii* 1-2, 2016.

_____ *Samoidentifikatsiia slavianskikh iazychnikov: sotsial'nyi portret, gosudarstvo i obraz lidera (po dannym polevykh issledovanii)"*. *Noveishaia istoriia Rossii* 1. Saint Petersburg, 2016.

Smul'sky, E.V. *"K razvitiu voprosa o poniatii 'neoiazychestvo'"*. *Colloquium Heptaplomeres* 1, 2014.

Sobolevsky, A. *"Nav'e i Verziulovo kolo"*. *Russkii filologicheskii vestnik XXIII*. Warsaw: 1890.

Speransky, N.N. (Velimir). *"Istoria i vera 'Koliady Viatichei'"*. *Informatsionnyi Portal Iazycheskoi Traditsii* [http://www.triglav.ru/forum/index.%20php?showtopic=236].

Speransky, N.N. (Volkhv Velimir). *Volkhvy protiv globalizma*. Moscow: Samoteka, 2014.

Speransky, N. and S. Ermakov. *Mesto. Bogovy stolpy. O sviashchennom meste v russkoi iazycheskoi traditsii*. Moscow: ITs Slava!, 2009.

Sreznevsky, I.I. *Issledovaniia o iazycheskom bogosluzhenii drevnikh slavian*. Moscow: Knizhnyi dom LIBROKOM, 2013.

Surovegina, E.S. "*Interv'iu s volkhvom Vadimom*". *Colloquium Heptaplomeres 3*, 2015.

Tishkov, V.A. "*Fenomen postsovetskikh diaspor v Rossii*". Paper presented at the Moscow conference "*Rossiiskaia diaspora v XIX-XX vv.: vyzhivanie ili ischesnovenie?*", 20-21 April 1999.

Tokarev, S.A. (ed.), *Mify narodov mira*. Moscow: Bol'shaia Rossiiskaia entsiklopedia, 1997.

Triglav. "*Religozni pomen pri Slovanih*". In: Matjaž Anžur (ed.), *Zbornik prispevkov šeste mednarodne conference "Slovanska dediščina" na gradu Struga od 8. do 9. avgusta 2009*. Ljubljana: Jutro, 2010.

Trinkūnas, Jonas. *Baltic Religions Today*. Vilnius: Senovės baltų religinė bendrija, 2011.

_____(ed.), *Of Gods and Holidays: The Baltic Heritage*. Tvermė: 1999.

_____ "*Vsemirnyi kongress ethnicheskikh religii v Vil'niuse*". *Nasledie predkov 6*.

Tupik, O.O. "*Neoiazichnitstvo na storinkakh presi*". *Visnik Akademii pratsi i sotsial'nykh vidnosin Federatsii profsilok Ukraini 2:15* (2002).

Union of Slavic Communities of Slavic Native Faith. *Slavianskaia Rodnaia Vera*. 2014.

Vagurina, L.M. (compil.). *Slavianskaia mifologiia. Slovar'-spravochnik*. Moscow: Linor, 1998.

Vasilev, M.S. "Our experience of religious building". In: *The Oaks: The Official Publication of the World Congress of Ethnic Religions 4*. Vilnius, Summer 2001.

Vasil'ev, M.S., D.Zh. Georgis, N.N. Speransky, and I.G. Toporkov. *Russkii iazycheskii manifest*. Moscow: Viatichi, 1997.

Vasil'ev, M.S., A.L. Potapov, N.N. Speransky. *Iazychniki otvechaiut 5*. Troitsk: Trovat, 1999.

Veleslav. *Kniga Velesovykh radenii*. Moscow: Veligor, 2008.

———*Osnovy Rodnoveriia. Obriadnik. Kologod*. Saint Petersburg: Vedicheskoe Nasledie, 2010.

———*Radeniia v Khrame Moreny*. Moscow: Amrita, 2014.

———*Rodnye Bogi Rusi*. Moscow: Rodoliubie, 2009.

———*Slavianskaia Kniga Mertvykh*. Moscow: Svet, 2015.

———*Uchenie volkhvov: Belaia kniga*. Moscow: Nauka, 2007.

———*Veshchii Slovnik: Slavleniia Rodnykh Bogov*. Moscow: Institut Obshchegumanitarnykh issledovanii, 2007.

Velimir. "*Boginia Lada v Doline Vodopadov*". *Derevo Zhizni. Gazeta etnicheskogo vozrozhdeniia 50*. Troitsk, 2010.

———*Darna - uchenie o zhizni v Prirode i obshchestve*. Troitsk: Trovant, 2009.

———*Dar shamanizma - dar volkhovaniia*. Moscow: Veligor, 2012.

———"*Iazycheskii religioznyi tsentr, ego zadachi i problemy sozdaniia*". *Informatsionnyi portal iazycheskoi traditsii*. [http://triglav.ru/forum/index.php?showtopic=399]

———"*Iazycheskaia tserkov', kto Za i kto Protiv? - vyskazyvaemsia*". *Informatsionnyi portal iazycheskoi traditsii*. [http://triglav.ru/forum/index.php?showtopic=428].

———"*Iazychestvo - subkul'tura?*". *Slavianskii Iazycheskii Portal Spravochnik po miru slavianskogo Rodnoveriia! Lichnyi blog pisatelia Stansislava Sviridova*. [http://slaviy.ru/problemnye-voprosy-rodnoveriya/yazychestvo-%E2%80%93-subkultura/].

———"*Kapishche Peruna*". *Derevo Zhizni. Gazeta etnicheskogo soprotivleniia 2*. Troitsk: Trovant.

_____ *Kniga prirodnoi very*. Moscow: Veligor, 2009.

_____ *Nravstvennaia kniga: hakim rodnoveru byt' i pochemu*. Pamphlet #11, Troitsk: 2012.

_____ "*O perspektivakh iazycheskogo dvizheniia, shkola*", *Informatsionnyi portal iazycheskoi traditsii*. [http://triglav.ru/forum/index.php.

_____ "*Poezdka v volshebnuiu derevniu*". *Derevo zhizni: Gazeta etnicheskogo vozrozhdeniia 41*, 2009.

_____ *Rodnoverie*. Moscow: Samoteka, 2012.

_____ *Russkoe iazychestvo i shamanizm*. Moscow: Institut obshchegumanitarnykh issledovanii, 2006.

_____ *Slovo ob idolakh i sviatykh mestakh iazycheskoi very*. Pamphlet #12, Troitsk: Koliada Viatichei, 2013.

_____ *Simvolika Drevnei Rusi*. Moscow: Koliada Viatichei 2008.

_____ "*Smysl i perspektivy iazycheskogo dvizheniia*. *Derevo zhizni 44*. Troitsk: 2009.

_____ "*Vozzvanie bogov. Slovo k russkim iazychnikam*". *Nasledie predkov: zhurnal pravoi perspektivy 6*. Moscow: OOO RUSPECHAT', 1998.

Velimir, Veleslav, and Vlasov. *Put' volkhva*. Donetsk: Kashtan, 2007.

Vereya (Svetlana Zobnina). *Russkaia vera - Rodoverie*. Moscow: Ladoga-100, 2006.

Vikernes, Varg. "Paganism: Part V - Sacrifices". 2005. [https://www.burzum.org/eng/library/paganism05.shtml].

_____ *Rechi Varga*. Tambov: Polius, 2007.

_____ *Skandinavskaia mifologiia i mirovozzrenie*. Tambov: Polius, 2006.

Vlasova, M. Novaia *ABEVEGA russkikh sueverii*. Saint Petersburg: Severo-Zapad, 1995.

Wirth, Herman Felix. *Khronika Ura Linda. Drevneishaia istoriia Evropy*. Translated into Russian with commentary by A.V. Kondrat'ev. Moscow: Veche, 2007.

Yggeld. "O permskom S'ezde Kruga Iazycheskoi Traditsii i priniatom na nem manifeste". *Drevo Zhizni: Gazeta etnicheskogo vozrozhdeniia* 28, 2007.

Yggeld, "Soveshchanie na 'baran'em Lbu'", *Drevo zhizni: Gazeta etnicheskogo vozrozhdeniia* 37, 2008.

Zalitailo, I.V. "Etnonatsional'nye diaspory i diasporal'nye obrazovaniia: sushchnost' i struktura". *Analitika Ku'turologii* 2, 2005.

Zlorovets, Y.I. and A.A. Mukhin. *Religioznye konfessii i sekty*. Moscow, 2015.

Znamensky, P.V "Gornye cheremisy Kazanskogo kraia". *Vestnik Evropy* 4. Saint Petersburg: 1868.

Zobnin, C.V., D.Zh. Georgis, D.A. Gavrilov, and V.Y. Vinnik. "Analiz sovremennogo mifotvorchestva v noveishikh issledovaniiakh po iazychestvu (kritika stat'i V.A. Schnirelmanna 'Ot 'Sovetskogo naroda' k 'organicheskoi obshchnosti': obraz mira russkikh i ukrainskich neoiazychnikov'". *Analitika kul'turologii*, 2015.

"Declaration", *European Congress of Ethnic Religions* (1998) [https://ecer-org.eu/about/declaration/].

"Neo-Paganism". *Encyclopedia Britannica* [https://www.britannica.com/topic/Neo-Paganism].

"Poniatie "Diaspora"". *Fond "Obeshchetvennoe mnenie"*. 15/11/2000. [https://bd.fom.ru/report/map/dd003030].

"Sovremennye neoiazycheskie partii i organizjatsii v Rossii i messianskaia ideologiia". *Slavianskii pravovoi tsentr* [http://www.rlinfo.ru/projects/seminar1200/13.html].

www.ingramcontent.com/pod-product-compliance
Lightning Source LLC
Chambersburg PA
CBHW060041230426
43661CB00004B/618